Amritasya Maa Narmada
Pada-Parikrama

Amritasya Maa Narmada

Pada-Parikrama

Vivek Ji

DK PRINTWORLD®
Publishers of Indian Traditions

ISBN: 978-81-246-1255-2 (Hb)
First Published in India in 2024

Printed and published by:
D.K. Printworld (P) Ltd.
Regd. Office: Vedaśrī, F-395, Sudarshan Park
ESI Hospital Metro Station, New Delhi - 110015
Phones : (011) 4172 2626, 98713 94815
e-mail : indology@dkprintworld.com
Web : www.dkprintworld.com

Preface

In the year 2022-23, I embarked on a remarkable journey known by the name "Amritasya Ma Narmada Pada-Parikrama". Accompanied by a group of seventeen individuals and a dedicated team of over fifty supporting staff, we set out to traverse the majestic banks of the Narmada River, spanning an impressive distance of over 3,000 km.

It has long been customary to walk along the banks of the holy River Narmada and complete its circumambulation. In the pages that follow, I shall recount the profound journey that unfolded before me during the sacred ritual known as the *parikrama*. Within the hallowed realms of this book, I shall endeavour to capture the essence of my extraordinary experience, as I embarked upon a spiritual odyssey like no other. With each step taken, I traversed the path of devotion, immersing myself in the timeless traditions and sacred practices. In the depths of my literary collection, there lies another book that delves into the sacred realm of knowledge, focusing solely on the hallowed tirtha-sthala that I, with great fervour, had the privilege of rediscovering during my profound parikrama. In the pages that follow, (I invite you, the reader, to embark on a remarkable journey alongside me.) Within the confines of this book, I shall recount the tale of one of the most arduous walks I have ever undertaken. It is a narrative that seeks to illuminate the depths of my experience, shedding light on the encounters I had with fellow travellers and the heartfelt conversations I shared with the innocent souls of children. In the pages of this book, you will find a captivating narrative that delves into the depths of my personal experiences, intricately woven with the rich tapestry of *tirtha*s' history. (However, should one's sole interest lie in the exploration of *tirtha*s, there exists another literary work dedicated solely to providing comprehensive details about the sacred *tirtha*s situated along the revered banks of the holy Narmada).

Vivek Ji

Contents

Preface v

Prologue 1

Holy Narmada in Indian Shastras 9

Historical Literature on Narmada 19

1. My Narmada Parikrama 21
2. Amritasya Ma Narmada Pada-Parikrama 23
3. Rund, Jalheri or Hanumani Parikrama 25
4. Mandhata-Omkareshwar 28
5. Mahant Mangal Das Tyagi 37
6. Truth Speaks 39
7. Parikrama Begins 41

OMKARESHWAR TO BAVANVAHINI

8. Khedighat: The Path That Was Not for Everyone 47
9. Gangeshwar Mahadev 52
10. Baji Rao Peshwa and Mother Narmada 57
11. Siyaram Baba Took Rs 200 Donation from Me 62
12. Tirtha and Bhakta 65
13. Names and the History 70
14. Water, Dams and Parikrama 73
15. Farmer and His Respite 75
16. Bavanvahini, Not Barwani 79

BAVANVAHINI TO GORA COLONY

17. Bhagavati 85
18. Shulpani Hills 88
19. Lakhan Giri Maharaj 91
20. There Was No Food 97
21. Back to Normal 103
22. Meeting and Greetings 105
23. Forest Band 108
24. The Song and the Singer 111
25. Arti and Bharti 115

GORA COLONY TO VIMLESHWAR

26. Rameshwaram 119
27. Someone Was Waiting for Me 127
28. Shakreshwar Maharaj and Laughter 134
29. Sea and Crossing 151

VIMLESHWAR TO GARUDESHWAR

30. Ego and Speed 161
31. Janya Jatis and Their Contribution 165
32. Bhrigukshetra 169
33. Educating India 171
34. Words, Feelings and Respect 176
35. Senapur 181
36. Gangeshwar Mahadev 192
37. Tirtha and Our Search 198
38. Shri Ram Nath Kovind 204

GARUDESHWAR TO JALUD

39. Fast Forwards 209
40. Giving Us Their Love 213

41. Panditji of Pura 215
42. Purity of Pura 217
43. Dev Path Linga 221
44. The Soldiers 225
45. Karoli to Bakaner 226
46. I Am Unknown 232
47. Dadhichi 234
48. Parashurama Temple 238
JALUD TO NAMAWAR
49. Pipleshwar Mahadev 249
50. No Passion for History 251
51. Cat and the Tea 253
52. What Is Forgotten 256
53. Ayodhyapuri 258
54. Namanpura 261
55. Debts Repaid 263
56. Nemawar 266
NAMAWAR TO SHOKALPURA
57. History Revisited 271
58. Let Us Make a Final Plan 273
59. Cold Winter 274
60. Maidan-e-Kichad 275
61. Vanara Bhalu Vana – Bandrabhan 277
62. Help Me to Walk 279
63. Bharkacch 281
64. Makara Sankranti 284
65. Ketudhana 286
66. Shokalpura 287

SHOKALPURA TO GWARIGHAT

67. Bilthari 291

68. State of Tirthas 293

69. Mrigkheda 294

70. The Path 295

71. Lamps to Shed Light On 296

72. Bil Pathar to Gopalpur 299

73. Gopalpur to Gwarighat 303

GWARIGHAT TO AMARKANTAK

74. Let Us Maintain Our Pace 309

75. Future of the Nation 311

76. Seeds to Be Sown 313

77. Ma Narmada Jayanti 314

78. Kids Are Not Kids 316

79. Nunkher to Dindori North 318

80. Book and Its Content 319

81. Money Matters 320

82. Penance 322

83. Jai Shri 324

84. Amarkantak 328

AMARKANTAK TO GADARWARA

85. Jai Hind 335

86. Madman 336

87. Mischievous Kids 337

88. Services Offered 339

89. Forest Camp 340

90. Brahmapuri 342

91. A Village of Soldiers 346

92. Truth Expresses 347

93. Green Efforts 349
94. Spirituality 350
95. None Knew the Distance 352
96. The Parikrama of Two Dogs 356
97. Shumbha and Nishumbha 359
98. Farmers Knowledge 361
99. Longest Route 363
100. Gadarwara 365

GADARWARA TO KOKHSAR

101. Walks in Gadarwara 369
102. Jai Shri Dadaji 371
103. Sandiya 373
104. Kubja Sangam 375
105. Satvasa to Sangakheda Kalan 377
106. Shri Gaurishankar Maharaj 378

KOKHSAR TO OMKARESHWAR

107. Cultural Obliteration 385
108. Bhandara for Patels 387
109. Hanuman Tekri 390
110. Punyaghat 393
111. Weather Changes 396
112. Maa Narmada Put to the Test 397
113. Submerged Tirthas 399
114. Returning to Omkareshwar 403
115. Omkar Maharaj 405

In Appreciation 407
Bibliography 427
Index 431

Prologue

Since the dawn of human civilization and historical literacy, the sacred River Narmada has been honoured with rituals of adoration and circumambulation in India. The River Narmada holds great spiritual significance for millions of people, who believe that bathing in her holy waters can cleanse their sins and bring them closer to salvation. Her revered status is further reinforced by the numerous temples and shrines that have been built along its banks, attracting pilgrims even from far and wide. According to the ancient Indian Shastras, there exists a profound act that is considered among the holiest endeavours one can undertake – the circumambulation of the revered Narmada River. The circumambulation, also known as *parikrama,* involves walking the entire length of the Narmada River on both banks, which spans over 3,000 km. This sacred journey is believed to purify the soul and grant blessings to those who undertake it. It has been my experience that completing the *parikrama* can bring immense spiritual growth and deepen one's connection with the divine.

This profound practice not only serves as a vital component of *sadhana,* but also entails the Hindu Sanatana history, accords these *tirtha*s (pilgrimage sites) a great deal of significance and credits various deities with blessing them. These sacred pilgrimage sites, established through countless religious endeavours and spiritual practices by a multitude of revered individuals, span across numerous epochs. The act of visiting those sacred *tirtha*s during the *parikrama* is the very essence that gave birth to this ancient tradition of *parikrama.*

I was following the footsteps of countless saints and other holy individuals when I started my walk of the *parikrama*. But I was also careful to adhere to the customs established by the Great Saint Shri Gaurishankar Maharaj, so I walked every day, made sure the pilgrims ate together and offered communal food (*saha-bhojana*) as it is known in India, wherever we spent the night. This practice of sharing a meal not only fostered a sense of unity among the pilgrims but also emphasized the importance of selflessness and compassion. It was a humbling experience to witness people from different walks of life coming together to partake in this sacred tradition. It had been many decades since the last time someone embarked on a *parikrama* (a sacred circumambulation), while also diligently organizing the *bhandara* or *saha-bhojana* (a communal feast) every night. As I made my way along the tranquil banks of the Narmada River, I could not help but notice the astonishment that flickered across the faces of the onlookers. It seemed that my meticulous preparations and the unique *parikrama* I had embarked upon had caught them off guard, as if they had never witnessed such devotion and dedication before. The locals were accustomed to offering food and assistance to the *parikramavasi*s, not receiving it themselves. It was a humbling experience for them to be on the receiving end of such devotion and dedication, and they were grateful for the feast we had got it prepared every night. For me it was a revival of ancient traditions right before their eyes. It was a humbling experience to see the impact my actions had on the community, inspiring them to reconnect with their spiritual roots and participate in the festivities with newfound enthusiasm.

The divine had its own plans and the events of my holy pilgrimage would eventually help educate the Indian people on the significance of the holy *tirtha*s located along the banks of the Sacred Narmada. What is more, it would be the impetus for the *tirtha-sthala*'s resuscitation and restoration, which was not an outcome I had anticipated.

I have written a book titled *Teerthas of Narmada Parikrama* with a heartfelt homage to the holy *tirtha-sthala* that was unearthed on the holy banks of the venerated Mother Narmada. This book is a thorough record of the many incidents and experiences of life that have touched my heart and mind during my travels. In addition, the fascinating history of *tirtha*s' locations, that have always held a special place in the hearts of many people but which have fallen into obscurity over the centuries, is woven throughout these narratives. This alternative volume provides a deeper exploration of the spiritual significance and historical context of the *tirtha*s. It offers a comprehensive understanding of the rituals, traditions and beliefs associated with these sacred sites, making them an invaluable resource for those seeking a more in-depth study of their surroundings.

Prior to British rule, the river that would become known as holy

Narmada was known as Narbuda or Nerbudda as the locals still call it. However, Ptolemy, a Greek traveller who landed in India around 2,000 years ago, dubbed the River Namadus. Ptolemy's name for the river, Namadus, is believed to have influenced by the Sanskrit name Narmada. This historical connection highlights the enduring significance of Ptolemy's observations and their impact on the region's cultural and geographical identity.[1]

The tale of Narmada unfolds through an array of enchanting landscapes, bustling trade routes, flourishing agriculture, verdant forests, and the ancient footprints of civilizations long past. It is a narrative that weaves together the intricate dance between the geography of the land and the ever-evolving fabric of its inhabitants, as they traverse the river's banks from one historical era to the next. The Holy River Narmada has witnessed the rise and fall of empires, the birth of legends, and the harmonious coexistence of diverse cultures along its shores. Its waters have quenched the thirst of countless generations, while its majestic presence continues to inspire awe and reverence. As time flows ceaselessly, the tale of Narmada remains an enduring testament to the enduring bond between humanity and divinity. The mighty Narmada not only carries within its waters the tales of civilization, but also the enchanting stories of divine gods, encapsulating the very essence of the life that once graced the sacred land of India. It was upon the tranquil banks of the Narmada River that one could witness the graceful ebb and flow of serenity, a sight that possessed a certain ethereal quality akin to the delicate strokes of an artist's brush. This sacred river, with its profound depth and unwavering current, had long served as a sanctuary for countless sages, revered *rishis*, and enlightened saints who sought solace and enlightenment within the vast expanse of India's spiritual landscape. Rare is the treatise on regions that fails to mention the illustrious Narmada.

Although the banks of this sacred river have attracted pilgrims for ages, the arrival and control of the British in particular was not motivated by religious fervour. The British were interested in the holy Narmada for one reason and one reason only: the treasures that lie concealed along its banks. They spent a long time in searching the banks of the Narmada for coal, iron, etc. and for the closest sea route through the Narmada, but they eventually gave up because Mother Narmada would not let her water be used in the transportation of minerals and other goods through her channel.

As much as a pilgrimage to the spiritual heart of a nation, Narmada *parikrama* is a journey of deep dialogue of silence, a meeting with the infinite inspirations of life, and a conversation with the history of nation worshipping on these *tirtha*s that remain after thousands of years of upheaval. The Narmada *parikrama* holds immense significance as it not only marks the beginning of a nation's existence but also symbolizes the eternal principles of Sanatana Dharma. It is a journey that connects individuals to their spiritual roots and fosters a deep sense of devotion and cultural identity.

With great anticipation and a spirit of adventure, I set forth on a magnificent *parikrama*, a sacred journey that would take me across an awe-inspiring expanse of nearly 3,000 km. However, this is not a mere account of passing days and distances traversed, nor is it a simple recitation of the commonplace wonders that have been documented by countless others. No, this expedition transcends mere significance. The essence of Sanatana Dharma, the living heritage of our nation, is beautifully captured in the exploration of the holy Narmada. This sacred river embodies the timeless spirit of Sanatana, serving as a profound symbol of our cultural and spiritual legacy.

***

In the heart of India, nestled amidst the lush green landscapes, flows the majestic river Mother Narmada. Emerging gracefully from the heart of Amarkantak, a colossal flat-topped hill, takes its rightful place as the eastern terminus of a majestic range that stretches across the very core of India, spanning from the eastern reaches to the western horizons.

Once upon a time, there existed a land of tranquillity and serenity. It was a place untouched by the chaos of contemporary society, where solitude was in charge supreme. However, in recent times, this once peaceful haven has transformed into a bustling city, adorned with towering structures, *ashrama*s, and various other establishments. It is quite astonishing to contemplate how this metamorphosis came to pass. In the days of British rule, this very land was deemed desolate, a barren expanse that only a handful of temple priests cared for, dutifully safeguarding the sacred source of the mighty Narmada River. In the bygone era, Amarkantak boasted an abundance of meandering waterways, each one contributing its precious flow to the mighty Narmada. Upon reaching the tip of the majestic Amarkantak plateau, the water cascades down a staggering height of approximately 70 ft, unveiling its enchanting presence to the world. With an exuberant display of vitality, it graces the surroundings with its resplendent beauty at Kapila Dhara. Continuing its journey, the water gracefully descends a little further, transforming into the ethereal Dudha Dhara, aptly named for its resemblance to the purest of milk. The sight of this milky-white water is truly a sight to behold, captivating all who are fortunate enough to witness its mesmerizing flow.

From the mountains of Amarkantak, the holy river plunges hundreds of feet in a series of falls and rapids where it meanders around the hills of Mandla and eventually passes under the remains of the palace at Ramnagar. The Sacred Narmada has now drained a large area of hilly terrain over its almost 100-mile journey. Its gushing waters branch out into a number of different tributaries, creating a natural border between the river's forested islands and the black trap-rock peaks and ledges that rise in the river's centre. No longer do the surrounding hills and dense vegetation conceal the horizon and the banks extend right down to the water's edge. Trees were cut down at an alarming measure, and forests were shrinking at a frightening rate. If this continues, the Narmada bank could lose much of its forest cover over the next decade. However, the river is a continuous blue ribbon of water from Ramnagar all the way down to Mandla, framed by towering tree-lined banks.

A crossroads where the Grand Trunk Road from Jabalpur to Nagpur passes below Mandla at Gwarighat. This crossroads at Gwarighat not only served as a strategic location for trade and transportation, but also held historical significance during the British colonial era. The felling and distribution of trees from this area played a crucial role in fuelling the growing demand for timber across various regions of India. From here a turbulent 30 ft drop occurs about 15 km south-west of Jabalpur at a place called Dhuandhara (Bhedaghat), where the Narmada then enters a narrow channel cut through a mass of marble and basalt for nearly 3-4 km, hence the name "Marble Rocks". The river narrows from a width of 100 m or so upstream to just 20 m or so downstream, winding its way between 50-80-ft tall marble rocks, before breaking free and returning to its former expansive state.

At this point, Mother Narmada descends from the hills and enters into the rich valley that stretches for more than 200 km and passing through the district of Narsinghpur and the Narmadapuram. The Narmada River, known as the lifeline of Madhya Pradesh, flows gracefully through this picturesque valley, nourishing the fertile lands and sustaining the local communities. This is the beginning of the river's journey through one of the large alluvial plains that will give the river its distinctive character as they alternate with the steep gorges. Farmers have found her blessings to grow various crops throughout four seasons, and it was here that the British once searched and located the coal belt and iron mines near Tendukheda. Crossing this section of the Narmada will lead one to the cities of Handia and Nemawar, which are located on the river's southern and northern banks respectively. The Narmada River gracefully winds its way through the formidable Satpura and Vindhya ranges, as if it has been dutifully safeguarding these majestic mountains since time immemorial. Recent findings have shed light on the age of these geological wonders, revealing that the Vindhya Mountains have stood tall for a staggering 1,400 million years, while the Satpura Mountains, though slightly younger, boast an impressive age of approximately 1,000 million years. It is as if the ancient Narmada has been a steadfast guardian, faithfully watching over both these mountain ranges throughout the ages.[2] Unni reveals a fascinating geological insight, asserting that the majestic rivers of Narmada and Tapti predate the renowned Ganges by a staggering 150 million years.

The hills on each side of the river begin to converge again just before Handia; in the early twentieth century, these were frequented by bandits like the Pindaris. The holy Narmada, having descended from the hills above Mandhata, is now flowing through Madhya Pradesh, where it will remain for the next 160 km or more. The Satpura Mountains are about 60-70 km south of here, and the Vindhya Mountains are around 25-28 km north of here. While passing through Maheshwar, the former Holkar capital, the river's northern bank is dotted with temples, palaces, and bathing *ghat*s, many of which were commissioned by Rani Ahilyabai.

The river flows from Shulpani and subsequently enters Gujarat via Rajpipla, Bharuch over the period of around 300 km. As it enters the Gulf of Kambhat below Bharuch, it develops into an estuary with a maximum width of 25 km.

Let us not forget that throughout the sacred river, numerous dams have been constructed, their presence significantly altering the natural course of the river. As a consequence, countless ancient sites have been submerged and villagers have been forced to abandon their ancestral lands due to the rising waters caused by these dams. Beginning with Bargi, then Punasa, Omkareshwar, Sardar Sarovar, and finally, nearing completion, another dam near Mandleshwar.

***

Many cultural and social characteristics of valley's life reflect the region's relative isolation. People have lived in the valley continuously from prehistory to the present day, and they have always created unique cultural traditions and legacies. However, the Narmada Valley has only recently been recognized as a unique cultural unit by archaeologists, art historians, and experts from related fields.

Numerous recent studies, both in the realm of scientific research and geographical exploration, have unveiled a captivating revelation: the Narmada Valley has been a site of uninterrupted human habitation for an astonishing span of 150,000 years. In the vicinity of Hathnora, a place of tranquil beauty where the Narmada River flows gently, an extraordinary revelation took place. It was there that the ancient remnants of a hominid skull, the oldest ever found in peninsular India, were unearthed.[3]

For countless generations, the Narmada Valley has been home to thriving settlements, each contributing to the development of a vibrant culture and the preservation of cherished traditions. In the annals of history, the true importance of the valley has remained shrouded in mystery until relatively recently, when archaeological discoveries shed light on its significance. These findings have revealed that the valley served as a hub for ancient civilizations, fostering cultural exchange and technological advancements that shaped the course of human development. It is only through the diligent efforts of archaeologists that the veil has begun to lift, revealing the valley's profound historical significance. Alas, the passage of time has not been kind, for soon after the nation emerged from the slumber of its colonial past, many dams were erected, forever altering the landscape. Regrettably, this noble endeavour has resulted in the submersion of numerous archaeological sites, rendering their treasures forever lost beneath the depths of water. These submerged archaeological sites held invaluable artefacts and remnants of ancient civilizations, providing insights into our rich history. The loss of these treasures not only deprives us of our cultural heritage but also hinders further exploration and understanding of our past.

In the heart of the valley lies the sacred Narmada River, revered as one of the holiest in all of existence. Its waters flow with a divine grace, carrying with them the essence of spirituality and ancient wisdom. This mystical river, known for its unparalleled sanctity, has witnessed countless souls embarking on a profound journey of devotion and introspection. Enveloping the Narmada River is a tradition that has stood the test of time – the *parikrama*, a sacred circumambulation that spans the length of this majestic waterway. This circumambulation, undertaken by devout pilgrims, serves as a testament to the enduring legacy of the valley. It is a testament to the unwavering faith and commitment of those who embark on this sacred journey. The circumambulation not only symbolizes their deep devotion, but also reinforces the profound spiritual connection they have with the valley and its significance in their lives.

Holy Narmada in Indian Shastras

The sacred entity, known as the holy mother Narmada, has been bestowed with mentions in various ancient scriptures of India. Throughout the ages, religious scholars, venerable sages, and devout saints have found themselves irresistibly drawn to the ethereal allure of the holy Narmada, as well as the majestic mountain ranges from which she gracefully originates, viz. Amarkantak on Maikal Hills. These scholars, sages, and saints have not only praised the spiritual significance of the Narmada River but also recognized its immense ecological importance. The river sustains a diverse range of flora and fauna, making it a vital lifeline for the surrounding ecosystems. The significance of Mother Narmada had led the establishment of numerous *tirtha*s along its course, attracting devotees from all over the country since ancient times.

In the Ramayana

In the epic tale of the *Valmiki Ramayana,* we are not only treated to the captivating narrative of Prince Rama's journey, but we are also granted a glimpse into the enchanting world of the Narmada River. In the *Valmiki Ramayana,* one finds a meticulous account of the diverse array of creatures that undoubtedly inhabited the enchanting forests surrounding Mother Narmada. Majestic tigers and regal lions, alongside formidable buffalos, graceful deer, and sturdy bears, all coexisted harmoniously amidst the verdant foliage. Moreover, the grandeur of the wilderness was further enhanced by the presence of magnificent elephants, their majestic presence adding an aura of awe-inspiring splendour. It is within this mystical setting that we encounter a myriad of bird-like creatures, each one more fascinating than the last. The *Ramayana,* in its timeless wisdom, takes us on a lyrical exploration of the diverse bird species that grace the waters of the Narmada.[1]

In the *Valmiki Ramayana,* the enchanting tale of Mother Narmada unfolds, portraying her as the epitome of riverine beauty. Her banks, adorned with resplendent trees, melodious birds and vibrant flowers, create a picturesque scene that captivates all who behold it. Moreover, the frothy bubbles that grace the surface of her waters resemble the graceful drapes of a flowing *sari*, adding an ethereal touch to her already mesmerizing charm. Ravana found himself utterly captivated by the ethereal beauty of the river before him. Her tranquil waters, flowing gracefully through the landscape, held an irresistible attraction. In the depths of his being, he could not help but draw comparisons to his previous encounter with the majestic Ganga, the river that had left an indelible mark on his soul. Ravana pleaded with those around him to immerse themselves in the sacred waters of the Narmada, promising them respite from their pains.[2]

Within the sacred text of *Ramacharitmanasa*, the esteemed sage Tulsidas artfully draws a parallel between the profound Ramakatha and the revered Narmada River. In doing so, he emphasizes the profound affinity that Lord Shiva holds for the Ramakatha, akin to his deep fondness for the holy Narmada.[3]

In the Mahabharata

In the Vana-Parva of the *Mahabharata*, there is a significant mention of the sacred river Narmada. Pulatsya Rishi provides Bhishma with valuable information about various *tirtha*s (sacred pilgrimage sites), including the banks of the Narmada. According to the text, performing *tarpana* (ritual offering) and *dana* (charitable giving) on the banks of this holy river holds immense merit for anyone who undertakes it.

The Vana-Parva serves as a guide for those embarking on a pilgrimage, emphasizing the importance of visiting specific *tirtha*s such as the Narmada to attain spiritual merit. By following in Bhishma's footsteps and partaking in *tarpana* and *dana* rituals on the banks of this revered river, one can hope to experience profound spiritual transformation and connect with ancient traditions that have stood the test of time.[4]

Again in the illustrious pages of the Vana-Parva there lies a mention, though a fleeting one, of the majestic mountain range known as Amarkantak. It is said that this range, adorned with the ethereal beauty of nature, was referred to as Vanshagulm Teerth, a sacred pilgrimage site of great significance.[5]

In the Vana-Parva, the merits of Mother Narmada are once again discussed, shedding light on the profound significance this holy river holds. Dhaumya Rishi provides a detailed account of the Narmada to Yudhishthira, emphasizing that every entity in the world seeks to have a sacred bath in its divine waters.

The narration highlights the revered status of the Narmada as a pilgrimage site, drawing people from all walks of life to experience its purifying and transformative powers. The description offered by Dhaumya Rishi underscores the belief that immersing oneself in the holy waters of the Narmada is an essential spiritual journey that transcends boundaries and connects individuals with their inner selves.[6]

The Vana-Parva's exploration of Mother Narmada's merits serves as a reminder of the transcendent power and universal appeal this sacred river holds. It encapsulates the profound reverence and devotion people have towards the Narmada, making it a cherished destination for seekers of spiritual solace and enlightenment.

The mention of the revered Narmada in the illustrious Shanti-Parva highlights the significance of this sacred river in Hindu mythology. It further emphasizes the spiritual importance and deep reverence that devotees hold for the Narmada, adding to the rich tapestry of religious beliefs depicted in the text. The Anushashana-Parva of *Mahabharata* also has various mentions of the Narmada specifically expressing that bathing in and living around the Narmada, spending life has merit on next life.[7]

The mention of the Narmada in this ancient scripture highlights her spiritual significance and reinforces the belief that performing religious rituals on her banks can bring great blessings and spiritual growth. This sacred river has been revered for millennia, attracting pilgrims from all over to seek solace, purification, and divine grace.

In the Bhagavata Purana

In the Sixth Skandha of the *Bhagavata Purana,* an ancient Hindu scripture, a significant event is mentioned on the banks of the Narmada River. According to this sacred text, a colossal battle took place between demons and divine beings in this very location.[8]

The mention of the Narmada River in such a context highlights its importance and significance in Hindu mythology. It serves as a backdrop for an epic clash between forces representing both good and evil. This account from the *Bhagavata Purana* not only showcases the rich mythological heritage of India but also emphasizes the spiritual and historical significance attached to the Narmada River. It provides a glimpse into ancient tales that have been passed down through generations, offering insights into our cultural roots.

The tale unfolds within the pages of the *Bhagavata Purana*, where a captivating narrative similar to that found in the *Vishnu Purana* reveals itself. It is within this sacred text that we encounter the enchanting account of Narmada, who emerges as the dear sister of the revered Naga beings.

In the sacred *Bhagavata Purana*, one can locate references to the illustrious Bhrigukaccha, known today as Bharuch, situated on the northern bank of the Narmada River. It is recounted that this very location served as the backdrop for the grand *yagya* of Bali, during which the divine manifestation of Sri Vishnu in the form of Vamanadeva graced the scene.[9]

According to the *Bhagavata*, Balarama once travelled all the way to the banks of the holy Narmada River. The spiritual significance of this occasion lies in its demonstration of the awe and respect that people have for this water body. When the bloody conflict between the arrogant Kauravas and the determined Pandavas broke out, Balarama was already on the holy waters of the Narmada. The story goes that he was able to take a holy dip in the Narmada River, not far from the dazzling metropolis of Mahishmati, and experienced the divine *darshana*.[10]

In the Vamana Purana

Within the sacred text of *Vamana Purana*, one encounters a captivating account that speaks of the revered Narmada River. It is in this narrative that we encounter the esteemed Chyavana Rishi, a sage of great wisdom and spiritual prowess. Drawn by an innate desire to purify his being, Chyavana Rishi embarks on a profound journey to immerse himself in the holy waters of the Narmada. As fate would have it, however, this spiritual sojourn takes an unexpected turn. For as Chyavana Rishi submerges himself in the tranquil embrace of the Narmada, a serpentine creature, with its powerful grip, seizes hold of him. In an instant, the sage finds himself transported to the ethereal realms beyond mortal comprehension. Undeterred by this unforeseen turn of events, Chyavana Rishi ventures forth in this mystical realm, traversing through the vast expanse of the ether world. It is amidst this other-worldly landscape that he encounters the illustrious Prahlada, a figure of great significance and spiritual enlightenment.

In the realm of the Narmada, a tale unfolds, whispered among the ancient winds. It is said that a mystical connection exists between this sacred river and the ethereal Sarasvati. Legend has it that those who venture to immerse themselves in the gentle embrace of Sarasvati's southern flow are bestowed with a profound experience akin to bathing in the very essence of Narmada herself.[11]

In the realm of ancient folklore, there exists yet another captivating tale, one that revolves around the legendary figures of Chanda and Munda. This particular narrative finds its roots in the mystical waters of the Narmada River, where the formidable duo of Chanda and Munda emerges, as if borne from the ethereal depths, with a singular purpose: to engage in a fierce battle against the indomitable Devi.[12]

In the illustrious *Vamana Purana*, it is recounted that the venerable Prahlada embarked upon a sacred pilgrimage to the revered Kapila Dhara. There, he partook in the purifying act of immersing himself in the holy waters and paid homage to the divine Narmada through the sacred ritual of *darshana puja*.[13]

In the *Vamana Purana*, Lord Vishnu unveils an array of names by which he is revered along the sacred banks of the Narmada River. Among these hallowed appellations are Vira, Shripati and a multitude of other revered titles.[14]

In the Vishnu Purana

In the ancient text known as the *Vishnu Purana*, a profound philosophical understanding of *Para-Brahmam* is said to have originated from the wise words of Parashara Rishi. It is believed that this knowledge was initially bestowed upon Daksha by the creator deity, Brahma. Daksha, in turn, passed down this sacred tale to Purukutsa, who had the privilege of hearing it on the serene banks of the holy River Narmada. In the ancient realm of knowledge, where wisdom flowed like a sacred river, a tale unfolded. It was Purukutsa, a learned sage with eyes that held the secrets of the universe, who took upon himself the task of narrating this tale. With utmost reverence, he began to weave the words, each syllable carrying the weight of centuries. As the story unfolded, Purukutsa found himself in the presence of Sarasvat, a revered scholar whose intellect shone like a beacon in the darkness. With great humility, Purukutsa shared his narrative, allowing the words to dance upon the air and find their way. In the tranquil embrace of the Narmada River, Raja Purukutsa found himself immersed in deep contemplation. It was on these very banks that a profound philosophical dialogue unfolded, forever etching its wisdom into the annals of time.[15]

It was Purukutsa who was helped by the Narmada and that is when the Nagaraja gave the blessings that no serpent poison would act against who worship the Narmada. From that day forward, Purukutsa became invincible to the venomous attacks of any snake. This divine intervention solidified Narmada's reputation as a revered deity, attracting countless devotees seeking protection from serpent bites.[16]

In the Agni Purana

Within the sacred pages of the *Agni Purana*, a brief yet captivating chapter unfolds, revealing the profound significance of the Narmada River and the enchanting realm of Amarkantak. With utmost grace and eloquence, this chapter delicately expounds upon the magnificence and sanctity that surrounds these revered destinations. The Amarkantak Parvat, known as Sri Parvat, is said to possess immense spiritual significance. It is believed that any action undertaken in this sacred place holds great merit, even the act of departing from this mortal realm. In the annals of this sacred place, it is inscribed that Lord Shiva and his divine consort, Parvati, have graced these hallowed grounds with their celestial presence. Not only have the divine beings sought solace in this ethereal abode, but even the formidable demon king, Hiranyakashyap, humbled himself before the divine altar, thereby attaining the desired boon bestowed by Lord Shiva himself. It also delves into the actions of the various *muni*'s who had undertaken the *tapasya* in this place.

The revered text of *Shraddha-kalpa* extols the virtues of performing the sacred ritual of *shraddha* on the banks of the mighty Narmada, as well as other revered locations.[17]

In the Narada Purana

In the enchanting chronicles of the *Narada Purana*, a vivid depiction emerges of the myriad *tirtha*s that grace the illustrious banks of the sacred Narmada River. A particular passage refers to the profound significance conferred upon each *sangama*, as it reveals the presence of precisely 108 *tirtha*s at these revered confluences. Fascinatingly, the *Narada Purana* delves into the intricate details of the numerous tributaries that gracefully converge with the mighty Narmada. In the epic tale of the *Narada Purana*, we find Mohini, the enchanting celestial being, embarking on a sacred pilgrimage to the revered Narmada *tirthas*. With grace and elegance, she traverses the sacred grounds of Amarkantak, where divinity intertwines with nature's splendour. From there, Mohini's journey leads her to the illustrious Mahishmati, a place known as Tripushkar Teerth, where spiritual seekers converge in search of enlightenment.[18]

It is the *Narada Purana* that refers to Galav Rishi and his son Bhadrashila. Detailed instructions for the Ekadashi Vrata practised on the banks of the Narmada are provided, as is the tale of the Galav Rishi and his son Bhadrashila, who is a devout devotee of Vishnu. Then, the *Narada Purana* discusses the several Puranas that extol the virtues of the holy Narmada.

In the Bhavishya Purana

The Holy River Narmada is mentioned multiple times in the *Bhavishya Purana*, including, most intriguingly, when the account of Surya's family is told.[19]

In the sacred *Bhavishya Purana*, there is a captivating account of a regal figure by the name of Chandrachuda, hailing from the illustrious city of Kashi. This noble king, driven by an unwavering devotion to the divine, undertakes the revered Satyanarayana Vrata, a sacred ritual that bestows immense spiritual merit upon its practitioner. Enveloped in the spiritual aura of his virtuous deeds, Chandrachuda embarks upon a pilgrimage to the hallowed banks of the revered Narmada River. It is here, amidst the sanctified surroundings, that he seeks to offer his heartfelt worship to the revered deity Sri Hari, the Supreme Lord.

In the Brahmavaivartta Purana

In the sacred text of the *Brahmavaivartta Purana*, the illustrious River Narmada finds mention in the context of Parashurama's arrival at its banks. It is during this momentous occasion that he sees a series of auspicious omens in his dream, foreshadowing his impending battle against the valiant Kartavirya Arjuna.[20]

In the Kurma Purana

In the glorious *Kurma Purana*, one can find numerous references to the sacred river Narmada. However, one particular account stands out, recounting the momentous occasion when the venerable sage

Markandeya engaged in a profound conversation with the noble Yudhisthira. Inquisitive about the most revered pilgrimage sites along the banks of the Narmada, Yudhishthira sought the sage's wisdom and guidance. In the sacred scriptures, Rishi Markandeya eloquently recounts the divine origins of the revered river Narmada. It is within these ancient texts that he reveals the profound truth that Narmada gracefully emerges from the very essence of Lord Shiva himself. It is this celestial connection that bestows upon Narmada an unparalleled magnificence, as her glory unfolds in all its resplendent grandeur. In the realm of spiritual liberation, it is widely proclaimed that the mere act of beholding the sacred Narmada River holds the power to emancipate one from the shackles of earthly existence. While other revered rivers such as the Sarasvati, the Yamuna and the Ganga require specific rituals and immersion to attain salvation, the Narmada bestows her divine grace solely through the act of witnessing her majestic presence.[21]

As the pages turned, the story took a profound turn, leading us into the enchanting world of the sacred. With each passing chapter, the narrative grew more captivating, unveiling the secrets of the revered Narmada River and the countless *tirtha*s that adorned its banks.

In the Brahmanda Purana

In the realm of Sanatana Dharma, the ancient scripture known as the *Brahmanda Purana* holds a prominent place. Within its sacred pages lies a tale that has woven its way into the very fabric of countless generations, captivating the hearts and minds of all who have encountered it. Once upon a time, in a land steeped in ancient legends and mystical tales, there existed a story that intertwined the fates of two remarkable individuals Kartavirya Arjuna and Rishi Jamadagni, and their extraordinary journey unfolded on the sacred banks of the mighty Narmada River.

In the Narasimha Purana

In the illustrious *Narasimha Purana*, a captivating tale unfolds wherein the valiant Pandavas, amidst their arduous journey, stumble upon a momentous encounter. Along the serene banks of the sacred Narmada River, they chance upon two enigmatic beings, veiled in the guise of ascetics, or as *sadhus*, two formidable demons known as Bahuroma and Sthulashira. Bahuroma and his cohorts harboured a sinister desire to abduct the illustrious Draupadi. There is a long story of Bahuroma and his life, but the interesting aspect is that it all happened in the Narmada Khanda.

In the Padma Purana

The *Padma Purana* recounts several tales from Sanatana Dharma, including those that focus on Mother Narmada. The history of the *tirtha*s on the Narmada bank and an in-depth description of the river itself may be found in the *Padma Purana*.

In the illustrious *Padma Purana*, great emphasis is placed upon the sacredness of the revered Narmada River, which is exalted as the holiest of rivers for the veneration of our esteemed ancestors, known as *pitr*.

The story of Rama, his wife Sita and his brother Lakshmana performing the *tarpana* for their parents on the banks of the Narmada is also told in the *Padma Purana*.[22] Amarkantak's glory and its holiness is again discussed in the Svarga Khanda of the *Padma Purana* by Narada.

In the sacred verses of the *Padma Purana*, a profound narrative unfolds, revealing the enchanting tale of Amarkantak. Within this mystical realm, we encounter the captivating story of Somasharma and his beloved wife, Sumana. Alas, their hearts were burdened by the absence of progeny, for they were bereft of sons to carry forth their lineage. It is amidst this poignant backdrop that a profound philosophical discourse takes shape, as Somasharma and Sumana engage in profound conversations that delve into the very essence of existence. Their souls intertwine, their minds entwine in a dance of intellectual exploration, as they seek solace and understanding in the face of their unfulfilled desires. Within the hallowed pages of the *Padma Purana*, the reader is transported to a realm where the boundaries between the mortal and the divine blur. In this sacred abode, a remarkable event got unfolded as their beloved offspring, a son named Subrata, came into existence. Subrata, a name that would soon resonate with reverence and awe, embarked on a spiritual journey that would forever alter the course of his life. It was through his unwavering devotion to the divine deity Vishnu that Subrata earned a distinguished place in the celestial realm of Vaikuntha.

In the illustrious *Padma Purana*, a treasure trove of ancient wisdom, one is bestowed with a plethora of intricate details pertaining to the sacred *tirtha*s adorning the hallowed banks of the revered Narmada River. Moreover, this sacred scripture graciously unveils the mystique surrounding the confluences that grace this divine waterway, while also shedding light on the esteemed sages and seers who have chosen to reside in close proximity to its ethereal banks.

In the Skanda and Vayu Purana

In the realm of ancient scriptures, the illustrious *Skanda Purana* and the venerable *Vayu Purana* grace us with their sacred verses. Within the depths of their profound wisdom, a chapter unfolds, dedicated to the enchanting tale of the holy river Narmada. This chapter, known as the Reva Khanda, stands as a testament to the reverence bestowed upon this sacred waterway by these esteemed texts. The Reva Khanda, a captivating realm, encompasses numerous *tirtha*s that have long evaded my quest for rediscovery. In the illustrious *Vasishtha Samhita*, one can delve into the sacred realm of *tirtha*s, where the ethereal exchange between the divine Lord Rama and the venerable sage Vasishtha resonates with timeless wisdom. Specifically, their dialogue reverberates with profound significance in relation to the revered Narmada *tirtha*s, ensuring its preservation for generations to come.

Historical Literature on Narmada

Mother Narmada is held in high esteem not only in religious and spiritual books, but also in many works of literature. Mother Narmada, whose presence is described as "awe-inspiring" in Kalidasa's *Raghuvansha*, is a real place.

Bharuch, historically known as Bhrigukaccha, was an essential stopping point for the adventurous travellers as they made their way across India. Crossing the mouth of the venerated Mother Narmada was one of the most difficult obstacles to reach the illustrious destination of Bharuch, and as such, it was frequently mentioned in stories about this bustling city.[1]

Even within the ancient manuscripts of the *Krityakalpataru* of Bhatta Lakshmidhara, a prominent figure in the court of Gahadavala king Govindacandra of Varanasi, one can find numerous references to the revered Mother Narmada. In the realm of literary treasures, there exist volumes that bestow upon us the sacred knowledge of the revered Mother Narmada. These books, meticulously crafted, bear within their pages the names and *tirtha*s (holy sites), associated with this divine entity.[2] In the eighth *kanda*, a profound tale unfolds, one that delves into the sacred *tirtha-yatra* (a pilgrimage of great significance). This ancient manuscript, penned nearly a millennium ago, unveils a vivid portrayal of the majestic river and the enchanting land of Amarkantak. It leaves one pondering over the ethereal beauty possessed by Mother Narmada, a beauty so captivating that it enticed even those residing along the banks of the revered Ganges to embark on this spiritual journey along her hallowed shores. On numerous occasions, along the banks of the sacred Narmada River, a divine phenomenon shall unfold. Narmada Maiya, the revered deity, shall beckon the souls of countless individuals to gather in her presence. Some shall embark on the sacred pilgrimage, known as *parikrama*, while others shall simply seek the blessings bestowed by her resplendent aura.

The rich tapestry of this nation's history revolves around the majestic figure of Mother Narmada. Whether chronicled in written accounts or passed down through generations via oral tradition, the essence of Narmada resonates deeply within the hearts and minds of its people.

Throughout the centuries, writers have been captivated by various texts that have managed to withstand the test of time. These texts, whether derived from ancient Puranas or inspired by the meandering path of the sacred River Narmada, continue to hold a prominent place within our cultural tapestry. One such writer, Virasimha, the ruler of Orcha, during the late sixteenth century, embarked on a remarkable journey that took him all the way from Amarkantak to the vast expanse of the sea. It is during this expedition that he encountered the profound wisdom encapsulated in the treatise known as the *Viramitrodaya*, authored by the esteemed Mitramishra. This remarkable work delves into the multifaceted aspects of the revered Narmada, offering a comprehensive exploration of its essence.

Rani Durgavati's husband, Dalapatraya, too, has contributed his narrative to the captivating tale of Mother Narmada. Within the text known as the *Narsimhaprasada*, one can discover a collection of approximately 172 eloquently crafted verses. These verses, carefully woven together, delve into the profound subject matter of the revered Narmada River and its interconnected *tirtha*s (holy pilgrimage sites).

1

My Narmada Parikrama

In the year 2016, I found myself in a tranquil setting, nestled upon the serene banks of the revered river Shipra. This majestic river gracefully meanders through the ancient city of Ujjain, India, a place where the divine deity Lord Shiva is venerated under the sacred terminology of Mahakala. It is here, in this sacred land, that the grand spectacle known as the Kumbha festival unfolds once every twelve years, drawing devotees from far and wide to participate in its sacred rituals and profound spiritual experiences. Kumbha holds a profound significance for individuals hailing from the Sanatana fold, as it stands as the most magnificent spectacle that humanity has ever witnessed. I had the immense privilege of participating in the sacred gathering known as Kumbha, where I resided in a camp for a duration exceeding two months.

Former Indian President Shri Ram Nath Kovind, the then governor of Bihar state, repeatedly invited me to come to Bihar shortly after the Kumbha. Even though I was exhausted from my two-month-long schedule, I finally decided to visit Bihar after receiving numerous calls from the Raj Bhavan, the official residence of governor of any state as it is known.

It was thanks to Shri Ram Nath Kovind that I was able to visit Bodh-Gaya and other important sites. Contrarily, I have long wanted to visit Bodhgaya. I was able to spend a considerable amount of time sitting under the Bodhi tree since Shri Ram Nath Kovind had everything perfectly planned. I had visited multiple locations in Bihar and arrived back in Patna late at night during the second week of June 2016.

On those warm June evenings, as I went off to sleep, I could not help but ponder over the fact that Lord Buddha, who had lived thousands of years ago and meditated in Bodh-Gaya, under the *bodhi* tree, and the places, still emanated energy. I thought it would be amazing to soak up the positive energy that floats around Mother Narmada, where millions of enlightened people have meditated over the course of millennia. This was my first thinking when considering performing the Narmada Parikrama.

It was an interesting anecdote that after spending a few days relaxing in the Raj Bhavan, I flew out of Patna and was waiting in the Mumbai airport when my phone rang. It was Dr Mohan Yadav who is now the Chief Minister of Madhya Pradesh, but was a member of the legislative assembly back then.

Dr Mohan Yadav had invited me to join the Shipra Parikrama that he was hosting in Ujjain. During the Kumbha, the water of the Mother Narmada was lifted and brought out in Shipra, reviving the long-dry Shipra River and making it possible for the Kumbha Mela, which featured many religious bathing ceremonies.

Since my first *parikrama* of the Narmada River's holy waters took place I have always felt that the benevolent Mother Narmada had bestowed upon me her blessings. As for the rest, it is all in the annals of history; everything fell into place in the year 2022-23, when I was finally able to go on Narmada Parikrama myself.

It is stated in Indian Shastras that by simply gazing upon the Narmada, one is liberated from this mortal realm and granted the Divine's gifts; the river is an integral aspect of India's cosmology.

Several rivers and cultures around the world celebrate their origin, many rivers in India are sacred, but the holy Narmada is the only one to be circumambulated where seekers finds spiritual enlightenment and purification.

2

Amritasya Ma Narmada Pada-Parikrama

From the very depths of my being, I have always possessed an inclination for meticulous planning. Even as I delved into the realms of spirituality and religion, I discovered that the art of planning held a profound significance within the sacred teachings of Sanatana Dharma. Within the vast tapestry of the Sanatana fold, each and every ritual, or any other sacred practice, possesses a profound sense of purpose and meticulous planning. This attention to detail and careful organization is not limited to rituals alone, but extends to all aspects of life within the Sanatana Dharma. Whether it is the construction of temples, the observance of festivals, or even personal daily routines, every action is thoughtfully planned and executed with utmost precision. This emphasis on meticulous planning not only ensures the smooth flow of events but also fosters a deep sense of mindfulness and reverence in every practitioner.

In the year 2021, I made an unequivocal announcement to embark on a remarkable journey – the completion of Ma Narmada Pada-Parikrama. With this declaration, a new chapter unfolded, initiating a meticulous and extensive planning process that would span several months.

Little did I know that countless revered saints and individuals embarked on the sacred journey of *parikrama*, completely oblivious to the mundane necessities of life such as food, water and logistical arrangements. On the auspicious occasion of Mahashivaratri, I found myself standing before a group of five individuals, with whom I had forged deep and enduring connections over the course of many years. With a heart filled with hope and determination, I humbly approached each of them, beseeching their support in funding the grand programme that lay before us. I wanted to make sure that every money that is spent has the purity and devotion that I required for the trip. It happened so that I was able to resist the desires of many people who wanted to fund the *parikrama*; interestingly, whose money I must have taken according to divine plan, their money got used. I saw this and felt that Mother Narmada has accepted the rules that I have established for the trip.

The entire thing was planned in the month of April in 2022, and it looked like a jumbo plan where a whole city would be walking along with me. There was a mobile kitchen, a water tanker, a truck stocked with any and all necessities for the trip. There was another truck with enough food to serve a huge number of people and enough infrastructure to set up small communities that can run on their own with their own lights and tents; a vehicle adapted as *ratha*, intended specifically to transport the sacred of *kalasha*'s of Mother Narmada's water. Amritasya Ma Narmada Pada-Parikrama is now a household name thanks to the River Goddess's help in organizing the journey around her mighty womb.

Amritasya means the holy nectar, and that is why the name of my *parikrama* I had chosen as Amritasya Ma Narmada Pada-Parikrama. The name of my *parikrama* symbolizes the spiritual journey I embarked upon along the sacred River Narmada, seeking the divine elixir of spirituality.

3

Rund, Jalheri or Hanumani Parikrama

In the bygone days, it was not customary for every *parikrama* to commence from Omkareshwar. However, as the tides of time have shifted, a significant number of Narmada *parikramas* now embark from this sacred site. Omkareshwar, nestled along the banks of the revered Narmada River, features the presence of one of the esteemed Jyotirlinga's in all of India.

In the annals of the late eighteenth century, the historical records that have come down to us indicate that the *parikrama* would commence from one of the three revered locations: Bharuch, Amarkantak and Vimaleshwar. In the annals of ancient scriptures, there exists a mention of the celestial deities embarking on a sacred journey, known as *parikrama*, commencing from the hallowed northern banks of the revered Narmada River. This momentous pilgrimage, which holds great significance, commenced from the sacred Devapatha *linga*, a topic that shall be dealt with in subsequent chapters.

Within the sacred scriptures that delve into the profound realm of *tirtha*s and the revered Narmada River, a certain ambiguity arises when attempting to ascertain the precise origin point from which one ought to commence the sacred *parikrama*. But as time has moved on, this has been included in a number of publications that outline the standards and locations where *parikrama* should be started. Even though I am well familiar with the historical and literary landscapes that have shaped the Narmada Parikrama, I still considered beginning the *parikrama* from Omkareshwar. An undeniable impulse compelled me to commence my narrative from this very point, as if the threads of destiny were intricately woven into the fabric of this moment. Deep within the depths of my being, I sensed that Mother Narmada contained a secret, a revelation of great significance. And so, with a profound sense of anticipation, I embarked upon my journey, being fully aware that the pivotal events were about to unfold right here, in this very place. Prior to my *parikrama*, I found myself acquainted with none but the revered Jyotirlinga in Omkareshwar. But now, I find myself in possession of a memory, a tangible connection to the vibrant city, its inhabitants, and the beautiful surroundings that have left an indelible mark on my being. It was not merely the beginning of my pilgrimage that I have embarked upon from this very place, but also a profound sense that a fragment of my essence remains rooted in this sacred town.

The readers, upon perusing these words, may find themselves pondering: who, among the countless souls, had the privilege of embarking upon the sacred pilgrimage of the Narmada River for the very first time? Several years ago, I had the privilege of being asked this very question. In response, I posited that it must have been the divine beings themselves who embarked on the sacred *parikrama*, as our scriptures indicate. Furthermore, the esteemed sage Markandeya recounted the tale of the Narmada River to Yudhishthira and his companions, providing us with invaluable records.

There are three kinds of *parikrama* that I come to know through scriptures – *Rund, jalahari* and *hanumani.*

Those who embark on the *rund parikrama* must meet the high seas and cross the river at the mouth, while those who take on the *jalahari* shall never have to set foot in a boat.

Indeed, within the realm of *jalahari*, one can discern the existence of two distinct types. In the initial form, the *parikrama* would commence at the sacred site of Hari ka Dham, also known as Reva Sagar Sangam. The pilgrims would embark on a journey that spanned the entirety of the terrain, traversing its vast expanse, until reaching the final destination of Vimleshwar, situated on the southern shore.

The second type begins from Amarkantak. In this scenario, it is necessary to undertake two separate journeys. The proposed itinerary involves travelling southward along the bank until reaching the sea, then returning to Amarkantak. Following this, the journey will continue northward along the opposite bank until reaching Hari ka Dham (Reva Sagar Sangam) before returning once again to Amarkantak.

In addition, the *hanumani* type was just recently launched, allowing for convenient river crossing at any chosen place. According to legend, it all kicks off in *sailani* which is to the north-west of Omkareshwar.

During the British occupation, they documented the *parikrama* they witnessed or heard about. Inaccuracies in British records may be found in the early days of their arrival when they were still seeking to understand the country and its customs. According to William Wilson Hunter's account in the initial edition of the *Imperial Gazetteer of India* published in 1881, the *parikrama* begins at the mouth and lasts for one to two years. However, Monier-Williams' report in 1883 indicates that the Narmada Parikrama commences at Amarkantak and lasts for almost three years. I believe they both have seen two different kinds of *parikrama* that we know as *jalahari.*

As we prepared ourselves, anticipation filled the air, for we were on the verge of embarking on the sacred *rund parikrama*. This spiritual journey would commence at the revered Omkareshwar, traversing southern bank and then crossing the confluence of holy mother with Ocean. And then meandering along the northern banks of the mighty Narmada, until finally reaching Amarkantak, the origin and then again traversing southern banks and culminating at the sacred grounds of Omkareshwar.

4

Mandhata-Omkareshwar

As the early days of November opened, the much-anticipated arrived Karttik Purnima. It was during this auspicious time that I found myself gracing the sacred banks of Omkareshwar, a place also known as Mandhata-Omkareshwar. The very name of this destination perfectly conveys the true essence that permeates its very being. The Omkareshwar fare has long been renowned for its peak season, which unfailingly arrives during the enchanting month of Karttik (October–November). It is during this time that a multitude of eager visitors, hailing from the neighbouring regions, flock to participate in the joyful festivities that abound. The tradition endures even in our modern times, as Karttik Purnima remains a momentous occasion that draws countless individuals to the sacred grounds of Mandhata-Omkareshwar. It is during this auspicious time that numerous pilgrims embark on their spiritual journey, engaging in the sacred practice of *parikrama*, much like I myself would engage in.

The region where Omkareshwar falls is known as Nimar, which has been inhabited for thousands of years, and many different cultures and dynasties have left their mark on the area. From the first century BCE until the fourth century CE, Nimar was a component of the powerful Satavahana Empire in southern and central India. The art, literature, and architecture of the Satavahanas were widely admired. Nimar probably saw first hand how their culture and government impacted other places. Nimar was ruled by the Vakataka dynasty, an important Indian dynasty notable for their support of Buddhism and the arts, between the fifth and tenth centuries. Under their leadership, the area saw major improvements in the fields of architecture and commerce. From the eleventh through the fourteenth centuries, Nimar was ruled by the Paramara dynasty, who originated in the neighbouring Malwa region. The exquisite temples of Mandu and Maheshwar are just two examples of the Paramaras' contributions to architecture. Between the years 1500 and 1800, Nimar was invaded multiple times by the Delhi Sultanate and the Mughal Empire. Wars broke out between local chieftains and Mughal soldiers, and the region as a whole became increasingly unstable politically. After Nimar was conquered by the Mughals, Islamic culture began to permeate the area. In the nineteenth century, as the Maratha Empire was consolidating its hold on central India, Nimar fell under its sway. The Marathas took control of Nimar and included it into their empire. This is when east Nimar came into the influence and was later occupied by the British forces. In the twentieth century, Nimar became a part to the state of Madhya Pradesh after India gained its freedom from the British colonial authority in 1947, and its borders were later changed to create new districts.

In the heart of Madhya Pradesh's East Nimar district, nestled within the majestic Narmada River, lies the enchanting island of Mandhata. Godarpura is the name given to the region that is across from Mandhata on the southern bank of the Narmada River. The holy Narmada caught the attention of European travellers to the enchanted kingdom of Mandhata for the first time in the late eighteenth century. This holy river, which was formerly full of life, attracted those who were eager to learn more about it because of its great depth. Many species of fish and alligators took refuge in its waters, fostering a balanced ecology that captivated anyone who got to see it. The courageous fish displayed such unwavering courage that they boldly arrived and grabbed the holy offerings from the devoted worshippers. There was no fear in them, and this intrigued the British officers who had never seen such a thing.[1]

As the site of the famous Jyotirlinga, Mandhata-Omkareshwar is an extremely important Hindu pilgrimage site in the Nimar area. Despite considerable archaeological remains on the island, its surroundings and the finding of several remarkable inscriptions, the historical role and significance of Mandhata have yet to be investigated in depth.

The narrative surrounding the nomenclature of Mandhata is intriguing. As per the Reva Khanda, which is the part of the *Skanda Purana*, the island was initially known as Baidurya Mani Parvat. It was later renamed to Mandhata as a result of a blessing bestowed upon Raja Mandhatri, the seventeenth ruler of the Solar dynasty, who had conducted a significant religious ceremony on the island in honour of the deity Sri Omkar.

King Mandhata's ancestry goes back to Chauhan Rajput Bharat Singh, who is said to have married the daughter of local chiefs Nathu Bhil at the invitation of the Daryo nath, the traditional chieftain of the Omkar temple. According to British records, the Raja of Mandhata was the legitimate custodian of all Mandhata temples in the past; today, however, his successors' claims lay with the Omkar trust.

Mandhata boasts a rich history and its seclusion has contributed to the creation of historical landscapes on the island. However, this same seclusion also made it vulnerable to the destructive actions of Muslim conquerors who ravaged the temples and architectural marvels of ancient times. It is unlikely that those responsible for the destruction of the temples possessed the ability to replicate or approximate their magnificence. However, the repercussions of such destruction have left a lasting impact on the nation, with India still recovering from the damage inflicted on her over centuries.

During the late eighteenth century, British officials documented in their internal correspondence an observation regarding the Mandhata region. Specifically, they noted that every ancient dome had been toppled and no deity, icon, or creature remained unscathed.[2]

In the year 1295 CE, Alauddin traversed this region upon his return from a Deccan raid. During his conquest of the nearby Asirgarh, he proceeded to pass over Mandhata and caused the destruction of numerous temples. This pattern of destruction was subsequently perpetuated by the Ghori prince of Malwa and ultimately culminated under the reign of the arch-iconoclast Aurangzeb.[3]

Despite the extensive devastation wrought upon this insular religious community, it remained akin to a veritable playground of historical significance. In this location, I have discovered remnants that encapsulate the entirety of India's cultural and spiritual essence.

After a comprehensive analysis that was done by many of the remains in Mandhata, it is apparent that the subject matter is extensive and has the potential to occupy an entire book. However, I will focus on the two temples I visited after completing the Narmada Parikrama, Siddheshwar Mahadev and Gauri Somnath.

The construction of the Siddheshwar Mahadev Temple showcases an exceptional level of skill and refinement, which is particularly striking in the remains. It is worth noting that the temple's dome has been substituted with a flat roof, which may have been subject to damage during a raid. The temple showcases the detrimental actions of invading forces that caused harm to the cultural heritage of the country. As a consequence, numerous images were mutilated, which involved the elimination of the ears of elephants.

Gauri Somnath boasts a sizeable Shivalinga as well as a large Nandi. The story dates back to a time when leaders of the Mohammedan community visited a temple repeatedly and were informed that the *linga*, which was previously white, had the ability to represent the metamorphosis that the soul would undergo in its subsequent lives. The leader was shown as a pig, which led to the *linga* turning jade bleak when he became enraged and set it on fire.

During the period of British history in 1870, the Nandi statue, crafted from high-quality green stone, was found without its head and an adjacent pillar was overturned, serving as a reminder of the destruction that had occurred. Currently, the Nandi artefact features a head that was added at a later time, without any known historical documentation.[4]

The buildings in the area are constructed from a combination of local stones and yellow sandstones that were likely transported from a distance. This suggests that the town employed skilled architects to construct the Sanatana temples or Hindu architecture on the island. The entire Narmada Valley was an area that was likely inhabited by a populous community at an early stage.[5]

During the seventeenth century, the southern bank was sparsely populated and covered by forest. However, over time, it became home to various *ashramas* of different branches, including Godars and Dashnamis. These *ashramas* were initially constructed with the assistance of Ahilyabai and other Maratha leaders. Omkareshwar has had a longstanding association with Maharashtra for quite some time.

As I ventured into the town, a profound sensation washed over me, as if the very essence of the city had suddenly awakened to its profound historical significance. The River Narmada, with its meandering course and the ancient secrets it guards within its banks, lends an air of mystery to the town, as if it will require a considerable amount of time for its inhabitants to unravel the hidden treasures that lie within their very own hometown.

The town was bustling with tourists and traffic, and I could not help but notice the police officers patiently explaining to some tourists that their car might get stuck if they continued on their current path. Omkareshwar is comparatively a small town and traffic is not the best here, having very small roads that do not allow the motorized traffic to pass smoothly. It was quite a scene, almost like watching a movie without any retakes.

The Omkareshwar is located in the inner part of Nimar, surrounded by a forest. Despite its previously inaccessible location, the Sanatanis have built numerous temples and have spent a significant amount of time here. Some of the recent historical mentions of this location appeared in British records in 1822, as noted in John Malcom's *A Memoir of Central India* (1823).

The *Indian Antiquary* featured an article on Mandhata in 1876, authored by Ravaji Vasudeva Tullu, who held the position of Superintendent of State Education in the Holkar State located in Indore. Tullu expounded upon the Indian viewpoint of Omkareshwar by citing Puranic sources that make reference to the Omkareshwar. Nonetheless, his literary compositions were predominantly disregarded for numerous decades. In contemporary times, there has been a resurgence of attention towards his literary works among scholars investigating the historical status of the Holkar dynasty.

In 1897, Henry Cousens published a report titled *Lists of Antiquarian Remains in the Central Provinces and Berar*. At the time of publication, the Siddhanatha and Gauri Somanath temples, along with a few other remains at Mandhata, had already been identified as monuments warranting different levels of protection. Additionally, two reliefs featuring elephants from the plinth of the Siddhanath Temple were acquired by the Museum in Nagpur.

The noble endeavour to safeguard the sanctity of the Siddhanatha Temple was set into motion in the year 1904, spurred by the auspicious occasion of Lord George Nathaniel Curzon's arrival. This statesman, serving as the Viceroy of India, came to the sacred grounds of Mandhata on the memorable day of 31 October 1902. Of particular significance is the fact that Curzon, in his discerning judgement, regarded the Siddhanath Temple as the solitary structure in the vicinity that merited substantial financial backing. This assertion is well-documented in the esteemed writings of Cousens (1903: 7; 1904: 20; 1906: 57). In accordance with the narrative provided by John H. Marshall in 1909, it is stated that all subsequent actions have been established based on the written message that was left by the aforementioned individual. It had huge impact that apart from this temple, no other temple structures were taken care of, and thus a great historical chapter of India was lost.

Although Forsyth's gazetteer report of 1870 indicated the presence of numerous archaeological remains at Mandhata, the unfavourable assessment of their historical significance by Lord Curzon appears to have hindered their thorough investigation. This is despite the discovery of several significant and unique epigraphs. Ah, poor Curzon! It seems his trip to the island left him feeling as deflated as a punctured beach ball. But let us be real, who would not break a sweat in that scorching October heat?

In 1904, Frederick Eden Pargiter made the first suggestion of Mandhata's historical significance. According to Pargiter, the *Devimahatmya* (chapters 81-93) of the *Markandeya Purana* may have been written in the ancient city of Mahishmati, according to them which was located on the island. Pargiter's research on the topic is where you may find these data.[6] Further excavations at Maheshwar had disproven this identification, notwithstanding John Faithful Fleet's initial endorsement for it. Despite the obvious futility of their efforts, both researchers should be commended for bringing Mandhata to the attention of the scholarly community. Since then, only publications focusing on the epigraphs discovered at Mandhata have been written by academics.

Even though there has only been a little amount of archaeological study, it is crucial that we familiarize ourselves with what we do know. Important epigraphs from the ninth century have been uncovered from the Amareshvara Temple.

In the depths of time, around the year 1100, there existed a collection of copper plates known as the Mandhata Grant. These ancient artefacts, with their intricate inscriptions, were discovered within the sacred walls of the Amareshvara Temple. It was a remarkable find, shedding light on the reign of Jayasimha I, a ruler of great significance. Bhima was one of the forty-two villages in the Maktula group in the Purnapathaka Mandala, and judging by the copper-plate records available, Jayasimha I authorized the allocation of its dues to the brahmanas associated with the *pathshala* located at the revered Amareshvara Temple.

It is dated the 13th of the dark half of Asadha in the year 1112, the term *svayamajna* indicates that the king personally gave this grant to the relevant individuals. It has been found via careful exploration of the neighbourhood that village Bhima and the adjacent region of Bhimpura are situated to the east of Godarpura. In addition, it is important to note that Maktula, located about 12 km to the south, is identical to the modern-day community of Mathela. Furthermore, Purnapathaka, which is around 30 km south-east of Mandhata, stands for Punasa.[7]

More inscriptions have been discovered from the Amareshvara Temple, now called Mamleshwara. These inscriptions are reported to have been discovered during the Jayamsimha I period (year 1068), hidden within the revered grounds of Amareshvara Temple. Stone inscriptions, weathered by the passage of countless years, were brought to light once more. It was the esteemed N.P. Chakravarti who, in the year 1948, unveiled this treasure to the world. In his seminal publication, he revealed with great reverence that he had meticulously transcribed a collection of Sanskrit strotras. These ancient verses, etched upon the side walls of the ardhamanandapa, held their silent vigil within the hallowed confines of the Amareshvara Temple at Mandhata. In addition, he made mention of having accomplished this particular task during the initial months of 1938. Adorning the Northern wall are three remarkable treasures, each possessing its own unique allure. Firstly, an exquisite eight-line stotra, resplendent with nine verses, gracefully extols the virtues of the revered river Narmada. Its mellifluous words weave a tapestry of adoration, paying homage to the sacred waters that flow with divine grace. Second, the renowned *Shiva-Mahimna Stotram*, a masterpiece of devotion, graces the wall with its profound presence. Comprising a grand total of forty verses, this masterpiece of spiritual expression spans an impressive twenty-two lines. Within its verses remain the power to transport one's soul to the ethereal realms, as it delves deep into the magnificence of Lord Shiva. Lastly, a modest yet profound three-line verse adorns the northern wall, offering heartfelt praise to the divine union of Shiva and Parvati. In its brevity, it captures the essence of their eternal love, resonating with the profound beauty that emanates from their celestial bond. Together, these three treasures form a harmonious symphony of devotion, enriching the northern wall with their sacred presence. Each item, in its own unique way, contributes to the tapestry of spiritual expression, inviting all who behold them to immerse themselves in the divine realms they represent. Within the vast expanse of literature, there exists but a solitary reference to an exquisitely inscribed *stotra* (a hymn of profound adulation) dedicated solely to the majestic Narmada River. In spite of its undeniable significance as the earliest documented testament to the veneration of the revered River Goddess Narmada, this particular piece of literature has regrettably yet to see the light of publication. The inscription unearthed at the Amareshvara Temple stands as a resolute testament, assuring scholars that within its sacred confines lies a realm filled with an abundance of invaluable knowledge awaiting their eager exploration.

Amareshvara, once a revered sanctuary, fell into obscurity amidst the tumultuous conflicts of the seventeenth and eighteenth centuries. The southern banks, once bustling with life, were abandoned and swallowed by the encroaching wilderness. As the eighteenth century drew to a close, the Peshwa, driven by a fervent desire to resurrect the temple's glory, embarked on a quest to rebuild it. Alas, both the sacred *linga* and its ancient abode had vanished, eluding their determined search. However, another temple was constructed alongside a group of smaller ones using slabs primarily sourced from the island's demolished temples. Subsequently, while excavating for bricks (many of which are of an old shape and can be found all over the neighbourhood), the ancient *linga* was discovered perched atop four *argha*s, proving its existence throughout each of the world's four epochs. Because it is aligned with Omkar and the Kapila Sangam, where a little stream flows into the Narmada, it has been deemed the authentic one by the Benares experts.[8] There is enough materials that have been found on the Mandhata-Omkareshwar but one cannot help but observe that the Mandhata-Omkareshwar Jyotirlinga in India has received relatively scant attention from researchers, thus arousing a sense of intrigue regarding the underlying factors contributing to this prevailing pattern.[9]

Omkareshwar is a sacred city in India that is renowned for its *ashrama*s and temples. The city has a rich history and continues to emanate a divine aura that is truly captivating. The city serves as the primary point of origin for the majority of pilgrims embarking on the *parikrama* of Mother Narmada. However, it is currently characterized by inadequate organization. This location attracts a significant number of tourists and spiritual pilgrims. However, the state of the public restrooms is unsatisfactory and the management of waste disposal is inadequate. Bad traffic control is a common occurrence.

Omkareshwar at one point was challenging to access due to its location in the remote Nimar region, which had changed in recent century. This area is bordered by the towering Satpura mountains on one side and the verdant Vindhya mountains on the other. The location boasts a breathtaking terrain and a culturally diverse atmosphere. Apart from the exceptional gastronomy and warm reception, tourists traversing the *parikrama* route in the Nimar areas will observe the deep reverence accorded to the Narmada River in the region.

The residents of the Nimar region exhibit a remarkable dedication towards assisting individuals who are embarking on the *parikrama* of Mother Narmada. Their unwavering commitment creates an atmosphere that can be likened to being indulged by an infinite reservoir of care and devotion. Without Nimar's presence, the *parikrama* route would have been significantly arid.

The Jyotirlinga is located on an island in Omkareshwar, which is shaped in a manner that accurately represents the Sanatana symbol for *OM*. The legend of Omkareshwar holds significant importance in the cultural and philosophical traditions of a community.

This is the place where Adi Shankaracharya arrived to seek knowledge and found his spiritual mentor. He remained for a period and authored the *Narmadashtakam*, a remarkable composition that is presently recited by numerous individuals during their veneration of the Narmada River.

The *Narmadashtakam* serves as a *mantra* and also delineates the attributes of the revered river and the saints who have dedicated themselves to the Sanatana Dharma. I have not come across any other *ashtakam* that has resonated with me as deeply in terms of its philosophical, ecological, and unifying themes as this one. This location is also a final resting place for numerous renowned spiritual figures. The entire environment is imbued with the rich heritage of Indian culture, serving as a vibrant representation of the country's unique identity.

A number of activities were scheduled for the *parikrama*, with the initial week of November 2022 being dedicated to Omkareshwar. It was later discovered that the communal food (*bhandara*) and the scheduled activities for the week were innovative concepts. As Mother Narmada served as our source of inspiration, it is evident that no other approach could have yielded such a comprehensive plan.

The initial week of the programme was structured to engage and facilitate all social, cultural and individual groups or volunteers who have offered their services to support the cause of Mother Narmada. I expressed my appreciation towards the individuals and organizations who have dedicated their efforts towards the preservation of Sanatana Dharma and the support of the *parikrama* of Maiya Narmada.

5

Mahant Mangal Das Tyagi

Prior to the *parikrama*, I did not have any acquaintances in Omkareshwar. Although I had previously visited the temple town with Dr Mohan Yadav, I did not have any established connections with individuals residing there. During the planning phase of the *parikrama*, I received a phone call from Lokesh Jharbade informing me that Mahant Mangal Das Tyagi wished to speak with me. I greeted the Mahant and then a resounding roar, that emanated from an individual with whom I was not yet acquainted, welcomed me for the *parikrama* and Omkareshwar. Little did I know that this encounter would mark the beginning of an intriguing relationship that would unfold over the course of the *parikrama*.

Upon my arrival at Omkareshwar, the itinerary dictated that on the initial day of the programme, we were to proceed to the main temples to engage in prayer and present offerings to the presiding deity of Omkareshwar. I shared my intention with Jitendra Sharma, who was overseeing the programme, to meet with Mahant Mangal Das Tyagi, who was expected to lead the programme. Jitendra Sharma informed me that Mahant Mangal Das would meet me during the procession.

However, I expressed my disapproval of this arrangement and insisted on meeting him prior to the commencement of the procession. I visited the ashram of the renowned Jod Ganpati temple and proceeded to the area where the Mahant was living. I encountered an individual in his early 50s who possessed a lengthy white beard and was not attired in any upper garments. This individual, known as Mahant Mangal Das Tyagi, has maintained this manner of living for an extended period of time. I respectfully greeted him, and he kindly invited me to take a seat. We engaged in general discussions, however, I anticipated an intriguing relationship with Mahant, which ultimately came to fruition.

Dr Mohan Yadav was in attendance during the procession, and while visiting Omkareshwar Jyotirlinga, we engaged in discussions pertaining to the procession. This is when Mahant Mangal Das Tyagi expressed that if we were to enhance the grandeur of the procession, it would be beyond our capabilities as it is solely dependent on the blessings of Mother Narmada, who bestows her blessings upon all that is destined to occur. I acknowledged his statement. This marked the inception of our relationship, which has remained amicable to date.

Mahant Mangal Das Tyagi is a highly recognised individual in Omkareshwar, and it is likely that he is known by a majority of the local population due to his prominent presence and notable character. He possesses a commanding vocal presence, yet maintains a humble demeanour. He exhibits unwavering dedication to the cause of Mother Narmada and consistently provides assistance to individuals embarking on the *parikrama* pilgrimage. He possesses a passion for providing food to the underprivileged. He and his team prepare daily meals and distribute them at various *ghat*s, with a special focus on Nagar Ghat, where Mahant Mangal Das Tyagi once spent his days in search of sustenance. He made the decision to continuously serve the underprivileged population for as long as he is able to do so.

During the first week of my stay in Omkareshwar, I frequently visited the *ashrama* of the Mahant, occasionally even making visits during the late hours which was proffered by him.

6

Truth Speaks

A few members of the press were waiting for me when I initially arrived at the Omkareshwar Dharmashala (where the seven days of events were taking place). I had just arrived in Omkareshwar and was feeling quite exhausted, but members of the press insisted that I give an interview anyway. I got the impression that at least one of them had a chip on his shoulder because he apparently assumed that, as a spiritual person, I would go on and on about how amazing the *parikrama* is that I am going into.

Upon my initial arrival at the Omkareshwar Dharmashala, where the seven-day events were being held, I was greeted by several members of the press who were waiting for me. Upon my arrival in Omkareshwar, despite feeling fatigued, I was approached by members of the press who requested for an interview. It appears that one of them harboured a negative attitude, presuming that my spiritual inclination would prompt me to excessively extol the virtues of the *parikrama* that I intend to undertake.

I respectfully requested that the organizing committee be responsible for addressing any inquiries and providing responses. I conveyed to the journalists that my purpose is not to provide answers to inquiries, but rather to engage in constructive dialogues with them. At the time of the event, a group of journalists assembled to observe my actions. I found it enjoyable when they attempted to intimidate me. The journalist, Vijay Jain, inquired about my objectives for conducting *parikrama*.

Upon discerning that the individual in question was not inquiring for the purpose of obtaining information, but rather was assessing my level of knowledge, I directed my attention to his gaze and responded that the act of *parikrama* is solely intended to revolve around Mother Narmada. Any assertion to the contrary would be deemed fraudulent.

The individual was taken aback by the response and had assumed that, given the scope of the programme, the speaker would elaborate on the specific objectives and strategies for leading the initiative. This was not part of my original plan. However, the undeniable weight of truth compelled every journalist present to transcend their professional roles and become friends. We had many responsibilities to fulfil, but the journalists would often visit me for meals during our stay in Omkareshwar.

It is noteworthy that several spiritual figures, during their *parikrama*, tend to discuss their aspirations and objectives, while overlooking the fundamental purpose of the practice, which is to perform *parikrama* itself. I have consistently expressed my beliefs in a direct and honest manner. Regrettably, in contemporary society, candour is a scarce commodity, which has had a significant impact on numerous journalists who have encountered my candid approach.

The programme's first day was commenced as per the scheduled plan.

7

Parikrama Begins

The seven days leading up to our *parikrama* were packed with events, the highlight of which was the evening *arti* on the Maiya Narmada, followed by a programme and *bhandara*. During one *bhandara*, we invited all of the priests from the several Omkareshwar temples to attend. The *pujari*s are the first people I think of when I consider those who have been hurt or killed by Sanatana Dharma's enemies. The priestly class was expected to defend the temple at all costs, regardless of whether they lived or died doing so. It was crucial, in my opinion, that we invited the Omkareshwar priestly class to demonstrate our appreciation to the Pujaris all across the globe who have labored ceaselessly for ages to preserve the holy places and rituals.

In honour of the saints of Omkareshwar, who have assisted innumerable pilgrims on their way to *sannyasa* and through the *parikrama*, we set aside a special day to honour them. The *bhandara* was the culmination of Mahant Mangal Das Tyagi's attempts to gather all of the saints of the region. On this particular day, Minister of Cultural and Religious Affairs Usha Thakur had attended the evening *arti* as well.

Many worshippers of Omkar Maharaj have relied on the assistance of local boatmen to safely cross the sacred Narmada River. Previously, pilgrims to Omkar Mountain would have to rely solely on boatmen to make the journey across the holy Narmada, but a recently constructed bridge has made the journey much simpler. Many *parikramavasi*s have been assisted by the Kevats in their journey through the many streams that flow into Mother Narmada, and we must not forget their contributions. We wanted to show our gratitude to the entire family of those who have sacrificed so much for Sanatana Dharma, therefore, we extended the invitation to them as well.

Without the *sevadara*s of numerous temples, it would be difficult to obtain temple services, thus they were given a day set apart just for them. It was my responsibility to host a programme and *bhandara* for temple officials and *sevadara*s before my *parikrama* began.

It is a vital part of Sanatana Dharma that, upon going into any temple, one is greeted by a plethora of shops selling the necessary items for performing the *puja*. These stores may seem unremarkable at first glance, but upon reflection, it is clear that they perform a truly invaluable service; without them, our ritual system would collapse. The next day, we invited everyone in Omkareshwar to a feast, including shopkeepers selling puja items, believing that this would be the best way to express our gratitude and connect with as many people as possible.

Kanya-pujana was performed on the first day, and it was also performed again on 7 November 2022. On the evening of 7 November 2022, devotees gathered at the Brahmpuri Ghat to perform a special *puja* to Narmada Maiya and later on a *bhandara*.

The *bhandara*s I conducted over the course of the week were my way of expressing my thanks to the many persons and organizations who have contributed so much to advancing the *dharma* in this country. It was not until much later that I learned from journalists and priests in Omkareshwar that our seven-day stay and *bhandara* offerings were not actually part of the many religious people who had gone in *parikrama*. Let us see whether others adopt the practice that was established.

The event on 7 November evening was graced by the presence of members of the coordination committee as well as Dr Mohan Yadav, Chandrashekhar Bawankule, his wife, and several families of those who will be embarking on the *parikrama*, including mine.

The objective of the *puja* was to undertake the *sankalpa* of *parikrama*. This indicates that we will conduct the *parikrama* with utmost respect and avoid any form of vehicle or transportation to move between locations, except when crossing tributaries of Narmada. In such cases, we will utilize small boats (*dongis*). Similarly, we will use boats to cross the *sangama*, where holy Narmada meets the ocean, to reach the other side. Our daily routine will involve walking on foot, including traversing both banks of the esteemed Narmada River. After the conclusion of our *sankalpa*, we will proceed back to this location and pay homage to Mother Narmada once more.

In our *sankalpa*, we embarked on a sacred quest to obtain the revered Narmada water, carefully collecting it in a number of vessels. These containers ranged from small portable *kalasha*s (which will be kept in pockets of those who will walk on *parikrama*) to larger *kalasha*s (water pots) that could be conveniently transported by vehicles and would be used for evening and morning ceremony of *arti*.

The vehicle had been specifically designed to accommodate the sizeable *kalasha*s, which would serve as a crucial component of our daily devotional rituals. These practices were conducted twice a day – once prior to embarking on our journey, during which a 40-minute *puja* was performed, and again in the evening upon our return to our lodging, during which an hour-long *puja* was conducted. Our endeavours to design a miniature shrine-like vehicle garnered significant interest.

As par the *parikrama* pledge, individuals undertaking a pilgrimage to the Narmada are required to collect a portion of the sacred water that they will be venerating during their journey. This practice has a long history spanning across centuries and has given rise to intriguing narratives about the transportation of the Narmada waters by pilgrims. In the event that the topography of the area prevents one from visiting the holy banks of the Narmada River during *parikrama*, it is possible to perform all requisite rituals by the *kalasha*s, accordingly. I later heard from many people that individuals would intercept the *ratha* during their journeys and perform *puja* rituals of the sacred Narmada water transported by the *kalasha*s. This used to happen when the contingent of vehicles used to move from one location to another while we walked on the banks of Mother Narmada.

It is intriguing to note that the devotees undertaking a *parikrama* of Mother Narmada carry water from the river with them during their journey, and ultimately offer it to the Goddess upon returning to the starting point of the *parikrama*. The water sourced from the River Narmada is returned to its original location on the sacred banks from where it was collected, signifying the completion of the *parikrama*.

During the spiritual resolution (*sankalpa)* ceremony on the banks of the Narmada River, we filled seven large water pots. The Mahant Mangal Das Tyagi entrusted me with the largest pot to transport it to the vehicle which was stationed outside the *ghat*s. The task was arduous, prompting me to seek the assistance of Mahant Mangal Das Tyagi in transporting the *kalasha*. Although my request was spontaneous, I now perceive it as a divine indication, as Mahant Mangal Das's presence remained with us throughout the *parikrama* and even afterwards.

Omkareshwar to Bavanvahini

8

Khedighat: The Path That was not for Everyone

It was on 8 November that we finally embarked on thousands of kilometres journey that would mean crossing a whole landscapes, languages, customs, and traditions that change in every few kilometres while on walking.

On this day we started from the *ghat*s of Mother Narmada and reached to Mahant Mangal Das Tyagi's *ashrama* where he had asked us to stop and to have our breakfast. My own family and a significant group of followers have come to see us off in the days leading up to today. Most of them had a rough time of it since they understood we were engaging in one of the most strenuous spiritual practices possible. I sensed that everyone around me was on an emotional high, so I quieted myself down internally.

From the outset of my *parikrama* planning, I made it abundantly clear that I intended to walk in close proximity to Mother Narmada. As I embarked on the sacred journey of circumambulation, I found myself diverting from the common path of well-trodden roads which people walk for easiness. Instead, my eyes were drawn to the tranquil banks of the Narmada River, where the divine waters beckoned me with their serene beauty. However, it was more difficult than walking on well-trodden paths, but I have not come here to walk on well-trodden paths, had I?

The Narmada River's banks have undergone a significant transformation. Numerous banks have been encroached upon and obstructed, while farmers have taken over those areas where the water has receded. These farmers have fenced off the land and begun farming, resulting in a slippery terrain when irrigated. A few *ashrama*s or similar establishments offer prompt services, and the terrain is not conducive to swift walking as it lacks proper roads. But I was certain that I would have to walk alongside the holy water if I had to create the digital map of Narmada Parikrama. Numerous individuals have expressed that the Narmada Parikrama would be arduous, but I was aware beforehand that it is not a journey meant to be effortless. It is not necessary to walk the entire circumference if one is looking for the quickest route.

On the inaugural day, a captivating occurrence unfolded as Mahant Mangal Das Tyagi presciently observed my forthcoming pilgrimage from the sacred shores of Narmada. However, if another individual inquired about the route, he refrained from suggesting the path that began at the banks of Omkareshwar, as it proved to be arduous and he was hesitant to undermine their confidence. However, he did not insist upon it; rather, he persistently encouraged me to walk along the shoreline from the day one. And so, on the inaugural day, that is precisely what I did.

At the Sri Jod Ganapati Ashram, I had the pleasure of meeting Tapan Bhaumik, who had embarked on the *parikrama* alongside another esteemed religious figures a year prior. He inquired of several individuals who were accompanying me as to why they had not changed their attire, yet he refrained from posing the question directly to me. When participating in *parikrama*, many people make a conscious effort to change their appearance, typically donning white *dhoti*s and either a *kurta* (blouse) to let those around them know they are participating in *parikrama*. Wearing this outfit aided in attracting support along the way. I have made it abundantly clear that religious and spiritual principles do not necessitate a distinct mode of dress. No deity has ever inquired about one's attire as a prerequisite for bestowing blessings. Traditionally, *dhoti*s have been the customary attire for individuals partaking in such a spiritual foot march. However, I found myself accompanied by an unprecedented number of young people on this particular journey. In order to encourage even more youth to join us on this enlightening path, it was imperative that I ensure their comfort with the chosen attire. No specific dress code had been established, save for the expectation that all participants dress appropriately and in a manner befitting the grandeur of the monumental trek ahead of them.

Tapan Bhaumik, a former politician, initially perceived my *parikrama* to be similar to the one conducted last year, which was accompanied by much fanfare but had left many to take care of things on the way, which was not the case with me. Tapan Bhaumik possesses a remarkable sense of humour that never fails to elicit laughter from those around him. However, I cannot help but ponder on how he manages to cope with his severe diabetic condition.

Following a meeting with Tapan Bhaumik and a heavy breakfast at Mahant's *ashrama*, we embarked on our first day of walking. As I embarked on my journey from the edge of the Naramda River, I was joined by none other than Mahant Mangal Das Tyagi, who graciously accompanied me on my walk for a brief period. Our journey began with a visit to Bangali Baba, a saint whose humorous demeanour and antics were so captivating that they warrant an entire chapter dedicated to his persona.

Bangali Baba is a nomadic saint who resides in a humble *kutiya* (small abode) situated along the serene banks of the Narmada River. Upon our arrival, he graciously presented us with an array of sweets and dry fruits, urging each member of our troupe to indulge in the delectable offerings. Amusingly, he quipped, "These items were all dropped by Tapan here yesterday, so I am merely serving as their temporary caretaker. They do not belong to me" and chuckled. In his early fifties, Bangali Baba possesses a deep, resonant voice that commands attention. He resides in a modest hut and dedicates himself to the care of those who traverse the nearby paths. Next, we remained at Mauni Baba Ashram, where we had tea and other refreshments and this is here Mahant Mangal Das Tyagi parted ways with us; at the time, we had no notion that the road ahead of us would be the most challenging of our lives. In truth, there existed no discernible path for us to traverse. Our journey entailed treading precariously along the very edge of the Narmada River, where a single misstep could have sent us plummeting into the waters some 50 ft below. Each step required utmost care and attention, as we carefully navigated the treacherous terrain with one foot placed gingerly before the other.

During the first day, numerous individuals accompanied us on our initial journey, either to bid us farewell or to walk alongside us for a day at the very least. On the initial day, the majority of them traversed by foot, and subsequently made their way back to their individual abodes. As they ventured into the jungle, their cameras were the centre of attention, capturing every moment of their first trek through this unfamiliar terrain. However, after an hour of walking, a newfound understanding began to settle in. The group fell silent, realizing the true depth of what it meant to walk alongside me. After walking for about 1 km, we arrived at a desolate area where only stones lay ahead. Progressing through these small stones required a delicate balance, as a misstep could result in a twisted ankle. We walked for more than two hours, each step taking us further down a path of thirst and hunger. It was becoming increasingly apparent that the decision I had made would have far-reaching consequences for our journey ahead.

One of the person who was walking with us, Sunil Junankar in his sixties, nearly lost consciousness. To cope with his distress, he resorted to keeping a lemon in his mouth. The *parikrama* proved to be a challenging undertaking, causing many who had initially planned to participate for a few days now thinking to bid farewell. They came to the realization that the journey would require great effort and dedication.

The sights we saw on the first day of our trip were incredible. There was the abandoned Omkareshwar Mountain, the pristine forest, and the deserted Narmada banks that looked untouched for decades. Like Shri Kamal Bharti who would have likely rested on these banks for a while, we had rested. It seemed like I was treading where Shri Gaurishankar ji Maharaj and his *jamat* must had gone before me. Walking alongside the river gave me the impression that I was floating, as if she were a permanent companion.

We had to make a dangerous descent from a hilltop as our quest progressed. Unfortunately, there was nothing but a dangerous, slick stone in front of us. I seized the initiative and we started down without delay. When we got to the bottom, I looked back at the trail we had just come down. That was like jumping from a cliff into a pit full of sharp stones, all of which could have hurt us. In appreciation for Mother Narmada's protection, I extended my hand towards the tiny *kalasha* I was carrying in my pocket.

On that fateful first day, a series of intriguing encounters unfolded, one of them I must share. In the midst of our *parikramavasi*s team, there was a man named Pramod Bambal who had walked alongside us for many days. As the scorching sun beat down upon us, Pramod's thirst grew unbearable. It was at this very moment that a miraculous encounter unfolded before his eyes. From the towering hills that stood proudly in the distance, a figure emerged, descending towards us with purpose. The imposing presence of the hills seemed to lend an air of mystique to this stranger. In his hands, he held a humble bottle of water. Without hesitation, Pramod accepted the offering, his trembling hands clutching the bottle tightly. As the cool liquid cascaded down his throat, a wave of relief rushed over him. The stranger, having fulfilled his purpose, swiftly reclaimed the bottle and vanished into the hills once more, leaving behind a sense of awe and wonder. In that fleeting moment, Pramod had experienced a divine intervention, a brief encounter with a benevolent force that had quenched his thirst and renewed his spirit. The memory of this encounter would forever be etched in his mind, a testament to the inexplicable wonders that can unfold amidst the trials and tribulations of our journey. This was something I learned about after we had already completed the *parikrama* and I had begun asking questions about the trip's early days.

As we arrived at our intended destination, we were taken aback by an unforeseen alteration in our lodging arrangements. Regrettably, we received word that the vehicles tasked with transporting vital provisions, including water and sustenance, as well as two vans intended for rest and hygiene, were unable to secure parking and entry. Consequently, the team responsible for coordinating our arrangements with Jitendra Sharma was compelled to relocate from the previously designated site. Our lodging was at Dada Darbar, a place of reverence dedicated to the esteemed Dhuniwale Dadaji. On the momentous occasion, it was made unequivocally evident by Mother Narmada that the choice of our abode would be solely subject to her discretion, irrespective of our personal preferences or the arrangements orchestrated by the event organizers, and this persisted until the completion of the *parikrama*.

9

Gangeshwar Mahadev

We began a ritual on our *parikrama* that would continue for the next 120 days and beyond. This necessitated arising at an ungodly hour to perform the sacrosanct *puja* of all the *kalasha*s and the Shivalinga bestowed upon us by Thakurji of Omkareshwar just prior to our *parikrama*.

The event in the morning was a grand ceremony that required the presence of all participants upon my arrival. Following this, a 40-minute solemn religious ceremony commenced. It took me a bit to figure out that this was not the standard procedure followed by any preceding groups. Grand *puja* ceremonies are typically not held in the morning. Instead, it is customary to perform the *arti* of *kalasha*s in the evening. But we were performing the complete *puja* in the morning and evening, as this is what we were required to do prior to begin our walk and when we returned at the end of the day.

We had established a routine in which each morning began with *puja* and the offering of *prasada* to Maiya Narmada, followed by our breakfast. During midday, once the food had been prepared at the campsite in our absence, the cooking team would first offer to holy Narmada with and then send it to us wherever we were by locating our location, which was the tough work for Lokesh who was responsible for food delivery and refreshments all through the day. Evening rituals included preparing a full *thali* of the food for Mother Narmada and presenting it to her during the *arti* ceremony. The *thali* that was offered to Mother Narmada then was graciously presented to a small girl. In addition, a *sari* and *shringara*, which were offered to Mother Narmada every evening, were donated to a less privileged family. This was my way of being socially conscious and evolve certain practices that were rooted in our religion but at present many people who have no clear idea of Sanatana fold have started to criticize it.

In the rich tapestry of Indian traditions, every act of worship is imbued with a sense of social responsibility. The ancient wisdom of Sanatana

Dharma recognized that by making offerings to the divine, one can also fulfil their obligations to the society. Thus, these two important tasks can be accomplished simultaneously, with due care and attention given to both. During my *parikrama*, it was imperative to me that the provision of spiritual and religious services be re-established and upheld. One could argue that any offering made to the divine is only truly meaningful if it serves to benefit another being on this planet.

As we set out on our journey, we commenced our walks and treks with the accompaniment of *bhajana*s, music, and divine play. I imparted to our fellow walkers the significance of this particular *yatra* – it was imperative that we maintain an upbeat mood and keep our spirits high. For in the face of the most arduous trek, without these two divine gifts, we risked losing not only our dignity but also the joy of the experience. To me, the essence of humour lies in the divine. The presence of music, laughter, and joy is a testament to this belief, and it is through these elements that our *parikrama* can be defined.

After walking for a few kilometres, an intriguing occurrence transpired, leaving me certain of what we would not undertake. After walking several kilometres, exhaustion had set in. As we trudged along, an *ashrama* came into view. We contemplated waiting in this spot for Lokesh, who was expected to bring our lunch from the base camp. Upon our arrival at the *ashrama*, the youths who were walking with me were promptly requested to present their certificate of *parikrama* and get affixed a seal. Bewilderment overtook me as I pondered over the matter at hand and asked from Yogesh what was happening. Until this very moment, I remained entirely ignorant of its nature. Upon enquiry, it dawned on me that the *parikramavasi*s (individuals who have embarked on the sacred pilgrimage of *parikrama*) are obligated to possess certain certificates. These certificates contain pertinent information such as their names and other relevant details. It is mandatory for them to present these certificates during meal service or before where they are stamped, as failure to do so would result in the denial of food and boarding.

I had also carried a certificate from Mahant Mangal Das Tyagi but that was for me a spiritual process through which I had obliged to a system which was in practice since day but I was not aware that this was the use. Upon witnessing this, I promptly departed the premises and ruminated on the nature of the enterprise. It occurred to me that when one provides food in exchange for certain certificates, it is not long days for them to eventually inquire about one's social standing or lineage before offering food. Such an imposition was unacceptable to me and shall not be entertained. And on that day, I resolved that from then on, we would eat all of our meals outdoors, in fields, under trees, and having a good time, rather than in *ashramas* or other such locations. This was great enough to give a message to all through *parikrama* banks that this is not okay with me and I was surprised that many people were quite happy by my stand. I agreed that many people do walk on *parikrama* only as they have tough life and by doing it they get some money and sustenance. There are stories of forgeries along the path of Narmada Parikrama where some individuals get involved in fraudulent behaviour but that had nothing to do with certificates. I believe something ought to change and that must.

An intriguing phenomenon occurs when one embarks on a journey along the banks of Mother Narmada. After traversing a few kilometres, the river's restorative powers begin to take effect, as was the case with Brahmachari-ji, who accompanied us on our trek. His shoes were causing him discomfort, and in a fit of frustration, he abandoned them on the path. I observed this, but refrained from intervening. In the days that followed, he traversed the terrain with bare feet, coming to the realization that he had made some missteps. However, it was not until another week had passed that he was finally reunited with a fresh pair of shoes.

We traversed a considerable distance until we reached a pivotal juncture where we paused to partake in our inaugural *tirtha*s. The site of our devotion was none other than the hallowed banks of the holy Narmada, where the Divine Mother once again revealed her benevolent presence to us.

Having meticulously marked all the *tirtha*s that line the banks of the revered mother Narmada, I was taken aback to discover that the local populace was not privy to this knowledge. Nonetheless, I proceeded to document my findings in a video and subsequently indulged in a delicious meal. As I was going to take small rest, I conversed with my fellow *parikramavasi*s, mainly youths. I expressed my fervent desire to have *darshana* of the Shivalinga of Gangeshwar Mahadev. Alas, our attempts to visit the sacred site during the *parikrama* were thwarted, as it is situated in the middle of the mighty Narmada River. According to an ancient Indian story, it is said that Rishi Matanga had performed his *tapasya* at this very location.

After taking a brief respite, I awoke approximately thirty minutes later and nonchalantly inquired of Atul whether he might procure some tea. It was strange for me because it was not tea time, but I still wanted some. Upon hearing this, Yogesh replied that there was no nearby establishment from which to procure tea. I returned to rest once more, and upon rising at approximately 2:00 p.m., I was greeted by the presence of an individual named Sobhag Chandra Patel seated before me, offering a cup of tea. In a mere 15 minutes, an impossible feat was accomplished. The tea had arrived, and where just moments before there had been no one, now a group of people eagerly awaited me to get up to partake in the hot beverage.

As I engaged in casual conversation, I found myself sipping on a warm cup of tea, contemplating the profound notion that the great Mother Narmada was attentively listening to our every word. However, the tale did not conclude there. This individual happened to be a member of the team responsible for the upkeep of Gangeshwar Mahadev, and proceeded to present me with a series of photographs. My request to see Gangeshwar Mahadev, which I had expressed to my group an hour earlier, was granted by Mother Narmada, who guided us on the trek in her own special way.

According to Sanatana legend, Maharishi Matanga was doing *tapasya* here and this is where the some other *rishi*s had come here. Rishi Matanga wanted to give a healthy welcome to the arrived saint as per the ritual but the *rishi* said that first we will have bath in the Ganga and then we would receive the welcome and food. But there was no mighty Ganga but Mother Narmada was flowing around. But Matanga Rishi by his meditative powers called Mother Ganga who appeared here. Mother Narmada flows in western direction but here where the Gangeshwar Mahadev rests in the middle of the Narmada River the stream of Narmada flows eastwards with heavy flow which marked the arrival of the Ganges here. This is when the *rishi* accepted the offer of Matanga Muni and after bath had food in his *ashrama*.[1]

Lalaram Chakravarti, a member of Narmada Samagra, had been participating in various locations as an integral member of our *parikrama*. He was present with us at the commencement of our *parikrama*. On that day, he provided me with an *asana* to sit. During the initial days, there was some uncertainty regarding what items to bring along while walking and my volunteers had not brought everything that was needed and *asana* was one of those things. I had utilized the *asana* on a daily basis and it continues to remain in my possession. In my perspective, I received the *asana* from Mother Narmada through one of her most dedicated devotees, which I utilized daily during the *parikrama* and continue to possess as a cherished possession. It is my belief that this was a manifestation of Mother Narmada's benevolence towards me.

During our journey through the Nimar region, we had the opportunity to interact with several individuals. Our first day concluded at Raverkhedi, which was our second stop. Here, we visited the *samadhi* of Bajirao Peshwa, a renowned leader who played a significant role in unifying Indian sentiments. He passed away at this location, situated on the sacred banks of Mother Narmada.

On that day, I delivered a discourse on the spiritual dimension of the Kingdom of Baji Rao Peshwa.

10

Baji Rao Peshwa and Mother Narmada

In many societies, particularly in India, it is a prevalent practice to overlook the contributions made by individuals who have enriched the lives of others through their exemplary actions. Baji Rao Peshwa is a notable political figure in Indian history, renowned for his efforts in unifying India 300 years ago, who reinstated the Sanatana Dharma in the regions under his control. This exceptional individual was renowned for his intelligence and military prowess, having never lost a battle. He was also the first to defeat the Mughals and establish himself as a king in Delhi.

The political contributions of Baji Rao Peshwa are still well known, but little is known about his dedication to Mother Narmada or his spiritual side. What little is known is because so many people visit his tiny *samadhi* on the banks of Mother Narmada. By all accounts, Raver is a town that has yet to discover and accept the historical value of its land, which is where the great Baji Rao Peshwa had his final resting place and *samadhi*.

Baji Rao's life was relatively brief, spanning only 40 years. However, during this time, he succeeded in instilling a sense of national consciousness and self-rule, known as *swarajya*, which became a recurring theme among political freedom fighters and spiritual leaders in nineteenth- and twentieth-century India. He was the first of his kind to propose the concept of national dominance and to restore Indian dominion to its original form of governance after many, many centuries of occupation.

Despite his life journey, there was one aspect of his inspiration that remained steadfast – his devotion to Mother Narmada, where he ultimately passed away.

Throughout the 1700s, the political landscape of India was largely defined by the Mughal Empire, which, despite its rapid decline due to corruption, degeneration, and courtly power struggles, remained a dominant force in Delhi, albeit on the brink of anarchy. Despite the absence of any dissenting voices or insurrectionary movements, no individual has thus far exhibited the temerity to contest its legitimacy. Even the Maratha Chhatrapati, Shahu – the illustrious descendant of Shivaji – demonstrated his acquiescence towards the rightful authority of the Padshah of Delhi but to capture it was a dream. Baji Rao was the visionary who recognized the potential of inheriting the Grand Mughal's estate and establishing a Maratha Empire in Hindustan.

He created two potent tools for his objective: the Maratha cavalry and the idea of a Hindu Pad Padshahi. The military force that Shivaji had established and refined had, over time, lost its status as the primary armed force of the Maratha renaissance. The situation involved the fragmentation of various factions into smaller groups, each with their own agenda related to the ongoing civil war. These groups engaged in activities such as asserting competing claims and conducting raids on the surrounding areas. Over time, Baji Rao successfully solidified the dominance of his master by diminishing the aspirations of the Kolhapur claimant and dismantling the excessive influence of feudal aristocrats such as Shripat Rao Pratinidhi and the Dhabades. He achieved this by establishing a unified military force, led by individuals such as Ranoji Sindia, Malhar Rao Holkar and Anand Rao Pawar, who were promoted from within the ranks and operated as commanders of a centrally-governed army. The ideology behind the dream of re-establishing Hindu sovereignty was facilitated by the army.

Similar to Shivaji before him, Baji Rao's actions were not merely political rhetoric. Through his interactions with the rulers of Rajasthan and his assistance to Chhatrasal in Bundelkhand, Baji Rao demonstrated a sincere commitment to the ideology of a Hindu Pad Padshahi. It is indeed true that during the later period of their authority in upper India, the Marathas seemed to have forgotten this doctrine. However, it is important not to underestimate its significance during the initial period of Maratha advancement towards the north, as well as Baji Rao's personal commitment to this ideal.

Baji Rao wanted to reassert Hindu authority over the holy sites in the Gangetic Valley because he saw himself as a defender of Hindu Dharma. It was a source of great sadness for him that the renowned Hindu pilgrimage sites of Benares and Prayag were under Muslim domination. As a sacred obligation, his father had left him the task of "regenerating Hindu religion and the sacred places of Hindu religion like Benares". The remarkable preparations made for Baji Rao's mother's visit to Benares show how strongly he felt the shame of the Hindus' holy places being under Muslim rule. Even Muslim Viceroys like Muhammad Khan Bangash acted like they were attending a royal court as they waited on and served the widow of Balaji Vishwanath.

The ascent of the Peshwas to authority is a captivating narrative. There have been a few instances in Indian history where a single family has exerted as much political dominance as the Peshwas. They achieved this feat not by challenging the authority of the ruling monarch or inciting unrest against the Chhatrapati, but by demonstrating utmost obedience and respect towards him while also emerging as the most influential and resolute leaders of the people of Maharashtra. Their primary objective was to enhance and fortify the empire, and they steadfastly defended it against external threats. A number of factors contributed to this intriguing phenomenon. Despite Emperor Aurangzeb's capture and execution of their King Sambhaji in 1689, he was unable to completely crush the Marathas. The Emperor exhausted all possible means at his disposal to eradicate the Maratha power, but to no avail. Upon the passing of the Emperor in February 1707, the predicament of the Marathas remained as arduous as it had been when he initially resolved to confront and assemble the empire's resources towards that end. Shahu Maharaj, son of Sambhaji Maharaj, had been raised in the Mughal court. He was eventually released with the intention of exacerbating the Marathas' difficulties and accelerating their fragmentation in Maharashtra. However, such an occurrence failed to transpire. Contrarily, the forces of integration gained greater dominance. In fact, it was during Shahu's reign that the Marathas achieved a string of triumphs.

During a challenging period of Sahu's reign, he appointed Balaji Vishwanath as his Peshwa and entrusted him with a significant task. This decision had a profound impact on the history of the Maratha region and India as a whole. Balaji Vishwanath facilitated numerous truces and garnered the support of several local chieftains to advance Shahu's cause. Despite facing several challenges along the way, he remained steadfast in his efforts to establish a sovereign rule for Shahu Maharaj.

The Raja remained a vassal of Delhi, and Balaji Vishwanath aspired to restore Shahu's sovereignty over all the territories previously under Shivaji's authority. The timing was ideal. The decline of the Mughal

Empire began after the passing of Aurangzeb, as disintegration gradually took hold. The Mughal throne was occupied by a succession of figurehead rulers, and during Farrukhsiyar's reign, the Syed brothers – Hussain Ali Khan and Abdullah Khan – wielded all the power.

In an effort to free himself from the influence of the Syed brothers, the emperor appointed Hussain Ali Khan as the viceroy of the Deccan. Hussain Ali Khan was unable to make any progress against the Maratha's depredations. In 1716, Khande Rao Dabhade, a seasoned Maratha leader, achieved a decisive victory over Hussain Ali Khan. As a result, the latter was required to initiate discussions with Shahu. This presented an opportunity for Balaji Vishwanath to challenge Shahu's demands for acknowledgement from the emperor in exchange for Maratha assistance. Hussain Ali Khan has concurred that the emperor should grant all the territories commonly referred to as Shivaji's *swarajya*, including the forts within, and that the Maratha entitlement to collect *chauth* and *saradeshamukhi* from the six provinces of the Deccan, Aurangabad, Berar, Khandesh, Bidar, Golkonda and Bijapur, which included the whole of Karnataka and the tributary states of Mysore, Tanjore and Trichinopoly should be acknowledged. Shahu agreed to pay a sum of one million rupees as tribute in exchange for the *swarajya* and 10 per cent of the annual income for the hereditary rights of *saradeshamukhi*. Additionally, he committed to maintaining a body of 15,000 horses in the emperor's service in exchange for the *chauth*, and pledged to safeguard the country from any acts of depredation and robbery. The aforementioned treaty, which was a product of Balaji Vishwanath's astute political manoeuvring, solidified the position of Shahuji as the legitimate sovereign of Maharashtra, effectively refuting the contentions of his adversary. Soon after gaining a momentous victory for the Maratha Balaji Vishwanath passed away on 2 April 1720.

By his marriage to Radhabai Barve, Balaji Vishwanath fathered two sons and two daughters. Visaji, also known as Baji Rao, and Antaji, also known as Chimaji Appa, were their two sons. Balaji Vishwanath's children had all settled down with spouses by the time he passed away. Radhabai, their mother, was a highly esteemed woman who raised her children righteously and watched over them for 33 years after her husband's death. From Jija Bai onward, the women of Maharashtra had a significant impact on the actions of Maratha leaders and the development of the Maratha Empire. The eldest son, Baji Rao, was born on 18 August 1700. He and his brother

Chimaji Appa were subject to their father's severe discipline from an early age, and their father passed on to them his political acumen and military leadership skills. Their father had begun a policy of territorial expansion and consolidation, and when the time came, these sons were prepared to carry it forward, thanks to their extensive experience and training.

Baji Rao believed that he could only serve his country by joining the military, thus he devoted himself to that field at a young age. In 1710, he was with Balaji Vishwanath when the Senapati, Chandrasen, became enraged and chased him from house to house. In 1711, the rebel Damaji Thorat imprisoned him and his father, and they survived on dried out rice and *gur*. And throughout all of these excursions, he had carefully examined the passions that enflamed men, their frailties, and the means of reviving their affection and leading them to victory. More than that, he was the most excellently fitted leader in Shahu's court to inherit the Peshwaship by 1720, having acquired first-hand understanding of the deeper nuances of home and foreign politics via regular connection with his father.

It was deliberate on Maharaj Shahu's part to appoint Baji Rao as Peshwa. Therefore, the older and more experienced members of the Maratha elite – including Shripat Rao Pratinidhi, Anandrao Sumant, Naro Ram Mantri, Khanderao Dabhade, Kanhoji Bhonsle, and others – who had been eyeing the Peshwaship were very unhappy with the selection of a twenty-year-old youth.

During his twenty years as Peshwa, the Maratha country had nothing but success. The Marathas became unrivalled in the Deccan after defeating Nizam-ul-Mulk at Palkhed. The destruction of the *senapati* at Dabhai marked the final stage in the gradual subjugation of the smaller Maratha leaders. In the south, Baji Rao reclaimed land from the Sidis and the Portuguese, and in the north, he expanded Maratha authority in Malwa, Bundelkhand and Gujarat, all while sending shockwaves through the Mughal Empire and marching into imperial Delhi.

Upon my arrival in the evening from our walk, I experienced a sense of historical significance, as if I had entered a time where Baji Rao sought leaders who would draw inspiration from Mother Narmada to achieve national liberation and establish a sovereign rule. However, there remains a mission to re-establish national consciousness, which is essential for the growth and development of our country in all aspects of life.

11

Siyaram Baba Took Rs. 200 Donation from Me

I experienced a sense of emotional attachment as I departed from the historical site that has played a significant role in shaping our nation. I proceeded to pay my respects at the *samadhi* of Baji Rao, speaking in hushed tones. I expressed my confidence that the banks of the River Narmada will continue to produce heroes like Baji Rao, who will contribute towards the development of our society and foster a sense of national consciousness.

While en route from Raverkhedi, I encountered a group of young people who had constructed a bridge over Khadak stream that converges with the Mother Narmada. The water current in this stream is quite swift and, without the bridge, travel by foot would be impeded, necessitating a lengthy diversion. This would result in the loss of access to the holy banks and detract from the overall walking experience.

It is noteworthy that numerous innovative measures have been implemented along the Narmada Parikrama route to facilitate the pilgrims. My personal experience during the journey has revealed a diverse range of such innovations. I expressed gratitude for their social innovations and conveyed my willingness to provide contributions should they require them in the future. One observation I have made is that individuals performing *parikrama* exhibit a lack of gratitude towards the local community who undertakes the arduous tasks necessary for the achievement of their goal. It appears that participants may overlook their responsibilities in this regard to appreciate the help extended and try to motivate the local population. I wanted to ensure that I would not remain stagnant in my current state, and thus proposed that we undertake some form of work after our *parikrama*. I expressed my gratitude towards the youths who have worked hard to erect the temporary bridge and presented them with a letter of appreciation, which elicited a positive response and a smile on their countenance as it was happening probably first time in the route.

During the *parikrama* route, we received consistent requests from the locals who generously offered us with tea, food, and other necessities. Although I did not make frequent stops, some places were eagerly awaiting for our arrival. During a tea break, we had the pleasure of meeting Bhopali Baba, a former *pracharak* of RSS who has since devoted his life to Mother Narmada and become a prominent religious figure. He has been walking for several years, the individual in question possesses a diminutive stature, and upon visual inspection, one may not readily discern that they once held a prominent role within the RSS organization. Our initial interaction was pleasant and we have since maintained communication through phone calls facilitated by Yogesh.

As we sipped our tea, my eyes wandered to the litter strewn about. From day one, we made a pact to properly dispose of any waste generated during our tea and snack breaks. By the end of our *parikrama*, Lokesh had become a master of waste management.

Today marks the beginning of our journey to Bhattayan, a quaint village nestled along the banks of the revered Mother Narmada. Bhattayan is a place that is marred by filth, with telltale signs of litter strewn about. Even the banks of the Narmada River, where we had gathered to perform our *arti*, were not spared from the heaps of garbage that had accumulated. One cannot help but ponder upon the actions of the local villagers or *panchayat*.

Bhattayan is a place renowned for its connection to Siyaram Baba – a wise and revered saint who has made his home in the village for many years. Most *parikramavasis* are familiar with his name, as he is a mountain icon for the surrounding area.

On this day we had done our *arti* at the banks of Mother Narmada, where also the *ashrama* of Siyaram Baba is located. After our *arti* in the evening as I strolled along the riverbank, I stumbled upon a group of young children diligently crafting intricate Shivalingas out of sand. Intrigued, I could not resist taking a closer look at their impressive creations. It was truly a sight to behold as I watched a group of talented kids transform a pile of sand into a magnificent temple of Lord Shiva. I was amazed by the level of skill and creativity displayed by these local artists. The culture we once cherished as golden was a time when our art was considered a sacred offering to the divine.

I made a donation to the Shivalinga that kids have made, but unfortunately, one of the children took all of the money and ran away. The kid who was constructing the temple and Shivalinga looked at me and hesitated before asking what my intentions were as a donor? I presented a further donation to the temple's representative with a smile, which elicited a positive response from him. The gentleman child was in the company of several young girls who requested to have some confectionery by this donation. He promptly proceeded to a retail establishment and procured candies for each of them. I wish all our temples were built and managed by such a gracious heart.

After having had wonderful time with the kids, I proceeded to visit Siyaram Baba. The elderly saint appeared to be of advanced age, likely in his late nineties. He was seated in a modest room surrounded by copies of the *Ramacharitmanasa*, which he recited continuously. Upon entering, I observed that the individual appeared to be of a delicate physical constitution and was in the process of tallying the monetary contributions that are regularly bestowed upon him by numerous individuals. It has been commonly reported that he does not accept more than INR 10 from anyone. I was carrying an envelope containing INR 200, which I handed over to him. He opened the envelope, inspected its contents, and retained all the money. He initiated a conversation with me and we engaged in a dialogue. We had a great time with Siyaram Baba, despite the many urban legends that circulate about how he never speaks to anyone.

Following our religious rituals, we proceeded to the designated campsite where our overnight accommodations were arranged. At this location, an individual approached me and expressed interest in joining our group as a fellow *parikramavasi*. After careful consideration, I granted the request, marking the first instance during the entire route in which I had extended such permission without hesitation.

Travelling is like reading a book with endless fascinating characters. Ah, the fateful encounter with a stranger over our dinner. Daily *bhandara* was our ritual of our nomadic lifestyles, and it was always performed for all those in attendance. As I was indulging in a delicious meal, a man in vibrant orange garb walked by and took a seat. Naturally, being my senior, he was eager to take pleasure in my presence. This person sat in and demanded all his foods in one go and screamed that he takes all the food at one go so he shall be served properly. I couldn't help but chuckle as he devoured down a few bites of *chapattis*, only to then ask for salt. Bless him, he clearly missed the announcement of him about taking everything at once!

12

Tirtha and Bhakta

We departed from Bhattayan en route to Shalivahana, and it was on this day that I came to the realization that my *parikrama* would be centred around the *tirtha*s of Mother Narmada.

The sacred site of Saat Pipli Ghat lies beyond the boundaries of Bhattayan, as chronicled in the revered Reva Khanda. According to legend, a saint once embarked on a strenuous period of penance at this very site. The culmination of this spiritual endeavour was a magnificent *yagya* ceremony, the remnants of which were purportedly visible as recently as the 1970s. The story of this place goes to the time when on one occasion, a brahmana came forward to him with a solemn admission of a serious error. The brahmana voiced his apprehension that he would never attain absolution for his transgression. With a solemn nod, the *rishi* extended a *pipal* branch to him and imparted a crucial instruction. He was to embark on a journey across the length and breadth of the nation, immersing himself in water and submerging the branch alongside. Wherever the branch yields its seven shoots, it is there that you must embark on your *tapasya*, and by doing so, you shall attain absolution from your transgressions.

The brahmana traversed the length and breadth of the country, yet the shoots from the *pipal* branch eluded him. He eventually arrived at this *ghat* where he immersed himself in the water and then *pipal* branch too, to his amazement, seven shoots emerged. It was then that the brahmana realized that he had reached the place where he must undertake the inner work and *tapasya*. He planted the seven shoots, which grew into seven trees, and the *ghat* was henceforth known as Saat Pipli Ghat.[1]

After crossing the Saat Pipli Ghat, we encountered numerous individuals who expressed interest in joining our *parikrama* after observing our arrangements for food, lodging and other amenities. Despite their requests, I regretfully informed them that we were unable to accommodate additional participants on our journey. However, we did extend an invitation for them to join us for meals wherever they want. I made it clear that the walking group I am leading has some ground rules that everyone must follow. It is advisable that only individuals who have previously consented to the code of conduct participate in the *parikrama*. I respectfully excused myself, acknowledging that this decision may have caused disappointment to some. However, it was the most appropriate course of action.

Today, we walked all along the hallowed shores of the Narmada River and had lunch at one of the most esteemed pilgrimage sites, Veda Sangam. This is here the Mankneshwar Mahadev Temple is. It has two *tirtha*s one is known as Sarasvat Teerth[2] and another Markat Teerth.

According to the Sanatana legend, during the Dvapara Yuga, the merging of Sarasvati or Brahmi with Mother Narmada took place at this very location. Here is where Manknak Rishi undertook his austerities, and in due time, he was bestowed with a divine blessing, granting him a vision of the entire universe. With a powerful vision in mind, he was consumed by intense emotions and began to move with a mesmerizing dance. His movements were so captivating that they caused a seismic shift in the three worlds. The pantheon of deities approached Lord Shiva with a plea to intervene in the ecstatic dance of Manknak Rishi, lest the entire world be consumed by the fervour of his movements and join in his rapturous celebration. Lord Shiva approached the revered *rishi* and inquired as to the reason for his fervent dancing. The *rishi*, lost in the rhythm of his movements, explained that he had beheld the entirety of the cosmos within himself and was thus moved to dance. At that very moment, the saint was bestowed with the divine touch of Lord Shiva, who gently brushed his finger against the *rishi*'s body, causing ashes to emanate from it. As the ashes spilled from his mortal form, the *rishi* steadfastly continued with his sacred ritual, performing the *puja* of Lord Shiva and consecrating the divine presence of Mankneshwar Mahadev. Reva Khanda suggests that the performance of religious acts here can foster a sense of inner stability.[3]

Another story of the place says that once upon a time, in the ancient land of Veda Sangam, there existed a sacred site known as Markat Teerth.[4] Legend has it that during the Treta Yuga, a king named Satyasena ruled over this land with his wife, the stunningly beautiful Shringaravallavi. However, despite her physical beauty, her face bore a striking resemblance to that of a monkey. Once, the monarch and his consort ventured to this region for a hunting excursion. As the king set out on his hunting expedition, the queen opted to explore the surrounding area. As she wandered along the banks of the Narmada, memories of a past life flooded her mind. In that previous existence, she had been a monkey who had met her demise at this very spot. Though her body had been carried away by the waters of the sacred river, her head had remained ensnared in the thorny underbush. She arrived at the location and retrieved the remaining bones of the head, which were still lodged, before casting them into the sacred waters of Mother Narmada. In due time, her countenance underwent a transformation, assuming the appearance of a human visage replete with alluring qualities.

As the king returned, he beheld the subtle transformations that had taken hold of the queen's countenance. Puzzled by this metamorphosis, he inquired as to its cause. The queen, in turn, revealed the tale of her life and the actions she had taken. Upon hearing this, the entire group proceeded to perform a *puja* at the location, which subsequently became known as Markat Teerth. As per the Sanatana legend, those who make a pilgrimage to *tirtha* and engage in *tapasya* or immerse themselves in the holy *sangama* are bestowed with the blessings equivalent to those received from observing the Chandrayana Vrata. Furthermore, it is believed that any endeavour undertaken here is met with success upon the performance of charitable acts.[5]

The area encompassing Veda Sangam is aesthetically pleasing. An ancient banyan tree, whose branches and trunk bear witness to centuries of history, is situated there. It is plausible that this was the location where the esteemed Gaurishankar Maharaj sought respite during his tenure. I approached the tree and made physical contact with it. The tactile experience was reminiscent of touching the passage of numerous centuries. I experienced a sense of connection to the many individuals who have performed circumambulation on the sacred banks of Mother Narmada by remaining in close proximity to the tree.

A mere few kilometres of distance separate Veda Sangam / Markateshwar Teerth from Mandavya Ashram. Here lies the sacred abode of Mandavya Muni, where he once fervently practised his austerities. Once upon a time, there existed a river called Vishok, which flowed into the mighty Narmada, creating a confluence known as Vishok Sangam. This sacred site was also home to the revered Vishokeshwar Mahadev. This is the very site where Vibhandaka Muni, Devyani, Indrani, Rohini, Sambharayani, Dakshayani,

Lopamudra, Ratnavali, Dhruva, Tara, Ganeshvari Arundhati, Savitri, Aditi, Diti, Ratnavali, and numerous other women from the Sanatana Dharma have undergone rigorous penance and achieved blessings.[6]

Amongst all the places, I stumbled upon the Vishokeshwar Mahadev[7] site, and its name piqued my interest. Vishok is a term denoting the absence of sorrow. Interestingly, after embarking on a three to four-day journey into *parikrama*, one will eventually stumble upon this fascinating place. The name of this place holds a powerful meaning – it symbolizes the act of leaving behind all pain and suffering when coming here to pray. As I stood amidst the *tirtha*s, I could not help but ponder over the ancient tales of pain and suffering that these sacred sites hold. Countless pilgrims before me have walked the path of circumambulation, each one experiencing ones own unique struggles. Yet, in the embrace of these *tirtha*s, they found solace and comfort. Vishokeshwar Mahadev is situated on the banks of the revered Narmada River, boasting a picturesque location with vast, unencumbered grasslands where cows graze freely. During our *parikrama*, we spent a significant amount of time admiring the stunning landscapes and contemplating the beauty of this sacred site where Lord Shiva is believed to alleviate the suffering of *parikramavasi*s.

During our *parikrama* today, we encountered an individual who was performing *parikrama* while carrying a substantial amount of luggage. Upon observing that our luggage had been transported by trucks, he appeared to be perplexed and disheartened by the sight of young men enjoying themselves during their *parikrama*. In a fit of anger, he angrily asked the group of these young men to step away from the path, instead of politely asking to give him the way. I saw this happening and could not help but think that this man could benefit from visiting Vishokeshwar Mahadev to alleviate his distress, but unfortunately, he did not enter the temple. This individual frequently encountered our group at various locations and later expressed his desire to join us. However, I declined his request as it became apparent that his motives were not aligned with our group's religious objectives, but rather centred around having his belongings transported – a self-serving agenda.

One aspect that I found adverse was the lack of environmental awareness among the individuals participating in the *parikrama*. The surroundings were littered with garbage, and it was apparent that the aesthetic value of the area was not a priority for them. I took the initiative to gather a group of individuals and organized a clean-up effort to address this issue.

Approximately 6 km farther on is the site once known as Swarnadipa Teerth,[8] now called Shalivahana because of the presence of Shalivaheneshwar Shiva; this is also where the Hiranyagarbha River meets the Mother Narmada, not far from the Yagyagarbheshwar Mahadev Temple.

Reva Khanda claims that ancient *rishi*s like Harita, Gautama, Vishnu, Savarni and Kaushika, among many others, called the forested banks of the Narmada River home. The practice of *tapasya* and *sadhana* was common among them. That is why local called it Swarnadipa. It was Swarnadipa Teerth and Shalivahaneshwar Temple where we had stayed for the night. It is located on the southern shore of Mother Narmada, directly opposite to Maheshwar.

The temple is aesthetically pleasing and has a rich history dating back several millennia. Originally known as Swarnadipa Teerth (the pilgrimage site of gold), it is situated in close proximity to Maheshwar, the city of Rani Ahilyabai. The banks of the holy Narmada are particularly deep in this area, affording visitors a panoramic view of the entire Maheshwar town.

On this day, I had the opportunity to meet a significant number of individuals, including some who were affiliated with the organization, Narmada Samagra. However, I have yet to fully comprehend the nature of their work.

On this particular day, our driver, who was operating the *puja ratha*, shared an intriguing experience with me. He expressed that the beautiful energy of Devi, which was present in his house, had disappeared over the past few months. I advised him to pray to Mother Narmada, and he followed my suggestion. The following morning, the energy reappeared in his house. He attempted to inform me of the story the next evening, but I was occupied with other matters. I learned of this account only after a few days had passed. This occurrence exemplifies the affection and beauty that Mother Narmada exhibits.

13

Names and the History

India has a long history of colonization, and one of the worst things that foreign rulers have done is change the names of Indian cities that were formerly named in commemoration of their spiritual or cultural legacies.

The current situation throughout India may lead to instances where individuals may encounter unfamiliar names and struggle to comprehend their significance. Each village name in India is rooted in a rich history, culture and religion, serving as a reminder of our cultural and spiritual heritage. This ancient wisdom allows us to recall the tales of our past.

The nomenclature of several sites situated on the banks of the revered Narmada River has undergone alterations, and the reasons behind the same remain ambiguous. I endeavoured to elucidate the local community during the *parikrama* regarding the importance of their geographical location and the historical events that have occurred in its vicinity.

Today, we departed from Swarnadipa Teerth, which houses the Shalivahaneshwar Mahadev. Although the location has undergone a name change, I encountered the local *sarpanch* this morning after departing from the Shalivahana Temple. I made a monetary donation to facilitate the installation of a signboard for this specific *tirtha* and to encourage its proper nomenclature. The narrative will reach a profound conclusion as individuals residing along the Narmada River will gradually erect signboards indicating their sacred pilgrimage sites. Nevertheless, the narrative that will unfold during my *parikrama* is found further up in this book, and I shall return to it at a later point.

The previous day, I had the pleasure of encountering a group of spirited young individuals who, with great enthusiasm, implored me to pay a visit to their newly established *seva* centre. Intrigued by their earnest request, I graciously accepted their invitation.

The young individuals who go on *parikrama* route to help others fascinate me. It was impressive to see such young people so committed to their work and to helping others. Young people who are mindful of their duties to their communities and to the nation at large, especially in the realm of social wealth generation, are an asset to any society.

I stopped for a little break as I was making my way to the place that serves the *parikramavasi*s, and it warmed my heart to see so many young people actively engaged in community service.

As we reached our destination, Lokesh had already taken the initiative to procure and promptly serve us with a delightful assortment of morning refreshments, comprising of steaming cups of tea and delectable snacks. Note that we ran across the same angry person who had demanded, in a huff, that the younger people with me keep their distance and leave the path earlier.

Lokesh demonstrated proactive behaviour by offering tea and snacks to us. I requested him to distribute the remaining refreshments among other *parikramavasi*s present. It is noteworthy that Lokesh has likely provided services to a significant number of individuals. Upon the arrival of the aforementioned individual, it was noted that the supplies of both tea and snacks had been exhausted. Mother Narmada conducts herself in this way.

While passing through this particular area, I encountered individuals who referred to a location with an unusual name. I inquired as to the origin of such names, but they were unable to provide an explanation. From that day forward, I began to rename the places I visited in an effort to preserve the cultural and historical significance of the area. This action allowed me to feel a sense of justice in honouring the threads of the past.

One of the largest challenges for India's rivers is maintaining a clean and peaceful flow, and a robust water treatment system is essential in the river belt for this to be possible. Several places around here, including the area close to Bhilat Dev, now have waste treatment plants up and running, as far as I can tell. Numerous cases have come to my attention where waste water was cleaned with local methods and then released into the Narmada. It gives me great pleasure to report that work has begun to protect the natural flow of water in the Narmada River.

We reached Khal-bujurg tonight. I suggested to the local officials that they change the name to Khadag Ghat, as that is where legend has it that Lord Parashurama cleaned his Khadag upon his arrival. Here, the Satak River joins the sacred Mother Narmada. The name Sataklingi Ghat comes from the 60 Shivalingas that were erected here on the stone of Mother Narmada. Unfortunately, the existence of the Sardar Sarovar Dam means that the splendour of the spectacle will not be a permanent feature of the landscape.

I arrived at the destination of Khadag Ghat in a timely manner. The lodging for the evening was a government-operated guest house situated alongside the Narmada River. The serene and picturesque view of the flowing river was quite captivating. I received a significant number of visits from females, marking the first instance of women visiting me unaccompanied. In the majority of cases, it is a widely held belief that women anticipate the presence of their spouses or family members to accompany them on various outings or similar engagements. However, I have observed a distinct difference in this regard during my stay at Khadag Ghat. Upon my arrival at the guest house in the evening, I was promptly greeted by a group of women who had gathered to meet me. They presented me with flowers, confections and refreshments. I thoroughly enjoyed engaging with each individual and learning about their personal narratives, including their professional responsibilities and religious endeavours both within and beyond their households. I extended an invitation to all women for *bhandara*, which was a customary occurrence during our *parikrama* period. It was fascinating that the women wanted me to eat what they cooked, but I gently declined so that they could have tonight off to attend *puja* and *arti*, after which they would have shut down the kitchen and invited everyone in the family to join us, which they did.

I had the pleasure of meeting with Sumer Singh Solanki, a highly articulate and courteous politician, and a member of Rajya Sabha, along with Dr. Mohan Yadav; both of them decided to visit us tonight. Our interaction was enjoyable. It has been a few days since I was walking and Mohan Yadav observed that my skin tone has started to change due to the effects of the sun. I made a lighthearted comment about how the Mother Narmada is the ultimate beautician and we both had a good chuckle.

14

Water, Dams and Parikrama

Our day commenced at Khadag Ghat as per our routine. However, we had to traverse through the highways, which was not preferable to me for two reasons. First, it did not align with my intended *parikrama* route. Second, I was concerned about causing inconvenience to the commuters and travellers on the highways.

The peaceful *parikrama* route that used to encircle the holy Narmada River has been destroyed by modernity. Dams built along the river's path have drastically altered the landscape by flooding large sections of the river's historic path. There is an abundance of backwater where smaller streams join the larger Narmada, making it impossible for pilgrims to cross. As a result, there is no alternative but to walk a greater distance away from the sacred riverbanks.

The aforementioned situation has resulted in the disruption of the *parikrama* path and the submergence of numerous ancient *tirtha*s. I comprehend the imperative nature of modern societal progress and the requisite sacrifices that it entails. However, it is crucial to acknowledge that sacrifices also necessitate the implementation of alternative arrangements that can aid the segment of society that is impacted. The issue of backwater is prevalent throughout the Narmada belt, particularly in the regions of Madhya Pradesh and Maharashtra that are part of the Narmada Parikrama. The Bavanvahini region, also known as Barwani, has experienced flooding that has submerged the *tirtha*s and paths commonly used for *parikrama*. This has resulted in the inability to access these areas by foot from the highways. Despite my desire to walk in close proximity to Mother Narmada, I was unable to do so in these districts due to the presence of backwater in several streams and the lack of bridges, resulting in obstructed pathways. Bridges are constructed exclusively on highways from where most of the people cross.

But imagine if we had been walking on the banks of Mother Narmada, we would come across the Varkhad Sangam as our initial destination. Here, one would be able to witness the Gyarahalingi Teerth, situated directly across from Dharmapuri. Upon arriving at Brahmanganva, one would find oneself in the vicinity of the revered Brahmavart Teerth. Reva Khanda recounts that Lord Brahma has eternally resided in this sacred abode, where the revered Brahmeshwar Shiva is enshrined. The performance of Rudra *puja* in this revered area is believed to bestow immense spiritual rewards. In close proximity lies the revered Patreshwar Mahadev Teerth.[1] The establishment of the Shivalinga is attributed to none other than the son of Chitrasen Gandhara. The tale goes that Chitrasen was a dear companion of Indra. Patreshwar, the son of Chitrasen, was a strikingly handsome man. On one occasion, he accompanied his father to the grand assembly of Indra, where the renowned Menaka was performing a captivating dance. It was then that Patreshwar was overcome with a powerful feeling of infatuation, driven by the irresistible force of *kama* (lust). Upon witnessing the scene, Indra was filled with anger and cursed Patreshwar. He admonished him for succumbing to the same carnal desires that plague humanity and banished him to the mortal realm to live amongst them. Upon hearing these words, Patreshwar's body turned cold and his desire dissipated. He humbly sought forgiveness from Indra, who then revealed that Patreshwar must journey to Brahmavart Teerth[2] where the mighty and sacred river Narmada flows. Indra revealed to Patreshwar that he must journey to the banks of Brahmanganva, where Lord Brahma perpetually resides. There, he must practise *brahmacharya* and offer devotion to Lord Shiva for a period of twelve years. It is said that Patreshwara once arrived at this *ghat* and erected the Patreshawar Mahadev.[3] He then fervently prayed to Lord Shiva, and upon achieving a state of purity, ascended to the celestial realm again.

15

Farmer and His Respite

I commenced my journey early in the morning with the objective of arriving at Anjad, a town of moderate size along the route, where I intended to lodge for the night. During our journey, my fellow *parikramavasis* and I came across a petite shelter situated in close proximity to a stream. At this point, a couple from a nearby village graciously invited us to join them for tea.

As a standard practice, we avoided frequent stops during our journey as the camp provided us with tea and refreshments. I ensured that our group of pilgrims did not cause any undue burden on the local community. In order to facilitate our journey, we ensured that all essential amenities including food, refreshments, and lodging tents were provided. Additionally, a dedicated team was assigned to oversee these arrangements while we embarked on the *parikrama*.

On several occasions, I faced challenges in expressing my intention to perform *parikrama* without causing any inconvenience to the local community, who kindly extended their assistance. My objective was to demonstrate appreciation by offering communal meal (*bhandara*), each evening at our place of lodging. At the very least, this will allow me to express my gratitude to the locals, without whose assistance the *parikrama* would not have been feasible for so many people.

This small shelter was operated by three individuals, two women and one man, who provided essential services such as tea, water and food for the *parikramavasis*. The elderly couple kindly offered me tea and breakfast. Upon visiting the shelter, I observed that it was being operated with minimal resources. However, everyone there displayed a profound level of care and compassion. I suggested that we wait for a short while as breakfast was being prepared, packed and sent from our camp. This would allow us to share a snack together, as there was an ample quantity available. The elderly couple in charge of the small shelter pleaded with me to sit down with my entire entourage for a cup of tea. To avoid taking anything from the elderly couple, I waited for Lokesh to bring us breakfast. The shelter was run on love and affection, and while that was the reason enough for me to stay, I did not want to use up all their resources.

The individuals who managed the establishment during my stay were moved and subsequently contacted the village inhabitants, who gradually assembled here.

Meanwhile, our food transportation arrived and we proceeded to have breakfast and tea. There were women present who were serving the *parikramavasi*s, and a gentleman who had generously provided the tent for the entire establishment, as well as various forms of support to ensure the *parikramavasi*s could stay overnight.

Through the act of offering *paratha*s to the women, I observed a profound emotional response in them. The present moment is a poignant reminder to express gratitude towards Mother Narmada, who manifests herself in the form of these women to serve the *parikramavasi*s.

As part of our daily *puja*, it was customary for us to offer a *sari* and adornments to Mother Narmada. I asked Lokesh to retrieve these items from the camp in order to present them as a gift to the women. Upon presenting the gift to these women, it was evident that I was not merely offering them a *sari* and adornment, but rather a timeless gift that would endure for many years to come. Upon my departure, a woman conveyed her gratitude by performing a gesture of touching my feet, while another individual became emotional and exhibited signs of tearfulness. I conveyed my gratitude for their services and reciprocated their sentiments.

I departed promptly as extending my presence would have presented challenges, given the heightened emotional atmosphere. The effect of our interaction persisted throughout the day.

During the lunch hour, we proceeded with our customary search for a suitable location to sit beneath a tree and eat our meals. A farmer approached us with a request to stay on his farm, and we subsequently accepted his invitation. Gradually, we settled to our new surroundings. The farmer extended an invitation for us to visit his residence located on his farm. However, I respectfully declined. As we were preparing for our activities, he kindly provided a bed from his home for me to rest. Following our lunch, Sumer Singh Solanki, a member of the Rajya Sabha, happened to observe us from the main road and subsequently paid us a visit, I was pretty impressed by his eyesight.

After our lunch and rest, the farmer returned and I inquired about the dams that have been constructed in the surrounding area and any potential losses that farmers may have incurred. The individual expressed that a significant number of farmers have been impacted by the submergence of their land in water. Some have relocated to Gujarat where they were provided with land and employment opportunities, while others have chosen to remain in their current location. As a result of the construction of dams and the availability of water, the agricultural practices in the area have significantly improved. The individual recollects a time when water scarcity hindered farming activities, but now they are able to cultivate crops up to four times a year.

The farmer, a man in his fifties, was known to wear his heart on his sleeve and expressed his emotions freely. He confided in me that he had been eagerly awaiting a visit from a spiritual figure for several years. His emotions ran deep as he expressed his gratitude that I had made the effort to stop by. As he basked in the afterglow of his experience, he could not help but feel that his deepest yearning, his *manga*, had finally been satisfied. The person made a request for tea, but I initially refused. But the farmer in question acquired the tea within minutes like he had already got prepared while I rested. Because I could tell the person was emotionally exposed, and soon he started shedding tears in emotions, I extended a cup of tea, and gave him a scarf for my memory. The person's countenance was aglow with a palpable sense of joy, reminiscent of that of a young child. *Parikrama* is an experience that entails the creation of emotional bonds, the cultivation of new connections, and an education on the way of life. The process involves cultivating a profound sense of kinship by means of heartfelt affection and unwavering dedication. The farmers contacted his son, who was assisting him on the farm, as I was leaving and asked me to bless him, so I did.

As we ventured forth from the sacred banks of the Narmada, we encountered a number of small streams that would have proved quite challenging to traverse had we remained along the river's edge. The backwater had infiltrated these streams, rendering them impassable. Had the situation been different and we had strolled along the banks, our path would have led us to the charming village of Maru ki Chichli. Here, the

Devanadi River converges with the mighty Narmada, in close proximity to the picturesque Lohariya Ghat. Here are located the ancient temples of Narmadeshwar, Varuneshwar and Shivayogeshwar, all of which have deep roots in Sanatana Dharma. I looked for them but I think one of them is up on that hill now called Siddheshwar, and the other is called Kapileshwar. A third temple, Shivayogeshwar, may be found just a short distance away, and it goes by the name Siddheshwar. When the temple's origins are unknown, it is a standard practice along the Narmada banks to give it a new name. This is exactly what has transpired here.[1]

A few kilometres from this location lies a place known as Kesarpura, where the Nahili River converges with the Narmada. After traversing a few kilometres, one arrives at Mohipura, renowned as the Sahastrayagkhya Teerth.[2] Long ago, this land was inhabited by the revered Bhargava Rishi, who conducted the Sahastra Yagya, giving rise to the name of this place. A short distance away lies a place called Dattawada, where the revered Kapalamochana Teerth[3] is situated. It is believed that the divine Kapileshwar Shiva has been enshrined here, albeit now submerged in the waters of the Sardar Sarovar Dam. Continuing on, one will soon come across Chota Vardha Ghat, which is reputed to be the site of Agni Teerth.[4]

16

Bavanvahini, Not Barwani

Today we are in Barwani district which is situated in the hilly tracts of Madhya Pradesh bordering Khandesh, Maharashtra in this hilly terrain. Many regions of the districts exhibit picturesque landscapes, characterized by a sequence of mountain ranges and valleys adorned with forests which used to be very dense some 100 years back or so.

In the earlier stage before British taking control of the district it used to belong to Sisodia Rajputs who were associated with the Udaipur dynasty. According to tradition, they are descended from the second son of Bappa Rawal, who founded their house. The history goes back telling that one of his descendants migrated to the banks of Narmada districts between eleventh to fourteenth century and settled at Avasgarh, a hill fort. Paras Ram Singh, also known as Parsan Singh, was the thirty-fifth chief who was defeated by the Mohammedans and subsequently taken as a prisoner to Delhi. He converted to Islam under the condition that he would be permitted to keep his ancestral estates.[1]

Bhim Singh, the successor, and the two subsequent Ranas, while identifying as Hindus in name, were effectively adherents of the Islamic faith. In approximately 1650, Chandra Singh, the forty-first ruler in the lineage, determined that Avasgarh was not a sufficiently fortified location and subsequently relocated the capital to Barwani.

During the reign of Mohan Singh, the son and successor of Chandra Singh, a significant portion of the state was captured by the Marathas. During this era, there was a noticeable decrease in the prominence of the house. Despite the efforts of the Barwani Ranas to maintain their autonomy and avoid becoming subjects of the major Malwa leaders, they ultimately found themselves with only a limited area of land under their control, in contrast to their previous expansive territories.

In 1794, Rana Mohan Singh II assumed the throne and was in power during the Malwa settlement led by Sir John Malcolm. In 1839, he passed away and was succeeded by his son Jaswant Singh. However, in 1861, Jaswant Singh was removed from the administration due to his incapacity. He was later restored to power in 1873 but passed away in 1880. He was succeeded by his brother Indrajit, whose administration was also deemed unsuccessful. Upon the demise of the individual in 1894, his firstborn, Ranjit Singh, assumed the position of chief at the tender age of six. During his youth, he received his education at the Mayo College, Ajmer.

During the British era, Barwani, encompassed a significant geographical expanse. The state boasted a diverse range of flora, including the exquisite *anjan* tree species (*Hardwickia binata*), which is indigenous to India and was once abundant in the region. The vegetation once thrived on both slopes of Barwani State, however, by the late eighteenth century, a significant number of trees was destroyed, resulting in a decline in forest coverage and revenue.

Land clearing was a prevalent practice during the British era, which was gradually halted. However, it resulted in the destruction of numerous trees and forests on the slopes for several generations. The impact of this event is still being felt, and recovery has been slow.[2]

I spent most of the day walking along the highways because the *parikrama* path was blocked by the backwater or the backwater had entered in small streams which makes it impossible to pass. This was the day when I initiated a conversation with our pathfinder, Yogesh, to gain a better understanding of the type of *parikrama* I am undertaking. I was determined to walk closely alongside Mother Narmada despite any potential obstacles. My goal was to create a digital map of the entire route, which has not been accomplished before. With the blessings of Mother Narmada, I believed I could achieve this feat, which I did. If we had embarked on a journey from the sacred banks of Narmada, our footsteps would have led us to Kasrawad, the site where the illustrious sons of Daksha Prajapati once performed their rigorous penance. Continuing on our path, we would have eventually arrived at Barwani Rajghat, a destination we could have explored while sojourning in Barwani.

It was a pitiful experience for me to walk on highways and be distant from Mother Narmada, whose *parikrama* I am undertaking. It was late afternoon and walking on highways did not allow for finding a place to sit and have lunch. Taking a break for lunch and rest was essential for all of us who were walking over 25 km every day. It was a much-needed respite. Today, it seemed like we would not be able to find a suitable place to have lunch. However, sooner than we expected, we stumbled upon a deserted space where we could find some shade, and decided to have our lunch there.

The town of Barwani, as it is currently known, may undergo a historical name change following my recent visit during the *parikrama*. It is possible that the town will become more commonly referred to as Bavanvahini in the future. Bavanvahini is encompassed by the Janya Jatis, referring to the ancestral origins of its inhabitants. The term "tribals" is not preferred as it does not accurately convey the intended meaning. The area around it was significantly impacted during the construction of the Sardar Sarovar Dam in Gujarat, which served as the starting point for Medha Patkar's lifelong advocacy through the Narmada Bachao Andolan. Additionally, it illustrates the reasons for the movement's failure, and with the exception of a few individuals, the regional dynamics remain unchanged.

Based on the Sanatana text, it is believed that this location of Barwani Rajghat was where Rohini, the wife of Lord Moon, performed her *tapasya* and subsequently earned the privilege of being his favoured spouse.[3] The name Bavanvahini is derived from the presence of *tirtha*s (sacred pools) on both banks of the river where feminine deities are believed to have performed their *tapasya*. The term *bavan* translates to "fifty-two" in English, while *vahini* refers to that which carries.

Upon my arrival at Bavanvahini, I was delighted to receive a warm welcome from the city. Following a ten-day trek on foot, we eventually reached our assigned camping location where we planned to take a day of rest. As we continued on our journey, we expected to have fewer chances to take breaks. As soon as I arrived, a group of people started to gather around us. During our conversation, a young man interrupted us and mentioned some information he had read on Wikipedia about the name of the city. He explained that the area was named Barwani due to the abundance of banyan trees in the region. The conversation that ensued led to an exploration of the city's past and the importance of its name. As a result, I decided to make it the focal point of my speech for the evening. The event received considerable attention and was subsequently reported in the newspaper the next day.

We had a day off, which gave everyone in the team the opportunity to go to the market and gather all the necessary supplies for the Shulpani trek. There were frequent visitors for me, including state ministers, who were devoted to Mother Narmada. However, they seemed to pay little attention to the *tirtha*s located on the banks of the river. This made me contemplate the matter even more deeply.

As the evening descended upon us, a programme was arranged that celebrated the indomitable power of women. It was only fitting that we chose Bavanvahini as the venue for this event, for it was a place where women had long been revered and had undertaken rigorous spiritual practices to attain the pinnacle of existence. Their unwavering dedication had enabled them to achieve excellence in all spheres of life.

One programme had meticulously curated the entire *parikrama* route, leading people to believe that this particular *parikrama* would be unlike any other that had taken place before.

Bavanvahini is a remarkable location that boasts the breathtaking Shulapani forest, which I discovered to be among the most favoured destinations. The mountain's beauty was mesmerizing, and my thoughts were consumed by the rich history of the place. I found myself unable to resist the urge to continue forward, eager for the next leg of our *parikrama* journey. As the Shulapani loomed in the distance, our team sprang into action, making preparations for the journey ahead. It was to be our final encounter with civilization for the next fifteen days, as we ventured into the Shulapani forest, where the trees were sparse and the markets for goods such as shoes were scarce.

As I was preparing to retire for the evening, the Rashtriya Swayamsevak Sangh (RSS) commenced their *shakha* outside our camp. Initially, I regarded their formation with a sense of disapproval. However, as I observed their disciplined and orderly approach, my sentiment shifted to one of admiration.

Bavanvahini to Gora Colony

17

Bhagavati

In the morning, the local Member of Parliament, who had been unable to attend our previous gathering, arrived to meet me. As we had not yet been acquainted, it was worth noting that there was another individual in our group who shared my name. This was easily discernible, as each member of our party carried identification pages that prominently displayed the name of the bearer. The name caught the attention of the local Member of Parliament. As he caught sight of the name, he instinctively reached out to touch the feet of this fellow traveller, mistaking him for Vivekji. However, it was soon revealed that the man in question was actually another Vivek, walking with Vivekji, but not the Vivekji! Despite this realization, Gajendra Singh was unable to contain his embarrassment and proceeded to enter the room to meet me. The tale I came to learn only in due time, as each person gradually revealed the fun they had at my expense.

Our next destination after Bavanvahini was the Shulpani mountains, where we planned to spend the night in Bhagavati (Bhavati). I referred to the place as Bhagavati because it was originally named so, owing to the *sangam* of the Gauri River to the Narmada. Gauri, another name for Parvati, is also known as Bhagavati. Historically, the location was referred to as Bhagavati due to the belief that the Gauri River embodies the essence of the Goddess Bhagavati. This was here that Anangeshwar Mahadev Temple existed, but now it is also submerged.[1]

Meghnath Teerth is located not too far away in Bhavati, and legend has it that the son of Ravana, Meghnath, stopped here on his route back from Kailasha. After a long journey, he was thirsty and exhausted from transporting two Shivalingas from Kailasa to Lanka. Here he paused to drink some water and set down the two Shivalingas he had been carrying. Later, he reached out to take hold of a Shivalinga, but it slid out of his hand and fell into the water. As he readjusted, a second Shivalinga toppled into the water, and he headed back empty-handed. However, both sides of the Narmada River share the same name Meghnath Teerth because two Shivalingas fell into the Mother Narmada's waters.[2] Meghnath was a fervent follower of Lord Shiva and had a dedication to *dharma* at one time in his life. We should realized that naming a *ghat* by the name of him (i.e. Meghnath) can only happen in India.

India is a fascinating place, rich in history, where the names of its towns and villages conjure up legends from long ago. Each name pays tribute to the great diversity of our ancestors and serves as an evocative reminder of our shared history. Unfortunately, it is a sad truth that these beloved legacies, our entire soul, were the first ties that successive foreign rulers of our country attempted to break. As a result, we are estranged from the realities and narratives that characterize our past. Throughout the tapestry of my life, I have stayed on track with unshaken determination. And as I set off on the hallowed *parikrama*, I was firm in my resolve to revere and preserve the bygone chapters that were distinctively ours. Considering the vast historical fabric that surrounds us, we feel obligated to learn more about it. We go on a tremendous path of learning with this first step of self-discovery. Indeed, it is the pursuit of knowledge that fuels the fires of spirituality within us.

Upon arriving at the Bhagavati camp in the evening, it was apparent that the terrain of Shulpani would commence the following day. In preparation for this, additional personnel were requested to accompany us on our journey to Shulpani. One of the members of the coordination committee, Praveen Chauhan, generously provided us with a team to assist in transporting the various items we intended to share and donate in Shulpani. These items included books, pencils, *saris*, T-shirts and candies, which were highly favoured by the residents of Shulpani.

Bhagavati is a tiny village, unaware of the history of the land that surrounded it. We slept at one school where the camp was organized. The whole village participated in a huge *bhandara*, and it was great to see so many unfamiliar faces on the *parikrama* trek. On this occasion, I initiated a conversation with the locals regarding the construction of toilets. I emphasized the importance of ensuring that there are sufficient toilets for the *parikramavasis*. This topic will be a recurring theme throughout the *parikrama*, and we will endeavour to donate funds wherever possible. I consistently emphasized the importance of maintaining cleanliness during *parikrama* to fellow individuals, as it is imperative in contributing to the betterment of the local community. Neglecting this responsibility may result in the younger generation developing a negative perception towards us.

One common sight along the *parikrama* path is the presence of trash and excrement. This is due to the lack of adequate toilet facilities, and many *parikramavasis* do not seem to realize that a small donation of 10 rupees from each of them could help ensure that there are enough toilets for everyone in the future.

As *parikramavasis* exhibit a transient lifestyle, they may overlook certain matters. Therefore, I took it upon myself to ensure that the concerns regarding the maintenance of toilets were voiced by individuals such as myself who are engaged in *parikrama*. Upon initiating this endeavour, I received ample support from numerous individuals. I am for certain trying to make sure that in years to come there are enough toilets for the *parikramavasis*.

Bhagavati is the initial hill that provides access to Shulpani, a location that has been a source of fear for generations among the *parikramavasis*. And it is this dread that drives people away from holy banks and towards highways. As we approached the hills, I anticipated an enjoyable experience, which is precisely what we encountered.

18

Shulpani Hills

Our journey commenced at Bhagavati and our intended destination was Kuli, a hamlet located in the Shulpani region. Prior to commencing the task, I had reservations regarding the functionality of the digital map in the absence of signals. However, I am pleased to report that the map performed optimally, alleviating any concerns I may have had. It is noteworthy that during the *parikrama*, I was unable to obtain phone range due to my reliance on BSNL, the national network which is scarcely available along the *parikrama* route.

The news of my rediscovery of the ancient *tirtha*s mentioned in our Shastras had spread, and I had the pleasure of meeting a saint who sought me out to offer congratulations on this task. During our conversation, he expressed his excitement that someone was undertaking this important work. I felt that Mother Narmada had provided the guidance that would carry me through to the end.

After Bhagavati had traversed a few kilometres, one would come across Bijasen Teerth. This ancient temple has been relocated, but according to the *Vasishtha Samhita*, it holds a fascinating tale. Ravana, a devout follower of Lord Shiva, once performed a *puja* (ritual worship) of eleven Rudras and Rudranis. These divine beings then granted him the opportunity to ask for a boon of his choice. According to historical accounts, Ravana, a prominent figure in ancient mythology, is said to have had multiple wives and a sizeable family with numerous offspring. He requested the Rudranis to provide a daughter with the ability to eliminate any future children from his other wives. According to legends, it is believed that Rudrani, a divine deity, granted a boon to Ravana. As a result of this boon, a powerful being named Bijaseni was born. Tragically, Bijaseni began to systematically eliminate the descendants of Ravana. During the period following Ravana's defeat at the hands of Lord Rama and the subsequent conquest of Lanka, Lord Shiva summoned Bijaseni to the Narmada Ghat. He instructed her to remain there and protect the future generations instead of causing their demise. Bijasen Teerth is a renowned pilgrimage site known for its sacredness and the blessings it bestows upon devotees. The temple is dedicated to Devi, a revered deity believed to have the power to grant the prayers of those who seek her intervention. Many devotees visit this *tirtha* with the hope of securing the well-being and prosperity of their future generations. Additionally, women facing difficulties in conceiving have also sought solace and blessings at this holy place, with many reporting successful outcomes in their journey towards motherhood.[1]

After walking a few kilometres from Bijasen, as we embarked on our arduous journey to the sacred land of Kuli, little did we know that fate had a peculiar encounter in store for us. It was amidst the vast expanse of the mystical landscape that we crossed paths with a man named Hira Lal, a figure whose reputation preceded him. Whispers of his notorious deeds, particularly his penchant for confiscating the belongings of unsuspecting *parikrama* participants, had spread far and wide. However, a remarkable transformation has taken place within him, altering the course of his life's journey. No longer bound by the shackles of his past, he has embraced a new purpose – to serve the *parikramavasi*s, those who have chosen to dwell in the austere wilderness. With unwavering determination, he now dedicates himself to the arduous task of providing nourishment amidst the unforgiving terrain that surrounds him. As we ventured forth, the roads that lay before us seemed to offer a glimmer of hope, a semblance of ease in traversing the treacherous terrain that lay ahead. However, our optimism quickly waned as we soon discovered that these paths, though paved, were no match for the unforgiving nature of the land. With each step we took, it became abundantly clear that the challenges we faced were far from over. The terrain, rugged and unyielding, tested our resolve and pushed us to our limits. The once promising roads now seemed like mere illusions, taunting us with their false promises. As the sun reached its zenith, casting its golden rays upon the land, we sought respite in a quaint village nestled amidst the rugged terrain. The month of November, though heralding the approach of winter, had not yet relinquished its grasp on the land of Shulpani, for the air still carried a gentle warmth. With weary bodies and parched throats, we yearned for a moment of respite from our arduous journey. And there, like an oasis in the desert, we discovered a haven of solace beneath the sheltering embrace of a mighty tree. Its branches stretched outwards, offering a sanctuary from the relentless sun, as if nature herself had conspired to provide us with much-needed shade. And we settled ourselves upon the cool earth.

We made a stop at a farm where a member of the Bhil Janya Jatis community, who holds influence in the area, kindly offered us a place to have our meal and take a break. However, it was evident that our host was very talkative, and we expected that our rest would be disturbed. I have yet to encounter an individual who does not require someone to communicate with. This person was capable of conversing with anyone, even if they were in a state of deep slumber. Yogesh, the pathfinder, was attempting to rest after a challenging day when the gentleman persistently engaged him in conversation. Despite Yogesh's request for silence the person continued to speak, causing disturbance to others in the vicinity. My eyes were closed and I was soaking up all the joy going on around me as I lay in the bed I had been given. Some individuals chose to relocate to a more peaceful location, but this was not a viable option for all. This marks the commencement of the Shulpani recreational activity.

In the vast expanse of the Shulpani region, where the land is unforgiving and the soil is barren, a population of extraordinary resilience thrives. Despite the challenges posed by the infertile terrain, the people of Shulpani have managed to carve out a life for themselves, defying the odds and embodying the indomitable spirit of human perseverance. In the vast expanse of this sacred land, there exists a group of resilient individuals who lead a humble existence, relying on scarce resources to sustain themselves. Despite their own meagre means, they possess a remarkable quality that sets them apart – an innate generosity that knows no bounds. It is this very generosity that compels them to offer sustenance to those who embark on the arduous journey of the *parikrama*. On a serene day, a band of *parikramavasi* meandered along, their weary figures hinting at a lack of nourishment. Lokesh was dispatched with a lunchtime call as per my instructions. It was impossible not to consider the daunting task of sustaining themselves amidst the harsh realities of this untamed land. And so it came to pass, exactly as it had been foretold. Once more, I found myself graced with the privilege of experiencing in the warm embrace of Mother Narmada. In a curious turn of events, the provisions that had been carefully set aside to sustain a modest group of thirty individuals found themselves in the hands of nearly fifty people. Despite this unexpected increase in numbers, it was a remarkable sight to behold as each and every person was adequately fed.

19

Lakhan Giri Maharaj

This morning, we departed from Kuli and made our way towards Semlet, a quaint hamlet nestled in Shulpani. It dawned on us that this would be the final day we would have access to many of our arrangements that were carried in vehicles by the management group before we reach to Dhadgaon which could take four-five days from here.

The path we were to embark on for our foot march in *parikrama* was vastly different from the roads our vehicles would traverse. It was clear that once we reached Semlet, we would part ways with our trusty automobiles, with no chance of reuniting them for several days. We had made prior arrangements for the transportation of the *puja*'s *kalasha* to our location on the following day, when vehicles would be unable to traverse the route.

Additionally, we had also arranged for the provision of food for the day. I had spoken with my devout follower, who presently holds the esteemed position in Maharashtra. He assured me that he has meticulously arranged everything for our upcoming *parikrama* days. For it is said that the River Goddess had her own grand design, one that surpassed our mortal understanding. In the realm of mortals, we often find solace in our meticulously laid plans, believing that they will guide us towards our desired destination. Yet, in the presence of Mother Narmada, our plans were but feeble attempts to navigate.

As we ventured further into the wilderness, the landscape began to undergo a remarkable metamorphosis. The once clear and well-defined path that had guided our steps was now fading into obscurity, leaving us with an unsettling sense of uncertainty. No longer could we rely on the familiar markers and signs that had guided our journey thus far. The terrain, once predictable and accommodating, now presented itself as a formidable challenge, shrouded in ambiguity. With each passing step, the path seemed to dissolve before our very eyes, leaving us to navigate through an uncharted wilderness. In the heart of this sacred mountain range, lies the tranquil abode of the revered Mother Narmada.

Her presence, a mere few kilometres away, casts a divine aura over the surrounding landscape. The mountains, standing tall and proud, seem to bow in reverence to her sacred being. It is here, in this invisible realm, that devotees from far and wide seek solace and spiritual enlightenment. As we ventured forth, we encountered many residents of Shulpani each having radiant features. It was not their affluence that brought about this radiance, but rather the beauty of their smiles. The murals, adorning the walls or any other surface the children could lay their hands on, were a sight to behold. Their artistic features left me completely mesmerized. As I made my way through the impoverished community, I encountered a multitude of children who were without proper clothing. Moved by their plight, I distributed a number of T-shirts to these young ones. Later on, we came across a group of women whose *saris* had been completely spoilt. We approached them and offered some new *saris*. As I stood there, my eyes widened in astonishment. Before me stood a group of children, seemingly around the age of ten, yet they lacked a fundamental skill that I had taken for granted – the ability to operate a simple pencil and sharpener. It was a sight that left me both perplexed and concerned. How could it be that these young ones, who should have been well-versed in the ways of the written word, were so unfamiliar with such a basic tool of expression? It was a stark reminder of the disparities that exist in our world, where some are afforded every opportunity to learn and grow, while others are left behind, their potential untapped. And so, with a sense of duty and determination, we embarked on the task of showing them the way to use it. As our weary bodies made their way down the rugged mountain path, the anticipation of a much-needed meal filled the air. Our trusty companion, the motorbike that faithfully carried our supplies, had always been a reliable source of sustenance during our midday breaks. However, to our dismay, as we reached the end of our arduous descent, the sight of the motorbike was nowhere to be found. Left with only the snacks we had brought along, we found ourselves in a state of collective hunger. The provisions we had packed, once a mere afterthought, now became our sole sustenance in this moment of need. With a sense of unity, we gathered together, each contributing what little we had, and shared in the meagre feast before us. The taste of the snacks, though simple and unassuming, brought a temporary respite to our growling stomachs, as we savoured every bite in a silent acknowledgement of our shared difficulty.

Shulpani is a place that holds a significant place in the history of Narmada Parikrama. One man's experience changed the course of events in this area. While doing the *parikrama*, Lakhan Giri Maharaj was robbed by the locals. He decided to stay put and began to share his knowledge and love with the people. His efforts brought about a sense of peace that still exists among the *parikramavasi*s today. In my view, the Shulpani Bhils did not engage in looting the *parikramavasi*s. In the past, it was common for Bhils to go about without any clothing. When encountering those who were clothed, such as the *parikramavasi*s, they would seize their garments and other possessions. Despite this, they would still offer them sustenance in the form of tough bread or a spicy bread (*roti*). From my perspective, the underlying motive of the action was to assimilate into the Bhil community by promoting the adoption of the dominant group's attire.

The impact of Lakhan Giri Maharaj's teachings has been profound, transforming the way in which people perceive themselves and their relationship with the sacred practice of *parikrama*. Through his teachings, numerous Bhils have come to comprehend the *parikrama* of Mother Narmada, whom they affectionately refer to as their sister. Lakhan Giri Maharaj revolutionized the approach to providing *sewa* in this area, resulting in a serene atmosphere throughout Shulpani. As we traversed the area, joyous countenances abounded. As we journeyed along the path, we came upon the *ashrama* of Lakhan Giri Maharaj. We took a moment to offer our prayers before continuing on our way.

Shulpani is renowned for its ability to bring about clarity in individuals. This phenomenon has been observed in numerous people, resulting in either a strengthened and blessed state or a realization of their mistakes, which they carry with them throughout their *parikrama*. A case of the latter came to pass with Nanga Baba, who happened to be trailing a few days behind me. Standing atop the Shivalinga at Lakhan Giri Maharaj is considered to have done one of the gravest sins one can commit. However, it was this very act that revealed his true nature.

Shulpani villages nestled in the midst of dense forests and towering mountains. The houses are scattered far apart, with several kilometres of walking distance between them. One could walk from house to house all day and still not reach the end of this village. Inquiring about the name of the village we had departed from six hours prior, its appellation still lingered on our tongues.

While walking under the scorching sun, we came across a place where there was no shade on the mountain. However, we found a small tree and decided to gather around it and rest for a while. From that spot, I was able to observe my surroundings. The view of Mother Narmada was breathtaking, with a visibility of several kilometres in the range. The mountains resembled ocean waves, and the terrain was an endless expanse of hills with small houses scattered throughout the area. I expressed a desire to stay overnight, however, the other individuals were hesitant due to the lack of prior arrangements made for accommodations. During our conversation, a farmer who did not speak Hindi, Marathi, or any other language approached us to offer water. Although we already had water, we appreciated his humility and kindness in offering us water that he had fetched from a distant location. I engaged in conversation with him and utilized nonverbal communication to convey my thoughts. Upon conclusion, we provided the gentleman's family with *saris*, T-shirts, and other miscellaneous items. Throughout the entire afternoon, we did not encounter any individuals except for one person. This emphasizes the individual experience of walking without the presence of a group.

A significant number of *parikramavasis* opt to traverse the roads that are situated at a considerable distance, while only a handful choose to journey towards Shulpani due to the challenging terrain and the scarcity of amenities and rest stops. However, I made a conscious decision to embark on the latter route as I desired to be in close proximity to Mother Narmada and follow the path that has been taken for centuries before. Earlier in the plan, the organizing committee had not discussed this route, and its alteration came as an unexpected development. Consequently, it became apparent that any aspect of the plan could be subject to change, and, thus, it was imperative to remain prepared for any eventualities. As a result, the team made a conscious effort to be ready for any changes that might arise on a daily basis. During this period, we adhered to our regular routine, but gradually began to exceed our expected timeline. Many *parikramavasis* express apprehension regarding potential delays while traversing through the Shulpani forests. However, I maintain that those who embark on this journey are bestowed with the divine blessings of Mother Narmada, which serves as a motivating force for them to continue. This is precisely what occurred with our team.

After walking a few kilometres in the afternoon, with two children who accompanied us to show the route after lunch. I engaged in conversation and enjoyed their company. They mentioned that they have not attended school much due to the distance of several kilometres. However, they displayed keen observation skills and remarkable stamina, akin to that of an athlete. They were also very mindful of their surroundings and ensured the safety of everyone during the challenging hill crossings. This continued throughout the journey. This refers to the level of compassion that the local community perceives in you.

While traversing a challenging terrain flanked by small trees, we ascended approximately 400 m from the base. Along the way, we encountered an elderly woman who appeared feeble, carrying a water pitcher. Initially, we were perplexed as to why she was in the forest. However, upon reaching her, she kindly offered us water. We were all taken aback by her presence, but upon realizing her intention, I encouraged my fellow *parikrama* companions to partake in her generosity and accept the water. Upon receiving the water, I offered a donation to the old lady who initially hesitated. I clarified that the donation was not in exchange for the water, but rather a gesture for her to purchase candies for the children in the village who may be anticipating her arrival.

As we proceeded further, we came across a tea store. It is common to find tea stores in various locations along the holy banks of Narmada. At times, the store owners invite you to sit and enjoy some tea. However, during our walk, I noticed that in addition to tea, some weeds were being served. Consequently, I declined to stop at that particular store. During my walk, I conversed with Kumar and expressed my concern that if this were the type of route taken during the Narmada Parikrama, it would defeat the purpose of the entire journey. It is noteworthy that during the Narmada Parikrama, individuals from various parts of the country embark on this pilgrimage. In fact, the entire nation is unified on the banks of holy Narmada.

As we continued our journey, a chance encounter brought us face to face with a couple hailing from the beautiful state of Jharkhand. They were accompanied by their two young children, who were joyfully engaged in the sacred act of *parikrama*. As I engaged in conversation with them, I discovered their deep longing to embark on a sacred pilgrimage known as *parikrama*. However, their desire remained unfulfilled due to the presence of their beloved children, whom they could not bear to leave behind in the care of others. Hence, they made the decision to bring their little ones along on this journey. The situation at hand was undeniably intriguing. In the depths of my soul, I find myself disheartened by the sight of young children, innocent and unaware of the profound teachings of religious faith, embarking on a journey on foot. Their tender feet tread upon the earth, following the footsteps of their parents who too walk this arduous path. Yet, within their young hearts, they may not comprehend the spiritual significance that lies within the sacred *parikrama* of Mother Narmada.

There have been instances where young girls, as young as five or six years old, have been referred to as "baby Narmada" while walking with their parents on the holy banks for Narmada Parikrama. I experienced a significant degree of sadness regarding that matter. As I believe that children should be equipped with an understanding of life's journey. It is imperative that they possess an understanding of both spirituality and religion.

Furthermore, this phenomenon is observed in numerous locations. Upon learning about this kind of practice, I expressed my disapproval of this particular syndrome. I firmly believe that the *parikrama* represents a profound spiritual odyssey, and it is crucial that we comprehend its significance before introducing children to it. In the realm of sanctity, a crucial aspect to consider is the necessity of allowing a child to comprehend the intricacies of life before bestowing upon them the esteemed title of a saint. It is imperative that they traverse the path to adulthood, embracing the wisdom and experiences that accompany this transformative journey. Moreover, it is of utmost importance that the child be granted the freedom to forge their own destiny, unencumbered by the desires and aspirations of their parents, for true sanctity can only be attained through a personal and conscious choice.

During our walk, we encountered several small hamlets within the village where we distributed notebooks, pens, shorts, and T-shirts. Additionally, we made a donation to the women who were providing water along the route.

It was becoming dark outside and that was when we spotted Praveen Chauhan on his way to provide water; unfortunately, the motorbike had not made it that day, so we had gone without water and tea. Because the route did not allow the truck carrying the food arrangement to drive in the direction we had anticipated, we had to have food brought in through the night from a point some 50 km behind.

20

There Was No Food

It was 20 November. As we departed from Semlet en route to Bhabri, our journey led us across the border into Maharashtra. Prior to embarking on our *parikrama*, I had conversed with one of the devotees residing in Maharashtra to ensure that arrangements had been made for our stay in the region.

The role of Shulpani area in Maharashtra proved to be a formidable challenge as the location was inaccessible by vehicles. We had to traverse a path for us which was 100 km further away from any motor route, all the while being surrounded by the majestic presence of Mother Narmada. After conversing with Chandrashekhar Bawankule, I was assured that all matters would be tended to upon my arrival in the Maharashtra region of Shulpani.

As we strolled along, we stumbled upon a desolate region devoid of any cellular reception. Our vehicles and the entire camp team had journeyed 150 km away from us, as the walking path we were on presented an extremely challenging terrain that made it nearly impossible for the vehicles to follow. The vehicles must traverse a route diametrically opposit to our own, ultimately arriving at a destination that we shall not reach for another three days, having surmounted the arduous terrain of Shulpani. To all intents and purposes, we *parikramavasi*s were on our own, as the region's borders are set deep and the routes are difficult to navigate. The harsh and uneven landscape poses a daunting obstacle. In the midst of a rough and formidable terrain, where the elements test the limits of human endurance, there lies an array of imposing hills. These majestic formations, with their sheer magnitude and commanding presence, stand as a testament to the enduring strength of nature. Yet, among this awe-inspiring panorama, there exists a solitary peak that towers above all others, inviting to those who dare to venture near. It is a summit that demands not only physical prowess, but also an unwavering resolve and unyielding determination. In the heartland of India, where the states of Maharashtra and Madhya Pradesh meet, there exists a mystical mountain trail. This trail, with its rugged terrain and awe-inspiring vistas, calls out to those brave souls who seek both challenge and enlightenment. It is a path that promises not only physical exertion, but also the opportunity to uncover hidden truths and unravel the mysteries of the natural world.

As a result, we made sure to bring along some breakfast provisions as we departed in the morning. As I journeyed towards the uncharted territories, my fellow adventurers and I found ourselves amusingly contemplating the possibility of subsisting solely on the provisions we had brought along for the day. It was getting dark when we unexpectedly ran across Praveen Chauhan, who had made his way to where we were heading. He eventually came up with us and, in a sombre mood, broke the news that nothing had been done to prepare for our arrival. No one has ever arrived and made any arrangements. I was unable to comprehend what had occurred and I was unable to accept it.

The first thing I did was consider the potential causes of what might have transpired. As I contemplated the workings of Holy Mother Narmada, it became clear that her divine influence ensured the failure of our carefully crafted plan. It was a humbling realization, yet one that reinforced the notion that her plans always come to fruition.

I had already hiked a hard 25 km, but now I was on the verge of climbing yet another peak because there was no cellphone reception anywhere in sight. I was hoping to reach Chandrashekhar Bawankule, but I knew I would have to walk for another kilometre or two into the mountains before I could even call him. A group of young people who were travelling with me and the rest of the team appeared exhausted and hungry, and my mood began to plummet. In these mountains, Chandrashekhar Bawankule has promised me that I need not worry about anything. In a stroke of luck, I found myself successfully sending the message to Chandrashekhar Bawankule and had spoken to Vijay Chaudhari. To my surprise, he too was taken aback by the lack of arrangements in place. However, as the sun began to set, I realized that time was of the essence. I yearned for a refreshing shower and to commence with the *pujana*, rather than dwelling on the absence of amenities.

Mother Narmada's *kalasha* was carried by Praveen Chauhan, along with Panditji, for the *pujana*. We were left without food or rest in a barren landscape. Even though we had nothing, we still had the Mother Narmada *kalasha* and all the other things we needed to perform the sacred *puja*, which made up for our lack of material belongings. I was completely enthralled. By the time dinner was ready, I was all by myself, sitting on a shaky wooden bench and eating *khichadi* that had been prepared in some mysterious fashion.

Scanty water supply was all that was available for my nightly and morning ablutions. We departed with a sense of contentment, as Mother Narmada's method of imparting the lesson that meticulous planning does not always guarantee fulfilment was truly enlightening to us all. Her wisdom and energy are inseparable. Truly, it is a blessing. It is the driving force behind all occurrences.

Following a captivating evening of dialogue with Vijay Chaudhari, I became the focus of a search conducted by a determined police officer who had journeyed a distance of 80 km to rendezvous with me. The officer arrived with provisions of food and water, despite the lateness of the hour. Despite the district administration's exhaustive search, it took them a considerable amount of time to locate us. For the first time, a considerable group of law enforcement officers had come to search for us. As I succumbed to slumber, provisions for the night had been brought forth – water, food, and blankets among them. Nevertheless, their recurrent disruptions endured. Praveen Chauhan lay peacefully outside, his slumber undisturbed by the world around him. The night was still, the air cool and calm. But suddenly, the tranquillity was shattered by the sound of police jeeps approaching. Their arrival pulled Praveen from his deep sleep, his eyes fluttering open to the sight of flashing lights and uniformed officers. As he unconsciously rose to his feet, Praveen realized that the police had come carrying supplies. Throughout the night, an eruption of sound reverberated through the stillness of the village, as the relentless arrival of police jeeps disrupted the peaceful sleep of its residents.

The events unfolding beyond my immediate surroundings were a complete mystery to me. The following morning, I became aware of the presence of police vans that had arrived and left provisions at our place of stay. However, there was no agony present within any of us. With hearts full of joy and gratitude towards Mother Narmada, we embarked on a journey towards the magnificent Khapparmal. The spectacular peak of Khapparmal can be seen far out in the distance, dominating the landscape. The journey to reach the pinnacle of its summit is an arduous endeavour, demanding immense expertise and unwavering perseverance.

As one embarks on the journey to Khapparmal, the act of ascending is not a mere walk, but rather an appealing attempt that looks like a form of climbing. Our luggage was abundant, as we were transporting all the items designated for donation. The track proved to be quite challenging. After a couple of hours of trekking, we finally reached the summit of Khapparmal. After a long and tiring trek, everyone finally reached the edge of the mountain. They were all exhausted, but the view that awaited them was breathtakingly expansive. They went ahead and sat on the edge, taking in the beauty of the vista before them. As we stood there, the vast expanse of Shulpani stretched out before our eyes. The rolling hills and sprawling fields seemed to go on forever, and the distant mountains loomed on the horizon. We took a deep breath, feeling the cool breeze on our face and the sun warming our skin. It was a moment of pure awe and wonder, as we took in the beauty of this incredible landscape.

As I sat very close to the path on the backside, I was wandering around, my eyes caught sight of a young girl standing a few feet away from me. She was between the ages of 8 and 10, but her beauty was beyond her years. I could not help but keep my gaze fixed upon her. Instantly upon locking gazes with her, I felt compelled to present her with a handful of sweets. As I rummaged through the bag on my right side, I could not help but wonder who it could be. When I whirled around to get a better look at her, she had vanished.

I shut my eyes and sat there in silence for a while, overwhelmed. I realized with tremendous clarity as I stared at the regal form before me that it was the holy Mother Narmada. The obvious aura of her spiritual blessing filled me with amazement and adoration at that very moment.

Once again, we set out on our journey by foot. As we ambled along, a feeling of hunger gradually permeated in everyone. The provisions for lunch were non-existent. Despite the coordinator's promise to provide us with lunch, his current whereabouts remain a mystery. The lack of cellular coverage had rendered all phones inoperable. After a considerable amount of time had elapsed, I approached Atul, our esteemed cameraman, and inquired about his plans for lunch? He responded with humility, stating that he would deem himself most fortunate if he were to be granted a portion of *chapattis*. "Very well", I replied. "Please proceed to Mother Narmada and convey this message to her." He proceeds in hushed footsteps, offering up a prayer to Mother Narmada for a bountiful meal. The time was approximately two o'clock.

The *parikramavasi* caught sight of a swiftly flowing stream amidst the lush greenery of the forest and turned to me with a query as to whether they could take a rejuvenating plunge. "Of course, you may", I readily assented.

I settled into the plush seat, my gaze drawn to the breathtaking majesty of the mountains. The surroundings were eerily tranquil, with scarcely any sign of vehicular activity owing to the lack of interconnecting roads. However, my attention was drawn to a pair of vehicles that materialized before me – one being a police jeep and the other adorned with a political sticker. I held onto the conviction that a team had been deployed to track me down, but alas, their endeavours were in vain as they could not establish my true identity. Remarkable was their speed. They passed by me, and after half an hour, they retraced their steps and returned to the very spot where I was seated. Vijay Chaudhari, a prominent politician from the area, made his presence known. He emerged from his vehicle with a weighty heart, and with a humble tone, conveyed his remorse for his lack of familiarity with the surroundings. Unbeknownst to him, the true nature of the obstacles that awaited him remained shrouded in mystery. He lamented the failed arrangements he had orchestrated. My mood was elevated and I felt rather jovial. I declined, confidently assuring that no failure had occurred. All was well. However, he persisted in shedding tears incessantly. Suddenly, the road we were travelling on became inundated with an abundance of food. As I gazed upon Atul, I inquired, "Did you not beseech the great lunch from Mother Narmada?". His eyes welled up with tears, for his supplications had been answered in full. This is the manner in which Mother Narmada carries out her duties.

In our company was Vijay Chaudhari, who diligently endeavoured to arrange our accommodations for the night. Upon arrival at a certain locale, it was deemed a suitable abode for my repose. As I arrived at the humble abode of a farmer, I could not help but think of the popular notion of "The Good Place". It seemed that this modest accommodation was a fitting representation of that idyllic concept, and I eagerly made my way inside. As I gazed upon the pastoral scene before me, my eyes were met with the sight of numerous goats. However, my enjoyment of the moment was somewhat dampened by the fact that I suffer from an allergy to these creatures. This affliction was first acquired during a stay in France, where I had the misfortune of sharing sleeping quarters with a group of goats. Their tendency to jump and frolic about had made it difficult for me to find rest, and the experience had left a lasting impression.

As I reminisced about my time spent in France, memories of goats flooded my mind. With a resolute tone, I declared that I could not possibly rest in this place. We began our journey at a leisurely pace, taking measured steps as we embarked on a 6-km trek to our next potential lodging destination. Pramod Bambal, Rahul, and several others accompanied us on our journey, though they lagged behind and assumed we were nearing our destination. As our nocturnal arrangements had been altered, the encroaching darkness had begun to unsettle Pramod Bambal, who was increasingly apprehensive about the diverse array of wildlife inhabiting the surrounding woods.

As we arrived at Sawariyadigar, the place where we were lodging, we were struck by the history of the school that stood before us. Constructed by Medha Patkar many years ago, the school was in a state of great adversity. The absence of walls in their school allowed for an unobstructed view of every corner. I was assigned a small, makeshift room that doubled as a classroom, with my bed serving as a makeshift desk made by joining several school tables together. Our dinner had to be sourced from a location that was 100 km away from our current whereabouts. Up ahead where our vehicle was located, there were no connecting roads. Praveen Chauhan had transported a car atop a boat. The connectivity between Sawariyadigar and Belgaon leaves much to be desired, as one must resort to traversing by boat during the months of November through January due to the abundance of backwater. However, come summer, the route is once again open for travel. Praveen Chauhan arrived with provisions, including food, blankets and other necessities. I retired for the night in a humble abode that had been fashioned out of makeshift materials. It was a marked improvement from the alternative, which likely would have been a space previously occupied by goats. On that day, it dawned on me that Mother Narmada intended to convey a powerful message: every successful plan owes its triumph to a single individual, and that individual is none other than oneself.

21

Back to Normal

Our journey commenced from Sawariyadigar towards Dhadgaon, requiring us to traverse the backwater by boat. This was due to the ongoing construction of a bridge that would connect this part of charming Shulpani to other regions, a project that has been in progress for the past twelve years. I wonder why this had taken such a long time?

The vessel transported our entire party, including an automobile that had traversed an alternate path and now required passage. We travelled in boat for a few minutes and it dropped us at Belgaon from where again we resumed our walk on foot.

As we strolled along, Vijay Chaudhari remained by our side, his presence unwavering. It was on this particular day that fate smiled upon him, as he received a well-deserved promotion within his esteemed political party. The anticipation for this long-awaited promotion had been building up for what felt like an eternity. However, as soon as he became a part of our team, fate smiled upon him and conferred upon him the well-deserved recognition he had been yearning for. In the midst of our journey, I suggested to Vijay Chaudhari that he should take a vehicle ride and relax instead of continuing on foot. It proved advantageous that he departed by car, as the journey on foot proved arduous and he was unaccustomed to traversing such a distance by foot. He pressed on, determined to better arrange our lodging for the night. Soon enough, the camp was once again abuzz with the welcome aroma of food and tea.

As I sat on the roadside in my chair, a group of men approached me, their eyes scanning the area as they inquired, "Excuse us, but do you happen to know the whereabouts of Babaji?" I mentioned that there exist numerous Babajis, and inquired as to which one specifically the individual is seeking? He, confused and with mixed emotions departed abruptly, yet later that evening, he crossed my path once more. Being a prominent figure in the local political scene, I could not resist the urge to jest with him. Throughout my life, I have often encountered situations where my youthfulness has caused others to doubt my identity. People frequently approach me, seeking confirmation that I am indeed the person they are searching for.

Amidst great anticipation, I arrived in Dhadgaon to a grand reception. Upon reaching the guest house where I was to reside, a series of events were scheduled for the day. During one such event, I delivered a speech on the significance of Shulpani and recounted my personal encounter with the place, which I aptly titled "Shulpani Kailasa".

Legend has it that the divine abode of Lord Shiva lies nestled in the majestic Kailasa, a place of immense sanctity. However, the sovereignty of this holy site is currently under the jurisdiction of China. Legend has it that Shulpani bears witness to Lord Shiva's holy footsteps, as he traversed the region for miles and miles through the area. It is said that the deity even paused to cleanse his trident in the waters of an ancient temple that once stood in the area, now submerged beneath the depths of the Sardar Sarovar Dam. It was here that he united with Devi. I could not help but feel that Lord Shiva was present in these mountains, as he must surely be where his devotees are. The appeal was truly captivating, and I had already made my decision beforehand. However, today I took the liberty of publicly announcing my annual pilgrimage to the enchanting Shulpani forest. It is a time for me to connect with the locals, exchange warm greetings, and strengthen the bonds that tie us together.

As the sun slowly descended below the horizon, I was joined by none other than the Superintendent of Police and a distinguished judge from the area. During this encounter, a profound bond was forged with the esteemed judge, which would ultimately lead to a plethora of exciting relationships.

22

Meeting and Greetings

As the sun rose over the horizon, casting a warm golden glow upon the quaint town of Dhadgaon, our weary group moved from a much-needed day of rest. It was time to resume our journey. As we stepped out, the town seemed to bid us farewell, its charming buildings standing as silent witnesses to our departure. As we embarked on our journey, the sun stood proudly in the heavens, its radiant beams cascading down upon the worn path that lay ahead. Filled with a newfound vigour and an eager anticipation, we embarked on our journey towards the captivating village of Molgi. Stretching out as far as the eye could see, the vast expanse of topography lay before them, its undulating contours remaining unchanged and unyielding. As far as the eye could see, the landscape was adorned with gentle, rolling hills that stretched out into the horizon, seemingly without end. Their undulating forms created a mesmerizing pattern, a dance of curves and bends that captivated the senses. Against the backdrop of the vast blue sky, this picturesque scene painted a picture of tranquillity and serenity. In the midst of this peaceful setting, one could find an abundance of charming hamlets, spread across the landscape like precious gems adorning a grand tapestry of nature. The air was filled with the sweet scent of wild flowers, and the gentle breeze whispered secrets passed down through generations. As one wandered through these humble settlements, it was impossible not to be captivated by their quaint charm. Each dwelling seemed to have a story to tell, its weathered exterior bearing witness to the history. As we strolled through the chilly morning, a familiar sensation of coldness crept over me. Vijay Chaudhari, our companion, was present and I urged him to continue with his usual routine. However, to my surprise, he opted to remain with us for an additional two days.

As we arrived, we were greeted by the Vanavasi *samaja*, who presented us with a beautiful bouquet of forest flowers. During our visit, we had the pleasure of meeting Ashok, a young and passionate teacher who had since transitioned into the realm of politics. In the small, close-knit community, his wife was a revered presence. With her unwavering dedication and tireless efforts, she had earned the esteemed position of *sarpanch*. This post bestowed upon her a great responsibility, as she was entrusted with the task of leading and representing the community. Her role as *sarpanch* not only commanded respect, but also carried immense influence and authority. It was a position that demanded wisdom, integrity, and a deep understanding of the people. As I engaged in conversation with her, it swiftly became apparent that she possessed an extraordinary measure of courage and fearlessness. Her words were imbued with enthusiasm and a certain manner that bespoke years of experience. Her confidence was palpable, as if it had been honed over the course of many decades. Overall, I was quite content with the fact that the Vanavasi *samaja* had immense faith in them. Once again, the entirety of the road was decorated with magnificent murals. Each stroke seemed to dance across, capturing the essence of the young artists who had created them. It was as if the space had been transformed into a gallery, showcasing the boundless creativity and imagination of these children. The paintings were everywhere, their presence impossible to ignore. From the smallest brushstrokes to the grandest masterpieces, they filled every inch of space with their kaleidoscope of hues. As I sat in quiet contemplation, my mind began to wander, seeking ways to elevate the artwork before me beyond the confines of this humble location. The vibrant strokes and intricate details of each piece seemed to beckon for a wider audience, a grander stage on which their beauty could be fully appreciated. I pondered over the possibilities, my thoughts dancing like brushstrokes across the canvas of my imagination.

As I journeyed, I encountered the individuals from the Reva Foundation. Their tale and their mischievous scheme will be revealed in subsequent chapters. However, upon my initial encounter with this gentleman, I was overcome with a sense of unease. I promptly warned my fellow travellers to exercise caution in their presence, as it was evident on that day.

As we continued our stroll, we were halted by an unexpected interruption. As we made our way to the *ashrama,* we were halted by a revered local saint. It was there that I once again encountered the gentleman from the Reva Foundation who had previously attempted to usher me inside. Despite his insistence, I politely declined his offer and respectfully refused the garland he had intended for me. As a personal practice, I reserve the act of garlanding for divine entities, unless specifically requested by a closely affiliated saint during a programme.

We travelled a couple of kilometres and stayed in an old temple with a gorgeous Shivalinga and a tiny village. This is where we ate lunch and relaxed for a while. As we arrived at the village, a heartwarming sight awaited us. The women, adorned in vibrant traditional attire, gracefully approached us, accompanied by the innocent laughter of children. Their eyes sparkled with genuine joy as they extended their hands in warm welcome, their humble greetings resonating with sincerity. To our delight, they presented us with a breathtaking bouquet of flowers, carefully gathered from the enchanting depths of the nearby forest. I offered them to join us for lunch and they gratefully accepted.

After a satisfying lunch, we embarked on a journey that took us a few kilometres away. Our next stop was Kathi, a place that held a remarkable treasure: a magnificent temple dedicated to the revered deities Hanuman and Ramalala. This temple, with its ancient origins, served as a testament to the rich tapestry of Sanatana Dharma and the profound stories of *jayanti*s. It was nestled along the route to Molgi, beckoning us with its grandeur and historical significance.

We were drawing near Molgi, a beautiful place with perfect weather that also turned out to be a snake paradise. As our conversation unfolded, our eyes were drawn to a captivating sight. There, in full view, lay several serpents, soaking in the inviting warmth of the sun.

Once more, we found ourselves lodged in the charming Molgi guest house, where a splendid event was held. During the gathering, I had the opportunity to expound upon the exquisite allure and profound spiritual significance of the Shulpani's forest.

23

Forest Band

I had a slight temperature when I left Molgi that morning, but I decided to keep walking nonetheless. In the company of an identified gathering of local politicians, we ended up finding ourselves engaged in a lively exchange of stories, each one sharing tales from their own unique life experiences of Shulpani. We encountered a stunning musical ensemble that graciously received us. Upon my inquiry for further insight, I learnt that the indigenous populace employs the *dhol* throughout the entirety of the evening in some festivals specially Shivaratri. Though not particularly weighty, this instrument yields an exceptional auditory experience. The melodious strains of music resonate deeply within the rustic environs of Indian villages. In the vicinity of the revered Mother Narmada, one can witness the enchanting spectacle of local musicians regaling the audience with their soulful renditions, paying homage to the benevolent deity and other local gods.

At one point, I encountered Ramdas. He had ingeniously discovered a shorter route for the *parikramavasi*s. With great determination, Ramdas had painstakingly chipped away at the earth, carving out a path that shaved off several kilometres from the original route. As I walked along this newly forged trail, I could not help but admire Ramdas for his unwavering devotion to the cause of the Narmada Parikrama. He stayed with us for the remainder of the day and shared his thoughts and feelings with us while he was at work. The services that locals provide for *parikramavasi*s are the most intriguing aspects of the Narmada Parikrama belt, although they are rarely talked about or documented. Among them was Bhila Seth, a name unfamiliar to many, yet his deeds spoke volumes of his noble character. For nearly half a year, Bhila Seth dedicates himself to the arduous task of aiding *parikramavasi*s along the sacred *parikrama* route. It mattered not that he was a stranger to those he assisted, for his charitable giving knew no boundaries. It is a tale that speaks of a profound tribute to the mighty Mother Narmada. As the sun began to set, we finally arrived at Pimpalkhunte. Our shelter for the night was an abandoned house, but it provided a breathtaking view of the nearby mountains. I found solace in the embrace of the majestic mountains, seeking refuge as close to their towering peaks as I possibly could. It was in this sacred place that the locals whispered tales of Bhima, a legendary figure from the ancient epic *Mahabharata*, who was said to have once graced this very land alongside his valiant brothers. Legend has it that with the passing of each year, a remarkable tradition unfolds, as the people gather to honour his arrival by embarking on a daring expedition up the towering mountain.

In the vast expanse of the Shulpani region, nestled amidst the rolling hills, lies a treasure trove of ancient tales waiting to be discovered. These majestic geological formations, standing tall and proud, hold within their very essence the echoes of a history that stretches back through the memoirs of time. For countless millennia, these hills have stood witness to the shift and move of civilizations, silently observing the rise and fall of empires, the passing of generations, and the evolution of of society. Take, for instance, the hill that loomed near us. It reverberated with the tales of Mogi Mata, whom I perceive as a manifestation of Bhagavati/Parvati. Her veneration is everywhere, as evidenced by the ubiquitous "Yaha Mogi" inscriptions on passing vehicles.

Nestled in the heart of Hela Dab, a word that translates to "cold" in the Bhil language, lies the revered Mogi Mata Temple. This sacred site holds great significance as it marks the origin of the Deva Ganga River, a waterway that has been mentioned in ancient Shastras. It is said that the old Shoolpaneshwar Temple once stood at the confluence of the Deva Ganga River and the Narmada River, a location that holds deep historical and spiritual significance.

The Bhil inhabitants hold Mogi Mata in high esteem, revering her as a deity who bestows blessings upon their crops. I was taken aback by the profound philosophy underlying the worship of Mogi Mata, as I perceived her to be a manifestation of the revered Mata Parvati.

I had made a promise to myself that upon completing the *parikrama*, I would visit Mogi Mata in Hela Dab which is situated in a direction opposite to our *parikrama* route.

Mogi Mata is regarded as the *kuladevi* of the Bhil society, every other vehicle that crosses the mountain ranges of Shulpani and surrounding in any state you would see "Yaha Mogi" written on the vehicle. Highly revered by the local society which is also the place from where Deva

Ganga originates. I had gone to the Mogi Mata Temple and Hela Dab after finishing my *parikrama* and had wonderful *darshana* as well as *bhandara* at the location. The Hela Dab valley is situated in the top of Shulpani hills and the temperature of the local area is so good that even in summer one does not need any fan here. Deva Ganga finds her place in the *Skanda Purana* where it is mentioned that the Deva Ganga's meeting place with the Narmada was the original spot of Shoolpaneshwar Temple which is now submerged in the water.

24

The Song and the Singer

As the day begun drew to a close, we realized that it was our final day in Maharashtra. Our departure from Maharashtra was scheduled for today, en route to the neighbouring state of Gujarat. Our journey will take us to the border, which is demarcated by the Dab River, formerly referred to as the Deva Ganga. Here, in the Shulpani area, is where the tale of Mogi Mata first began. Mother Parvati's metamorphosis into a revered figure of the community became the theme of local lore. At the confluence of the Dab Ganga and the Narmada River was a sacred site known as Shoolpaneshwar, named after the divine Shivalinga that was enshrined there. It is from this holy place that the surrounding area derived its name.

Reva Khanda in the *Skanda Purana* and the *Vayu Purana* indicate that the story covers a significant period of time. The Shoolpaneshwar Teerth[1] has been meticulously expounded upon in roughly fifteen chapters of the *Skanda Purana*, and in nearly twelve chapters in the *Vayu Purana*. Allow me to recount the tale of the Shoolpaneshwar Temple, a sacred site now engulfed by the waters of the Maiya Narmada due to the expansion of the Sardar Sarovar Dam. Although the temple has been submerged beneath the waters, it is my responsibility to ensure that its story lives on.

In the vast Hindu pantheon, Lord Brahma's progeny included the highly revered Rishi Kashyap. His two wives, Diti and Aditi, were held in great esteem as they were considered the mothers of both celestial deities and malevolent entities. Diti was bestowed with a precious gift, a son named Andhakasura, who embarked on a remarkable journey of penance. For an incredible duration of 4,000 years, he committed himself to a rigorous discipline of *tapa*, unlike any that had ever been witnessed before. For 1,000 years, a dense veil of smoke enshrouded him, concealing his figure from sight. For a millennium thereafter, he remained steadfast on one leg, his poise unyielding despite the relentless march of time. For another 1,000 years, he perfected the art of controlling the essential flames, his mastery over the basic elements unwavering. The previous millennium was dedicated to the profound introspection attained through the practice of *yoga*. The great penance was taking its toll, as evidenced by the fumes wafting from his head. The fumes were of such a potent quality that they managed to reach Kailasa, completely engulfing it.

Mother Parvati queried Lord Shiva regarding its nature. As Lord Shiva engaged in conversation with Parvati, he disclosed that the billowing smoke emanated from Andhakasura, who had been steadfastly engaged in his arduous penance for countless aeons. Mother Parvati inquired, "Why have you not granted your boon to the destitute Andhakasura, who fervently seeks your favour?" Lord Shiva responded that he was currently in a state of deep meditation, which accounted for the delay.

Then Lord Shiva and Parvati arrived at the location where Andhakasura was deeply immersed in his penance. As soon as Lord Shiva arrived, he humbly requested Andhakasura for a boon. Andhakasura was overwhelmed with joy as he beheld the divine form of Lord Shiva. He humbly requested the deity to grant him the power to weaken anyone who dared to stand against him, if his austerities had found favour in the eyes of the Lord. Initially, Lord Shiva refused to grant the boon, however, Andhakasura remained unwavering in his demand and would settle for nothing less. In that very moment, Lord Shiva granted him the boon that such a circumstance would indeed come to pass. However, it was made clear that the efficacy of the boon would be nullified in the presence of Lord Vishnu.

Andhakasura was overjoyed with the boon he had received. He wasted no time in setting his sights on conquering all three worlds within his realm. With great force, he defeated Indra and claimed Indrani as his own. It was a moment when the vanquished deities sought the aid of Lord Vishnu. Lord Shiva had granted this demon a blessing, and Lord Vishnu said that since Lord Shiva had blessed him, he is unable to do anything. "Go to Lord Shiva for help", commanded Lord Vishnu to all. At this point, Andhakasura, who was now filled with pride, even requested a battle with Lord Shiva. As Lord Shiva engaged in a fierce battle with the demon Andhakasura, he thrust his trident with great fury, causing the demon's pride to crumble. Overwhelmed with defeat, Andhakasura fervently recited numerous *stotras* in an effort to appease Lord Shiva. Moved by his devotion, Lord Shiva was pleased once again. At this moment, the Lord bestowed upon Andhakasura his own form, which became integrated into his *ganas*. The demon expressed gratitude, however, Lord Shiva's trident bore a bold stain from Andhakasura and seemed to be unyielding.

Lord Shiva made every effort to remove the stain, piercing it wherever he went, but to no avail. The stain remained steadfast, defying all attempts to eradicate it. The divine deities revealed that Andhakasura, despite being a demon, was the grandson of Brahma. The restoration of his trident requires complete purification. With all the gods in tow, Lord Shiva journeyed to various *tirtha*s and locales, endeavouring to eradicate the determined bloodstain. However, despite his efforts, the stain remained steadfast. In a divine moment, Lord Shiva and Parvati journeyed to the majestic Bhrigu Parvat. With the company of the gods, Lord Shiva thrust his trident into the mountain once more. To his astonishment, the trident's tip penetrated the netherworld, and with a single strike, the stain was removed. The topography of the terrain narrates a tale that reverberates with the vitality of the trident. Legend has it that the undulating slopes of Shulpani were formed by the mighty trident, which was plunged into the earth and lifted the terrain as it surged forward.

Legend has it that the mighty trident of Lord Shiva struck the earth, giving rise to the sacred Sarasvati Ganga. This holy river eventually merged with the revered Narmada, creating a divine pool known as Chakratirtha, nestled within the bosom of Mother Narmada. Here, in this sacred place, Lord Brahma erected a Shivalinga in his own name, revered as the Brahmaeshvara Shivalinga. Towards the southern end, a temple was dedicated to Lord Vishnu. In close proximity was Rudra Kunda and the cave of Markandeya Muni. A small distance away stood the temple of Ranchodadas, which had fallen into disrepair over a century ago and now lay submerged in water.

In the vicinity of Mokhdi, there is a river renowned as the Moksha Ganga. The place was deemed a *tirtha*, as per the accounts of Reva Khanda, and it was believed that performing *pitri-tarpana* was highly recommended there. The village of Mokhdi has been engulfed by the waters of the Sardar Sarovar Dam, leaving no trace of its existence.

Intriguing reports of the *sangama* of the Deva River with the Narmada and the temple of Shoolpaneshwar were recorded by an English lieutenant who visited in 1828. He was astounded by the presence of the temple in a region covered entirely by trees.[2] The lieutenant known as E.P. Del'hoste also mentioned that trees were plenty in the area of Shulpani, and that the local Bhils populace sold their timber-cutting services to buyers from Chandod and Bharuch. The best method of transportation for the logs was through river current, where they were floated.[3]

The erstwhile temple now lies submerged beneath the waters, and I prayed from distance. A new temple has been erected at a distance in Gora Colony. The Gora Colony emerged during the construction of the dam, serving as a provisional residence for the labourers and other workers.

The police personnel who had been accompanying us for several days were bidding us farewell on the last day of their stay. Their duties were concluding as we approached the border of Gujarat, where state protocol dictated a change in personnel. The law enforcement officers joined us for a midday meal, and we thoroughly enjoyed their company.

We savoured our midday meal on the serene banks of the Dab Ganga, as was our custom. However, a peculiar sensation stirred within me, prompting me to forego our customary post-lunch respite. As I departed and made my way towards the main road, where we intended to continue on our walk, I received word that two funeral processions were en route to the riverbanks, awaiting our departure. Once more, I was overwhelmed by the immense tenderness of Mother Narmada.

We arrived at Mathasar on this particular day and found lodging in a school. As the elections loomed in Gujarat, the state had provided ample cover for our border crossing. During our stay in Mathasar, we lodged in a school for the night. On this particular evening, an intriguing incident occurred. Following our meal, a surplus of sustenance remained. As a member of the organizing committee and the individual responsible for the culinary arrangements, Nandlal's keen eye detected a modest quantity of sustenance that had yet to be consumed and still in the cooking vessels. Under the cover of darkness, a group of individuals, who were familiar with our organization and the provisions we carried, noticed our presence. Among them were *parikramavasi*s who had taken up residence nearby and were in dire need of food. Approaching Nandlal, they inquired if we had any food to spare. Nandlal confirmed that we did, but only for a few. However, upon inspecting the pots, Nandlal was surprised to find them replenished once again. Nandlal was taken aback by the event that unfolded before him. He fervently prayed for the blessings of Mother Narmada, who, on that day, like every other day, provided food to a multitude of individuals. After a week or so, Nandlal recounted this tale to me. I reassured him that he could take solace in the fact that Mother Narmada is in charge of the entire entourage.

25

Arti and Bharti

As we journeyed from Mathasar towards Gora Colony, the majestic hills of Shulpani gradually receded, revealing an increasingly urban landscape. On the right-hand side, we beheld the embodiment of unity in the form of a colossal statue of Sardar Patel, the man who is renowned for his role in unifying India. As I laid my eyes upon the statue for the very first time, I could not help but feel captivated by the grandeur of the scene before me.

The platform, elevated alongside the mighty Mother Narmada, served as a unifying force for the entire Sanatana Dharma. The Statue of Unity that it exuded was reminiscent of our national unity post-Independence, leaving me in awe of the seemingly great story being played out before me.

The condition of the road was quite poor, leaving me to ponder how the State of Gujarat intends to entice tourists, who are drawn to the area's main attractions, with such dusty and substandard thoroughfares. As we traversed, we come across numerous dwellings that bear no relevance to the rich geographical history of our nation. It is disheartening to note that the *parikrama*, a significant aspect of this region, has been all but forgotten in Gujarat. We have passed by countless buses filled with tourists heading towards the Statue of Unity, a magnificent attraction in Gujarat. It is ironic that in a state where alcohol is banned, we encountered several drunken men. The abundance of alcohol bottles and pouches that I discovered in Gujarat surpasses that of any other region along the *parikrama* where alcohol is not prohibited. I am left to ponder over the impact it may have had on the local populace. Nearly every path we traversed revealed traces of illicit alcohol, surreptitiously transported across the adjoining borders.

Our journey led us to an *ashrama* where we encountered Somnath Bharti, a youthful ascetic with a captivating persona. He possessed a humorous disposition, yet his patience was easily exhausted. As the evening descended upon us, we partook in the customary *arti* before embarking on a journey to perform the sacred *achamana* ritual for the water of Maiya Narmda.

As we arrived at the banks of Mother Narmada in Gora Colony, we were promptly advised to hasten our pace and maintain a safe distance from the water's edge. The reason being the presence of numerous crocodiles in the vicinity, a fact that would hold true for the duration of our stay in Gujarat spanning several weeks.

The Gora Colony has undergone a transformation, shedding its former identity as a makeshift dwelling for labourers. Now, hotels and the State of Gujarat have taken over many of the *ashrama*s that once lined the banks. It is curious to think whether development truly means progress, as it seems to have failed in preserving the existing elements that were part of the Narmada banks. In fact, it appears to have caused a dichotomy rather than a unification, which is hardly what one would consider true development.

Once a great supporter of *parikrama*, the State of Gujarat has since strayed from its original path. Nowadays, the practice has become heavily commercialized, with opportunities to pay for rest stops available at every turn. In this particular state, we found that the majority of establishments required payment for lodging, despite our having all necessary amenities. Our group had everything we needed for a comfortable stay – from a food truck to our own sleeping arrangements and even a water tanker. All we required was a suitable location to park and spend the night. However, during our time in Gujarat, we encountered several *ashrama*s that required us to pay a fee for parking. The contrast in question warrants further investigation as a potential research topic.

Gora Colony to Vimleshwar

26

Rameshwaram

I was scheduled to spend a day at the Gora Colony *ashrama* of Somnath Bharti, but the atmosphere did not suite well with me. Consequently, I expressed to Jitendra Sharma my intention to leave the following day. At the crack of dawn, we departed after relishing a delightful breakfast, as was our custom. We then spent a while in the company of Somnath Bharti, sharing laughter and good cheer. With a remarkable ability to find humour in the world around him, he was a funny individual indeed. Despite his youth, he was entrusted with the management of an *ashrama*, leaving one to wonder how he found the time to fulfil his spiritual duties. Having settled the agreed-upon sum in advance, we departed.

We started our journey to the holy site of Rameshwaram from the picturesque Gora Colony. We had a long journey ahead of us, one that would take us through beautiful scenery and historic settlements, all of which were steeped in myth and legends. During our grand expedition across the vast expanse of the land, we embarked on a series of enchanting pilgrimages to various sacred *tirtha*s.

At the first *tirtha*, known as Pippalada Teerth, here Pippalada Muni did *tapasya* and Lord Shiva appeared; Pippalada Muni, in gratitude, requested a favour from the Lord and asked that he remain here forever, which He did since and was known as Pippalada Teerth.[1] Before *parikrama*, while I was poring through historical records and drawing out a map of the *tirtha*s, I had not been able to find the Sakrtatirtha, although records from long ago indicated that it was close to the Pippalada Teerth. We (the *parikramavasi*s and I) began exploring the holy banks, and eventually came across Sakrtatirtha. According to Reva Khanda, there once was a demon named Jambhasura who, via extensive *tapasya*, gained such immense power that he was able to overthrow Indra and assume control of the world. Indra performed *tapasya* here to appease Lord Shiva, the God he worships. Indra prayed to Lord Shiva for the power of Shakti so that he may vanquish his foe Jambhasura. Here, at this spot, is where Lord Indra installed the Sakreshwar Shivalinga.[2]

We continued our walk along the same route we had originally planned to travel to get to Vyasheshwar and Vaidyanath Teerth. Vyasheshwar Mahadev was set up to the west of the Vaidyanath Teerth when the Vedavyasa came to pay a visit to the Shoolpaneshwar. After several years of meditation, the Ashvinikumaras attained the status of knowledge necessary to become *vaidya*s of the divine. In other words, Vaidyanath was established when its founders achieved the wisdom encapsulated by the term *vaidya vidya*. We stayed there for what seemed like forever, yet we never encountered any other *parikramavasi* or even locals. This temple gives the sense of being rarely visited, which is confirmed by the absence of tourists. I do not think many *parikramavasi*s, especially those from Maharashtra, have the intestinal strength to venture to such locations, preferring instead to stick to more tame walking routes without any unexpected turns. It seemed that those who had gathered the Maharashtrian crowd for *parikrama* had neglected to impart a crucial piece of knowledge, which is to visit holy *tirtha*s. For one, *parikrama* is not merely a matter of traversing the distance from one end to the other, as if it were a mere formality. No, it is a profound experience that entails drawing near to the revered Narmada River and paying homage to the sacred *tirthasthala*s that grace her banks.[3]

We left the temple and Lokesh brought us tea; after relaxing for a while, we resumed our journey to the next *tirtha*, which, according to the Sanatana legend, was only a short distance away.

After a 6 km walk, we arrived at what we believe to be the site of Anandeshwar Teerth, but I could not uncover any remnants of the ancient temple. Nothing was discovered during our search of the area. It was here that the demons Chandrapida and Surantaka planned to abduct Goddess Parvati, according to legend. Lord Shiva, upon hearing this, immediately went to war with the arrogant demons. Mother Parvati pleaded with Lord Shiva to use his trident to destroy the demons as the conflict continued. After defeating the demons, Lord Shiva was so overjoyed that he danced with his *gana*s in the Bhairava form and then erected a Shivalinga, which he named Anandeshwara Shivalinga.[4]

After another kilometre or so, we reached the confluence of the Anadwahi River and Mother Narmada. There is a lovely tale to be told here, one that bears witness to the ancient Sanatana history that shaped the landscape in which it is set. In the vast expanse of this nation, every landscape holds within it a rich tapestry of history. From the towering mountains to the serene valleys, from the bustling cities to the tranquil countryside, each corner of this land is imbued with the essence of Indian Sanatana traditions. These ancient traditions, deeply rooted in the fabric of society, have stood the test of time, preserving the stories and beliefs of generations past. They serve as a guiding light, illuminating the significance of every hill, river, and forest that graces this diverse land. There was a time when Lord Shiva and Mata Parvati were sleeping on this spot, and Nandi was guarding them. A group of demons came and started making noise, so Nandi told them to be quiet because Lord Shiva and Mata Parvati were asleep. When demons did not pay the heed, Nandi sparked a fight, and after spending the night fending off demons, a gigantic carter showed up. The night-time battles were witnessed by the divine lords, who expressed their respect by showering the earth with rain, the source of this river.

In addition, this river is where the sweat from Nandi's body met the Narmada. The fact that, as I crossed that area, I could still make out the carter mentioned in the Reva Khanda a proof that Indian *rishi*s had a deep awareness of the processes that shaped the terrain and the stories behind them. It is fascinating how the carter can suddenly be seen on landscapes where no one would expect to see it.[5]

There are two significant locations at a little distance from the point where the Anadwahi River and Mother Narmada meet; both have gone through numerous name changes over the years, but legend has it that here is the spot where Shiva hid himself from Bhasmasura. The story begins in the past, when Lord Shiva had accepted the *tapasya* of Kalavashpa (the original name of Bhasmasura) and appeared to him in gratitude. If Lord Shiva is pleased, Bhasmasura said, then Lord Shiva should grant him the blessing that anybody or anything he puts his hand on should be destroyed or turned to ashes instantly. After Lord Shiva gave his assent, Bhasmasura decided to give it a try by placing his palm on Shiva's head. After Nandi battled Bhasmasura, Lord Shiva realized he would not be easily defeated and headed south, eventually arriving at the Narmada Ghat. But Narada saw that wherever Lord Shiva went, Bhasmasura followed, and so he quickly informed Lord Vishnu, who then arrived to help. While Vishnu dealt with Bhasmasura, Shiva was instructed to take refuge inside Mother Narmada.

In a moment of divine intervention, Lord Vishnu assumed the form of Mohini, a being of unparalleled beauty and grace. As Mohini emerged, her ethereal radiance captivated all who beheld her. Her delicate features were sculpted with such a perfection that even the most hardened hearts were softened by her mere presence. Her eyes, shimmering like pools of liquid moonlight in a mischievous turn of events, she decided to amuse herself by imparting some dance knowledge upon Bhasmasura. Little did he know that these seemingly innocent movements would lead to a most unfortunate outcome. As fate would have it, during one particular step, he inadvertently placed his palm upon the crown of his head. In an instant, a transformation occurred that left him reduced to nothing more than a pile of ash.

Since then, this place, where Lord Shiva hid himself, was known as Lukeshwar Teerth.[6] Jateshwar Teerth is conveniently located nearby. It was a time when the malevolent Bhasmasura relentlessly pursued Lord Shiva, seeking to harm him. In the midst of this perilous chase, a moment of divine intervention occurred. Lord Shiva's magnificent *jata*, his matted locks of hair, unravelled at this very spot. Thus, this hallowed site came to be known as Jateshwar Teerth.[7] When the Lord of Wealth, Kubera, learned that Lord Shiva had been hiding nearby, he came to the same location to perform his *tapasya* and subsequently established Dhaneshwar Mahadev. Intriguingly, the temple grounds are littered with ancient statues that serve as reminders of the site's rich past, and it was here that we stopped for lunch and a respite. My companions and I ate our lunch among the statues, taking in the atmosphere of a location whose history has been preserved despite the passage of many centuries. The only difficulty with Sanatana Dharma is that its adherents do not take the initiative to record and maintain their traditions, instead hoping that some external force will serve as a constant reminder of their faith's long history.

As I ventured forth on this fine day, a profound realization washed over me like the gentle caress of a summer breeze. It became abundantly clear that the divine guidance of Mother Narmada was asking me towards a noble purpose – the preservation of the sacred *tirtha*s that grace her majestic banks. In this sacred mission, I sensed a calling to establish a system, a framework if you will, wherein these sacred places could be etched into the very fabric of our collective consciousness, ensuring that they do not fade away into the annals of forgotten history. They stood as the living embodiment of this nation's history.

After the delightful respite of our lunch break, we resumed our journey with renewed energy. Our feet carried us forward, step by step, as we ventured deeper into the unknown. Our first destination awaited us eagerly, beckoning us with its mystical allure. Mangaleshwar Teerth,[8] a place of spiritual significance, stood before us, ready to unveil its secrets. In this very place, Mangala arrived, seeking solace and enlightenment. With unwavering determination, he embarked on a journey of deep meditation and *tapasya*. By his relentless devotion and unwavering faith, he sought the blessings of Lord Shiva. Days turned into weeks, and weeks into months, as Mangala immersed himself in his spiritual quest. His commitment and dedication were unwavering, as he delved into the depths of his soul, seeking wisdom and enlightenment. And then, as if the heavens themselves had heard his plea, the blessings of Lord Shiva descended upon Mangala, who was given the place among the planets. The other planets, witnessing his unwavering devotion and the divine grace bestowed upon him, began to hold him in high regard. Since Mangala performed *tapasya* there, the locals have known it as Mangrol since time immemorial.

We continued on foot till we reached the Shankhchudeshwar Mahadev[9] Temple, where the Shivalinga dedicated to Shankhchuda Snake was first installed.

We continued on our way in an effort to go to Tejonath or Vaidyanath Teerth.[10] Skanda was told a tale about it by Lord Shiva. After the *pralaya* (last destruction), when the universe began to breathe again, Lord Brahma was tasked with remaking the planet. When Brahma began considering his options, Shiva suddenly materialized from his forehead (*brahmateja*) and began to weep aloud, prompting Brahma to give him the name Rudra, "the one who weeps aloud". Lord Brahma then asked him to begin helping with the creative process, at which point Rudra spawned millions of copies of himself, all of whom were just as angry as Lord Shiva. Lord Brahma then turned to Lord Shiva and said, "We need to create a world where everything is not like Rudra, furious and deadly". This was the place where *brahmateja* (illumination) had appeared and rested hence the name – Tejomaya Teerth.

It was here that Garuda had also performed his *tapasya*. At one time, Garuda was pleased with himself for being the world's pre-eminent bird and the steward of Lord Vishnu. Lord Vishnu sensed his pride and pinched him to remind him that it is not the Garuda's might, but Lord Vishnu's own modesty, that makes the Garuda his vehicle. Lord Vishnu began his explanation by saying that pride and haughtiness are the quickest way to ruin one's reputation. Garuda then inquired as to the location of the *tapasya* that would cause his ego to vanish. To obtain enlightenment from inside, Lord Vishnu instructed him to perform *tapasya* on the sacred ground of Tejomaya Teerth, located on the banks of the River Narmada.[11]

Ashvinikumar, according to later stories, had arrived here during the Varaha *kalpa*. Ashvinkumar travelled to Tejomaya Teerth to receive the divine guidance and blessings necessary to master all of the world's herbs and use them to heal not just people but even the divine gods. Thus, the current name of the location is Vaidyanath; nevertheless, Vaidyatanath is erroneous, as it has been around for much longer.

After hearing about Tejomaya Teerth from Lord Rama, Sugriva travelled there to seek the deity's favour. Not long after, nearby, Vandariya performed penance and founded Vanreshwar Teerth.[12] The temple appeared to be in a terrible state, with a few ancient statues lying around but no one seemingly caring about this important historical site. It was getting close to nightfall, and the state of the temple made me sad, so I set out for Brahmeshwar Teerth. It, over a perid of time, has been called by many other names. Lord Brahma created it during the first *kalpa*, therefore, from that point on, it was known as Brahmeshwar. As a result of Lord Vishnu's *tapasya* here in the second *kalpa*, the area came to be known as Chakreshwar. Shakreshwar was the name given to the area after Indra performed *tapasya* there in the third *kalpa*; Dharmeshwar was the name given to the area after Yamaraja performed *tapasya* there in the fourth *kalpa*; and Varuneshwar was the name given to the area after Varuna performed *tapasya* in the fifth *kalpa*. Kubera had performed *tapasya* here in the sixth *kalpa*, so the area became known as Dhaneshwar; in the seventh *kalpa*, Markandeya Muni did the same, and the area became known as Kumbheshwar. And it was here that Shani, at Brihaspati's direction, performed his *tapasya* and founded the city of Shanishchar. Many of the ancient statues that have taught us about our heritage are still displayed on the temple's walls. Although the town is small, the temple is kept in good condition.[13]

On the day end, our journey led us to the very location where, according to Sanatana history, Lord Rama undertook his *tapasya* after eliminating Ravana, known as Rameshwar Mahadev.[14] Lord Rama and his brother Lakshmana had come here after their victory over Ravana to perform *sadhana* and atone for the sin of killing a brahmana. Lord Rama abided by the societal conventions of his period, which said that anyone who committed the killing of a brahmana (Ravana was a brahmana) must perform penance. Lord Rama established Rameshwaram here, and Lakshmana prayed to the Shivalinga, which he renamed Lakshmaneshwar, while he sat with his brother for *sadhana*.

Since Lord Shiva himself performed Kumbhabhisheka to the Shivalinga here after Lord Rama completed his *tapasya*, Rameshwaram is also known as Kumbheshwara. In close proximity of this area, Matsyak Muni founded Matsyakeshwar, and Jeemut who belonged to the family of Yayati had offered prayers to Maheshwar.[15]

As I arrived at the desolate location in the evening, I came to the realization that a significant number of *parikramavasi*s did not make the journey to the temple, which was situated quite a distance from the *ashrama* where the majority of them stay. The establishment is overseen by a *grihastha sant*, a married couple who are quite intriguing. During my stay, I resided in at a distance from the main structure. As I laid my eyes upon the lady, it became apparent to me that she was not one to be associated with the spiritual realm. Her demeanour exuded a commanding presence, and she took it upon herself to assert her authority over us, a group of young individuals engaged in *parikrama*. Despite her domineering nature, I urged my companions to withhold judgement and remain in her company. I affectionately dubbed them "Baba and Babi". The Baba was a remarkable individual, always willing to serve those who crossed his path. He exuded a gentle and humble demeanour, and our time spent in his company was truly enjoyable. However, due to my relationship with him, he did scold his wife at one point. We had originally planned to spend only a single night in this place, but circumstances compelled us to extend our stay by an additional day.

I approached the Shivalinga for *darshana*, a sense of wonder enveloped me. The mere act of touching the same Shivalinga that Lord Rama had worshipped and Lord Shiva himself had done the *abhisheka* was a deeply moving experience. The Shivalinga that I came across during my *parikrama* was truly a sight to behold. Its exquisite beauty was unparalleled, and it was evident that both the temple and the Shivalinga had gracefully withstood the test of time, spanning tens of thousands of years. The temple is beautiful and holds the story of several generations but it is in bad condition from outside. Its upkeep is poor. As I approached the temple, rumours circulated that the individual taking care of the temple was impeding progress. However, upon further investigation, I discovered that this person was actually quite hardworking and was exceptionally pleased with our arrival. In fact, we were able to conduct our Naramda *kalasha pujana* within the temple's confines on the very night of our arrival.

The *puja* held on that day was of great depth and significance. I could not help but feel that it would not have been possible without the benevolent blessings of Devi Narmada. As the sun began to set, I encountered a youthful *sadhu* who happened to reside within the same compound. He expressed a desire to discuss matters pertaining to our national culture, but I gently conveyed to him that such a discourse was unnecessary. I explained that our *puja* rituals embody the entirety of our nation's heritage, leaving no need for further elucidation. Though initially taken aback, the *sadhu* eventually comprehended that my intentions were not to preach, but rather to embark upon a spiritual journey. The attendees that came to see us included Indar Hisaria, Purushottam Hisaria, Satyanarayan Dhoot, Om Soni, Abhishek and Rajiv. While we were in Gujarat, the *parikramavasi*s would often phone Rajiv, who is based in Baroda, whenever they needed something. They had all grown up in Rajasthan, where nobody knew anything about holy Narmada, and they did not understand a word I said about the temple's history, but when they finally got there, they were stunned by what they saw.

27

Someone Was Waiting for Me

Departing from Rameshwaram, our next destination was within a walking distance of approximately 30 km. Little did we know that our journey would take us to the enchanting town of Ori where Koteshwar is situated. Though a premonition had stirred within me, hinting at a stay in a divine *tirtha*. On this fateful day, we encountered a perplexing predicament – the inability to locate a suitable spot to have our midday meal. This unfortunate circumstance repeated itself thrice during our *parikrama*, each instance transpiring on a day of great significance to me.

Upon concluding my visit with Baba and Babi, I made a concerted effort to ensure Babi's contentment. I kindly requested that she join us for a photo session, which she found pleasing, as she may have previously felt overlooked. With Baba and Babi had as proud parents of two daughters, I generously gifted them with both monetary funds and clothing. It was with great pleasure that I learned one of the daughters was to get married in the upcoming month of January.

Gujarat, a land of great beauty, boasts an impressive collection of *tirtha*s that have been mentioned in the Shastras. It was a personal goal of mine to visit each and every one of these sacred sites. After conducting extensive research for a period of four months, I meticulously crafted a map of the *tirtha*s. The process was incredibly therapeutic, and my companions and I were able to visit each location that I had carefully marked on the map.

As we journeyed through the verdant expanse of Koteshwar, we encountered numerous individuals along the way. The landscape was dominated by vast swathes of fertile farmland, lending a bucolic charm to our travels. On either side, the land was adorned with either sugar cane or banana plantations. Both crops require copious amounts of water, but fortunately, Gujarat has been blessed by the benevolent Mother Narmada, rendering any concerns regarding water scarcity moot.

Our journey began with a visit to Hanumanteshwar Teerth,[1] a sacred site where the mighty Lord Hanuman is said to have performed his rigorous penance. It is the story of Lord Hanuman, a revered deity in the Hindu pantheon, who played a pivotal role in the epic war between good and evil. Alongside the noble Lord Rama, Hanuman embarked on a perilous journey to vanquish the malevolent demon king, Ravana, and his legion of wicked minions. With unwavering loyalty and boundless strength, Lord Hanuman fearlessly engaged in countless battles, displaying his prowess. However, in accordance with traditions and customs, it is worth noting that Ravana hailed from the esteemed lineage of brahmana *vansha*. Consequently, the need for purification arose, as dictated by the prevailing beliefs and practices of the time. It is said that Lord Rama, the courageous king and embodiment of righteousness, found himself engaged in a profound conversation with his devoted companion, Hanuman, the mighty God. In the midst of their dialogue, Lord Rama revealed a startling revelation to Hanuman. He spoke of a hidden truth, a burden that weighed heavily upon their noble souls. It was whispered that they, along with their loyal allies, had unknowingly accumulated a grave sin – the sin of slaying brahmanas. Lord Rama, with a heavy heart, disclosed that their adversary, the formidable Ravana, hailed from the very lineage of these revered brahmanas. He deemed it fitting that in his noble quest, the mighty Lord Hanuman should join him in paying homage to the revered deity, Lord Shiva. And so, it was decided that this sacred act of worship would take place upon the hallowed banks of the Narmada, a river revered for its sanctity. In the depths of his contemplation, Lord Hanuman knew his next course of action. The weight of his recent actions was heavy upon his conscience, and he sought a path towards redemption. With a resolute heart, he considered the possibility of bypassing the arduous journey of *tapasya*, the rigorous penance undertaken by the devout to attain divine favour. In his wisdom, Lord Hanuman contemplated the notion of approaching Lord Shiva directly, beseeching him for forgiveness and blessings. The thought of standing before the mighty deity, humbly acknowledging his transgressions, and the thought of seeking solace in Shiva's divine grace filled Lord Hanuman's mind. Lord Hanuman, the mighty and devoted disciple of Lord Rama, embarked on a sacred journey to Kailasa seeking the divine presence of Lord Shiva. With unwavering determination, Lord Hanuman approached the grand entrance of the chamber where Lord

Shiva resided. However, his path was obstructed by Nandi, the loyal and vigilant gatekeeper of Lord Shiva's abode. Nandi, with a solemn expression, informed Lord Hanuman that he could not enter the sacred chamber for *darshana*, the blessed sight of the divine deity. Nandi, ever wise and perceptive, revealed the reason behind his refusal. He spoke of a grave sin that Lord Hanuman had committed in the past – the sin of brahmana killing. This transgression, though unintentional, had left a mark on Lord Hanuman's soul. Nandi, in his wisdom, suggested that before seeking *darshana*, Lord Hanuman must first undertake a penance, a rigorous *tapasya*, to absolve himself of this sin. Having undergone this extraordinary experience, Lord Hanuman returned to Lord Rama and began to recount the incredible tale that had unfolded before his very eyes. Once more, Lord Rama gently reminded him of the very suggestion he had made from the outset – to embark on a rigorous penance in order to absolve his sins. It seemed that his words had fallen upon deaf ears before. In this particular instance, Hanuman proceeded with determination and settled himself down to engage in his spiritual practice. With unwavering focus, he diligently performed his rituals and rites, ultimately establishing the revered Hanumantehswar Teerth, a sacred place of pilgrimage.

As I approached the *tirtha*, it appeared to be nestled within the confines of private property. The temple itself was a sight to behold, meticulously maintained and exuding an air of tranquillity. However, despite its grandeur, there was an undeniable sense that this was not a public space. Throughout my time here, it became increasingly apparent that this place, steeped in rich history, was shrouded in an aura of peculiarity. The behaviours of the individuals residing in this vicinity were markedly unusual, leaving me with a lingering sense of intrigue and curiosity. The premises were met with indifference, as if trespassing upon private property had been committed. The disapproval of our presence was palpable among the people. However, their hands were tied, unable to take any action. I meticulously documented the scene through cameras, I proceeded to elucidate the significance of the location, adhering to our customary practices. Once my task was complete, I bid my farewell and departed from the premises. Once known as Kapisthitapura, this hallowed ground has since evolved into the enchanting realm of Kathora.

In the vicinity of this place, not too distant, is Purtikeshwar Mahadev.[2] It is said that during the time of Lord Rama, the mighty Jambavan, accompanied by his loyal companion Neel, sought solace and enlightenment through their rigorous penance at this very site. Miraculously, any afflictions and injuries they bore were miraculously healed, and even the burden of the grave sin of slaying brahmanas was absolved within these sacred grounds. In a land not too distant from here, lies the sacred Naleshwar Mahadev Teerth.[3] It is in this very place that Nal, a valiant warrior who had vanquished numerous sons of the mighty Ravana during a great war, embarked on a profound spiritual journey. It was here that he immersed himself in deep meditation and, through his unwavering devotion, established the revered Naleshwar Mahadev Temple.

Nal and Neel, these two extraordinary beings were not only renowned architects but also held the esteemed position of being the masterminds behind the formidable *vanara* army. Their indomitable spirit and unwavering dedication to their cause were legendary, as they embarked on a perilous journey to construct a bridge across the vast ocean, with the sole purpose of reaching the fabled land of Lanka. Nal, with his unparalleled expertise in the art of construction, possessed a keen eye for detail and an innate ability to envision grand structures. His mind was a treasure trove of architectural brilliance, and his hands possessed the skill to bring his visions to life. Neel, on the other hand, was a master engineer, well-versed as his brother.

As our journey progressed on this defining day, we found ourselves unexpectedly discovering a revered *tirtha* of Nageshwar. This sacred site lay nestled within the expansive stretch of farmland, its presence shrouded in an air of mystique and reverence. In a world ravaged by time and turmoil, there stood a temple, once grand and magnificent, its sacred halls echoed with the haunting whispers of a forgotten era. Yet, amidst this desolation, there was one portion of the temple that had miraculously escaped the clutches of destruction. It was a sight that caught the eye of all who ventured into the temples. The journey to discover this sacred *tirtha* had been a lengthy and challenging endeavour. Historical accounts had indicated that the temple no longer existed, yet deep within me, I held a steadfast belief that we would uncover its hidden presence. And our unwavering determination bore fruit as we stumbled upon its revered grounds. As we gazed out into the distance, our sight was hindered by the vast expanse of the banana plantation that stretched before us. Yet, it was as if a stroke of pure grace guided our steps, leading us along a hidden path that wound its way through the verdant foliage. And there, amidst the lush greenery, we stumbled upon a hidden gem – the magnificent Nageshwar Temple. In the annals of Sanatana legends, it is written that within the folds of time, there existed a sacred place where Vasuki Naga, (mighty serpent) embarked upon his arduous journey of penance. In the ancient tales, it is said that Ganga (sacred river) always rests upon the head of Lord Shiva. One day, Mother Parvati, the divine consort of Lord Shiva, expressed her desire for him to dance. Lord Shiva, ever eager to indulge in the joy of dance, began to sway and twirl with grace. As his divine movements intensified, a remarkable phenomenon occurred – the holy Gangajala (water of the Ganges) began to flow downwards from Lord Shiva's matted locks. Witnessing this extraordinary sight, Mother Parvati, in her wisdom, instructed Vasuki, the mighty serpent king, to consume all the flowing Gangajala. And so, Vasuki obediently drank the sacred waters, preventing them from cascading onto the earth. Ganga's eyes fell upon Vasuki, the serpent king who had been faithfully serving Lord Shiva for countless ages. However, something within her stirred, and a surge of anger coursed through her divine being. In a moment of intense fury, Ganga, unleashed a powerful curse upon Vasuki. She decreed that he would face failure and be stripped of his esteemed position in the service of Lord Shiva, a role he had held with unwavering devotion. The air crackled with the weight of her words as they hung in the atmosphere, leaving Vasuki stunned and bewildered. Vasuki begged Ganga for forgiveness out of fear, and she advised him to visit the revered Narmada River banks and perform his *tapasya* so that he may once more be of service to Lord Shiva. Vasuki took the advice and proceeded to the Narmada River banks where he built a Shivalinga and began worshipping Lord Shiva under the name Nageshwar. After a while, the Lord reappeared and gave Vasuki the instruction to pour all of the Ganga's water into one of the Karanjatarani caves in the holy Narmada. Vasuki obeyed. Vasuki took a bath and was purified at this confluence of the same river, which is now known as the Arjan River. In one *kunda*, known as Rudra Kunda, which was located inside the holy Narmada and from which the local name of the area Rundha was formed, Lord Shiva also enjoyed participating in aquatic activities. (Rundha is a deformed name of Rudra + Kunda).[4]

The son of Vyasa Sukeshwar performed his *tapasya* here, and after Lord Shiva was appeased by the *tapasya*, he was given the blessing not to experience another mortal birth and to remain in this location forever.

Since we were in *parikrama*, which forbids crossing to the centre of the Narmada, we were unable to access the well-known Markandeya Teerth, which is directly across on the island formed by the river. But the tale begins when Rishi Vyasa lived in this location. After visiting him, Rishi Markandeya stayed for a while and built a structure that he named Markandeshwara Shivalinga.[5]

As we traversed one of the small stream with difficulty, Yogesh came to the realization that I was in the process of creating a digital map. It became clear to him that I was not interested in following the commonly trodden path that fails to encompass all of the *tirtha*s. On that day, we encountered difficulty in locating a suitable location for lunch. We were walking at a slow pace and Lokesh in vehicle was ahead of us for searching for the place for lunch, after a long delay in finding the proper spot in the farmland or under a tree cover, I made a statement that if Lokesh with our food vehicle were to pass a certain curve, I would abandon the search for a lunching spot. As fate would have it, the vehicle did indeed pass the curve, and I upheld my statement by refraining from eating. I requested my fellow *parikrama* team members to partake in a meal as they were feeling hungry. However, out of respect for my own hunger pangs, they refrained from doing so. Subsequently, I called the camp to prepare some savoury items when we reach as I knew my young companions are struggling with hunger, which was an unprecedented request to Nandlal but made him extremely happy.

It is worth mentioning that I learned later on that Jitendra Sharma had escorted all the vehicles to Koteshwar. Upon our arrival, the lady who ran the *ashrama*, affectionately referred to as "Ma" by her followers, eagerly awaited us. She had prophesied the arrival of her beloved Rama, which she had named me so. Upon arriving at Koteshwar, I was greeted by Ma and her son. From that moment on, we formed a strong bond and our relationship flourished. Many years ago, Ma had completed her *parikrama* and subsequently became a saint. Under the loving care of her son, she wants for nothing. The temple, with its rich history of countless *yagya*s, is a sight to behold. It is no wonder that it has been given the name Koteshwar. After years without rain brought hardship to the Treta Yuga people, they all converged in this area, which became known as Kotinarpura. Koteshwar Mahadev was established here at the site of a *yagya* where the people prayed to the Almighty God Shiva for protection against starvation.[6]

As the evening drew to a close and the *arti* had been performed, Ma made a request to me. She asked that I sing for her, and though it was a rare occurrence, I obliged. As my voice filled the room, she was moved to tears. The inception of our formidable alliance was followed by a request from her and her son to assume control of the temple grounds. Despite my admiration for her, I declined the offer and pledged my unwavering support without assuming the mantle of leadership. The premises were truly stunning, and she had transformed them into a wonderland. A magnificent *bodhi* tree graced the landscape, covering nearly half an acre, while a variety of exquisite snakes made their home there.

28

Shakreshwar Maharaj and Laughter

Following our daily *puja* ritual, we set out on a journey that took us to countless *tirthas*. The sun shone brightly as we set off in the early morning, eager to visit the holy places we had heard so much about. Mukuteshwar was the first *tirtha* we saw today, and its story dates back to a time when Daksha held a *yagya* at which neither Lord Shiva nor Parvati Mata were invited. After hearing that Mother Parvati had burned herself into ashes, Lord Shiva destroyed Daksha's *yagya* and eventually made his way to this holy bank. When Lord Shiva's *ganas* realized he was no longer wearing the *mukuta* (crown), they came here expecting to find him, only to discover a Shivalinga in his place. Everyone then worshipped Lord Shiva and gave the crown to the Shivalinga. This is why this place is known as Mukuteshwar Teerth.[1]

In the vicinity, not too distant from our current location, lies a sacred place known as Skandeshwar Teerth.[2] Legend has it that it was here where the revered deity Skanda Swami, also known as Karttikeya, undertook a rigorous penance. As a testament to his divine presence, the *tirtha* was established and named Skandeshwar Mahadev.

As one strolls along for a mere few hundred metres, a magnificent destination of profound historical significance comes into view. Originally christened as Narmadeshwar Teerth,[3] this remarkable place has acquired a local moniker, Markandeya Teerth, owing to its deep connection with the revered figure, Markandeya. Once upon a time, in a realm where the celestial beings roamed and the cosmic energies intertwined, there existed a momentous event that would forever be etched in the annals of history. It was a time when Lord Brahma, the creator of all existence, decided to embark upon a grand *yagya*, a sacred ritual of immense power and significance. The celestial beings, with their ethereal grace, eagerly gathered around as Lord Brahma prepared for the *yagya*. This celestial congregation included not only the divine entities but also the enigmatic demons, whose presence added an air of intrigue and unpredictability to the proceedings. As the sacred fire blazed with a mesmerizing intensity, its radiant flames dancing in perfect harmony, every single entity of the universe was called upon to participate in this extraordinary event. From the celestial deities to the celestial nymphs, none was left to attend the this great event. In the realm of the divine, there was a gathering of *rishi*s and *muni*s. They engaged in deep discussions with the celestial gods, seeking to unravel the mystery that had captured their thoughts. The question that lingered in their minds was one of great significance – why had Lord Brahma (creator of the universe) chosen the sacred banks of the Narmada River for this grand *yagya*? It was a query that challenged their beliefs, for they had long revered the holy River Ganga as the pinnacle of reverence among all rivers. In the hushed gathering, a profound silence enveloped every individual. Each person pondered over the question at hand, searching for an answer that eluded them all. However, just as despair began to settle in, a remarkable phenomenon occurred. The vast expanse of the sea, with its mighty waves crashing against the shore, emerged as if summoned by an unseen force. All eyes turned towards the sea, anticipation and curiosity etched on every face. And then, in a voice that resonated with ancient wisdom, the sea spoke. It revealed a truth that had remained hidden from the minds of mortals. Only one among them possessed the power to absolve sins, to cleanse the souls of all beings, be the rivers or divine lords. That chosen one was none other than the sacred River Narmada. The revelation sent ripples of astonishment through the gathering. The significance of Narmada's role in the grand tapestry of existence became clear. Lord Brahma himself had bestowed upon her the honour of being the focal point of the *yagya*, the sacred ritual that held the power to purify and redeem. In that moment, the silence was broken, replaced by a chorus of murmurs and whispers. The revelation had stirred something deep within the hearts of those present. They marvelled at the divine wisdom that had guided Lord Brahma's decision, recognizing the profound importance of Narmada's presence in their lives. With hearts brimming with devotion, the crowd made their way towards the river, ready to immerse themselves in its hallowed depths. The anticipation was palpable as they prepared to partake in the sacred act of bathing, a ritual believed to cleanse the soul and renew one's spiritual connection. However, amidst the throng of eager devotees, there stood a solitary figure. Markandeya Muni, a sage known for his unwavering dedication to his spiritual path, stood apart from the rest. Instead of joining the multitude in the river, he chose to pay homage to the holy Narmada in his own unique way. With hands folded in reverence. When everyone else was taking the holy dip, holy Narmada wondered why Markandeya Muni was not among them? Markandeya Muni replied that when only by seeing her, or having the *darshana* of Mother Narmada one gets liberated so if one would take dip who knows what merit one will accumulate? Markandeya Muni said that he has only requested to be liberated, so, having her *darshana* is enough. Markandeya Muni and everyone else at the *yagya* were showered with blessings by Holy Mother Narmada after hearing this. Who afterwards built the temple dedicated to Narmadeshwar Mahadev.

Another location known as Brahmshila Teerth[4] is very close to this *tirtha*, and I had trouble finding it before *parikrama*. I asked the locals here if anyone knew anything about the temple as we continued the stroll, and I kept my eyes moving in all directions. Everyone had given up, but I kept looking, and when I finally found a Hindu flag on a hilltop, I asked the others to follow since this area of the farmland still had the ruins of the temple that formerly stood there. The temple is no longer there, and there are several statues, including one of Indra, but only time will tell how long it will remain in this state. Before establishing the world, Lord Brahma performed his *tapasya* and *yagya* here. Brahmshila Teerth is the name given to the place where the *yagya-vedi* was changed into a *shila*.

If one walked further and reached close to Indore there is Indreshwar Mahadev.[5] Once upon a time, in a land shrouded in mystique and ancient legends, there existed a place where the story of Devaguru Brihaspati unfolded. It was a time when respect and honour were cherished virtues, yet the mighty Indra, ruler of the divine lords, harboured a sense of pride that clouded his judgement. Unbeknownst to him, this arrogance would lead to a rift between him and the revered Brihaspati, causing the wise sage to abandon the side of the divine lords. In the world of the divine gods, Brihaspati held a position of great importance. He was none other than the main priest, the one responsible for carrying out the sacred rites that connected the gods. Without him, the performance of these rituals became a daunting task, for his knowledge and expertise were unparalleled. It was during a time when the trinity gods, in their infinite wisdom, recognized the need for a successor to this esteemed position. They looked upon the son of Tvasta, Vishvarupa, a man of exceptional character and devotion, and deemed him worthy of the title. Thus, by their divine decree, he was appointed as the *purohita*, the high priest of the divine lords. This appointment brought with it great responsibility and honour. The new *purohita* would now bear the weight of ensuring that the sacred rites were carried out with utmost precision and reverence. The gods themselves had placed their trust in him, knowing that he possessed the necessary qualities to fulfil this crucial role. It was a position that required not only deep knowledge of the rituals and traditions but also a profound understanding of the gods' desires and expectations. As fate would have it, this enigmatic figure found himself drawn to the side of darkness, offering his assistance to the very demons that sought to sow chaos and discord. It was a decision that would forever alter the course of his life. He was killed by the Indra which infuriated the father of Vishvarupa Tvasta. This infuriated Tvasta to no end. One day, while performing a sacred *yagya*, Tvasta decided to create a powerful being known as Vritrasura. Vritrasura was a formidable warrior, designed to challenge even the mightiest of gods. Tvasta had a specific purpose in mind for his creation – to engage in a fierce battle with the mighty Indra, the king of gods. As the news of Vritrasura's existence reached the heavens, Indra became aware of the impending challenge. He knew that he would have to rely on the blessings and grace of the trinity gods – Brahma, Vishnu and Shiva. This tale has been recounted countless times within the sacred texts of the Veda and Puranas. Vritrasura was no ordinary foe. He was a creation of Tvasta, a revered brahmana known for his mastery over the cosmic arts. This fact, however, would prove to be a double-edged sword for Indra, for in his fervour to vanquish his opponent, he had accumulated the sin of killing a brahmana. Indra had to perform *tapasya* in order to atone for his guilt, but no one could help him until he arrived at this location, where Lord Brahma blessed him and divided his sin into four parts. Water received one, earth received two, women received three, and those brahmanas who do not perform the labour in accordance with their inborn nature received four. After Indra was cleansed of his sins, Lord Shiva gave him instructions to build the temple of Indreshwar Mahadev.

We eventually go close to Sakreshwar Teerth, where we had planned to stay for the night. Unfortunately, our managing team was unable to establish a camp for the night due to the city's restricted accessibility and narrow streets. That is when Jitendra Sharma decided to move the camp to some farmland beyond the hamlet. It was a fascinating endeavour to stay in our very own city, built by management team everyday, particularly for those who were acquainted with the *parikrama* vicinity. There were always individuals on the Narmada banks to tell us that every day a whole new city appears out of nowhere!

As the sun began to dip below the horizon, and the time of *arti* approached, the *mahant* of Sakreshwar Teerth[6] emerged from the shadows. My gaze was drawn to him, seated slightly apart from the others, his eyes piercing and intense. With a subtle wave of my hand, I beckoned him to draw near and take his place amongst us at the forefront of the evening's *arti*. As I gazed upon him, I discerned the aura of a true master emanating from his being. After *arti* with a humble tone, I extended an invitation for him to join us for a meal. However, he politely declined, citing his responsibility to attend to the nourishment of the *parikramavasi*s at his *ashrama*. He asked without any hesitation if it would be appropriate to make a donation, and I agreed. He proceeded to unveil the complete extent of his financial assets.

The story of Sakseshwar Teerth goes to the time that one fateful day, a formidable demon named Jrimbhasura rose to power, challenging Indra's reign. With his dark forces, Jrimbhasura waged war against the gods, determined to claim the kingdom for himself. Indra, though valiant, found himself overwhelmed by the demon's might and was forced to retreat. In his despair, Indra sought solace and guidance. He embarked on a spiritual journey, traversing treacherous lands and enduring countless hardships. Finally, he arrived at this sacred place where the divine energy of Lord Shiva permeated the air. With unwavering devotion, Indra established the divine shrine of Sakreshwar Mahadev, a symbol of his faith and determination. Day and night, he fervently prayed, beseeching Lord Shiva for assistance in his quest to reclaim his kingdom. Moved by Indra's unwavering devotion and the sincerity of his prayers, Lord Shiva appeared before him and blessed him the power that he was needed. Radiating with in the realm of Sakreshwar Teerth, a sacred place of great significance, resides the esteemed Mahant Seetasharan. With wisdom and devotion, he carries the weighty responsibility of guiding the spiritual journey of those who in *parikrama* of Mother Narmada and runs a great place for the *parikramavasi*s.

Next day with the ascent of the morning sun, our journey led us to the *ashrama* of the venerated saint and Sakreshwar Teerth. The extent of his kindness knew no bounds, and it was apparent from the moment he humbly touched my feet as a sign of respect. In response, I mirrored his kind action and bestowed upon him the highest form of respect by humbly touching his feet. The moment we exchanged words marked the genesis of a profound bond between us, a connection that I frequently refer as a model of virtuous living.

He was one of the most humorous individuals I encountered on the *parikrama* route. He consistently elicited laughter from me whenever I contacted him, and there seemed to be no bounds to his ability to make me chuckle. I would even call him solely for the purpose of experiencing a good laugh. I initially believed that he was in his sixties, but when I went to see him after my *parikrama*, I learned that he is actually in his eighties.

As we departed from the sacred town of Sakreshwar, our journey took us first to the enchanting village of Ladva. This quaint village is home to the revered Kusumeshwar Mahadev, a divine deity worshipped by many. In the realm of ancient legends, the mighty Lord Shiva, known for his immense power and divine presence, embarked on a fateful encounter with Kusumayudha Kamadeva and had destroyed him. Kusumayudha Kamadeva, in a remarkable act of resilience, embarked on a *tapasya*. Through his astral body, he delved deep into the realms of meditation and self-discipline, seeking to attain enlightenment and this is where Lord Brahma was pleased and blessed him here.[7]

Sangameshwar Teerth,[8] located a little distance from Kusumeshwar Teerth in the midst of a farmland, is one of the most inconsequential places in all of India. The legends indicate its closeness to Kusumeshwar, but nobody expected to locate it on a private property, and the public temple was surrounded by a fence. This was the location of the legendary Sangameshwar Teerth, but we went in there regardless. From what I understand of the legend, there was a time when Kuber was present when Ravan sought out Lord Shiva for the Darshana. Ravana's deep voice and beating caused a honey-filled Kamandala to fall to the ground, and when Madhumati Ganga emerged from the honey to greet holy Narmada, Kubera erected Sangmeshwar Mahadev there.

If one continues forward, one will come to the location where Yamaraja performed his *tapasya* at the Anarkeshwar Mahadev. Once, when Yamaraja was worn out from work and bored enough to come here and do his *tapasya*, Lord Shiva appeared, smiled and asked Yamraja what was wrong, and the latter explained that he had grown weary of his labour and preferred that it be done by someone else. There is a lovely record of a conversation between Yamaraja and Lord Shiva, in which Shiva explains Yamaraja's function and responsibilities within the holy realms. Before continuing his work, he prayed to Lord Shiva, asking him to bless the area and the Shivalinga he had worshipped with the name Anarkeshwar, which means that those who worship here will not be damned to the underworld. Lord Shiva granted his request, and the area became known as Anarkeshwar. Even after looking for a while, no one showed up when we visited this stunning shrine. Even after looking for a while, no one showed up when we visited this stunning shrine. We had a great day, the venue was tranquil with stunning natural scenery, and it was well-managed.[9]

We were on our way to Sarpeshwar Mahadev when we first noticed the massive sugar-cane plantations that dotted the landscape. As we were walking through the thick vegetation, we spotted a herd of wild boars. They crossed the road without flinching, despite the fact that it was broad daylight and they knew we were around.

A story is told in the ethereal world of Sarpeshwar Mahadev,[10] a sacred location buried in old stories. It tells the story of the powerful serpent Dananjaya and his kin who took shelter in the sacred grounds of the sanctuary and established the Sarpeshwar Mahadev. Their goal was to escape the unrelenting pursuit of Garuda, the powerful bird deity who instilled fear in the hearts of all creatures with his very presence. In their frantic search for protection, Dananjaya and his fellow serpents found rest here and prayed to Lord Shiva. This holy place, served as their refuge and defence against the fury of Garuda. Because it was thought that Lord Shiva's presence prevented the terrifying bird deity from entering this holy place. This place which is named after the snakes had worshipped here Sarpeshwar Mahadev, thus developed into a paradise for snakes, a place where they could hide and flourish without the constant threat of Garuda.

My senses were heightened as I set out on my trek across Gujarat's enthralling villages, excitedly soaking up every detail that came into view. An environment abounding with fascination was created by the brilliant colours of the busy streets, the enticing fragrances emanating from street food vendors, and the beautiful sounds of the Gujarati language. But a strange observation caught my eye amid the alluring tapestry of this culturally diverse area. It seems that the locals were less likely to use the traditional greeting of *Narmade har*, which had long been an important element of the community's culture. I became curious to know the causes of this unusual change in social conventions. It seemed like a small detail, but it made me wonder about the cultural changes that had taken place in the region over time.

A recurrent realization has emerged as I have travelled and had conversations with many different people, including those of great spiritual significance. Many people choose to give up on the *parikrama* after the first twenty-five days, despite having travelled hundreds of kilometres on foot. Those who endure and successfully complete the journey are deemed to possess an exceptional degree of fortitude. As weariness takes hold, a dwindling confidence and a hint of unease begin to creep in. The unpleasant sensations seem to work together to hinder one's advancement, creating obstacles that make it challenging to persevere. The crux of the matter lies in relinquishing all factors to the lap of Mother Narmada, who dutifully tends to them. In the midst of the serene Shulpani forest, I was beset by the unwelcome maladies of cold and flu. Despite the persistent fever that had plagued me for a week, my indomitable spirit persevered and after a few days, I emerged unscathed. Every day, I strode forward with unwavering determination, resolute in my pursuit to surmount any obstacles that dared to impede my progress.

On my journey to Sarpeshwar Mahadev, I encountered a pair of individuals who were in a state of distress, bearing visible wounds in their legs. Despite their condition, they remained steadfast in their determination to complete the *parikrama*, and humbly requested my blessings. I offered them my sincerest wishes for success, while also advising that they need not exert themselves unnecessarily if they encounter difficulty in their leg, few days rest and time with Mother Narmada is that all will help.

As we journeyed along, we came across a fascinating group of individuals from Harda. They all donned matching attire and we encountered them twice during our travels. The first time we saw them, they were enjoying a delicious shake, and the second time they were indulging in *faluda*. I could not help but wonder how they were able to continue walking after consuming such a heavy meal.

On the day we were scheduled to cross the sea, we unexpectedly encountered the same group of *parikramavasis* we had met earlier. As we conversed with them, one of their members revealed that they hailed from Harda and had set a goal to complete the *parikrama* in just sixty days. I could not help but wonder how they planned to accomplish such a feat, I calculated in my mind that for this they need to walk 55-60 km a day which is pretty hard, as I was walking and knew the fatigue that comes. We saw them again in northern bank but most of them sitting in a vehicle. Little did they know that they would meet us again. At that time, the group did not say anything to us, not even a simple greeting like *Narmade har*! Probably they understood the gravity of the statement that they had made earlier. I looked at them innocently while we were walking but they all speed up the vehicle in a hurry.

In the dim light of the early morning, we embarked on our journey from the sacred Sarpeshwar Teerth. Our destination was further ahead, nestled beyond the bustling town of Ankleshwar, once known by the name Mandavyeshwar. In a time long ago, there existed a mighty king by the name of Devaraja. He was known throughout the land for his unwavering devotion to Devi Bhagavati, the divine Goddess. In the realm of divine intervention, a man found himself bestowed with an extraordinary gift. Through the benevolent grace of the Devi, he was blessed with the arrival of a precious daughter into his life. This precious tiny soul was given the name Kumudini, a name that would always have meaning and significance in the fabric of their lives. Once upon a time, Kumudini found herself lost in playful delight while surrounded by the peaceful surroundings of a placid water body. A malicious demon was drawn to her graceful presence and fell head over heels in love with her ethereal beauty. The devil cleverly assumed the appearance of a bird in an attempt to kidnap Kumudini and take her as his own because he was determined to possess her. The girl was crying while the demon carried her away. On the way she left some ornaments from sky and fell on Mandavya Ashram situated here. Mandavya Rishi was performing his daily meditative ritual and he did not know what was happening outside. On other side the soldiers from the kingdom arrived here searching for Kumudini and saw the ornaments here and they become doubtful on *rishi*. *Rishi* was the first to be questioned by soldiers, and his response that he knew nothing about the ornaments was expected. Soldiers got irritated and their doubt becomes more strong and they went to the king and informed of the situation king was infuriated and immediately asked the *rishi* to be hanged. *Rishi* was hanged but did not die, the younger brother of *rishi* was upset with the king about the act that was done. He cursed the king to have total destruction. Upon witnessing this, the Rishi Mandavya decided against cursing the king and instead explained that he must have sinned in a previous life, the consequences of which are now being felt. Several other *munis*, as well as a visiting *saptarshi*, had gathered at this point to assist the *muni* in coming down from its perch, but Mandavya Muni stubbornly refused to go. The *munis*, upon hearing his proposed method of resolving his karmic debt from previous lifetimes, departed the scene.

According to the legend, around this time, a woman named Shandili was transporting her ailing husband when she accidentally crashed with Mandavya Muni since it was dark outside. After Mandavya Muni cried out in agony, a large number of sages gathered. Mandavya Muni's enraged sibling repeated his earlier curse that the woman who struck his brother would never find love once the sun came up.

Hearing this the women Shandili started praying to Lord Shiva and the night covered the sky for many days. Seeing this, every divine Lord went to Lord Brahma and shared their anguish as the sun was not coming to sky and the earth inhabited the night sky all through the world which had taken down the natural phenomena. Lord Brahma advised that we all shall go to Shandili and they gave the assuredness to Shandili that they will help the woman to make sure that her husband lives. This is when the sun arises and the husband of Shandili died but again was made alive by Lord Brahma with full vigour and health. Simultaneously, the demon comes here with Kumudini, explaining that he was cursed to become a demon by a *rishi*, who also told him that if he abducts a female named Kumudini disguised as a bird, the curse will be lifted. After the devil spoke his tale and abandoned Kumudini, he disappeared.

The kings and the king's attendants, upon hearing this news, begged for pardon from Mandavya Muni. At this point, the *rishi* was released, and from then on, the *tirtha* was known as Mandavya Teerth. The tale remains incomplete, for it is the brother of Mandavya Rishi who, with a curse upon his lips, had cast the water not upon the ground, but into the vast expanse of the mighty Ocean. And it is this very act that birthed the venomous poison that was again brought into the world when sea was churned.[11]

In the mystical land of Ankleshwar, also known as Mandavya Teerth, there exists a sacred *kunda*. This revered site holds a profound significance, for it was constructed as a testament to a remarkable event that unfolded when gods defended here to aid Shandili. In commemoration of this extraordinary gathering of celestial beings, a sacred *kunda* was erected. It became a hallowed ground, forever etched in the memories of those who witnessed this divine intervention. Initially known as Deva-Kunda, it later came to be called Rama-Kunda, a name that resonated with the echoes of devotion and divine grace. Its significance continues to captivate the hearts and minds of pilgrims who journey to Ankleshwar, seeking solace and spiritual enlightenment.[12]

Balbala-Kunda is located near Ankleshwar, and legend has it that Lord Shiva took on his Dhanvantari form to grant the blessing requested by Kashyap Rishi when the sage seen the wretched state of the creatures he had encountered. When Kashyap Rishi told Lord Shiva his desire to learn *vaidya vidya* in order to treat illness, the Lord of the Universe gave his blessing. It was at this time that the Balbala-Kunda was created; so called, because it continues to eject bubbles to the surface. The *ashrama* of Kashyap Rishi can be found in the Balbala-Kunda.[13]

With hearts filled with anticipation and a sense of reverence, we embarked on our quest to uncover the sacred *tirtha*s, as described in the ancient Shastras. The weight of history and the whispers of legends guided our every step, urging us to tread carefully on this hallowed path. In the depths of our hearts, a fervent longing arose to catch a glimpse of the ethereal Siddheshwar Mahadev. Legends whispered that this divine being, so revered and mystifying, had chosen to conceal himself within the enchanting Sahjot. Before *parikrama*, I had tried to locate it by consulting both the contemporary computerized maps that are at our disposal and the map from the first phases of undivided India. However, I was not successful; this time, we made care to look for them during the *parikrama*. We then reached the settlement of Sahjot, and after a little search, we discovered the Siddheshwar Mahadev. When Lord Brahma and Lord Vishnu first fought among themselves and over who was more significant amongst them, that is when the legend of Siddheshwar Mahadev first began. Then, in the shape of light (*jyoti*), one Shivalinga came, and a single voice informed them that the person who can find the beginning or the end of the Shivalinga will be the one who can be called supreme among them. Both Lord Brahma and Lord Vishnu devoted a significant amount of time to find the beginning and the end of the Jyotilinga. After some time, Lord Shiva asked them again if they had found it. Lord Vishnu said that he had not, but Lord Brahma said that he had. However, this was incorrect, and Lord Shiva was not happy, so he pulled out Lord Brahma's fifth head, which made him responsible for the *brahmahatya*. He visited other locations but was not absolved of the *brahmahatya* sin. In the end, he came here and took a holy bath in the *kunda* where Siddheswar Mahadev is, and it was at this point that he was absolved of the guilt.[14] The large lake known as Deva ka Talab (which translates to "lake of the Divine Lords") was nearly dry when we visited.

We were strolling along at our usual pace when I was reminded that just a small fraction of *parikramavasi*s share my interest in finding and exploring the sacred sites that dot the banks of the Narmada. At this point, I resolved that we must follow a course that leads to the continued discovery of ancient *tirtha*s and the preservation of their significance in our culture.

The locations of Vaidyanath Teerth and Surya-Kunda are not far apart. Let us get into the tale of Surya-Kunda; Maharshi Kashyap was married to Aditi, from whom Surya was born; he was married Vishwakarma's daughter, Samjna; Samjna was unable to withstand the sun's heat and begged for relief for a few days so she could return to her father's home; however, Surya, the Lord of Rays, refused. Eventually, Samjna was unable to go on living, so she conjured a woman named Chaya from her shadow, sent her to live with Lord Surya, and begged Chaya to keep the secret to themselves. Samjna went to live with her father, but after a few days, her father Vishwakarma told her that she should return to Surya and his family because it was not appropriate for a married woman to continue to live with her father. Samjna was asked to go to Surya by her father, but instead she went to the forests and transformed into a Ghodi (Mare). Surya continued to have children with Chaya at this time. Yamaraja, Samjna's son, was not thrilled with Chaya's attitude because she clearly preferred her biological children to Samjna's. This is when Suryadeva scolded Yamaraja for his fury and running to hit Chaya, but Yamaraja stopped himself, saying that no mother could do what their mother in the appearance of Chaya was doing, and that it was probably not their mother but someone else. When Suryadeva inquired thus, Chaya revealed all, telling the fact that she was not Samjna but rather her shadow, Chaya.

Suryadeva went to Vishwakarma's home to inquire about Samjna, and Vishwakarma said, "Yes, she did come, but I sent her back to you", to which Surya replied, "She never got back". When Surya realized that Samjna had taken the form of a mare and was wandering in the forest, he changed into a horse and followed her. This is when Ashvinikumaras were born. The two then visited Vishwakarma, but the latter was so angered by the whole affair that he created twelve identical Suryas (Adityas) out of a single one, and diminished Surya's power and luminosity in the process. Surya felt guilty about what had happened, so he began doing *tapasya* in this spot by creating a *kunda*. Pashupati's lord, Shiva, made an appearance and bestowed his blessing on Surya, restoring the Sun God to his former grandeur. There was also a promise made that anyone who bathed in this particular *kunda* would emerge from the experience of purified and radiant like Surya. The *darshana* at the temple was stunning, but the *kunda* was poorly maintained and overgrown with bushes when we visited. Although they had seen numerous locals at the location, the locals themselves knew nothing about it until I told them the story and they contacted an elderly man who was rumoured to be familiar with it. The man became visibly moved when I told him the site's history, as he recalled hearing similar tales from his elders and, upon hearing them again from me, sixty-five years later, felt as though he had been transported to a different era. The man offered us to have tea, but I politely declined because I had another *tirtha* to find.[15]

Matrika Teerth was our subsequent *tirtha*. When Karttik Swami was born, Krittika was unable to feed him since he was always hungry. Devi came here and worshipped Mother Narmada, asking for her grace so they may be able to feed Karttik. Mother Narmada granted their request. The story goes back to the time of ancient ages and discovering this *tirtha* was something emotional for me.[16]

Matruka Teerth is not too far away, but before the *parikrama*, I always pictured the Matruka Temple in a different location. We arrived in Mothiya and started looking for the temple, but there was nothing there save for its ruins. A distinguished man stopped in front of us at that same time, intrigued by our focused search. He smiled kindly and asked what the goal of our search was. Yogesh eagerly started to tell the story of the temple, its importance, and the zeal with which we searched for it. I was surprised when the man intervened and said that the temple which was here had only been moved a few hundred metres from its original location. He was not aware of the history of it but had been a regular visitor to the temple. When we got there, we met some nice couples who were taking care of the area and temple. They told us that the old temple was deteriorating and that water logging was a continuous problem, so they had to bring all the idols from there. Once again, I felt Mother Narmada's blessings as we continued our journey to find the *tirtha*. In the meantime, the couple caring for the establishment arranged some curd and *lassi* for us, which was both a delight and a demonstration of their humility when we stopped over for lunch. I invited the whole group to join us for lunch, and they came. While we had lunch I sent Yogesh to the original location of the temple and take some photographs for the sake of history and he did.

The tale of this temple goes back to the time of Rishi Kashyap and his devoted wives. It is said that they embarked upon a spiritual journey, seeking solace and enlightenment in a sacred site. With unwavering determination, they arrived at this hallowed ground, ready to embark upon a profound *tapasya*. In their quest for spiritual transcendence, Rishi Kashyap and his wives undertook a remarkable endeavour. They laboured diligently, constructing a magnificent *kunda*, and filled it with the water of holy Narmada. Through their unwavering *tapasya*, she and her beloved husband were bestowed with a divine blessing, one that would shape the destiny of both gods and demons alike. Their fervent devotion had earned them the extraordinary privilege of becoming the parents of all celestial beings, as well as every living entity that graced the sacred earth. And thus, it came to be known as Matrika Teerth, a name bestowed upon it for this very reason.[17] Interestingly, the *kunda* that Kashyap and his wives Diti and Aditi are supposed to have constructed is still visible. This site also served as the location of the original temple.

From this point in our journey, we embarked towards the enchanting destination of Seera. It was in this captivating place that we discovered the sacred Narmadeshwar Teerth, a site of great significance and reverence. In the heart of the village stood a temple, its grandeur and splendour captivating all who laid eyes upon it. The villagers took great pride in maintaining its pristine condition, ensuring that every nook and corner was kept immaculate. It was said that within the sacred walls of this temple, a tale of divine significance unfolded. Legend whispered of a time long ago, when Lord Shiva, the supreme deity, assumed the guise of an aged bull. With grace and majesty, he traversed the sacred lands surrounding the holy river Narmada, meandering along its northern and southern banks. As he set foot upon the hallowed ground, a miraculous sight unfolded before his eyes. From the depths of the shimmering waters, a radiant figure emerged. It was Mother Narmada, the goddess of the holy river that bore her name. Her ethereal beauty and grace captivated Lord Shiva, and he was moved by her devotion. With utmost reverence, she approached him and offered her prayers. Touched by her unwavering faith, Lord Shiva felt compelled to grant her a boon. He asked her to name her desire, promising to fulfil it without hesitation. Without a moment's hesitation, Mother Narmada expressed her heartfelt wish – to have Lord Shiva's eternal presence in this very place. And so it came to pass. Lord Shiva, in his infinite benevolence, granted Mother Narmada's request. From that moment onward, the sacred site became known as Narmadeshwar Teerth.[18]

Our next destination beckoned us towards the enchanting city of Hansot, known in ancient Sanatana texts as Hanseshwar. In the vast tapestry of earth's history, there exists a captivating tale that traces the lineage of all living beings back to a revered figure known as Kashyap Rishi. This ancient sage, with his profound wisdom and spiritual prowess, held a significant place in the annals of time. Among his many wives, one was the mother of a majestic swan named Kanthishikha. This extraordinary swan, born of divine lineage, possessed a grace and elegance that surpassed all earthly creatures. Little did the world know that Kanthishikha's destiny was intricately intertwined with the cosmic forces that governed the universe. As the wheels of fate turned, Kanthishikha's purpose became clear – to serve as the celestial vehicle for none other than Lord Brahma, the revered deity responsible for creation itself. With each graceful flight, the swan carried Brahma, the embodiment of divine creativity, across the vast expanse of existence. In this enchanting tale story goes that once swan was neglectful in his duty when Lord Brahma was present at Prajapati's *yagya*, thus Lord Brahma cursed him to be reborn in the mortal world. When the swan Kanthishikha heard this, he was devastated and begged Lord Brahma for forgiveness, at which point Brahma instructed him to perform a *tapasya* in the holy waters of the nearby Narmada, where he eventually built a Shivalinga and gave it the name Hansheshwar Mahadev.[19] The temple was locked when we arrived, and it seems no one has visited in quite some time, but I counted myself lucky to have found it.

In the enchanting land of Hansot, nestled amidst its serene surroundings, one can discover the divine presence of Tiladeshwar Teerth,[20] a hallowed site that graces the landscape not too distant from the Hanseshwar. Once upon a time, in a bygone era, there lived a wise sage named Jabali. Though revered for his knowledge and spiritual prowess, Jabali carried a heavy burden upon his conscience. He was plagued by a sense of guilt and remorse, for he had committed grave errors in his past. Seeking redemption and solace, Jabali embarked on a journey to a sacred place, a realm where the divine presence of Lord Shiva could be felt. It was in this hallowed sanctuary that he hoped to find absolution for his sins. With a heart heavy with repentance, Jabali resolved to undertake a unique penance. He decided to sustain himself solely on sesame seeds, believing that this austere act would serve as a form of atonement and appease the mighty Lord Shiva. Day after day, Jabali would consume nothing but the humble sesame seeds, relying on their nourishment to sustain his body and spirit. Through this self-imposed deprivation, he sought to demonstrate his unwavering devotion and commitment to his quest for forgiveness. In the solitude every day, he partook in a ritual of consuming smaller portions of sesame, gradually diminishing his intake. With each passing day, his sins seemed to diminish *in tandem*, as if a weight was being lifted from his soul. And then, there came a day when he abstained from consuming anything at all, completely engrossed in his *tapasya*, a deep state of meditation and self-discipline. This is where Jabali Muni had established Tiladeshwar Mahadev.

Not very far from here Vasavatirtha is another *tirtha* in the nearby village of Vasnoli. It is said that eight Vasus, cursed by the *pitri*s, came here to perform *tapasya* and eastbaslihed under the name Vasaveshwar Mahadev.[21]

We were nearing to katpur where is situated Koteshwar Mahadev which was our final destination for the day. Many gods and *gandharva*s travelled here to witness this magnificent occurrence when the Reva/ holy Narmada meets the ocean. Everyone was blessed to witness the confluence of the Narmada with the sea, and it is at this time that they founded Koteshwar Mahadev.[22]

Once reaching Koteshwar, Alika Teerth[23] is not far away, but I doubt many people travel there since the terrain does not allow it and because it has altered so much that it is no longer navigable. The story of this place belongs to a time when Chitrasena, one of the rulers of *gandharva*s, had a daughter named Alika. She married Vidyananda, without the consent of her father, and after being away with him for a while, she returned to her father, but this time Chitrasena was not happy to see her and asked her to leave. Alika performed *tapasya* on the banks of the holy Narmada and thereby founded Alikeshwar Mahadev, after whom the *tirtha* is named. There is no sign of the temple currently, although the area is still called Alikabet.

29

Sea and Crossing

As the prospect of a sea crossing loomed, Praveen Chauhan and Ajay Vijayvargiya arrived in the company of several individuals such as, Deepak Rawal and his family, and Manish Rawal with his wife, Rajiv also took time and wanted to walk with us with his wife Ashita and kids. I had since the beginning said that even a few kilometres of walk on the banks of holy Narmada is a great spiritual activity and everyone shall do if they cannot perform all the *parikrama* in a go.

Everyone in the company started walking with us, some in high spirit wanted to walk barefoot, I just looked at each of them and did not say a word. As the sun began its descent, casting long shadows upon the land, the condition of the road deteriorated rapidly. What was once a well-maintained path now transformed into a rugged terrain, still in the process of being prepared. The ground beneath us became laden with coarse blue metal, posing a formidable challenge for those who had dared to shed their protective footwear. It was when I approached Kumar and others, requesting their harmonious voices to grace us with a rendition of the sacred *bhajana*. I knew that this melodic offering would propel our journey forward, igniting a surge of energy within me. And so, we commenced our melodious tribute to Mother Narmada, the divine river. Our voices resonated with such fervour that it seemed as though time itself quickened its pace. As a result, our fellow travellers found themselves trailing behind, a mere half kilometre distant. Eventually, they sought solace in the convenience of the cars that dutifully followed in our wake. As we reached Koteshwar, a place situated perilously close to the sea, we chanced upon a saint whose demeanour was akin to the vast expanse of the ocean. Throughout the night, he remained in a state of constant agitation, speaking to himself in a voice that reverberated loudly in the stillness of the surroundings.

This morning with a sense of determination, we embarked on our journey earlier than anticipated. The departure of our boat depended upon the delicate dance of the tides, and thus, we were compelled to adhere to its rhythmic ebb and flow. From our present whereabouts, we ventured forth towards the enchanting destination of Vimaleshwar. Its sacred land has stood the test of ages, its name whispered through the corridors of history. From time immemorial, Vimleshwar has been revered as a *tirtha*, a place of profound spiritual significance. In the realm of the sacred Narmada River, nestled upon its southern banks, it is the final *tirtha*. The legend of this sacred site, dates back centuries. It was during a time when Tvasta's son, a being named Trishira, had joined forces with the malignant demons. His deceitful alliance, however, was short-lived, since he was killed by the great Indra, the king of gods. Indra sought consolation and redemption, haunted by the weight of his deeds. So he set out on a voyage that would lead him right here, Vimaleshwara Teerth. Indra intended to alleviate the load of guilt that hung heavily on him for the death of Trishira here, amidst the tranquil surroundings. Indra took refuge in this sacred shelter from the unending strife within his soul. It was a place where the divine and mortal realms met, providing a haven for individuals seeking peace and forgiveness. For a time, Indra found peace in Vimleshwar Teerth's calm embrace, as he sought to wash himself of the sin that stained his conscience. This is the story that runs through the fabric of time, a story of gods and devils, redemption and forgiveness. Vimleshwar Teerth,[1] Lord Surya, the radiant Sun God, had graced this sacred place with his presence. Alongside him, Shringi Rishi, the illustrious son of Vibhandaka Muni, had also spent time here. Having spent countless years dwelling amidst kings, he carried the burden of sins accumulated from such association. Nevertheless, he too sought solace in this very place, embarking on a profound spiritual journey. In the sacred realm of Vimleshwar Teerth, Lord Shiva, the supreme deity of destruction and transformation, and Lord Brahma, the creator of the universe, have both descended upon this sacred abode. After paying our respects at the sacred Vimleshwar, we embarked on our journey towards the destination where our boat awaited us, ready to transport us to the enchanting northern shore.

As we eagerly awaited the arrival of the tides, our *parikrama kalasha* and other sacred items were carefully arranged on the grounds. Despite the solemn atmosphere that permeated the air, I could not help but feel that this was not the proper way to witness the meeting of Mother Narmada and the sea. With this in mind, I began to sing *bhajana*, hoping to infuse the gathering with a renewed sense of energy. To my delight, my efforts were met with enthusiastic participation from the most of the individuals in attendance, and soon the entire area was filled with the sound of our collective voices.

In the midst of the bustling *parikrama* days, where throngs of individuals eagerly await their turn for a sea crossing, I was taken aback by a disheartening revelation: the absence of individual lavatories, a circumstance that undeniably worsens the challenges faced by women. There was no water available for the thousands of people who waited hours for the tides to come. In my perception, it appeared as though the government had forsaken the entirety of the *parikramavasi*s. As I embarked upon the vessel, a disheartening revelation awaited me – its weary state of disrepair. Alas, the boat, once a beacon of maritime splendour, now bore the scars of neglect. My eyes, keen observers of detail, quickly discerned the conspicuous absence of life jackets and other indispensable safety accoutrements.

As we traversed the waters, our vessel was frequently impeded, requiring us to dock and tether to other boats. It was through this method that we ultimately arrived at the Mithitalai shore. To help me move this issue ahead and initiate the discourse to improve it, I imagined that Mother Narmada had shown me every difficulty associated with crossing the sea.

Excitement filled the air as we embarked on our journey to cross sea probably when the divine gods had come to see the mergence of Mother Narmada and ocean they would have been similarly excited. I smiled to myself because I knew that the enthusiasm of the ever-excited *parikramavasi*s would soon be dampened by the oppressive heat and the long boat voyage.

As I wrote in my diary, I could not help but think about how the tough conditions had tempered the *parikramavasi*s' early enthusiasm. When the boat halted in the middle of the ocean several times, I noticed the serious and anxious expressions on the *parikramavasi*s' faces. When the boat was having problems, I would make jokes to cheer them up, but I saw that Jitendra Sharma always seemed concerned that the boat would eventually just remain in the middle of the ocean and be carried away by the tides to some faraway place; fortunately his concern did not come true!

Upon arriving at the Port in Mithitalai, we were required to transport six *kalasha* (a large container for water) as well as all of our *rudraksha* beads and the Shivalinga that accompanied us on our *parikrama*. The procession of the gods and divine elements was a spectacle to behold. We carried them towards our *rath*, including the grand *kalasha*, as we made our way through the crowd. Even our small *kalasha*, which we kept in our pockets, required a full *puja* to be performed once again. The ceremony was a spectacle that had not been witnessed before, captivating the attention of all who were present.

Upon completing the *puja*, we resumed our journey towards Mithitalai. The place has transformed from a serene paradise to a concrete jungle with big roads and *parikramavasi*s lost in the chaos. It is like the industries took over and said, "Move over trees, we are the new cool kids in town!" It is like trying to find your way through a corn maze blindfolded, only to realize you are actually on the Narmada Parikrama.

A diminutive tea shop persistently beckoned us to partake in its offerings. However, in my customary fashion, I advised that he shall offer to those who may be in greater need than us.

As the *parikramavasi*s prepared to embark on their sea crossing, many of them had removed their shoes. Upon returning to the northern banks, most *parikramavasi*s were in need of a new pair of shoes. I empathized with those who had left their shoes behind and were now struggling to find a place to purchase new ones. In our midst was Ajay Vijayvargiya, who generously bestowed a sum of 500 rupees upon each *parikramavasi* to purchase shoes, until his funds were depleted, a period that spanned over an hour.

Upon arriving at our intended destination, we found ourselves disenchanted with the accommodations. Without hesitation, we promptly departed the premises, albeit not before Jitendra Sharma as coordinator of the *parikrama* had paid to the *sadhu*-robed manager for his "No" services. Our journey led us to a more tranquil abode, where we ultimately found solace. As the evening descended, a gathering of locals had convened, comprised predominantly of labourers hailing from various regions of the nation. As industries continue to flourish and develop, Gujarat has become a hub for migrant workers from various parts of the country. These individuals seek employment opportunities in a region where prosperity and industrialization provides ample job prospects. Coming from a distant land, they were initially unaccustomed to the *parikrama*. However, residing on the banks of Mother Narmada, where she merges with the sea, they gradually grew accustomed to this sacred ritual.

Despite our best efforts, we were unable to locate any of the numerous *tirtha-sthala* that had been lost to progress in this region; the sacred banks of the Narmada are now littered with industries rather than remnants of the region's rich Sanatana Dharma heritage. I do not know if these temples have been destroyed beyond repair or if they still stand within the industries that settled along the Narmada's banks.

But let us still remind ourselves of these stories that have been part of our culture and history.

In the enchanting realm of Loharaya, or perhaps the whimsically misspelt Luvara, lies a place of great significance known as Jamadagni Teerth.[2] Legends and tales have spoken of its existence, nestled near the sacred confluence or the revered Reva Sangam. It was here that the revered Parashurama, a saint of immense power and wisdom, received a visit from his beloved parents, Jamadagni and Mata Renuka. In the depths of his *tapasya,* Parashurama had immersed himself within. As I ventured into thriving industrial district, I found myself confronted with a perplexing challenge – the area had undergone a profound transformation, now concealed behind imposing gates. The task of locating my destination suddenly became a formidable undertaking, as the signs of progress and development had rendered the landscape unrecognizable.

In the annals of ancient history, a tale is whispered of a place not far from here. This sacred site was known as Rama Teerth, a place steeped in legends and mysteries. It is said that long ago, when the mighty warrior Parashurama had vanquished the kshatriyas, he was guided to this very spot by the command of his revered parents. In obedience to their wishes, Parashurama arrived at this sacred land and performed a solemn ritual known as *pitri tarpana,* an act of homage to his ancestors. Such was the significance of this act that the place came to be known as Narmada Kurukshetra, a name that echoed through the ages. The echoes of this ancient tale resonate through time, reminding us of the profound connection between the past and the present. As we stand here today, we cannot help but feel the weight of history that once unfolded in this very place. The whispers of the past beckon us to explore the depths of its secrets, to unravel the enigmatic stories that lie hidden within sacred shores.[3]

In the vicinity of our current location lies a quaint village by the name of Lakhi. It is said that within this village, there once stood a magnificent temple known as Luntheshwar Teerth.[4] Although our search yielded no evidence of this temple's existence, allow me to recount the tale that has been passed down through generations. In the ancient era of Satya Yuga, a time when the world was believed to be pure and divine, a remarkable event unfolded. The mighty Ocean, ever watchful and wise, observed as the sacred river, Mother Narmada, gracefully flowed towards him. A sense of joy and excitement filled the air as the Ocean eagerly embraced her arrival, causing waves of elation to ripple through his vast expanse. As the Ocean welcomed the river into his watery embrace, a wondrous sight unfolded. Amidst the swirling sands that accompanied the river's journey, a magnificent Shivalinga emerged, seemingly materializing out of thin air. This divine manifestation, a symbol of Lord Shiva's presence, stood tall and resplendent, radiating an aura of spiritual energy. Meanwhile, in the proximity of the Shivalinga, Nandi, the loyal and devoted bull who served as Lord Shiva's faithful companion, was present. Unaware of the sacred object before him, Nandi inadvertently stepped upon the Shivalinga with his mighty hoof. This unintentional act, though seemingly insignificant, held great significance in the grand tapestry of events that were unfolding. Little did anyone know at that moment, but this seemingly accidental encounter between Nandi's foot and the Shivalinga would set in motion a series of events that would shape the course of history and leave an indelible mark on the world as we know it. And thus, in that moment, the Shivalinga transformed into a magnificent sight resembling the sacred Gaumukha. It was at this precise juncture that the mighty river Narmada gracefully flowed into the Shivalinga, its pristine waters serving as a divine offering, as *achaman*, to this revered symbol of Lord Shiva. As the cool liquid cascaded down devotees throat, it was as if they were partaking in the sacred elixir of ancient India, known as *soma*. As one delves into the story, a captivating narrative unfolds, revealing the profound wisdom embedded within the ancient teachings of Sanatana Dharma. It is within this rich fabric that the elucidation of earlier *rishi*s, who possessed a keen insight into the workings of the natural world, comes to light. These enlightened souls, through their deep contemplation and profound experiences, were able to decipher the intricate causes behind various natural phenomena. Such is the exquisite beauty that permeates the essence of Sanatana Dharma, where the timeless wisdom of the past seamlessly intertwines with the present. In the realm where the mighty Narmada River converges with the vast expanse of the sea, a remarkable phenomenon unfolds. It is an undeniable truth that the sea, in all its grandeur, ventures forth into the embrace of Mother Narmada, traversing a considerable distance. This extraordinary occurrence stands as a testament to the ancient and timeless tale that has been passed down through the ages. There is a lake and a building in Lakhi; the *kunda* may have formerly been here, but the area has undergone recent development, and I cannot attest to the *tirtha*'s authenticity.[5]

Vimleshwar to Garudeshwar

30

Ego and Speed

As our weary feet carried us further into the heart of the bustling city of Dahej, known far and wide for its industrial prowess, a longing stirred within me. Amidst the clamour of machinery and the ceaseless hum of progress, I yearned for a respite, a moment of solace amidst the chaos. And so, my thoughts turned to the tranquil banks of the Narmada River, a place where time seemed to stand still. The Narmada, the lifeline of countless generations, held within its depths a sense of ancient wisdom, a connection to a world untouched by the relentless march of modernity. In the ancient land of Dahej, nestled amidst the serene surroundings, there existed a sacred *ashrama*. This *ashrama* was none other than the abode of the revered sage Dadhichi Muni. It was within the hallowed grounds of this *ashrama* that the origins of the name Dahej were rooted. Long ago, when the land was still untouched by the passage of time, Dadhichi Muni chose this tranquil spot to establish his spiritual sanctuary. The *ashrama* became a haven for seekers of wisdom and solace, drawing people from far and wide who sought the sage's divine guidance. As the millennium passed, the name of this sacred place underwent a transformation.

Our departure was scheduled for the early hours of the morning, as we were aware that the numerous *tirtha*s that once adorned the area had been replaced by the relentless march of industrialization. Amidst the pursuit of profit by the industry, do we still hold reverence for the spiritual wonders of our *dharma*? As we strolled along the lesser-travelled paths, eschewing the bustling highways, a familiar figure came into view.

It has become customary for numerous fraudulent individuals to infiltrate the spiritual realm, lacking in education, morals, and entirely lost in their ways, donning the saffron robes of *bhagava*, all the while believing they are upholding the principles of Sanatana Dharma. The Sanatana Dharma that I have come to know is not reflected in this. To me, Sanatana Dharma embodies a pursuit of knowledge, ethical conduct, humility, and a willingness to share life's grandest ideas with all. It involves deciphering ancient texts, preparing for the future, and imparting wisdom for living a fulfilling life. Vishnu, as he is known, presents himself as the reincarnation of the revered Dhuniwale Dadaji, a prominent figure of the early twentieth century who commanded a significant following. He was well aware of my presence and seemed eager to impress me. With a confident stride, he began to walk at an impressive speed of 10 km/h, breezing past me. It was rather surprising, considering he had initially expressed interest in sharing a cup of tea with me to one of the *parikramavasis*. As he passed by, I could not help but notice that he neglected to offer the customary greeting of *Narmade har*, which is typically extended to those you encounter while walking. "Who is this gentleman?", I inquired. As my fellow travellers divulged, the individual in question is none other than Vishnu, the notorious fraudster whom I was familiar with. On a previous occasion, I had implored numerous followers of the revered Dhuniwale Dadaji to rectify his behaviour. Laughter rippled through the group, infecting us all with its contagious joy. We shall not encounter this individual again, for his sole purpose was to exhibit his ability to walk. Curiously, I found myself ruminating on the notion that if the mere sight of my presence could inspire individuals like Vishnu to traverse the banks of Mother Naramda, then surely it is a testament to the blessings bestowed upon us. Interestingly, we did not see Vishnu anywhere after this, I did not know if he was on *parikrama* or just wanted to show off to me for a few kilometres.

As we traversed through the heavily industrialized area, the air was thick with pollution that seemed to be making its way towards the nearby sea. The landscape was devoid of any significant tree cover, prompting me to ponder upon the extent of our social responsibilities towards nurturing the environment's greenery and aesthetics. Does our existence solely revolve around accumulating wealth while disregarding the depletion of our planet? As I pondered the idea, it occurred to me to convene with the industrial professionals of this locale and engage in discourse regarding their personal growth. It is a curious thing that despite the prevalence of religion among the populace, many fail to recognize the vital importance of maintaining a healthy tree cover alongside industrial progress.

As the day dawned in the quaint village of Jageshwar, we embarked on a journey through the picturesque village of Ambheta, where the air was filled with the sweet fragrance of blooming flowers and the gentle rustling of leaves. It was here that they encountered their first sacred site, a place of profound significance known as Kolyada. Nestled amidst the serene surroundings, Kolyada revealed its hidden treasure – in the ancient tale of Sanatana Dharma, it is said that Kapila Muni arrived at this very place, guided by a profound sense of purpose and a yearning for tranquillity. The convergence of the mighty Narmada River and the vast expanse of the ocean lay within close proximity, offering an ideal setting for his spiritual endeavours. The village temple stood proudly, its beauty captivating all who laid eyes upon it. It was a place of tranquillity and solace, where weary souls sought respite from the chaos of everyday life. Nestled within this serene haven was a quaint old house, its weathered exterior telling tales of years gone by. As we entered the house, a sense of nostalgia washed over us. It seemed as though time had stood still within these walls, preserving the essence of a bygone era. The caretaker kindly directed us to the first floor, where we would find much-needed reprieve and had our lunch.

The presence of the Erandi Sangam lends additional significance to this location. Erand was a *muni*, but he had no children, so he did *tapasya* to Mata Jagadamba in order to have a child. As a result of his devotion and *tapasya*, Mata Jagadamba herself was born into his home, and his daughter excelled in every way. She refused to get married, so she fled home and began performing *tapasya* on the banks of the Narmada, and it was there that she met Ocean, hence the name Erandi Sangam.[1] Since industrial debris may have filled the stream that joined the holy Narmada, we had not discovered any signs of Sangam.

By the time it was evening, we had made it to Kapaleshwar Teerth, which is the location where Lord Shiva is said to have reset his *kapala*. The story goes that Lord Shiva had travelled with his *kapala* to each and every *tirtha*, and when he arrived here, he placed it on the ground, and it turned into a Shivalinga which bears the name.[2]

The desolate village lay before me, its once-bustling streets now eerily quiet. Upon our arrival, the residents of the village showed a tremendous deal of excitement. It was clear that the majority of its inhabitants had long since departed, seeking refuge in more hospitable locales. The water, once a source of life and sustenance, had become tainted and unpredictable, forcing the villagers to abandon their homes and seek a safer existence elsewhere. The temple, an ancient landmark and *tirtha* of Mother Narmada, is situated in a prime location. It is a site where *arti* was performed and a grand *bhandara* was held.

It was a day when I found it necessary to establish some guidelines to ensure that everyone comprehended the importance of dining together and rising only after all had finished. Sharing a meal with others is a gesture of care and consideration. It entails accommodating the pace of others, even if you happen to have a lesser appetite, and waiting patiently for everyone to conclude their meal before rising. *Pangat* is a practice that fosters empathy and compassion, allowing individuals to gain a deeper understanding of their fellow human beings. Through this tradition, one can cultivate virtues such as patience and kindness towards others. The act of sharing a meal transforms it into a communal space for the exchange of energy among all present. After a few days, I noticed a lack of respect among the group for *pangat*. In response, I proposed that they all wait to eat until everyone had finished, with the exception of two *parikramavasi*s who understood the importance of communal dining. For a week, I dined along with these two *parikramavasi*s and then everyone was set right. Now, our *pangat* began to receive recognition.

31

Janya Jatis and Their Contribution

We started on this day from Kapaleshwar and going towards Bharuch, the ancient Bhrigu Teerth. The town's name change is just another indication that the nation's efforts to forge a stronger historical link to its past are ongoing. Until relatively recently, this area was known by the name Bhrigukaccha.[1]

In the captivating land of Navetha, nestled amidst the ethereal beauty of nature, lies the sacred *tirtha* known as Apsareshwar Mahadev.[2] This divine abode holds great significance, for it is here that numerous celestial beings, known as *apsaras*es (damsels), have sought solace and enlightenment through the divine presence of holy Narmada. With hearts brimming with unwavering devotion, these celestial maidens embarked on a sacred mission to establish this *tirtha*, a place where they could pay homage to the mighty Narmada and seek her divine blessings. Apsareshwar Mahadev stands as a testament to their profound faith and unwavering commitment. It is a place where the celestial and mortal realms intertwine, where the veil between the ethereal and the earthly is lifted, allowing devotees to witness the divine grace of Mother Narmada first hand. As we approached the temple, its magnificent location took our breath away. It stood proudly a testament to the devotion and craftsmanship of those who built it. The temple grounds were meticulously maintained. The stillness in the air hinted at the absence of human presence. Undeterred, we ventured forth, our curiosity guiding us towards the temple's entrance. With each step, anticipation grew within us, eager to witness the divine beauty that awaited us inside. As we crossed the threshold, a hushed silence greeted us. The temple's interior was a sight to behold, with intricate carvings adorning the walls and ceilings. This is here I pulled Kumar to join me. With utmost openness, I urged him to seek solace in prayer, requesting the divine for a happy family life that would be both enchanting and profound, capable of uplifting not only his own spirit but also that of his beloved family.

A little temple that was formerly called as Dindeshwar Teerth in Sanatana Dharma is located very close by. The Sanatana story claims that

Lord Shiva came to this location with his Dindi and pounded his *damaru* (drum) in order to determine whether or not the residents of this village have any empathy. Nobody offered Lord Shiva any *bhiksha* (alms) when he went door to door seeking for it. Whenever Lord Shiva in guise of *sadhu* visited a home and was not provided *bhiksha* in exchange, that home would be set on fire. As a result, most of the homes in the community were destroyed. After witnessing this, many locals approached the *sadhu*, only to discover that he was actually Lord Shiva. They pleaded with *sadhu* for pardon, and the satisfied Lord Shiva restored their homes to their previous states, requesting only that they be generous to those in need.[3]

Manad Temple of Munyalaya Teerth[4] is not too far away. Munyalaya Teerth got its name from the fact that seven sages (*saptarshis*), visited this area long ago, along with many other sages (*rishis*). Since it was here that many *munis* and *rishis* resided the name was given Munyalaya Teerth.

Ganita Teerth,[5] located further in Mahgana, was formerly recognized as Bhagavati Siddha Pitha. Here is where Sanatana Shastras claim Lord Shiva and Mata Bhagavati were engaged in some sort of divinely inspired mathematics. As they began praising each other, Lord Shiva eventually conceded to Shakti's superiority and stopped calling out his own praises. This is Bhagavati's territory for this same reason. Markandeya Teerth is located nearby; it was named after him because, during his visit to Ganita Teerth, he erected a Shivalinga in his memory. Lord Shiva is said to have appeared to Markandeya Muni at the *tirtha* and blessed him, making the site famous.[6]

The lovely Kantheshwar Temple[7] can be found farther inside Kosava. It is said that Lord Shiva, accompanied by his *ganas*, rested here and placed his *kantha*, from which the Shivalinga subsequently materialized, hence the temple's name. The Shivalinga is in the form of a *kantha* and may be found in the temple, which is itself an interesting sight. We had lunch and took a break in the temple, which is tucked away on a peaceful side street.

Now, following the completion of our meal, we were prepared to continue our journey and arrived at Bhadbhut.[8] There was a period when Bhadbhut was well-known for its education, and at that time there were a lot of educators living and working here. At that time, there was a teacher who was well-known not only for his teaching but also for serving the pupils; even if they did not have anything to offer, he would still teach them. The educator who was known as Vishnu Sharma was also a fantastic *guru* who would donate food to a large number of people.

It was at this point that Lord Shiva decided to put him to the test because of all the attention that had been drawn to him. Lord Shiva assumed the role of a student and travelled all the way to Vishnu Sharma to receive his education. Vishnu Sharma was unaware that Lord Shiva himself had arrived to serve as the student for him when he made the student agree to the conditions that the *guru-seva* must be completed in order to receive instruction at this location.

The student was given the responsibility of preparing the meal, which he complied with on a daily basis. However, it was Lord Shiva, and not anybody else, who would call Kamadhenu to prepare the food so that he may go and play with the other students. Once, the pupils cautioned him that he needed to give his full attention to preparing the food, or else the *guru* would become angry with everyone. When the question was put to him in the shape of a student, Lord Shiva responded by asking, "Why are you worried about food?" He indicated that once you get at *gurukula*, you will be provided with food at right time. When this occurred, some students questioned whether or not this was the fact by inquiring, "If this is the case, who is making the food while you are engaging with us?" Upon hearing this, Lord Shiva gave the following response: "Since you do not think the food in *gurukula* is prepared, I made everything before coming over to play with you. So when we go to *gurukula* and everyone has found something to eat for evening, I will dump everyone into the water of Narmada." Lord Shiva said this because he saw that they did not believe that the food was ready in *gurukula*.

When all of the students arrived at the *gurukula* and saw that the food was prepared and being served, they were a little surprised but didn't expect that they would all be dumped in water the following day; yet, this is exactly what happened. When Lord Shiva, in the shape of a student, tosses the other pupils off a cliff into the River Narmada.

It is at this point that he makes his way back to *gurukula*, where he reports the events that took place to his Guru Vishnu Sharma. The *guru* stated that it was not good and that it could not be accepted. Vishnu Sharma then instructed the student to retrieve his classmates from the Narmada River in the same manner in which he had tossed them. At this point, Lord Shiva emerged from the guise of pupils and smiled. In his place, a Shivalinga materialized, and all of the children suddenly materialized inside of a sack bag while still being alive.[9]

We had picked up the tempo and were now on our way to Vadava, where we were planning to locate and look for Rinmochan Teerth.[10] It was one of the first Rinmukteshwar temples in the country, and it stood on the holy banks of the Narmada River. When I arrived here, I found the due temple, but it had been moved by the locals – specifically, the fifteen *janya jati* families – to save it from a another structure that was built in 1970, at a time when the Narmada River was at its highest level. These families were responsible for protecting the temple. Following the flood that occurred in the 1970s, the previous location of the temple was taken by members of another faith, and these individuals began mistreating the God idols, so they were relocated to the current location of the temple. I learned that there are young people who take care of the temple. One of the girls in particular captured my heart, and because of this, I sat there and made donations to the other children, and I even provided some money to the girl's parents while she was at school. I also promised that I will return there once more with the necessary items to do some form of *puja* and to leave some of other necessary items.

There are three different sorts of obligations, known as *rin*, that mankind owes. The first is to the Divine gods; the second is to the *pitru*, (progenitors); and the third is to the *rishi*s, or *guru*s. By doing a *yagya*, a person can be freed from the obligation of the Divine; by having children, a person can be freed from *pitri-rin*; and by teaching and studying, a person can be freed from the *rin* of *rishi*s or *guru*s. In the distant past, there was a king whose name was Dusharavan, and he did not have any kids. He came to this area and prayed for a boon via *tapasya* to have a child, and after a long time, Lord Shiva arrived and blessed him to have sons, and at that point, the king was free from all of his debts and this is when the Rinmukteshwar was established.

Nandlal had a difficult time finding this temple because the entire hamlet is dominated by Muslims, and despite the fact that he requested multiple times, no one was willing to provide the appropriate guidance to reach the temple. On this particular day, we found ourselves nestled within the sacred grounds of Suvarneshwar Teerth.[11] Legend has it that within these hallowed grounds, a prosperous businessman once bestowed numerous golden rings upon the brahmanas. It is said that his act of immense charity granted him passage to the divine realm of Vaikuntha. Thus, in honour of this noble deed, the *tirtha* came to be known as Suvarneshwar. This is here, in the close promixity, we had stayed the night and visited the temple twice.

32

Bhrigukshetra

On this particular day, we embarked from Suvarneshwar Teerth and traversed through Bharuch. After leaving Suvarneshwar, our first visit was to Dashan, where we looked for the Dash Kanya Teerth. The story here is about Lord Shiva testing ten brahmanas who were ascetic-like travelling along the banks of the holy Narmada. In order to determine whether or not they were ready to follow the path of *sannyasa*, Lord Shiva wished to test their innermost beings. This is when he created ten lovely women, and by assuming the appearance of elderly brahmanas, he visited these young brahmanas. "Look, I am becoming old, I have these daughters, and now who knows when I will be gone, therefore, I am asking all of you to marry my daughters", he said to the young brahmanas. The brahmanas had taken a vow of chastity, but they had not completed their *tapasya* and had merely been dressed in *sannyasi* garb. However, after spotting the girls' attractiveness, they became engaged and got married. This *tirtha* serves as a powerful reminder that *sannyasa* is not for people who still possess the fire of the world inside them. Since Lord Shiva brought ten young women here to create this *tirtha*, it is also known as the Dashan or Dashkanyeshwar Teerth.[1]

The city of Bharuch, which has forty-six prominent Teerth nearby, has undergone significant transformation in recent years, and it can be challenging to travel there at times to reach the banks of Mother Narmada. Bharuch was the old Bhrigukshetra,[2] which had been under the heavy domination of Islamic armies for many centuries. This is one of the reasons why the area, which was once filled with *tirtha*s, is now strewn with several varied landscapes. We travelled through Bharuch and tried to look for different temples there, but the terrain prevented us from doing so, and many of the temples had undergone name changes that made it impossible to even determine their location. I vowed to return to Bharuch and find the local *tirtha*s, but today I pushed on.

Our ultimate destination was a breathtaking location, which had been meticulously developed by Mufatbhai Patel, a prominent industrialist hailing from the local region. His farmhouse had been transformed into an *ashrama*, providing solace to numerous *parikramavasi*s, including myself. As we arrived at the *ashrama*, the intention was to take a day's respite. However, I found myself hesitant, as my priority was to ensure our timely arrival to Garudeshwar.

It was the day when I received a call from the honourable former president of India, Shri Ram Nath Kovind, expressing his desire to join us on our *parikrama*. Initially, the arrangement was for him to arrive in Jabalpur on 10 February. However, the esteemed former president made the decision to arrive earlier than anticipated. As a former president, his presence would undoubtedly be a remarkable addition to our journey.

It was decided that the honourable former president would be visiting us in Garudeshwar in the coming days. However, I felt it was imperative that I arrive ahead of time to ensure everything was in order. Garudeshwar is a sacred location that is situated nearby, and in close proximity lies the Statue of Unity. The symbolism was truly remarkable, and it struck me that my *parikrama* was not only a physical journey but also a symbolic one. National unity demands the unification of our spiritual heritage, and this was exemplified by the honourable former president's participation in the *parikrama* and *puja* at this sacred site.

With modern amenities and a calm ambiance, Mufatbhai's development is genuinely impressive. Speakers placed all around the space produce the spiritual *bhajana*s or divine *om* sound, which filled the entire area with a beat. One might sense the presence of a divine entity at the *ashrama* and the tunes were calming.

33

Educating India

On that particular day, we set off later than planned after enjoying a delightful lunch with Mufatbhai and his family, with whom we had the pleasure of spending most of the day. A dedicated being, wholly devoted to the sacred cause of India.

Mufatbhai was deeply troubled upon learning that I had come across a photograph of Nanga Baba standing atop the sacred Shivalinga. As a result, he promptly abandoned the idea of accommodating this fraudulent individual in his farmhouse. A man arrived to make arrangements for Nanga Baba, unaware of the events that had transpired. Mufatbhai initiated a conversation with him and presented the photograph that I had previously viewed. The man in question then expressed to Mufatbhai that they may not be aware of the playful nature of *babaji*. At that point, I corrected him, asking, "Why the hell do not I get that sort of playfulness or any other saints or figures?" I conveyed to him that only an individual of a morally corrupt nature could find gratification in such pursuits. Is it possible that other highly spiritual people have done something similarly disrespectful to a representation of God? He fell silent and Mufatbhai was able to perceive the topic of my discussion.

Just before I left, Mufatbhai and I continued talking about the philosophy of Gorakhnath and other Nath saints. When I started singing some of Gorakhnath's couplets, Mufatbhai started crying in the backseat. After that, something interesting happened and we all departed. After walking with us for a while, Mufatbhai and his wife eventually left in their car after being asked repeatedly to do so.

On this beautiful day, we set out on a spectacular adventure, exploring a plethora of holy pilgrimage *tirtha*s. We happened upon Shukla Teerth,[1] a site steeped in legend, within these sacred grounds. The legendary King Chanayaka of Avanti is said to have ruled with great bravery and wisdom. This great king had sworn an oath, promising to give up his mortal body if anyone dared to trick him. In the realm of the divine, numerous celestial beings embarked on a quest to put their powers to the ultimate test. Alas, despite their formidable abilities, they found themselves unable to accomplish this seemingly insurmountable feat. In a realm shrouded by darkness, there existed two formidable demons known as Sunda and Upasunda. Bound by a malevolent curse, these once fearsome beings were transformed into crows, their majestic forms reduced to mere avian creatures. However, their cunning and deceitful nature remained unscathed, allowing them to navigate the treacherous paths of their existence. It so happened that these cunning crows devised a wicked plan to deceive the unsuspecting king of their realm. And so it came to pass that they, through cunning and artifice, succeeded in deceiving the king. It was at this pivotal moment that he made the fateful decision to depart from his mortal body. In his quest for guidance, he sought the wisdom of the revered Dharmaraja. With great reverence, he approached the wise, seeking solace and direction. In response, the Dharmaraja bestowed upon him a small ball of cotton thread. With a gentle voice, Dharmaraja advised him to embark on a pilgrimage to the sacred *tirtha*, a place of spiritual significance. It was there, amidst the divine aura of the *tirtha*, that he was to unravel the true purpose of the cotton thread. Dharmaraja revealed that as he journeyed through the *tirtha*, the black cotton thread would undergo a transformation, turning white at a specific location. This transcendent transformation held great significance, for it would mark the place where he was destined to leave his mortal body behind. The monarch travelled everywhere, yet no matter where he went, the cotton remained the same dark colour. It was a momentous occasion when he descended upon this sacred place known as Shukla Teerth. The cotton thread draped around him, shimmering in a pristine white colour, perfectly capturing the essence of Shukla, from which the *tirtha* derived its name. It was a truly magnificent experience as we were granted a divine glimpse of the sacred Shukla Teerth.[2]

In the vicinity of this very place lies Hunkareshwar Teerth,[3] where a captivating tale unfolds. Legend has it that a group of brahmanas once ventured to this sacred site, drawn by its mystical aura. Intriguingly, it is said that the revered Mother Narmada herself devised a test to assess the temperament of these learned individuals. Would they succumb to anger, or would they exhibit the utmost composure in the face of her divine examination? The mighty Narmada, her waters surging with increasing intensity, swept away everything in her path, including the sacred *asana* and *kamandala* of the devoted brahmanas. Helpless in the face of this relentless force of nature, the brahmanas could only watch as their cherished possessions were carried away by the powerful currents. However, in a moment of divine intervention, a resounding sound, a *hunkara*, echoed in the air. Miraculously, the Narmada, heeding the call, diverted her course several kilometres away from her original path. It is this extraordinary event that has bestowed upon the place the name Hunkar Teerth, forever commemorating the divine intervention that ensured the safety of all those present.[4] In the midst of this enigmatic realm lies a temple, its exact location shrouded in uncertainty. Though I cannot claim absolute certainty, it is believed to be the very same place that now bears the name Omkarnath Temple, where a resplendent Vishnu Murti resides. In the realm of ancient lore, there exists a tale that speaks of the proximity between the illustrious Hunkar Teerth and the revered Adityeshwar Teerth. It is said that these sacred sites were situated in such close proximity to one another, as if they were intimately intertwined in the fabric of their existence.

In close proximity to the illustrious Hunkar Teerth lies the esteemed Adityeshwar Teerth,[5] also known as Ravi Teerth. This sacred site holds great significance, as it was once inhabited by a righteous soul named Jabali during the era of Satya Yuga. Jabali, a man of unwavering devotion to his religious pursuits, tragically lost his beloved wife due to his inadvertent neglect of her and his domestic responsibilities. As a consequence of this unfortunate turn of events, the brahmana found himself afflicted with the debilitating condition of leprosy. Desperate for redemption and seeking guidance, he humbly sought counsel on how to atone for his sins. It was then that he received a solemn recommendation to embark on a pilgrimage to the sacred land of Shuklateertha. The brahmana, aware of his physical limitations, had embarked upon a rigorous *tapasya* in this very place. Through the benevolence of the sun, he was bestowed with divine blessings. The *tirtha*, known as Adityeshwar Mahadev, gained its renowned status through the ages.

In the vicinity lies a quaint village, renowned by the name of Mangaleshwar. Interestingly, this hamlet was once known as Bhargaleshwar,[6] owing to a fascinating tale rooted in ancient mythology. Legend has it that Bhargal, the illustrious son of Kashyap, embarked upon a rigorous penance in this very place, thus bestowing upon it its original appellation. In the vicinity of Bhargeshwar lies a quaint village by the name of Nikora, a place steeped in history and legend. Once renowned as Svetavarah Teerth,[7] it earned its name from the divine presence of Bhagavan Varaha, who graced this sacred land and blessed it with his divine touch. In this very location, Bhagavan Varaha found respite beneath the majestic *ankole* tree, and it was here that the revered Linkeshwar Mahadev was established.

As we ventured deeper into our journey, we stumbled upon the hallowed dwelling of Mangala *graha*, a place renowned as Angareshwar.[8] In this sacred place, Mangala had diligently performed his *tapasya*, a rigorous spiritual practice, seeking divine intervention and guidance. Through his unwavering devotion and perseverance, he was bestowed with the grace and blessings that would enable him to be embraced by the celestial realm of *graha*. As we stumbled upon this ancient temple, a sense of wonder enveloped us, beckoning us to explore its sacred grounds. With reverence in our hearts, we embarked on a *puja*, a ritualistic ceremony that promised to transport us to a realm beyond the mundane. Little did we know that this spiritual endeavour would soon captivate our senses, leaving an indelible mark on our souls. Curiously, the temple stood in a state of abandonment, mirroring the countless other *tirtha*s that had crossed our path during our arduous expedition. In spite of everything, we revelled in the tranquillity of the day, immersing ourselves in the act of paying homage to the celestial deity. As our weary feet traversed the winding path, we eventually arrived at the enchanting destination of Dharmashala, a place renowned for its spiritual significance, often referred to as Amahak Teerth,[9] or the Sacred Pilgrimage of the *pitr*s. Undeterred by the arduous journey thus far, we pressed on, eager to explore the mysteries that lay beyond.

As the sun started to recede below the horizon, our journey led us to Jhanor. It was there that we found a break in the Sri Aurobindo school, where the very air seemed to hum with the spiritual energy of Mother and Sri Aurobindo. In my morning meeting with students, I stressed the significance of their current educational setting. In the 1960s, a generous devotee of Sri Aurobindo donated the land upon which the school now stands. I was struck with wonder at the realization that even during that era, the principles of Sri Aurobindo's philosophy and educational approach were already being put into practice. Education was deemed by both Sri Aurobindo and Mother as the pivotal criterion of their *ashrama*, with the ultimate goal of forging a novel being. Until or unless the education is given properly there is no way the new kind of men and women could emerge. As I walked along the *parikrama* path, I caught sight of Sri Aurobindo's school and could not help but feel a glimmer of hope for the realization of the prophecy he once made. It is another tale that many of the educators I encountered were unfamiliar with the educational principles of Sri Aurobindo, but I figured they were doing the best they could with the information at hand.

34

Words, Feelings and Respect

On that fateful day, our departure from the hallowed grounds of the school premises marked the beginning of an extraordinary journey. Our first destination, a sacred place known as Nanda Devi Teerth, awaited us in the enchanting realm of Nandgram. In this sacred abode, Mahishasuramardini once sought solace to pay homage to Lord Shiva. It is said that the holy Narmada herself graced this hallowed ground to offer her devotion to the revered Goddess. The temple, it appears, has undergone a meticulous restoration, breathing a new life into its ancient walls. According to the ancient Shastras, Bhairava, Rudra, and Kedara Mahalaya once resided within these sacred precincts. Alas, their traces have become elusive, perhaps forever enshrouded in the annals of history.[1]

Venturing deeper into the realm of exploration, one shall stumble upon the enigmatic Somaj. According to the annals of Sanatana history, this sacred place was known as Somatirtha,[2] a name that carries profound significance. It is said that within the confines of Somaj, the sin of Moon or Soma from his *gurutalpa,* he had found liberation, as if the very essence of freedom permeated the air. In this sacred place, one would discover three additional *tirthas*, each holding its own mystical significance. Among them is Sakratirtha,[3] a sacred site where the formidable curse of Gautama Rishi found its resolution. It was here that Indra, the celestial deity, embarked upon a profound penance, seeking redemption and absolution. In the annals of ancient history, a tale unfolds, revealing the presence of Karkateshwar Mahadev.[4] It is said that during a time when the King of Kashi, Jayant, was burdened with the weight of his sins, a remarkable transformation occurred. Upon his demise, his soul found rebirth in the form of a humble bird, destined to traverse the realms of existence. However, even in his avian form, he clung to his ingrained behaviours, causing distress among the other birds in the vicinity. It was during this tumultuous period that Pakshiraja, the king of birds, took decisive action, ending his life and leaving his lifeless body on the serene banks of the sacred Narmada River. After quenching his thirst with the sacred water, Pakshiraja's eyes beheld a remarkable transformation. In place of the bird that had once perched before him, now stood a magnificent Shivalinga, an object of divine worship. Enthralled by the tale, Balakhilya Rishi graced this place with his presence, regaling numerous souls with the captivating narrative. As one ventures forth, a captivating sight awaits: the quaint village of Oz, once hailed as Ayodhyapuri. The tale transports us to a bygone era, when Lord Rama had graced the land of Ahilyapuri. As he ventured along the sacred banks of the holy Narmada, a profound realization dawned upon him – a resplendent Ayodhya ought to be erected in this very vicinity. Thus, the city sprang into existence. To imprint the memory of this hallowed ground into the annals of time, his brothers, in a gesture of reverence, consecrated the revered Rameshwar Shivalinga within its confines.[5]

As one ventures forth, a path unfolds leading to the enchanting realm of Koral. Within its sacred confines lies the revered Kubera Teerth, a sanctuary of divine energy. Here, one encounters the esteemed deities Varuneshwar, Vayaveshwar, and Yameshwar,[6] whose names resonate with ancient power. It is within these hallowed grounds that Kubera, Varuna, Vayu, and Yama, embodiments of celestial authority, embarked upon arduous penance, beseeching the heavens for their ascension as guardians of the realms. With the acquisition of the wealth, Kubera ascended to the illustrious throne of the *yaksha*s, assuming the mantle of their revered king. In a grand turn of events, Varuna ascended to the illustrious throne of water, his dominion extending over vast oceans and mighty rivers. With his newfound power, he commanded the tides and controlled the very essence of life itself. Meanwhile, Vayu, the once humble deity, underwent a remarkable transformation, becoming omnipresent in every corner of the world. His ethereal presence could be felt in the gentle breeze that caressed the land, the powerful gusts that swept across the mountains, and the whispers that carried secrets through the air. Yama, in his unwavering pursuit of justice, assumed the role of the arbiter of righteousness, the enforcer of *dharma*. In the realm of antiquity lies Koral, a place steeped in history and lore. As recounted in the revered Reva Khanda, this village was not only home to Kuber itself, but also harboured other sacred *tirtha*s (pilgrimage sites). Among them, Aashapuri Devi Teerth stood resplendent in the eastern expanse of this mystical land. Legend has it that it was none other than Lord Shiva himself who personally established the presence of Devi Bhagavati in this hallowed ground. Koral, a place of great significance, was once graced by the presence of Adivaraha Teerth. It was at this sacred site that Adivaraha,[7] in a valiant act, rescued the earth from impending doom. In the sacred realm of Koral, a profound event unfolded wherein Lord Vishnu himself graced the land and offered reverence to his divine Varaha incarnation. This remarkable occurrence drew the presence of numerous revered sages, infusing the place with an aura of sanctity and earning it the distinguished epithet of Kotitirtha.[8] Here is where Lord Vishnu freed Vishnudas from the bonds of mortality by teaching him the Satyanarayana Katha. In this sacred realm, known as Brahmaprasada Teerth, the divine presence of Lord Brahma himself established its foundations. With benevolence and grace, he bestowed upon this hallowed ground his divine blessing, ensuring that all who partake in the religious rituals held here shall be bestowed with abundant merits. According to legend, Lord Vishnu commanded Rishi Markandeya to build Markandeya Teerth so that all the gods and goddesses who visited the area could see the River Narmada. Narada, who was also present at the time, was asked where the holiest place in India was, and he replied, "Jambudvipa". In the realm of rivers, three prominent goddesses reign supreme: Brahmi, also known as Sarasvati, Vaishnavi, affectionately referred to as Bhagirathi, and Raudri, known as Narmada. While all three possess remarkable qualities, it is Narmada who stands as the epitome of auspiciousness among them. These words of Narmada had spread far and wide of the sacred destination where *rishis* and divine lords alike embarked on their spiritual quests, fulfilling their religious obligations with utmost devotion. Due to the fact that the divine Lord had established all of Kashi's divine beings there, this area became known as Kashi of the Narmada banks.

Koral also had some other *tirthas*, viz. Bhrigishwar Teerth is where Bhrigu performed his *tapasya* for his progeny and became known as Bhrigishwar Teerth.[9] Then Pingaleshwar Teerth[10] – when Ruchka Rishi witnessed his wife being burned by Agni, he cursed Agni, saying that he would not receive a portion of himself in *yagya*. This is when Agni arrived and performed his *tapasya*. This was one of Agnihotris' most well-known locations. Ayonij Teerth[11] – once upon a time in *pradosh kala*, a *rishi* by the name of Shaunik began worshipping Lord Shiva, and it was then that one Shivalinga appeared here, signifying that Shaunik Rishi had completed his *tapasya* and received Lord Shiva's favour. When the world was at peace, Lord Sun came here to perform *tapasya* and established this *tirtha*, which is known as the Ravi Teerth.[12] These all *tirtha*s were located in Koral village which is known as Kashi of the Narmada bank. While the temples of Ravi Teerth, Kubera Teerth (or Panchakubera), and Ashapuri Devi remain, I was unable to locate any traces of any additional temples since that might have changed names or disappeared.

Just a few kilometres away from this very spot, in the realm of spiritual significance, Nareshwar has risen to great prominence, owing to the presence of the revered sage Rang Avadhut on the tranquil banks of the Narmada River. However, in times past, this sacred place was known as Kapardeshwar Mahadev,[13] a name steeped in ancient lore. Legend has it that it was here that Lord Ganesha, embarked upon his arduous penance. Furthermore, Nareshwar of yore was referred to Narmadeshwar,[14] a name that carries with it a tale from the annals of Sanatana Dharma. It is said that Lord Shiva and Mata Parvati graced this hallowed ground with their divine presence, and it was at this very spot that the holy Narmada River, in a remarkable display of devotion, emerged from the depths of the water to offer her heartfelt prayers to the divine couple. Thus, this sacred site came to be known as *punya tirtha*, a place of immense sanctity and virtue.

Our journey today was towards Kohna. However, our expedition was not without its fair share of intriguing occurrences. Jitendra Sharma and Vinay Chauhan had made all necessary arrangements and parked, and developed a camp at a nearby *ashrama*. However, they were dissatisfied with the location and decided to seek out an alternative. They eventually stumbled upon a Hanuman Temple and approached a *sadhu* for permission to set up a camp there. The *sadhu* kindly granted their request. It was none other than Sitaram Bapu with whom we were destined to have yet another intriguing relationship.

At the evening *puja* time, when I still did not know where we were or who ran the *ahsrama*, I spotted a *sadhu* with innocent eyes and invited him to join us in *arti*. He stayed for a while but eventually went. As per my routine, I would perform *arti* of Mother Narmada and subsequently proceed to every temple situated in the vicinity to conduct another *arti* of all the deities. Expressing gratitude to the divine entities of the land that have bestowed their blessings upon us during the *parikrama*, was my humble gesture of appreciation. We visited the temple to pay our respects to the divine Hanuman and other gods. Accompanying us was Sitaram Bapu, who initiated a conversation with me. He kindly offered me his *asana* to sit on, but I respectfully declined, as it was his rightful place, Sitaram Bapu also declined to sit if I did not. However, he then suggested that we sit together, which led to an interesting turn of events. As dinner time arrived, Bapu began to speak and we gradually eased into a lively discussion, enjoying each other's company. Bapu was quite the debater, but I responded in my own unique way, which seemed to amuse him greatly. We laughed heartily for quite some time, and our mutual respect for one another grew stronger as a result.

As the morning sun began to peek over the horizon, I made a request for breakfast to be prepared for all, including Sitaram Bapu and myself. Additionally, I asked that plates be thoughtfully arranged for each of us. According to Nandlal Tayal, Sitaram Babu will not be joining us as it is not yet time for his breakfast. I reminded Nandlal that regardless of his absence, we must still prepare a plate and set a place for him at the breakfast table. Failing to do so would be a sign of disrespect towards him. In a matter of moments, Sitaram Bapu arrived and took notice of his meticulously arranged seat and plates. His eyes conveyed a message to me, as if to say, "I never imagined I would have a place at the breakfast table". We proceeded to engage in a captivating conversation that lasted for quite some time. With his keen sense of humour and logical thinking, he quipped that winning against lawyers in court was impossible, much like how he found it impossible to outsmart me. Our relationship had blossomed into something truly special. Our friendship grew to the point where onlookers would assume we are each other's devoted followers. Sitaram Bapu is a cherished offspring of Mother Narmada whom we have had the pleasure of encountering, and with whom I maintain a strong connection.

Kohna, a hallowed ground where the esteemed Kohan Rishi[15] once immersed himself in arduous *tapasya*, holds a profound significance. As Kohana Rishi's mortal journey neared its end, he recited the sacred verses of the *mahamrityunjaya patha*, invoking the benevolence of Lord Shiva. In his divine grace, Lord Shiva bestowed upon the *rishi* the *siddhi* of *mahamrityunjaya*. It is said that within the sacred confines of Kohna, the recitation of a single Rudra *patha* holds the power equivalent to 100 such *pathas*, as performed by the venerable *rishi* himself. Revered as one of the sacred *tirthas* of Narmada Maiya, this place holds great significance in the hearts of devotees. In this very moment, Sitaram Bapu carries forward the noble legacy of a revered historical saint of Sanatana Dharma.[16]

35

Senapur

After paying our solemn respects to the revered Sitaram Bapu, our journey commenced at the break of dawn. As we ventured forth, the path unfurled before us, revealing a multitude of sacred *tirtha*s that graced our path. As the pilgrim embarks on their sacred journey, the first *tirtha* that graces their path is none other than the illustrious Chandraprabhash Teerth. Nestled within its hallowed grounds, one discovers the divine presence of Chandreshwar Mahadev, a deity of great reverence and awe. In the captivating tale of Sanatana Dharma, it is revealed that Chandra, the celestial embodiment of the moon, graced the realms of existence in various *kalpa*s (cosmic cycles). The enigmatic Chandra's origin is shrouded in mystique, as he first emerged from the ethereal recesses of Lord Brahma's mind. However, the Moon deity's ethereal presence was not confined to this singular genesis, for he was subsequently reborn from the vast expanse of the ocean, once again brought forth by the divine hands of Lord Brahma. In the illustrious Varaha Kalpa, a time of great significance, Chandra experienced yet another birth, this time under the auspices of the revered Anusuya and Atri Rishi.[1] This divine couple, renowned for their spiritual prowess, played a pivotal role in ushering Chandra into existence once more. Such is the intricate tapestry of Chandra's existence, woven with threads of divine intervention and cosmic happenstance. In this particular *kalpa*, he found himself in this place, guided by the divine command of Mahakala. It was in response to the sin of *gurupatni-gamana* that he had committed, and through his rigorous *tapasya* performed in numerous locations, including this one.[2]

In the vicinity of this enchanting locale lies the quaint village of Ranapur, where a hidden gem known as Kambhukeshwar Teerth awaits.[3] In the annals of ancient lore, a tale unfolds within the lineage of the formidable Hiranyakashyapu demon. It is said that amidst this fearsome family, there resided a demon of great renown, known as Kambuka. Gripped by an overwhelming trepidation of the mighty Lord Vishnu,

Kambuka embarked upon a rigorous penance, delving deep into the realms of spiritual austerity. For an extended duration, he immersed himself in this arduous practice, seeking divine favour and solace. As Lord Shiva beseeched him for a boon, the divine mother Sarasvati gracefully perched upon his tongue, and in that sacred moment, he fervently requested that only Lord Vishnu, the supreme deity, possess the power to vanquish him. And his plea was granted, sealing his invincibility against all but the mighty Vishnu. It was he who had established the sacred Kambhukeshwar Mahadev in this very place. In the annals of history, there exists a tale of a precious Shivalinga vanished into the mists of time, only to resurface through the efforts of enlightened sages. This Shivalinga, once lost to the world, was miraculously discovered once more, resting peacefully in the depths of a flowing river. Legend has it that bestowing the sacred *abhisheka* of *linga* through the resonant conch holds profound significance. As I stepped into the sacred temple, my eyes were immediately drawn to a weathered conch resting gracefully upon the ancient stone floor. It exuded an aura of timeless wisdom, as if it had witnessed countless rituals and prayers over the centuries. Intrigued by its presence, I felt compelled to take part in the *abhisheka puja*, an act of reverence and devotion, using the very conch that had captivated my attention.[4]

Legend whispered of the existence of Kapileshwar Teerth and Trilochan Teerth[5] in the quaint village of Diver. Intrigued by these tales, I embarked on a quest to uncover their hidden splendour. Alas, despite my fervent search, these mystical sites eluded my grasp, leaving me yearning for the ethereal wonders that were said to reside within their sacred grounds. As I ventured forth, my eyes beheld a plethora of temples, each one more magnificent than the last. Alas, despite their grandeur, none possessed the antiquity I sought nor the rich tapestry of historical significance that would satiate my thirst for knowledge. Kapileshwar, a sacred place of worship, was established by the revered sage Kapila Muni. Similarly, Trilochan, another significant site of spiritual significance, was founded by the illustrious son of Pundarika Trilochana.

In the vicinity of this place, known as Malsar, lies a sacred site called Pandutirtha.[6] Legend has it that long ago, a tragic incident occurred involving Pandu, a noble king. It is said that Pandu, in a moment of misfortune, unknowingly slew a revered sage who had taken the form of a majestic deer. Overwhelmed with remorse and seeking redemption, Pandu sought solace in the tranquil surroundings of Malsar, where he performed *tapasya*. This act of atonement was believed to cleanse his soul and bring him closer to absolution. In this enchanting land, there exists a place steeped in history and mystique. It is none other than the sacred Angareshwar Teerth,[7] where the mighty planet Mars, known as Mangala, once performed his rigorous penance for an extended duration. The echoes of his devotion still resonate through the ages, leaving an indelible mark on this hallowed ground. Not far from Angareshwar Teerth lies another sacred site known as Ayonij Teerth.[8] It is here that the revered sage Tijyananda, born of divine origins, first graced the world with his presence. The very essence of his being seemed to radiate an ethereal aura, captivating all who encountered him. These two *tirtha*s, with their rich histories and profound significance, stand as testaments to the deep spiritual heritage of this remarkable place.

From where I was standing we set out on an adventure, travelling the miles to reach the beautiful city of Senapur. This location carried a lot of promise for us because it had piqued our interest and inspired speculation. This location can claim a genuinely unique past thanks to its intricate tapestry of Sanatana Dharma. Numerous *tirtha*s, each with its own special meaning, have graced its sacred grounds.

This ancient settlement, steeped in the mists of time, holds a captivating allure. It is James Forbes, a distinguished officer serving under the East India Company, who appeared on the city with his presence and chronicled its wonders in his esteemed book. Forbes, a man of discerning taste and keen observation, was captivated by the myriad temples that adorned the landscape of Senapur. These architectural marvels, standing as testaments to the devotion and craftsmanship of the ancients, cast a spell on all who beheld them. Each temple, with its intricate carvings and sacred aura, whispered tales of a bygone era. But it was not only the temples that enchanted Forbes; the town itself pulsated with the vibrant energy of its inhabitants. Senapur was a hub of skilled weavers and artisans, their nimble fingers transforming threads into exquisite fabrics. The air was alive with the rhythmic clatter of looms and the vibrant hues of dyed yarns. The town's streets, bustling with the comings and goings of these talented individuals, painted a vivid picture of a community deeply rooted in its craft. Thus, through the eloquent words of James Forbes, we are transported to a time when Senapur, or Sinore as it is now known, flourished as a city of resplendent temples and skilled weavers. It is a testament to the rich tapestry of history that we are fortunate enough to glimpse through the eyes of this esteemed author. In this region, cotton reigned supreme as the primary crop.[9]

Sinore, or perhaps more famously known as Senapur, held a distinguished reputation akin to that of Chandod, for it served as an esteemed centre of erudition, particularly in the realm of Sanskrit teachings encompassing the profound wisdom of the Vedas and the revered *gurukula*s. The towns nestled along the serene banks of the Narmada River were renowned for their esteemed *gurukula*s, attracting eager learners from far and wide. These erudite teachers, who imparted wisdom and knowledge, had themselves received their education in the illustrious city of Benares, which served as a veritable hub of learning for these scholarly mentors.

The journey from Sinore to Chandod along the sacred Narmada River was steeped in profound spirituality. Revered for its sanctity, this majestic waterway held a special place in the hearts of many. Renowned chronicler James Forbes, in his meticulous accounts, documented the river's purported ability to alleviate a myriad of ailments. One must recall that Sinore was a locale abundant with *vaidya*, those esteemed healers whose presence rendered the environs more pristine, fostering an atmosphere conducive to the absence of maladies.[10]

In his accounts, James Forbes eloquently recounts his observations of the profound reverence bestowed upon the bull in this particular region. According to his recollections, whenever these majestic creatures would venture into the farmland, they were not met with hostility or chased away. Instead, the locals perceived their presence as a divine.

Some of the *tirtha*s proved to be quite challenging to locate, as if each had been concealed for centuries and we were the first to rediscover them. As we arrived in Senapur, or what is now referred to as Sinore, we were greeted by the charming architecture of the old town. However, it was disheartening to witness the state of disrepair that these beautiful buildings had fallen into. Many of them had been dismantled, and their exquisite windows and doors had been replaced with modern concrete structures. It seemed as though no one in the town was aware of the place they called home. As per the ancient Sanatana chronicles, Senapur was the sacred site where Skanda, the son of Lord Shiva, received the divine blessing to become the commander of the celestial army. Henceforth, the place came to be known as Senapur.

In the heart of a mystical land, stood the ancient temple of Dhutpapeshwar.[11] Legends whispered of its sacred origins, tracing back to a time when gods and demons clashed in epic battles. It was said that the mighty Lord of the divine army, Skanda, had once graced the hallowed grounds of Dhutpapeshwar. After emerging victorious from countless battles, where he vanquished fearsome demons and laid waste to their wicked schemes, Skanda sought solace and purification within the temple's sacred walls. Within the temple's ancient halls, adorned with intricate carvings and adorned with shimmering tapestries, Skanda sought to cleanse himself of the darkness.[12] The temple had fallen into disrepair and was on the verge of being taken over by another religion. Despite our best efforts to locate it, the temple remained elusive and out of reach. It was only through the kindness of a local boatman, who had noticed our search, that we were able to find our way to the temple's hidden location. Upon arrival, we were dismayed to find the temple doors locked and the sacred Nandi statue missing. The duration of its preservation may be uncertain, yet I am grateful for having had the opportunity to behold the temple's divine presence.

As you approach the town, it appears to be a formidable fortress with its high walls and sturdy gates. However, upon closer inspection, you notice that the upkeep of the town is quite poor. The temples scattered throughout the town are in a state of disrepair, with crumbling walls and broken statues. Despite the town's appearance of strength, it seems to be struggling to maintain its once-great splendour.

As I embarked further on my journey, my feet led me to an *ashrama* nestled amidst the tranquil surroundings. However, to my surprise, it appeared that the *ashrama* had somehow forgotten the significance of the sacred *tirtha*. It was here, in this very place, that Bhogeshwar,[13] the divine lords, had once organized a grand feast in honour of Lord Shiva. The temple they established stood as a testament to this divine celebration. The surrounding *tirtha*s were in a state of disrepair, yet the inhabitants of the *ashrama* were fervently devoted to the construction and maintenance of a fairly new temple. The *ashrama sadhu* extended an invitation for us to remain in his presence. I acquiesced, but soon found that he had little to impart. Our exchange felt devoid of substance, and I took my leave with courtesy. In the winter months, the Kedareshwar Temple[14] of Senapur is believed to be graced by the presence of Lord Kedara. The temple was a sight to behold, with the revered *pancha-kedara* enshrined within. They bore an uncanny resemblance to their Himalayan counterparts.

The ancient landmark's sheer magnificence and splendour left me utterly spellbound. Our journey to the temple was aided by a woman. It was not until we had paid a visit that we came to realize that she held the role of caretaker for the revered location. With a fervent longing to leave a lasting impact on the revered site, eagerly offered a donation. Despite my persistent persuasion, she initially declined my offering. I found myself in a delicate situation, tasked with explaining to her that the contributions were not intended for her personal gain. Rather, they were meant to honour the divine deity by supporting the oil lamp that she was dutifully tending to. Following a thoughtful exchange, she arrived at a comprehension of the matter and ultimately consented to accept the contribution.

As our expedition pressed on from the majestic *ghat*s, our eyes fell upon the awe-inspiring sight of Markandeyeshwar Mahadev.[15] Legend has it that this sacred temple was established by the revered Markandeya Muni himself, driven by his fervent desire to secure victory for Skanda, the divine warrior, in his valiant battle against the malevolent demons.

During our visit to Senapur to explore the *tirtha*s, we had the pleasure of encountering a wise *jyotisha* very close to Markandeyeshwar Teerth where we were sitting and having our tea. Despite his advanced age of 80 years and near-blindness, he graciously extended his generosity towards us by offering a donation from his wallet. It was a remarkable display of respect for those who undertake the sacred *parikrama*. We shared a cup of tea with him, and in return, I offered a donation which he initially declined but eventually accepted.

As the journey continues, one encounters the sacred sites of Nishkalankeshwar, where the revered Lord Parashurama once embarked on his spiritual quest. It was here that he sought solace and enlightenment through his rigorous *tapasya* or deep meditation. Moving along the path of Narmada Parikrama, the next stop is Rohineshwar, a place of great significance. It is said that Rohini, a devout devotee, chose this very spot to engage in her own *tapasya*. With unwavering devotion and a heart filled with reverence, she immersed herself in spiritual practices, seeking divine blessings and guidance. And then, there is Chakratirtha, a hallowed site that holds a tale of triumph over darkness. Legend has it that after the fervent prayers of Skanda, the mighty Lord Vishnu vanquished the demons and then washed his *chakra* here in the holy water of the Narmada, and thus the name. These three sacred sites, Nishkalankeshwar, Rohineshwar, and Chakratirtha, stand as beacons of spiritual energy along the path of Narmada Parikrama. They offer pilgrims a chance to connect with the divine, to seek solace, and to witness the profound grace that flows through the sacred river.[16]

As our journey led us to the enchanting destination of Kanjetha, we were bestowed with a remarkable opportunity to visit the sacred Dhanakubera Teerth.[17] According to a legend, Dhanakubera, a revered deity, once performed intense penance in this very place. It is believed that offering prayers to Dhanakubera at this *tirtha* brings forth abundant prosperity and blessings into the lives of those who seek his divine intervention. The temple's surroundings exuded an air of historical significance. Ancient Shivalingas were scattered here and there, remnants of a bygone era. Some of the old structures, once grand and imposing, had succumbed to the passage of time, making room for newer ones to take their place. In the vast expanse of time, where millennia have come and gone, the presence of the divine deities remains steadfast. Their enduring existence serves as a testament to the unbroken continuity of Sanatana Dharma.

Our hard journey eventually led us to the picturesque city of Kanjetha. Here we discovered the holy site of Saubhagya Sundari Mata,[18] which is a sanctuary with a reputation for being a source of many benefits. Intrigued by the stories handed down through the ages, we discovered that Khyati, with the help of Arundhati's counsel, had begun a profound spiritual quest on these very grounds. Her heart's deepest wish was to become a mother, and she worked tirelessly towards that end.

On the sacred temple grounds, one can discover the illustrious Nageshwar Teerth, Bharteshwar and Karanjeshwar Teerth. It is within these hallowed premises that the remarkable tale unfolds, where Pundarika Nag, the esteemed offspring of Tvasta, embarked upon a rigorous penance to liberate Lord Indra from the shackles of a formidable curse, and is known as Nageshwar Teerth.[19] Bharteshwar Teerth came to existence when, Bharat, the illustrious son of Shakuntala, diligently engaged in a multitude of *yagya*s and fervent prayers, beseeching the divine favour of the gods.[20] Karanjeshwar,[21] is a place steeped in spiritual devotion, where the *tapasya* (intense meditation) is unfolded. This hallowed ground, known for its profound significance, was established by none other than the revered *brahmachari rishi* Karanj Rishi.

The next day, our journey led us on a delightful walk towards the enchanting Badrikashram, nestled in the vicinity. However, our path to this sacred destination was graced with an unexpected discovery in the charming village of Ambika. It was there that we stumbled upon the magnificent Ambikeshwar Mahadev,[22] a divine sanctuary believed to have been established by none other than the illustrious daughter of king of Kashi, Ambika herself. Perched atop a gentle incline, overlooking the sacred banks of the revered Narmada River, lay the temple we sought. To reach this hallowed place, we embarked on a journey that required us to ascend, step by step, until we reached its lofty heights. The temple stood in a state of abandonment, its once bustling atmosphere now replaced by a haunting stillness. The absence of visitors was palpable, as if the temple had been forgotten by time itself. Yet, amidst this desolation, the surroundings were adorned with a plethora of ancient artefacts, strewn about as if left behind by a forgotten era. These remnants bore witness to the temple's profound historical significance, serving as a testament to the grandeur it once possessed. In this sacred place, it is believed that if unwedded women grace its honoured grounds and engage in the ritualistic *puja*, they may possibly find a suitable life partner. As we made our way back to the tranquil banks of the sacred Narmada River, a captivating sight unfolded before our eyes. A group of youthful maidens, their vibrant presence imbued with an air of anticipation, embarked on a pilgrimage to partake in the sacred *puja*. If the nearby community still remembers this temple's past, I wondered! It appears that if we do not start conserving now, the temple may completely vanish from this area in a few years.

As the journey persists, a path shall unfold, leading the wanderer to the sacred Suvarnashila Teerth.[23] It is here, amidst the tranquil embrace of nature's sanctuary, that countless revered *rishi*s once embarked upon their arduous spiritual quests. In a divine display of cosmic orchestration, Lord Shiva, the supreme deity, chose to send forth a woman as a vessel for a profound experiment. It was through `this chosen one that the *rishi* (a sage of great wisdom) would be put to the ultimate test. As the *rishi*'s mind, steadfast and unwavering, remained in a state of serene tranquillity, a momentous event unfolded before their very eyes – the birth of the sacred Shivalinga, a symbol of divine power and eternal consciousness.

The Erandi Sangam, a place of great significance, was originally intended to be situated in close proximity. However, due to the myriad alterations that have taken place, its precise location has become quite elusive and challenging to ascertain. In this very spot once stood the revered Anusuya Mata Mandir. According to the captivating Sanatana legend, it is said that the revered Anusuya Mata, guided by the wise counsel of her beloved husband, embarked upon a profound *tapasya* in this very place. As a testament to her unwavering devotion and spiritual discipline, she was blessed with a series of extraordinary events, culminating in the birth of her illustrious son, Dattatreya.[24]

Venturing further from this point, one would stumble upon the enigmatic Manmatheshwar Mahadev,[25] a place shrouded in desolation. A sense of eerie stillness permeates the air, as if time itself has come to a standstill in this forsaken location. It is whispered that the land's proprietor had once embarked upon the ambitious endeavour of constructing a grand resort amidst these vacant surroundings, only to abandon the project midway, leaving behind a haunting reminder of unfulfilled dreams. Intriguing indeed is the landmark, for it is here that Kamadeva (deity of desire) embarked upon his arduous penance subsequent to being vanquished by Lord Shiva's all-seeing third eye, which reduced him to mere ashes. In a remarkable display of ethereal existence, Kamadeva assumed an astral form to engage in his rigorous spiritual practice and established Manmatheshwar Mahadev.

Being in this place was truly a marvel. We embarked on an extensive exploration of the entire vicinity, eagerly seeking out remnants of the past, particularly historical records. It so happened that the temple we sought was nestled in a land where another temple stood, just a stone's throw away distance. Intrigued, we ventured forth to that neighbouring temple as well. Alas, the state of affairs there was rather disheartening. It appeared as though the passage of time had not been kind, for the temple had languished in neglect, devoid of any renovations for what seemed like an eternity. Regrettably, it had become a receptacle for all manner of refuse, a sad fate indeed. The temple architecture, exquisitely renovated several centuries ago, stands as a testament to the resplendent era of the Narmada riverbanks.

We departed from our current location and arrived at the sacred Janakeshwar Teerth,[26] situated in close proximity. It is here that the revered Maharaja Janak embarked upon his arduous spiritual journey, engaging in profound meditation to appease the mighty Lord Shiva.

In the vicinity lies the quaint village of Batkal, once renowned as Batkal Teerth or Sankarshan Teerth.[27] It is here that Yadu, the illustrious son of Yayati, sought solace through rigorous penance, ultimately liberating himself from the shackles of his father's curse. In this very place, Lord Balarama graced us with his divine presence, engaging in profound meditation in this sacred *tirtha*. Within the confines of this very village, there exists a sacred place known as Prabha Teerth,[28] where the esteemed Prabha, spouse of the illustrious Surya, had embarked upon her arduous spiritual journey. The temple, with its meticulous management and exquisite beauty, appears to have been bestowed with utmost care and attention, ensuring its preservation and tranquillity.

As one continues to stroll along the picturesque banks of the magnificent Narmada River, it is impossible to overlook the emergence of a captivating island. This enchanting landmass, gracefully taking shape within the flowing waters of the Narmada, is none other than the revered abode of Vyaseshwar Teerth.[29] In the tranquil embrace of the southern shore, Maharshi Vyasa, the illustrious son of Parashara Muni, immersed himself in the sacred practice of *tapasya*. It was during this profound period of spiritual contemplation that a multitude of *rishi*s, drawn by his divine presence, sought the blessed opportunity to have *darshan* of the revered sage.

Upon the arrival of the esteemed *rishi*s, an offering of food was graciously presented to them. However, to the surprise of all, the *rishi*s declined the food as they did not want to have the food on the southern shore of Narmada. It was at this moment that, on the request of Maharshi Vyas, the mighty river Narmada, with its divine power, began to split, creating an island where the revered sage's *ashrama* now resided. In light of this extraordinary occurrence, Vyas Rishi kindly urged the *rishi*s to partake of their meal wherever they pleased as now they could have lunch in northern shore. With the River Narmada now flowing also on the north side of the *ashrama*, the *rishi*s gratefully accepted the invitation and enjoyed their food in that direction. It was during this time that Vyasa Rishi's name reverberated throughout the nation, his unwavering devotion and rigorous spiritual practices earning him widespread recognition.

A short distance lies ahead, where one may find the revered Koteshwar Teerth.[30] It is said that numerous sages, who had embarked on a pilgrimage from the sacred land of Badrikashram, arrived at this hallowed place to pay homage to the great sage Vyasa. It was during their visit that these venerable sages, in their wisdom, established the *tirthas* for future generations to seek solace and spiritual enlightenment.

In the vicinity of Koteshwar lies the quaint village of Nandoriya, a place imbued with a sense of tranquillity. It is here that one can find the sacred site of Badrikashram, a hallowed ground where the revered figures of Nara and Narayana once graced with their presence. In their quest for spiritual enlightenment, these divine beings chose to engage in rigorous penance along the serene banks of the holy Narmada, infusing the surroundings with an aura of sanctity. In the vicinity of Badrikashram,[31] a place steeped in mysticism and spirituality, we stumbled upon a humble *ashrama* that would become our sanctuary for the night. It was within the walls of this sacred abode that we had the privilege of crossing paths with a remarkable *sadhu*, whose aura radiated an unparalleled level of humility. In the face of his laboured breaths, he clung steadfastly to his unwavering determination to be of service to those in his midst. His modesty struck a chord within me, stirring a profound sense of admiration.

36

Gangeshwar Mahadev

Today, we embarked on a sacred pilgrimage to the revered Gangeshwar Mahadev, our first *tirtha* of the day. In the enchanting tale of Sanatana, it is recounted that this very place served as the sacred abode where the revered Ganga, the embodiment of purity, descended upon the mortal realm. It was here that the divine Gangeshwar Mahadev,[1] in all his resplendent glory, manifested himself, offering solace to the holy River Ganga as she sought liberation from the burdensome sins that humanity had bestowed upon her sacred waters. Perched gracefully upon the elevated banks of the majestic Narmada River, it finds itself in a lofty position.

It was within these hallowed walls that Sri Aurobindo's path fortuitously crossed with that of Swami Brahmananda, an encounter that would forever alter the course of his spiritual journey. The latter gazed deeply into Sri Aurobindo's eyes, their gaze penetrating the depths of his soul, forging a profound and intimate connection. After experiencing the divine *darshana* of Gangeshwar Mahadev, I felt as though I had been transported back in time to when Sri Aurobindo had visited this sacred place. I imagined how he must have been enchanted by the ethereal beauty that surely captivated his discerning gaze.

We were en route to our intended destination. As we journeyed along, we chanced upon the ancient Yamhas Temple.[2] The *tirtha*, a sacred place of great significance, was said to have been established by none other than Yamaraja himself, the deity of death. Perched atop a lofty hill, the temple stands in humble proportions, its size diminutive, yet its significance immense.

Its structural integrity perilously compromised by the relentless erosion of the Narmada River's banks. The temple, once a bastion of grandeur and piety, now teetered on the brink of collapse, a poignant reminder of the fleeting nature of all things. I encountered a group of journalists who were eager to hear my thoughts on a political matter. However, I politely declined to engage in such discussions. Despite my reluctance, they persisted in their request for me to speak on the topic. Eventually, I acquiesced and shared my perspective. Unfortunately, it seemed to go over their heads, leaving them with little to ask in follow-up. One journalist, in particular, seemed to have a sense of what I might say and refrained from posing any further questions.

Afterward, our journey led us to the enchanting town of Chandod, a place steeped in ancient lore and imbued with a sense of mystique. According to the revered Sanatana story, Chandod boasts not just one, but seven sacred *tirtha*s, each holding its own significance and captivating tales.

Chandatiya – In the aftermath of Indra's triumphant victory over Chanda–Munda, a profound transformation took place. They embarked on a sacred journey, immersing themselves in the divine worship of Surya, the radiant Sun God. Through this profound act of devotion, they sought solace and sought to secure their future. In the wake of their unwavering dedication, they were bestowed with a divine blessing – a formidable shield against any potential threat. It was decreed that no force, save for the mighty Kali herself, would possess the power to vanquish them.[3]

Chandika Teerth[4] – According to this captivating narrative, it is believed that the mighty Lord Surya, the radiant sun deity, bestowed his divine blessings upon Chanda and Munda. These formidable beings were granted a unique safeguard, rendering them impervious to harm at the hands of any being, save for women. Such was the extraordinary nature of their invincibility, an enigma that would shape their destiny in unforeseen ways and they will be killed by Kali.

Chakratirtha – In the annals of ancient history, it is recorded that it was at this very location where the fateful demise of Talamegha transpired, at the hands of none other than the mighty Lord Vishnu himself. In the ancient land of Bharat, there once lived a learned brahmana named Talamegha. Known for his deep knowledge of the sacred scriptures and rituals, he held a position of great respect within the community. However, fate had a different plan for him. In a surprising turn of events, Talamegha deviated from the path of righteousness. Instead of faithfully performing the *yagya bhaga*, the sacred offering to the gods, he began indulging in practices that were in direct opposition to the religious customs he had once upheld. This audacious act did not go unnoticed by the divine forces governing the universe. It was at this critical juncture that

Lord Vishnu, the preserver and protector of all creation, intervened. In his infinite wisdom, he recognized the grave consequences of Talamegha's actions. With a heavy heart, Lord Vishnu resolved to put an end to the brahmana's transgressions, for the harmony of the cosmos depended on it. Thus, in a divine display, because he was a brahmana and Lord Vishnu had committed the *brahmahatya* sin, he came here to cleanse his *chakra* and perform *tapasya*. In the tranquil embrace of Mother Narmada, Lord Vishnu too found solace.[5]

Kapila Teerth – According to the historical texts, when Kapila Muni was on his *tirtha-yatra*, he performed his *tapasya*.[6]

Rinmochan Teerth – For half a year, *devarshi*'s faithfully performed the sacred ritual of *tarpana*, paying homage to their ancestors. And with a stroke of fortune, found themselves liberated from the shackles of not one, not two, but three burdensome debts. *Brahmarshi* (wise sage) imparted a profound wisdom upon the world – the art of liberating oneself from the shackles of debt in this place which is second Rinmochan Tirtha along the banks of holy Narmada.[7]

Pingaleshwar Teerth – In a tale of divine displeasure, we find Lord Shiva, the mighty deity of destruction and transformation, perturbed by the audacity of Agnideva. It is said that Agnideva (God of Fire) had brazenly trespassed into Lord Shiva's sacred abode, disregarding the sanctity of his presence. This arrogant act had the power to unsettle even the most composed of gods, and Lord Shiva was no exception. The equilibrium of his divine realm had been disrupted, and the consequences of such transgression were bound to be severe. In that moment, the countenance of Agni underwent a remarkable transformation, assuming a resplendent shade similar to the rich earthy tones of *pingala* (a deep shade of brown). It is then that Agnideva spent several years in intense meditation. Later Agni beseeched the divine presence of Lord Shiva, seeking his benevolent blessings.[8]

Nandahad – On Lord Shiva's direct instruction, Nanda Devi had annihilated the demonic forces that threatened the Somnath Tirtha. Lord Shiva himself constructed Nandahad Tirtha after vanquishing the demons, and it was here that Kashyap Rishi performed his *tapasya*.[9]

This is from where we left from Karnali to see the Kali Mata Temple there was a beautiful image of Kali that Sri Aurobindo had seen here and had a divine glimpse of Kali. The temple, situated on the banks of Narmada, has undergone a transformation. It is now under the occupation of the priestly class who conduct their business there. I payed my respect and departed from the premises.

The Chandrama or Soma who performed his *tapasya* in Karnali is credited with installing Someshwar Mahadev there. Chandrama is reported to have shown a great deal of fondness towards Rohini, much to the dismay of his other wives, who were all daughters of Daksha. At this point, Daksha unleashed his wrath against Chandra and he was cursed to slowly begin shedding and being destroyed. At this point in time, Chandrama began to feel the same way about each of his wives. He completed his *tapasya* here, established the Someshwar Mahadev, and was blessed by Lord Shiva, allowing him to finally break free of the curse.[10]

In close proximity lies the esteemed Kubereshwar Mahadev Temple, steeped in legend and mystique. The tale whispered through the ages recounts a fateful encounter between Kubera (the deity of wealth) and a woman hailing from the illustrious brahmana lineage. It is said that Kubera, driven by his insatiable desire, cast an envious gaze upon this fair maiden, unwittingly inviting upon himself a curse of profound magnitude. The woman, her heart aflame with righteous anger, beseeched the heavens to afflict Kubera with the ravages of time and ultimate ruin. He had arrived at this very spot with the sole purpose of embarking on his *tapasya*.[11]

Exploring more deeply into the distance lies Pavakeshwar Mahadev, a place steeped in legend. The tale unfolds with the renowned Rishi Bhrigu, whose curse befell Agni (God of Fire). Seeking redemption, Agni sought solace in this very spot, engaging in rigorous penance to cleanse his spirit and regain his divine purity.[12] The tale unfolds with a captivating twist: prior to her union with Bhrigu, his beloved wife had been betrothed to a denizen of the demonic realm. However, her father, upon discovering this unholy alliance, swiftly intervened, dissolving the engagement and orchestrating her marriage to Bhrigu instead. In the passage of time, Puloma, the wife of Bhrigu, found herself secluded in the *ashrama*, carrying the precious gift of life within her. It was during this vulnerable moment that a malevolent demon, cunningly disguised as Brahmana, made his presence known. With nefarious intent, he brazenly attempted to abduct Puloma, disregarding the sanctity of her condition. In a display of courage, Puloma vehemently protested, denouncing the demon's immoral act. In response, the audacious creature turned to Agni, the sacred fire ablaze in the *yagyashala*, seeking validation for his actions. He questioned whether Puloma's marriage had indeed been arranged with him, as if to justify his sinister deeds. "Yes", Agni replied with a solemn nod, acknowledging the gravity of the situation. It was at that very moment, when the air was thick with tension, that the malevolent demon seized Puloma, snatching her away from their midst. In the midst of this chaos, Puloma went into labour, and out of her body came Rishi Chyavana, who single-handedly annihilated the demon with his observant gaze. The youthful Chyavana, newly brought into this world, was escorted back to the tranquil *ashrama* alongside his nurturing mother. Once settled, he proceeded to recount the intricate events to the venerable Bhrigu Rishi, who, in his wisdom, sought an explanation from the enigmatic Agni as to why he failed to maintain a state of quietness. In a tumultuous display of emotions, Bhrigu Rishi, consumed by anger, unleashed a curse on Agni. It was an unfortunate consequence of Agni's unwavering commitment to truth. From that moment forward, Agni, the divine fire, would no longer discriminate between the pure and the impure, indiscriminately consuming all that came before it. It was a moment of great upheaval, a time when Agni, the divine force that had long guided and protected us, ceased to function. The consequences of this unexpected turn of events were nothing short of catastrophic, as chaos engulfed the entire world. Under the divine guidance of Lord Brahma, Agni was bestowed with profound wisdom, enabling him to comprehend the intricacies of his existence. Engrossed in a captivating conversation, Lord Brahma's words resonated deeply within Agni's being, leaving an indelible impact on his consciousness. Encouraged by this newfound understanding, Agni was implored by Lord Brahma to descend upon the mortal realm and embark upon a sacred mission – the establishment of the revered Shivalinga. With unwavering determination, Agni embarked upon his arduous journey, prepared to undertake rigorous penance in pursuit of spiritual enlightenment. This is where he established the Pavakeshwar Mahadev. Having departed from the dilapidated temple, its once resplendent image of the divine now marred by neglect, one could not help but marvel at the exquisite carvings that adorned its weathered façade. It was evident that this sacred sanctuary, at one time, had held a position of prominence, renowned throughout the surrounding region.

We stumbled upon a charming establishment owned by Gita Press where we decided to take a break for lunch and rest. We stumbled upon a charming colonial-style edifice, complete with a picturesque garden that beckoned us to explore further. Our curiosity piqued, we were halted by a caretaker who kindly requested our presence within the premises. I apprised the gentleman of my intention to partake of my midday meal amidst the verdant splendour of the garden, steadfast in my resolve to avoid the indoors. Lokesh had already arrived with our lunch and began setting up our dining area in the garden.

The entire premises lay barren, leaving me to ponder over the underlying intention behind its construction. Amidst the tranquil mango orchard, there resided a comical individual who seemed to be oblivious to his surroundings. This young chap, in his early twenties, commenced watering the garden just as I had retired for a brief respite after my meal. Atul slumbered amidst a cluster of mangoes and implored the young lad to see to the irrigation duties once they had departed. The boy acquiesced with a nonchalant "okay" but failed to follow through. As Atul drifted off into slumber, he soon became aware of the presence of water surrounding him. Attempting to relocate his sleeping spot, he found that wherever he lays his head, the water would follow and form a trench around him. Atul simply gazed at the man, his expression inscrutable. Yogesh requested a few moments to rest, but despite the boy's agreement, he persisted with his irrigation efforts. As I roused from slumber, a cacophony of mirthful sounds reached my ears, prompting our departure from the premises.

As we ventured forth, our path was strewn with small shrubs that blanketed the terrain. Little did we know that we were not alone in this wilderness, for the elusive leopard had claimed this territory as its own.

We arrived at the Meera Ashram, a tranquil abode managed by a former Indian military personnel. On the night of our stay, all inhabitants, including the guard of our vehicle, were sound asleep. It was reported that a leopard had been sighted on the premises, but we were fortunate enough to have missed the sighting. However, two days later, we received a video of the elusive leopard visiting the *ashrama*. As the night wore on, the manager's announcement seemed to have a profound effect on the group. No one dared to venture out, and those who did so did it in the company of others, seeking solace in the shared experience.

37

Tirtha and Our Search

Our journey commenced from the serene Meera Ashram, which was nestled on the banks of the revered Mother Narmada.

The initial pilgrimage site we embarked upon in our quest was none other than the revered Nandikeshwar Teerth.[1] After Nandi visited the sacred site of Dadhi-Madhu Kshetra[2] without first alerting Lord Shiva, the latter condemned him to spend eternity as a bull on earth. Nandi did *tapasya* and built the *tirtha* in his memory at this location. The setting of the temple is breathtaking, but the building itself is in such disrepair that I have to worry how much longer the *tirtha* will remain.

It was around this time that I began to consider the feasibility of forming a non-profit organizations whose primary mission would be to improve the state of the *tirtha* and educate the locals on its history with the hope that doing so would help improve the *tirthas*' current precarious condition and inspire them to pitch in with maintenance.

The next logical step was to make our way to cross the Ashvaparni River. The Ashvaparni's *sangama* (confluence) with the Narmada is revered as a holy site, and it is not far from here that Chandrama's vehicle Ashvaparna performed his *tapasya*. The Sanatana tradition tells us that after the ocean was churned, Ucchaishrava emerged on his horse and proceeded to sire four sons: Ashvaparna, Suparna, Madhuparna, and Marudha. Chandra chose Ashvaparna to be his vehicle. When Chandradeva performed this *tapasya*, Ashvaparna fasted and did his duty as well. When he collapsed one day, Lord Shiva appeared in a tiny *linga* form and brought him back to life; the temple where this happened was called Vatveshwar Mahadev, and the river that runs through it is called the Ashvaparni after the horse that inspired it.[3] It is sad that we had the confluence, but we did not find the trace of the temple.

After a little more exploring, we came across the Chandreshwar Mahadev Temple, popularly known as Gupta Prayag. During the Mayura Kalpa, Chandrama was cursed, but after performing *tapasya*, he was rewarded with the favour of Mother Narmada and Lord Shiva.[4]

We were often sent to establishments while we tried to locate the Saptamatrika Mandir.[5] It is interesting to note that in the Narmada belt, asking about a temple is often interpreted as a search for the meals that was traditionally served there. However, given the current state of affairs, temples no longer provide sustenance, and many communities have instead started establishments to provide meals for *parikramavasis*. Our main concern was with the temple itself, not with eating. As part of our investigation, we looked for old temples mentioned in the Puranas. We made a concerted effort to rediscover these holy places and instill them with meaning into our *parikrama*. We looked for quite some time before discovering the temple, which was hidden behind a row of homes. Both the Gautameshwar Teerth[6] and the Saptamatrika Temple can be found on the same property. Since Gautama Rishi performed his *tapasya* here, asking for a wonderful companion for the rest of his life, and since Lord Shiva foretold that, in the Treta Yuga, when Lord Rama would come to earth, he would get a wife who would not have even the tiniest amount of sin in her, hence her name Ahilya, this location is significant. (*Hal* means *papa* and *a+hilya* meaning without any *papa*.)

In the illustrious era of Treta Yuga, the venerable Gautama Rishi found himself in a fateful encounter with the enchanting Ahilya. Alas, a grievous curse befell her, transforming her very being into cold, unyielding stone. However, it was through the benevolent intervention of Lord Rama, Ahilya was restored to her former state, breathing life into her petrified form once more and this is when Saptamatrika had brought her here in this place and later stayed back for the locals' welfare, hence the name.

Tilakeshwar Mahadev Teerth is a holy pilgrimage place that may be found within the enchanted land of Tilakbada. It was said that the name by which it was known changed with each passing *manvantara* in the wide span of time as the cosmic cycles unfolded. The story of how Tilakeshwar Mahadev came to be is a fascinating one in the realm of myths and folklore. Legend has it that when the son of the great sage Vaivasvata Manu heard the enthralling story of this holy site, told by none other than the revered Gautama Rishi, he was compelled to visit for himself. So he made the journey to this holy site, where he participated in the magnificent *darshana* and *puja*, and felt the profound spirituality all around him. He named this holy place Tilakeshwar Mahadev as a token of respect and homage, permanently establishing his personal imprint on this place of worship.[7] In the vastness of *manvantara*, the holy pilgrimage spot is known by many different names, each with its own special resonance. The *manvantara* is a notion found in the rich tapestry of Hindu cosmology. This ethereal concept defines a cyclical period of time in which the rule, longevity, and age of a Manu – the venerated progenitor of mankind – establish the fundamental essence of existence.

In Svayambhuva Manvantara, Priyavrat Mahraj had called this Priyavrateshwar; in Svarochit Manvantara, it was called by Chaitra Maharaj Chaitreshwar. In the time of Uttama Manu, Ajastra king had called it Ajastreshwar. In Tapas Manvantara, it was called by Shantiraj Shantireshwar. In Raivata Manu, it was called by Satyak Maharaj Satyakeshwar. In Chakshu Manu, Shatrughan Maharaj had called Shatrughaneshwar and in Vaivasvata Manu, it is called Tilakeshwar.

Continuing on this path, one would eventually arrive at the sacred confluence where the mighty Man River merges with the divine Narmada. It is here that the Maninageshwar Teerth resides, a place steeped in ancient lore. Legend has it that this *tirtha* owes its name to the poignant tale of Mani Nag, who was cursed by Kadru herself. Among the numerous sites in this vicinity, Mani Nag had chosen this very spot to embark on a profound spiritual journey (*tapasya*). It is said that his tears, shed in sorrow after being rejected by his own mother, gave birth to a river that came to be known as Man.[8]

In close proximity to our current location lies the quaint village of Vasna, renowned throughout the vast expanse of India for its historical significance. It was within the confines of this very village that the illustrious Kapila Muni, known for his extraordinary feat of vanquishing the mighty Sagar's son, sought solace and embarked upon a profound journey of self-discovery through the practice of *tapasya*, ultimately attaining a state of unparalleled tranquillity.[9]

We ventured deeper into the realm of Raingan, a sacred site where Kameshwar Ganapati had embarked on his arduous journey of *tapasya*. It was here that he sought the divine blessings of Mother Narmada and Lord Shiva, immersing himself in their divine presence.[10] In the vicinity lies a quaint village, known as Sanjroli, which once bore the name Ravi Teerth. In the realm of Bhanumati, a captivating woman, Suryadeva found himself ensnared by the whims of fortune. This encounter had bewitched him, leading him down a path of temptation and desire. It was within this very moment that he embarked upon his arduous journey of self-discipline, known as *tapasya*.[11]

In the vicinity, not too distant from this very location, lies the sacred Agastyeshwar, where one can discover the awe-inspiring Agastyeshwar and Kedareshwar Mahadev temples. The tale harks back to a bygone era, when the venerable sage of the Shandilya *gotra*, hailing from the illustrious land of Andhra Pradesh, embarked on a momentous pilgrimage to the sacred abode of Kedarnath. After traversing countless days on foot, weary and famished, the sage finally arrived at his destination. Overwhelmed by exhaustion, he succumbed to slumber, only to be visited by a divine vision in his dreams. In this ethereal encounter, Lord Kedara himself beckoned the brahmana to awaken, proclaiming his divine presence in this very place, solely for the sage's sake. He could not believe it at first, but before long, a magnificent Shivalinga appeared by his side, steadily growing in size. It was at this very moment that he found himself compelled to offer his worship to the divine Lord Shiva, in the sacred form of Kedara.[12]

In this very place, nestled within the realm of promises, lies the sacred temple of Agastyeshwar Mahadev. The tale transports us to a bygone era, where Vindhyachal, with a heart full of curiosity, dared to approach the mighty Lord Sun. In his audacity, he posed a question to the radiant deity, expressing his desire for the Sun to encircle him just as it does the illustrious Mount Sumeru. However, Surya, in his wisdom, gently reminded Vindhyachal that the esteemed permission to traverse the celestial heavens had been bestowed solely upon Mount Sumeru by the divine Brahmaji. It was at this juncture that Vindhyachal commenced its remarkable expansion, displaying an unwavering determination to reach new heights. In a grand assembly of celestial beings, the divine entourage gathered before the venerable Brahmaji. However, to their dismay, he revealed that Vindhyachal, a formidable force of nature, remained impervious to the pleas and counsel of all but his esteemed *guru*. In light of this revelation, the divine beings, in their wisdom, summoned the revered sage Agastya to intervene. As Agastya graced the presence of Vindhyachal, the majestic mountain range humbly bowed in reverence, adhering to the timeless customs that dictate one must remain in prostration until the *guru* grants permission to rise. Thus, Vindhyachal remained in a state of deep obeisance, patiently awaiting Agastya's return from his journey to the southern lands. Agastya Rishi embarked on a journey towards the southern lands, guided by a profound purpose. It was there that he encountered a wise *rishi* who beseeched him to remain in that sacred place indefinitely. The reason behind this plea was to ensure that the majestic Vindhyachal mountain range, with all its grandeur, would remain in its current state and not expand any further. Prior to his departure towards the southern realms, Agastya Rishi had established a divine manifestation of Lord Shiva, known as Agastyeshwar Mahadev, in the eastern lands.

As we continued our journey, we arrived upon the captivating town of Garudehswar. In the days that lay ahead, we were on the verge of an extraordinary journey, a temporary adventure as we readied ourselves to embrace an unfamiliar place. We were overjoyed to have the honor of welcoming Shri Ram Nath Kovind, the acclaimed former President of India, and we eagerly anticipated his arrival.

Nestled amidst the folds of time, Garudeshwar stands as a testament to the ancient wonders that have captivated the hearts and minds of countless souls. This hallowed place, steeped in history and shrouded in mystery, has earned its rightful place among the pantheon of renowned destinations. A prominent attribute that captivates attention is the majestic Lord Dattatreya Mandir, gracing the surroundings with its divine presence. Furthermore, nestled within this sacred abode lies the hallowed resting place of the esteemed sage, Vasudevanand Saraswati. Renowned for bestowing profound insights upon countless ardent followers of the divine deity, Lord Dattatreya, his *samadhi* stands as a testament to his spiritual legacy.

In the realm of divinity, nestled amidst the ethereal beauty of the cosmos, lies the hallowed grounds of Garudeshwar. It is here that the celestial deity, Lord Karttikeya, in all his resplendent glory, chose to bestow upon the mortal realm the divine presence of Lord Kumareshwar.[13]

Legend has it that the divine Lord Shiva, in all His magnificence, assumed the sacred form of Garuda, gracing this very hallowed site with His divine presence. It is widely believed that He, in His benevolence, showers His blessings upon the devoted souls who seek solace and enlightenment in this sacred abode. Garudeshwar, a sacred place of profound significance, is renowned for being the divine dwelling place of none other than Lord Mahadeva himself.

When we arrived at Garudehswar, we gave money to the Temple Trust in order to arrange rooms at the *ashrama* for the entire crew as well as the guests who had gathered to observe the programme of the honourable former president of India. The area was in a state of disarray and required a full day's work to ensure the grounds were pristine in time for the distinguished arrival of the honourable former president.

Why the former president of the nation would wish to meet with a small, obscure religious figure like myself was beyond the comprehension of the populace.

38

Shri Ram Nath Kovind

Garudeshwar was the destination where we extended an invitation to the honourable former president to join us in paying homage to Mother Narmada during our *parikrama*. The esteemed former president had confirmed the date of 17 November.

It was a programme in which he was participating for the first time. The atmosphere was electric as the city bustled with preparations for the grand arrival of the VVIP. The police personnel, district collector, and SP held a meeting with our staff, although they had not yet had the pleasure of meeting me. The significance of the VVIP's visit in India was not lost on anyone, and the excitement was palpable. What are the tasks that we ought to undertake and those that we should avoid? Internally, I was chuckling, yet simultaneously, I could not help but appreciate their unwavering commitment to their responsibilities. The Garudeshwar Temple and its surroundings were in a state of disarray, prompting us to dedicate an entire day to its clean-up. The task required the assistance of numerous individuals from the local *panchayat* and private sector. I had taken great care to ensure that I did not require any assistance from the local government in funding the entire affair, as it was my own initiative that I had spearheaded.

My association with the former president dates back to his tenure as the governor of the Bihar State. During this time, he had a wonderful experience in Bihar. Even after he assumed the presidency, our relationship remained unchanged. Prior to the *parikrama*, I had the opportunity to meet with him and extend an invitation to attend our programme at any location of his choosing.

When the honourable former president arrived at the location, I proceeded to receive him at the entrance of the temple, where we first went to have *darshana* of Lord Dattatreya. As I approached the honourable former president, I noticed a flicker of confusion in his eyes. It appeared that my slightly altered appearance had momentarily caught him off guard. With my newly grown beard, a departure from my usual clean-shaven look, it was understandable that he may not have immediately recognized me. However, after a brief moment of searching, his eyes finally settled on me and a smile spread across his face. In that instant, he not only recognized me but also let out a chuckle as if to acknowledge the unexpected change in my appearance. This small interaction served as a reminder of the familiarity and rapport we shared. Despite the physical alteration, our connection remained intact. It was a testament to the depth of our relationship and the bond we had developed over time.

In moments like these, it becomes evident that true connections transcend external changes. Our shared experiences and understanding allow us to see beyond appearances and recognize each other on a deeper level.

The *pandit*'s face betrayed a hint of unease as he embarked on the sacred ritual of *puja* for the distinguished VVIP. The atmosphere was charged with an air of anticipation, heightened by the meticulous scrutiny of every detail by the vigilant special forces of security. Even the simplest of offerings, such as water, underwent a thorough examination before being presented for *achamana* to the esteemed former president. In the midst of it all, a charming encounter unfolded between superintendent and myself. At first, SP struggled to identify me, as his preconceived notion of my age had clouded his perception. As I entered the room, a hush fell over the crowd. I could feel their eyes upon me, their curious gazes filled with anticipation. It was as if they had all expected me to be a wise elder, someone with decades of life experience etched upon my face. Little did they know, I was very very far from being in my seventies.

The atmosphere was stressful as the security measures were stringent. Police officers stood guard, their presence serving as a formidable barrier, limiting entry to the programme area. The honourable former president's private secretary was resolute in his insistence that the *parikramavasi*s, who were accompanying me on our walk, be seated in close proximity to the former president. However, due to protocol constraints, the local administration was reluctant to comply with this request. But it was Maiya who stepped in, her determination shining through as she deftly orchestrated a plan. With her unwavering resolve, she managed to secure seating arrangements that brought all the attendees, even the esteemed *parikramavasi*s, into close proximity with the former president.

The day had been long and arduous for the former president. The *puja*, a sacred ritual of worship, was about to commence. It was a new experience for him, as his busy schedule rarely allowed for such moments of spiritual reflection. The air was thick with the scent of incense, and the soft chants of the priests filled the space, creating an atmosphere of serenity. As the *puja* unfolded, the former president closed his eyes, allowing himself to be immersed in the rituals and prayers. The hour seemed to pass in a timeless haze, as he found solace in the rhythm of the chants and he spent an entire hour on the ritual, giving his full attention to it.

After the *puja* as the former president commenced his speech, a subtle shift in attention occurred, and suddenly, all eyes were fixed upon none other than myself. In a momentous gathering, the former president, with an air of candour, expressed his belief that the vibrant youth, such as myself, embody the very essence of India's ideals. It was with great joy and anticipation that I, in turn, was bestowed the honour of carrying forward the profound philosophies of the revered Swami Vivekananda. This announcement was met with resounding applause and a palpable sense of excitement among those present. (He clubbed up my name with the organization *vivek* + *ananda hi ananda* thus Vivekananda.)

In a momentous address, the esteemed former president eloquently expounded upon the paramount importance of unity within the great nation of India. With a profound sense of purpose, he urged his fellow countrymen to embark upon a collective journey of self-assessment, delving deep into the very essence of their national progress. In his stirring words, he implored them to reflect upon the profound significance of carrying the sacred flag of Sanatana Dharma, the eternal principles that have guided their civilization through the annals of time.

Garudeshwar to Jalud

39

Fast Forwards

After a fruitful visit with the esteemed former president, we departed Garudeshwar after a three-day stay. As the morning sun rose, we were graced with the presence of Mangal Das Tyagi. Mangal Das Tyagi requested that I join him for *darshana* at the temple before departing. Garudeshwar held a significant place in his heart. However, soon after, he departed for Omkareshwar while we continued on our journey along our designated route.

In the sacred land of Garudeshwar Teerth, a divine presence known of Lord Kumareshwar reigns supreme. It is within the depths of this holy abode that Kumaraswami, immersed himself in rigorous spiritual practices. Through his unwavering dedication, he managed to secure the profound blessings of none other than Lord Shiva. In this enchanting realm, nestled amidst the ethereal beauty, lies Karoteshwar Mahadev. Legend weaves a tale that transcends time, transporting us to an era where a formidable demon, known as Gajasura, once roamed these very lands. Garuda, with majestic wings outstretched, had arrived at this humble abode in search of a refreshing drink of water. Little did he know that fate had a grand plan in store for him on this very day. With a graceful leap into the sky, Garuda soared high above, carrying with him an unexpected passenger – the mighty Gajasura. As the Garuda savoured his newfound feast, the majestic head of the *gaja* made its way to the sacred Narmada River. There, in the tranquil embrace of the flowing waters, a divine transformation took place. The head, now imbued with a profound sense of reverence, began to offer heartfelt prayers to the mighty Lord Shiva. And lo and behold, the benevolent deity bestowed his blessings upon the humble creature. When Lord Shiva made his request for a boon, the man responded with a profound declaration. He proclaimed that the mighty deity should adorn himself with the majestic hide of the revered elephant, Gaja. It was in that very moment that the head of the man, filled with divine wisdom, foretold that Lord Shiva would forever reside in that sacred place. In the realm of Karoteshwar Rupa, a sacred abode where Lord Shiva has chosen to reside, the passage of time holds a profound significance. It is within these hallowed grounds that the divine deity bestows his blessings upon devoted souls who seek solace and spiritual enlightenment.[2]

Vasudevanand Saraswati's visit to perform *tapasya* is one of the city's most notable historical events. His parents, Ganesh Bhatt Tembe and Ramabai, gave birth to Swamiji in 1854 in the city of Malegaon. Swamiji was devoted to Dutt Bhagvan from a young age. He married Annapurnabai at age 21 and spent the next twenty-five years in the *grihastha ashrama*. He became a *sannyasi* after the death of his wife around 1891 and was initiated by Shri Narayan Swami of Ujjain. After that, he travelled throughout India, eventually settling at Garudeshwar, where he established a simple hut in a ground not far from Holy Narmada's riverbank in 1913. Later local people laboriously constructed a dwelling for him, and word of his extraordinary fame spread gradually from there. He was well-versed in Ayurveda and Sanskrit. Twenty-two *granthas*, written by him in Sanskrit and Marathi, survive. The Duttatreya Temple in Gurudeshwar, Gujarat was built and he attained *samadhi* in the subsequent year.[3]

As one ventures further up from this point, a magnificent sight awaits: the Statue of Unity and the mighty Sardar Sarovar Dam. These remarkable landmarks have had a profound impact on the surrounding area, submerging numerous sacred sites (*tirthas*). The rising water table has made it challenging to traverse these once-accessible paths, forcing us to take a longer route that veers away from the riverbanks. It is unfortunate that we are unable to walk directly from here, for it would have allowed us to encounter these revered *tirthas* along our journey. In the land of Gamona, a place of ancient legends and mystical wonders, there existed a sacred site known as Bhimkulya Sangam.[4] It was said that long ago, the mighty warrior Bhima himself had graced this hallowed ground, accompanied by a retinue of divine gods. Together, they vanquished countless demons and established this very *tirtha* (holy place). In this sacred realm, there existed a revered sage known as Markandeya Muni. Deeply devoted to the divine, he sought to honour the mighty deity Shiva by establishing a sacred symbol in his name. Thus, a magnificent Shivalinga was carefully crafted and placed, serving as a testament to Markandeya Muni's unwavering faith and devotion. The sacred Shivalinga, a symbol of Lord Shiva's divine presence, remains nestled just a few kilometres from here. Its mystical aura beckons devotees, offering them the opportunity to behold its divine form and receive blessings. In the distant land of Bagadiya, nestled near the enchanting Statue of Unity, lie three sacred sites of great significance. Adityeshwar, Kambaleshwar, and Pushkarni Teerth stand proudly, beckoning pilgrims from far and wide.

Adityeshwar Teerth[5] is the place where many *rishi*s have found peace, according to Sanatana fold legends. There was a famine, so the legend goes, and many *rishi*s, including *saptarshi*s, came here to live temporarily. At this point, they saw that a woman with a terrifying appearance was approaching in a red dress, accompanied by a legion of demons. When the frightened *rishi*s went to Adityeshwar Mahadev for help, she granted them the ability to face their fears without hesitation. After this, Agni took all five of them to heaven, including the terrifying women. At this point, the *rishi*s began to comprehend the immense value of this *tirtha*. The other two *tirtha*s were located in the same complex; one was Kambaleshwar, where charitable acts such as the distribution of clothing and blankets rank among the highest, and the other was Pushkarni, where it is believed that Surya Bhagavan always dwelt.

Some of the *tirtha*s that once stood in that area are now hidden beneath the surface of the water in the Sardar Sarovar Dam, including the Vimaleshwar Teerth, which was located directly in front of Mokhdi, at the highest point of the reservoir. It is said that Gopal, a cowherd man, accidentally killed a cow, but after performing *tapasya* he was cleansed of his sin and later reborn as Vimleshwar, one of Lord Shiva's *gana*s. Lord Shiva gave the divine command that this *tirtha* be built.[6]

Not far from here lies Kapila Teerth, a sacred site established by Kapila Muni during his meditation, submerged in the water right in front of the old Shulpani Temple. This *tirtha* held immense significance due to its association with Kapila Muni's spiritual practices. The Pushkarni Teerth was located here on the northern bank, and it was here that Lord Shiva's *trishula* was struck by Surya's horses as he attempted to comprehend the magnitude of Shulbhed. The Pushkarni Teerth, also known as the Lotus Pond, became a sacred site for devotees seeking blessings and spiritual purification. The small stream that originated from the fallen lotus created a serene and tranquil atmosphere, attracting pilgrims from far and wide.[7]

As we arrived at the opposite bank of Shulpani, our gaze was drawn to the majestic mountains that loomed before us, providing a truly enchanting experience. As night fell, we arrived at a humble school that would serve as our lodging. Our team had already communicated with the principal, who selflessly ran the institution for the benefit of the local villagers' children. In this particular region, schools hold significance only if they can provide adequate space and nutrition. Given that the nearby villages are situated at a considerable distance, it is likely that a significant number of children would be deterred from pursuing their studies if they were required to travel back and forth to their homes. Therefore, having a school that also provides lodging ensures that these children have access to education without any hindrances. Additionally, the principal's dedication to the well-being of the students is evident in his efforts to provide nutritious meals, further enhancing the overall learning experience for the children in this region.

The pupils of this institution possessed an impressive ability to recite numerous *mantra*s and were well-versed in the subject matter being taught in their classes. The school had humble beginnings, with contributions from well-wishers. The man in charge of running the school was dedicated to serving the community, which left a lasting impression on me. We engaged in delightful conversation both in the evening and the following morning. I also addressed the children regarding their future responsibilities. The best rendition of the *mantra* was delivered by a timid young girl. Her soft voice carried a sense of vulnerability, yet her delivery was filled with unwavering conviction. The way she effortlessly connected with the audience left everyone in awe, creating a profound and lasting impact. A group of skilled musicians adept at playing Indian instruments convened for a music session. Their expertise and mastery of their respective instruments added depth and richness to the rendition, enhancing the overall experience for the listeners. The harmonious blend of traditional sounds and the girl's mesmerizing voice created a captivating atmosphere that transported everyone to a different realm. I found solace in the fact that there are places in the country where children are permitted to explore their pursuit of purpose and meaning in life. The place that lingers in my memory is Nakhalpura Gurukul. As the evening approached, we summoned Rajiv to bring forth his culinary expertise in the form of Italian dishes. The monotony of our regular fare had left us feeling fatigued, and Rajiv arrived with a plethora of delectable dishes, each one carefully packaged and presented.

Vivek ji in the *Samadhi* of Shri Gaurishankar Maharaj

Vivek ji in Holy Narmada banks

Vivek ji in Shulpani Region one of the most difficult region which many *parikramavasi*s leave due to its terrain and difficulty

Daily *aarti* of the *Kalsh* of Holy Narmada water that was carried in the *parikrama*

Vivek ji bowing himself in the *samadhi* of Shri Gaurishankar Maharaj

Vivek ji in the *samadhi* of Shri Gaurishankar Maharaj

Vivek ji speaking to the audience in the *samadhi* of Shri Gaurishankar Maharaj

Vivek ji in
Shulpani region

Vivek ji and other sitting waiting for the tides to come with the *Parikrama Kalsh* and other participants of the *parikrama*

Vivek ji en route with others from Southern banks of Narmada to Northern banks

Vivek ji walking with others in Narmada *parikrama*

Vivek ji welcoming former President of India Shri Ram Nath Kovind ji in Garudeshwar when he came to participate in the Narmada *parikrama*

Vivek ji and former president of India Shri Ram Nath Kovind ji in the stage as well as the member of *parikrama* committee

Shri Ram Nath Kovind ji, a former Indian President, and Vivek ji, during the *aarti* of the Holy *Kalash* of the Narmada

Performing the sacred ritual of Holy Narmada *Kalash* in Garudeshwar with Vivek ji and the former Indian President

Vivek ji offering Memento to the former President of India in Garudeshwar when he came to participate in Narmada *parikrama*

During the *parikrama*, a saree was offered daily to the Holy Narmada and then distributed to families in need. In Garudeshar, the former President praised the humanitarian initiatives and present a saree to underprivileged girl

Bhandara by Amritasya Ma Narmada Parikrama Committee. Such initiatives by *parikramavasi*s were first seen after a long time.

The mobile kitchen which carried the supplies and kitchen items.

Vivek ji with Chandrashekhar Bawankule, President of BJP, Maharashtra, Ajay Vijayvargiya, Arvind Patankar, Jitendra Sharma, Sanjay Singh, Praveen Chauhan, Hemant Patil

Vivek ji having breakfast with other saints

Every day, lunch was brought to Vivek ji and everyone else from the camp to wherever he happened to be wandering.

Vivek ji in *Agni teerha*, rediscovered by him in the *parikrama*

Vivek ji in Diptikeshwar Teertha which was rediscovered by him during the *parikrama*

Vivek ji in Devpatha linga Teertha which was rediscovered by him during his *parikrama*

Vivek ji in Vishokeshwar Mahadev teertha, rediscovered by him during his *parikrama*

Vivek ji in Dhutpapeshwar Teertha, rediscovered by him during *parikrama*

Vivek ji in *Mai ki Bagiya* in Amrkantak

After completing his Narmada *parikrama,* Vivek ji entering the Sri Jod Ganpati Hanuman Temple at Omkareshwar

Mahant Mangal Das Tyagi and Vivek ji met in Omkareshwar on Vivekji's return from the 3,000 kilometer Narmada *parikrama*

After finishing his Narmada *parikrama,* Vivek ji returned to Omkareshwar and bowing, offering *pranam* to the holy *kalash* of Narmada.

Mahant Mangal Das Tyagi and Vivek ji met in Omkareshwar on Vivekji's return from the 3,000 kilometer Narmada *parikrama*

Mahant Mangal Das Tyagi and Vivek ji met in Omkareshwar on Vivekji's return from the 3,000 kilometer Narmada *parikrama*

Vivek ji, along with Dr Mohan Yadav, who is now the Chief Minister of Madhya Pradesh, and others, are heading towards the Omkareshwar temple to offer the sacred water of Narmada *Parikrama.*

Vivek ji, Mahant Mangal Das Tyagi, along with Dr Mohan Yadav, the Chief Minister of Madhya Pradesh, and others, are heading towards the Omkareshwar temple to offer the sacred water of Narmada *Parikrama.*

At Brahmpuri *Ghat* in Omkareshwar, Vivek ji performing the *acamana* from the sacred Narmada River after completing his *parikrama*

Vivek ji in the celebration that happened when he returned from *parikrama* and it was Holi festival.

After a long period, someone like Vivek ji had returned from his *Pada Parikrama* of the Holy Narmada on the auspicious day of Holi. Vivek ji had made a request to Mother Narmada during the early days of *parikrama*. He wished to complete his *parikrama* on the day of Holi, and his request was granted. The grand holy celebration in Omkareshwar was a momentous occasion.

Vivek ji with Maa of Koteshwar Teerha

Vivek ji with Mahant of Koyna Sitaram Das Maharaj

Vivek ji with the Mahant Seetasharan of Shakreshwar teertha

Vivek ji speaking to audience in Brahmpuri ghat after completion of his Narmada *parikrama*

The fleet of Vehicles that accompanied Vivek ji in his *parikrama*

The fleet of vehicles that supported the entire *parikrama* and volunteers who helped in doing various other works while Vivek ji walked in Narmada *parikrama*

Vivek ji trekking a mountain
in Shulpani region

Vivek ji trekking a mountain
in Shulpani region

Vivek ji in Shulpani area

Vivek ji with young child who walked with him fewkilometers in Shulpani region

Vivek ji offering the notebooks, etc. to a poor child

Vivek ji offering the saree to a woman who didn't have much means

The group of Amrutasya Maa Narmada Pada-Parikrama

Vivek ji and others walking in Narmada *parikrama*

Vivek ji taking rest
during Narmada *parikrama*

Vivek ji and others walking in Narmada *parikrama*

Vivek ji walking with others in Narmada *parikrama*

Vivek ji walking with others in Narmada *parikrama*, crossing farmland and mother Narmada just beside

Vivek ji speaking with Women during his *parikrama*

Vivek ji walking with others in Narmada *parikrama* and devotees meet him on the way

Vivek ji walking with others in Narmada *parikrama*

Vivek ji walking with others in Narmada *parikrama*

Vivek ji in Shulpani region with Vijay Chaudhury and others

Vivek ji in the 120th day of his parikrama, returning to Omkareshwar after travelling on foot 3000 kms

Vivek ji speaking with Saints from Omkareshwar

Vivek ji speaking with school children during his *parikrama* in Gujarat

Vivek ji discussing with villagers many issues such as toilets on the *parikrama* path

Vivek ji doing aarti of Holy Narmada in Omkareshwar with
Mahant Mangaldas Tyagi, Usha Thakur the former Minister of Culture, MP

Vivek ji in Gaurishankar Maharaj *Samadhi*, bowing to the towering figure of Narmada *Khanda*

Vivek ji in Amrkantak

Vivek ji with Ajay Vijayvargiya, Praveen Chauhan members of Amrutasya Maa Narmada *Pada Parikrama* steering body

Vivek ji with a farmer who requested him to spend some time in his farm

Vivek ji with multitudes of people who came to see him while in *Parikrama*

Vivek ji with Dr Mohan Yadav, now the chief minister of Madhya Pradesh,
Dr Sumer Singh Solanki, M.P. Rajya Sabha and others,
who came to see him during his *parikrama*

Vivek ji walking with others in Narmada *parikrama*

Vivek ji in the *Samadhi* of Baji Rao Peshwa

Vivek ji crossing the makeshift bridge

Vivek ji with kids from Shulpani region

Vivek ji with kids from Shulpani region

Vivek ji with local MP of Badwani, Gajendra Singh

Vivek ji facilitating woman on her contribution for Holy Narmada

Vivek ji and other in Amarkantak the place where holy Narmada emerged

Vivek ji Amarkantak,
Holy Narmada *Kunda*

40

Giving Us Their Love

Our journey began from the Gurukula, and today we ventured towards the hilly track, reminiscent of Shulpani. As we trekked, we caught a glimpse of the towering peaks that we had likely crossed while on the southern bank. On this particular day, we encountered numerous individuals who were persistently attempting to bestow gifts upon us. During a moment of repose, a gentleman passed by. With lightning speed, he darted past me before turning around and doing it again. I could not help but wonder what he was up to. Moments later, he returned, holding a pack of biscuits. When I politely declined, suggesting he save it for others since we were well-stocked, he insisted that it was a gift just for me. Gratefully, I accepted his kind gesture and took a few of the biscuits. In return, I offered him some fresh fruit, and we shared a moment of camaraderie over our mutual generosity. He implored us to venture forth in search of a more suitable location to rest. After a brief sojourn, we comprehended the wisdom behind his request. In the heart of the village stood an old man, proprietor of a humble grocery store. His dialect bore the unmistakable cadence of Uttar Pradesh, and it was he who tended to the needs of every *parikramavasi*s. As I conversed with him, he humbly requested my blessings so that he may embark on a sacred pilgrimage to Narmada.

We were walking from a bit far from the Narmada banks but if we had walked from the ancient route we had encountered the great temple which is now submerged in Narmada's risen water from the Sardar Sarovar Dam which was known as Hapeshwar Teerth.[1] Now, a temple honouring Hapeshwar stands a little distance above the floodplain of the Narmada River, but before you visit, you should hear the area's fascinating backstory from me. After Indra killed Vritrasura and did *tapasya* to atone for his guilt, Lord Brahma split the sin into four pieces, with one going to the element of water (Varuna). This caused God Varuna much sorrow, so he came to this site to perform *tapasya* in order to be cleansed of his sin. He established this *tirtha* at this time on Lord Shiva's divine command. The history of the Hapeshwar Teerth predates our recollection of the Pandavas by a long shot, and the tales of those long-ago days have all but been lost. My experience in the Narmada belt has shown me that whenever the locals want to make something historical, they would inevitably bring up the name of the Pandavas, seemingly unaware that the time of the Pandavas is not that distant from us, but the Sanatana story that the region has preserved dates back thousands of years. Interestingly, the Pandavas' visit to the Narmada bank was inspired by the stories they had heard from Markandeya Muni.

As night fell, we sought refuge in a humble schoolhouse. The following morning, we were greeted by two young children who kindly offered to guide us along a more direct route. As the day progressed, we traversed through Gujarat and eventually arrived in Madhya Pradesh. As we journeyed towards Sondhwa, the majestic Shulpani hills came into view intermittently. That evening, we found ourselves lodged beside a school in Sondhwa, adjacent to a towering schools that has a special place in chief minister's list and funded by him, the school was really well maintained.

Tikkad is a thick *chapatti* that is made by hand, and from this point my love for the *tikkad* started to blossom. Girish proposed the idea of having *tikkad* for a week. He was only looking to have a good time, and he was aware that some (or even most) *parikramavasi*s disliked *tikkad*.

41

Panditji of Pura

When Jitendra Sharma and his companions arrived to make preparations ahead of the *parikrama*, they found themselves in the presence of a man whom they respectfully addressed as Panditji. In the realm of fleeting connections, there was a singular occasion when our voices intertwined through the ethereal wires of communication. It was a mere moment, a solitary encounter, yet it left an indelible mark upon my memory. For, on the other end of that telephone line resided a man of profound cultivation, a being whose very essence exuded an aura of fascination. Though our conversation was brief, it was enough to glean a glimpse into the depths of his captivating personality. His enthusiasm radiated from him, tangible and infectious. It was as if he had been eagerly awaiting our arrival, counting down the days until this momentous occasion. The *parikrama* (a sacred journey) seemed to have been etched into his very being, a pilgrimage he had longed for with every fibre of his being. In the crisp and wintry month of December, our weary journey led us to the very environs that he called home.

We encountered Panditji of Pura as we embarked on our journey from Sondhwa to Dahi, and since that day he has been keeping a watchful eye on the paths we tread.

Dahi, a quaint town nestled in the *janya jati*s belt, exudes a bustling energy that centres around its vibrant marketplace. The town's atmosphere is imbued with the essence of Nimar, and its inhabitants are renowned for their warm hospitality. Upon arrival, a grand welcome awaited, further testament to the town's gracious spirit. Our journey through the city was a lengthy one, with throngs of people lining the streets to greet us upon our arrival. That evening marked my inaugural discussion on the topics of agriculture and Indian spirituality. The significance of the farming community and their produce in the context of the Sanatana Dharma has been widely acknowledged and deeply contemplated upon by the masses. As we journeyed through the city, we encountered the customary *bhandara*, which was a familiar sight. However, the morning brought with it a sense of intrigue as we found ourselves delayed by the eager locals who wished to greet us and offer their respects. This unexpected delay added to the enigma of our travels.

Upon departing from Dahi, we were guided by the Panditji to our next destination, which happened to be the abode of the Kuladevi of the brahmana community. We were walking little bit further up as this time in December the water of holy Narmada had still submerged many *tirtha*s due to Sardar Sarovar Dam which I visited in my car trip soon after my return from foot *parikrama*.

We could have reached the opposite of Meghnath Teerth on the southern banks if we had continued travelling before the *tirtha*s were flooded and made our way to Dharmarai, where the Pandavas had performed their *yagya*.[1] Located on the northern banks, this spot is also known as Meghnath Teerth and is a great spot to spend a few days. If we had made it to Koteshwar Kundeshwar Teerth, we would have learned that Kundhar, the son of Vishrava, also known as Kubera, was a very intelligent and powerful individual. In order to gain Lord Shiva's favour, he performed extensive *tapasya* and, once given blessings, had established this *tirtha*.[2]

Upon arriving at Banvariya, the place where we were lodged for the night and where both Brahmans and Rajpurs have their Kuldevi's, it was evident that careful consideration had been given to our accommodations. However, on this particular day, my thoughts turned to the concept of Indian unity. During my evening discourse, I conveyed the notion that a Kuladevi or Kuladevata, venerated by a particular group, could be held in equal reverence by another group, without any differentiation between the two. The discourse I presented on the unification of Indian Sanatana Dharma was received with great admiration, signifying the initial instance in which I approached this subject matter.

The following day, we embarked on a journey towards Pura, the birthplace of Panditji. Although it was a slight deviation from our intended route, I felt compelled to honour Panditji's emotional attachment. His sentiments held great significance to me.

42

Purity of Pura

As the sun rose on the horizon, our group was keenly aware that our journey would be a short one, covering a mere 15 km with the ultimate destination of Pura in our sights. Contrary to our initial assumptions, the day seemed to drag on as Panditji had meticulously planned multiple halts en route, where enthusiastic individuals eagerly anticipated our arrival, eager to make our interaction. This marks the commencement of a journey that will unveil numerous *tirtha*s, etching a new chapter in the history of the region. As we embark on this *parikrama*, the land of Nimar will embark on a journey of introspection, delving deeper into the Narmada Parikrama and its associated *tirtha*s.

As we bid farewell to Banvariya, our expedition took us through a series of recognizable villages. Yet, there was a certain village (Pipaliya) that left a deep impression on me. Nestled within this idyllic countryside lay a quaint village, inhabited by the esteemed Patidar community. Revered for their pioneering agricultural methods and their exceptional aptitude for preserving communal harmony, this group of individuals has inherited a legacy of social cohesion that spans across generations.

The Patidar community thrives in the expansive nomadic region, where their culture is renowned for its remarkable vitality. Upon my arrival at Pipaliya, a charming village enclosed in the idyllic countryside, I was cordially welcomed by Patidars, a native inhabitant. They informed me with an uplifting tale of how the village had united to safeguard its well-being and protection. A resolute cohort of youthful individuals had assumed the responsibility of safeguarding their community, while the remaining inhabitants of the hamlet banded together to furnish assistance to both the group and their kin. An organization had been established, officially recognized and widely known. Its impressive chain of command was a spectacle to behold. The display of unity and cooperation was truly heartwarming and left a lasting impression on me.

Once upon a time, the village provided a humble ration of two *chapattis* and vegetables to the *parikramavasis*. A new arrangement has arisen, though, in which groups of women take turns going to the *parikramavasi*s resting place to cook them a more substantial dinner. The group functions in a self-sufficient manner.

Upon further investigation, it was revealed that they possess a unique internal lending system for the welfare of the community. This system allows members to provide financial support to one another without any interest being charged on the borrowed amount. By engaging in this practice, they are able to attend to one another's financial requirements.

As our journey led us closer to the village, a vibrant sense of eagerness enveloped us. As we arrived, the entire community had assembled to greet us, their palpable enthusiasm filling the air. The village was a spectacle to behold. Every temple had been adorned with intricate decorations, a testament to the unwavering dedication of the Patidar community. The temples were maintained in all their splendour, with no expense spared, thanks to the generosity of those who supported them.

Upon that fateful day, I solemnly pledged to embark upon the sacred and time-honoured journey of *parikrama*, renouncing the modern invention of Mandu. The focus of my pilgrimage was of utmost importance, as I sought to centre myself upon the ancient *tirtha*s that grace the banks of the Narmada. I was not interested in indulging in fanciful tales that lacked any foundation.

The chronicle of Mandu and Baz Bahadur is a contemporary account that lacks any empirical foundation. Through my research, I have come to learn that the inception of this can be attributed to Christian missionaries. Throughout the course of the last fifty years, this departure from authenticity has gained significant traction in society. In the 1970s, *parikramavasi*s were few and far between at this location. Moreover, the Shastra's dictate against venturing too far from the Narmada River's banks for an extended duration.

Two individuals and a publication played a significant role in the development of this story. The first was a publication authored by Major William Sterling, while the second was written by agent W. Kinkaid. Major William Sterling was deeply invested in his Christian faith and devoted much of his attention to exploring the origins of his religion. His quest led him to search for the homeland of Abraham, whom he believed to have been born in the vicinity of the Narmada River. Major William regarded the vast expanse of holy Narmada and her surrounding regions as integral components of the biblical narrative. He was convinced that Maheshwar was the same as Mesh, a name referenced in the book of Genesis in the Old Testament. Major William Sterling was thoroughly convinced that the Narmada River in question was none other than the Pison mentioned in the Bible.[1]

He was fully engrossed in proving that a significant portion of the Indian population had ties to the Christian community, and he was willing to go to great lengths to do so. He meticulously examined every aspect of the situation, including the prevalence of cattle rearing in the Nimar region since ancient times. He was struck by the notion that this was the very place where Abraham, as mentioned in the Old Testament, had once tended to his own herds.[2]

To him, the entire Narmada region holds a significance akin to the places mentioned in the Bible. In my belief, the individual responsible for originating the theory of Mandu and Reva-Kunda is none other than him. However, the complete narrative was not disclosed by him. Baz Bahadur may have abducted or somehow coerced the daughter of the Patels of Dharmpuri into falling in love with him. Major William Stirling and his story had a profound influence on the Narmada Parikrama. As a result of this narrative, many individuals nowadays refrain from visiting the ancient *tirtha*s situated along the Narmada's banks, instead choosing to sustain baseless legends. Regrettably, such is the state of affairs in India, where a spurious narrative was introduced and gradually gained traction, ultimately leading to widespread acceptance.[3]

Curiously, Major General John Welcom, compiler of the memoirs of India, makes no mention of Reva-Kunda or any similar subject. In his literary works, he solely highlights the imprudent actions of Baz Bahadur. As per his account, Rupamati hailed from Saharanpur and was known for her dancing skills. The origin of Rupamati remains a topic of contention, and I defer to the expertise of historians on this matter. However, it is evident to me that the story has been fabricated, and since the 1970s, numerous individuals have begun to embrace this fiction as an integral aspect of the tale.[4]

It is my belief that if Rupamati were a true devotee of Mother Narmada, she would not have taken on the position of mistress to Baz Bahadur. On the other hand, had she assumed such a role, it would have been improbable for her to sustain her allegiance to Mother Narmada.

It is noteworthy to mention that historical accounts consistently portray Lord Rama embarking on a journey to the banks of the Narmada, as opposed to the river itself making its way towards him. Why would Mother Narmada, who did not follow Lord Rama to Ayodhya, suddenly decide to follow Rupamati and Mandu instead? As I readied myself to articulate my contemplations during the *parikrama*, an impediment presented itself in the figure of Mangal Das Tyagi Maharaj. His advice was to complete the *parikrama* prior to engaging in any other activities or discussing it further.

43

Dev Path Linga

Right from the beginning, I made it evident that my *parikrama* was not a mere customary pilgrimage. It was not just any journey, but a sacred pilgrimage with a noble purpose – to restore the *tirtha*s that grace the revered banks of Mother Narmada. With a steadfast conviction, I held the belief that it was a noble intention that led me to the right path along the river's banks. Despite the numerous individuals who urged me to venture towards Mandu, I remained steadfast in my resolve to stay the course, for to do otherwise would have compromised the very essence of my undertaking. I am convinced that it was the benevolent grace of Mother Narmada that guided me to remain steadfast in my pursuit.

The day began in Pura after a wonderful city-wide celebration. I tried my best to visit every household, but unfortunately, there were a few that I could not make it to. I expressed my sincere apologies and assured them that I would make things right during my next visit. I had the pleasure of encountering a group of individuals during my journey to Karoli who were in the process of constructing a *dharmashala*. I was requested to perform the *bhumi-pujana*, a traditional ceremony, which I agreed to with some hesitation. I was invited by a group of doctors to visit their residences, and I happily accepted their invitation. I wanted to express my gratitude for their valuable services that were essential to the well-being of the entire community. As we embarked on this particular route to visit significant *tirtha*s, we made the conscious decision to quicken our pace in order to arrive at our destinations with haste.

Our next destination was Dev Path Linga Teerth,[1] a sacred site renowned for its spiritual significance. However, we were informed that our intended visit to Panchakunda Teerth had to be postponed as it was still submerged in water. After completing a sacred circumambulation on foot, I embarked on a journey to seek *darshana* at the revered *tirtha*. The revered Chikhaldha Teerth, formerly known as Panchakunda Teerth,[2] derives its name from the presence of five distinct pools within the river. These pools were meticulously crafted by ancient sages, including the esteemed *saptarshi*s, who sought solace and enlightenment through their rigorous penance. Rather than immersing themselves directly in the sacred waters of the mighty Narmada River, these wise souls chose to purify themselves by bathing in the pristine waters of these *kunda*s. In this enchanting realm, one can find the divine presence of Nilkantheshwar Mahadev, the majestic Harihareshwar Mahadev, and the fiery Agnishwar Mahadev. In this sacred abode, Agnideva, the divine deity of fire, has perpetually dwelled. It was here that the venerable *rishi*, with utmost devotion, sought to appease Agnideva through profound prayers, assuming the resplendent form of Brahma Svarupa. In a time long ago, Agnideva, the divine deity of fire, bestowed his blessings upon this sacred place. It was here, amidst the tranquil surroundings, that the revered *rishi*s and *saptarshi*s came together and established the divine presence of Agnishwar Mahadev.

In my ongoing quest, I find myself in pursuit of an elusive palace known as Devmay Teerth.[3] This sacred abode holds great significance, for it was the very place where the divine gods convened before embarking on their sacred pilgrimage along the revered Narmada River. Alas, the precise whereabouts of this hallowed site remain shrouded in mystery, evading my diligent efforts thus far.

However, my desire to reach the very spot where the divine gods had commenced their sacred *parikrama* was evident. Before my arrival, numerous teams had been dispatched to scout the temple. Vaibhav Yadav, who had been on the *parikrama* with us for a couple of days, had just arrived here the day before to reassure us that we could indeed make it to the temple. Astonishingly, the locals remained oblivious to the profound significance that this sacred place held. However, it was only upon my arrival that the true essence of the temple began to unfold.

It was imperative that we reach these sites as soon as possible, as some of them required traversing through muddy and watery terrain that had been affected by the Sardar Sarovar Dam's water. Our destination Dev Path Linga, was partially engulfed by water. The temple was only accessible by wading through water that reached up to our waists. The temple stood before me, a magnificent sight to behold. Its ancientness was palpable, evident in the remnants of past generations that surrounded it. Before us stood the Shivalinga, its towering enormity inspiring a sense of awe. On this momentous day, one that would undoubtedly leave an indelible mark, I found myself recounting the captivating tale of the Indian Sanatana Shastra and delving into the rich history of the temple. From this very spot, the divine deities had commenced their *parikrama*. We remained there for what felt like an interminable amount of time, and my thoughts drifted to an era when the divine beings had concluded their *parikrama* and enshrined the resplendent Shivalinga.

As the mighty Sardar Sarovar Dam inundated the surrounding landscape, the memory of the once-vibrant temples gradually receded into obscurity. Occasionally, the local department of archaeology would relocate the ancient walls by simply removing them from their original location and transporting them elsewhere. In their endeavour, they appropriated the architecture, yet failed to preserve the very essence that had given rise to it – the Shivalinga, nestled deep within the waters.

As time passed, the narrative and truthfulness surrounding these temples slowly disappeared from recollection. Indian firmly believes that the historical significance of a location is what bestows upon it the revered title of *tirtha-sthana*, which translates to "the place that had the *tirtha*s". I too hold the belief that temples ought to be preserved in their natural state. The gradual decrease in water levels every month presents an opportunity for the locals to undertake maintenance activities. The stone temples have endured the test of time, standing tall for centuries and remaining unscathed to this very day. Several idols have been displaced from their original locations when the dam was being constructed and the water started to rise but then within the confines of this sacred temple, the unwavering denizens have ardently opposed any endeavours to relocate it, resolutely convinced that it rightfully occupies its designated location.

Prior to embarking on my journey, I meticulously perused numerous literary works that made reference to the illustrious temple. The accounts vividly depicted an era of unparalleled grandeur, a time that I yearned to witness first hand. And now, I found myself in the presence of the Shivalinga, a sacred symbol established by the gods themselves, seated beside the gentle current of Mother Narmada. As I learned of the numerous artefacts that had been acquired by the esteemed archaeology department, I could not help but contemplate their true purpose, extending far beyond mere exhibition within the walls of a museum.

Articulating the notion that Indian cultures are not confined to museums, but rather exist within the collective memory of society and the hearts of devotees, proves to be a challenging task for me.

As we ventured forth from the sacred grounds of Dev Path Linga, our path was leading us to the enchanting Bagad Sangam. However, upon our arrival, we were met with a formidable obstacle – the waters of Bagad were swollen and impassable on foot. Thus, we were compelled to seek an alternative route, traversing the river from a higher vantage point. In this captivating location, situated among the celestial Ganglade Ghat, lies a sacred site of profound significance. It is here that the revered Nandi, the divine vehicle of Lord Shiva, graced this hallowed ground with his presence, engaging in deep penance and thereby establishing this sacred *tirtha*.

We continued on, but this time we hit a snag: Bageshwar Teerth[4] was inaccessible because the dam farther upstream has caused the Narmada River to flood. Sanatana legend has it, however, that this is where Suryavanshi Maharaja Brahmadutt performed the largest *yagya* ever recorded, donating an enormous sum of money in the process. The Bagu and Narmada rivers come together at this point.

44

The Soldiers

On this particular day, I encountered Suraj, a man who appeared to be in his thirties and had long been a fervent advocate for the preservation of Mother Narmada. Despite his unwavering dedication to the cause, he had unfortunately found himself without any significant opportunities to contribute. Numerous young individuals and others have dedicated themselves to the noble cause of Mother Narmada. However, they have been neglected and their potential remains untapped. As a result, the Narmada riverbank is bereft of their valuable contributions. Suraj, who had often accompanied us on our walks, joined us for the initial leg of our journey, which was set to last for a duration of seven days.

During an extensive conversation with Suraj, I expounded upon the significance of the Narmada Parikrama and the precarious state of its divine *tirtha*s. Regrettably, many individuals remain uninformed of this critical matter. Furthermore, there appears to be a gradual shift in the focus of the *parikrama*, which is leading people astray from its true purpose. As I conversed with my fellow devotees, a concern arose regarding the continuation of the *parikrama* in its current form. The services provided in various locations for the *parikramavasi*s may not yield the same merit as before. In the past, pilgrims would be nourished as they journeyed to visit divine sites, becoming reinvigorated with the divine light that permeated the area. They themselves would become a beacon of light, carrying it with them to both the banks of the river. As a result, people would offer them sustenance and worship them as if they were lords. Should this fail to come to fruition, it shall be akin to any other march devoid of significance and the benefits it may yield.

As I comprehended Suraj's understanding, my mind conjured up the potential of creating an extensive community of individuals like him. It is imperative that we guide them along the same path that Suraj had once taken, so that their deep reverence for Mother Narmada may flow effortlessly in its intended direction.

45

Karoli to Bakaner

The day in question shall forever be etched in the annals of our *parikrama* as a momentous occasion, one that symbolized the very essence of our pilgrimage – the discovery of the *tirtha*s. I would be willing to traverse an additional 15-18 km in order to discover the *tirtha*s, despite the availability of a shorter path leading to the designated destination. The pursuit of this objective would serve as an instructive experience for my fellow *parikramavasi*s, as it would demonstrate my unshakable dedication to its achievement.

The day prior, as we arrived in Karoli, a magnificent reception awaited us, greeting us with warmth and grandeur. The villagers had been eagerly anticipating our arrival for several days, eagerly awaiting our passage through their quaint village.

The plan of *parikrama* was crafted with great care and attention to detail, considering the prevailing sentiments and historical contexts. The process was carried out meticulously. The planning of the journey to Mandu followed the customary approach of *parikramavasi*s, including the revered saints of contemporary society. Decisions over whether to travel to Mandu or investigate the sacred Narmada riverbank occupied my thoughts. Whilst residing in Pura, I received a clear message from Mother Narmada, discouraging us from proceeding with our planned itinerary, which entailed disregarding Mandu from our travels.

Amidst the meandering river of Narmada, lie numerous ancient *tirtha*s that have stood the test of time. Regrettably, a considerable number of individuals fail to acknowledge the profound importance of these *tirtha*s. Instead, they opt to gravitate towards a spurious narrative of Mandu that lacks any foundation, yet manages to lure the *parikramavasi*s in that direction.

In a bygone era, the path that led to Mandu was seldom traversed. Pilgrims embarking on the sacred *parikrama* pilgrimage would prefer to journey along the path of the revered Narmada River. During the mid-nineteenth century, a curious rumour emerged, allegedly disseminated by a Christian missionary. As time passed, the rumour began to spread and soon enough, people who were travelling along *parikrama* path started to make their way towards Mandu. In a bygone era, the influx of *parikramavasi*s to Mandu was rather restricted. Over the course of the last two to three decades, there has been a noteworthy surge in their ranks. As they diverge from the well-trodden path, they leave behind a trail of sacred *tirtha*s. These holy sites now lie unattended, occupied by other religious forces who do not share the same reverence for Sanatana Dharma. The current state of the temples serves as a powerful testament to the fact that a single falsehood can uproot an entire narrative of history. As a nation, India must remain vigilant in safeguarding the integrity of Sanatana Dharma. To ensure authenticity, it is crucial to carefully examine any claims made about it.

Once more, we embarked from Karoli on a pilgrimage towards the sacred shores of Mother Narmada. The road less taken, for the majority of travellers tends to head towards Bakaner, a mere 18-km distant. Our pursuit of the sacred *tirtha*s had brought us to Semalda, where we set out on a mission to locate the enigmatic Diptikeshwar Teerth.[1] Despite the unfamiliarity of the location to the locals, I ultimately unearthed the sacred sanctuary nestled alongside the Narmada River. Atop the hill, the archaeology department has relocated the ancient walls. Regrettably, the original Shivalinga and other remnants within the temple have been left to fade into obscurity.

As per the annals of Sanatana history, this hallowed terrain served as the very site where the divine trinity of Brahma, Vishnu and Mahesh descended to alleviate the apprehensions of the celestial deities at the onset of their *parikrama*. Throughout the centuries, the location has been graced with the name Diptikeshwar Teerth , a designation that has endured the trials of time.

Upon our arrival at the designated location, the vestiges of the once-splendid temple grounds came into view, beckoning us forward. Regrettably, the walls of the temple had already been dismantled by the archaeology department, leaving behind only a handful of remnants in a state of disrepair. The remnants of the ancient temple had been ingeniously transformed into functional pump houses by the resourceful farmers. As I delved deeper into the space, my gaze fell upon the time-worn effigies of Lord Ganesha and Chamunda Devi, steeped in antiquity. Furthermore, amidst the array of idols, there was a particularly ancient-looking Shivalinga. As I stood in the temple, my eyes were drawn to the various idols present, including the revered Vishnu. However, my thoughts were consumed by the ancient Shivalinga. Suddenly, a man emerged from the nearby Narmada River, having just completed his bath. He informed us that the Shivalinga now lay submerged in the water due to the construction of the Sardar Sarovar Dam. It was a poignant reminder that had the temple not been relocated to a higher position, we may have still been able to witness the divine presence of the Shivalinga today. As the archaeology department meticulously removed the walls of the temple, they inadvertently caused the destruction of the mound that had previously cradled the ancient structure.

The Narmada region has witnessed the submergence of several temples and cities that extend over a distance of several hundred kilometres. The individual who revealed the original Shivalinga's location declined my initial offer of 100 rupee note. I humbly requested that he consider accepting my proposal and kindly acquire a coconut for me during his upcoming trip when he plans to take a bath in the sacred waters of Mother Narmada and offer on my behalf.

The temple remains stood tall and regal, situated by the tranquil banks. Its walls were embellished with exquisite depictions of the revered deities Ganapati and Chamunda Devi. Furthermore, the premises were adorned with a venerable *lingam* that had been mentioned in the Shastras. Standing by the tranquil waters of the Narmada, my gaze is irresistibly drawn to the rich and enduring history of this great nation. The landscape bears witness to the passage of time, its features weathered and worn. However, the tales of yesteryear endure, etched into the very fabric of this hallowed ground.

I respectfully pleaded with people gathered to accept responsibility for the act of whitewashing the temple's ruins as I left the area in a gloomy tone. The state of our Sanatana Dharma's history left me incredulous, as it appeared to be in a state of disrepair without any apparent concern from anyone.

Our quest to search for *tirtha*s led us to the Vishnu Teerth,[2] a place that had long been forgotten. Our search began, but we soon discovered that the once-familiar landscapes and backwaters of the dams had undergone significant changes. Everything, including the local scenery, had been transformed. The once-beautiful banks of Mother Narmada are now adorned with thorny bushes, instead of lush trees. My companions were well aware that I possessed an unwavering determination to locate the temple. Our journey involved traversing numerous small hills, navigating through murky backwaters, and overcoming various obstacles. Despite the challenges, we finally arrived at our destination, a place that exuded an aura of ancient beauty. Perched atop a hillock, the temple resonated with the rich history of the land. It was here that Lord Brahma had undertaken his *tapasya*, and where demons had attempted to disrupt his meditation and *yagya*. In his time of need, Lord Brahma had called upon Lord Vishnu, since he himself serving as a priest in a *yagya* and was unable to engage in battle. Lord Vishnu had answered the call and come to Lord Brahma's aid and destroyed the demons.

Within the temple grounds, I chanced upon a magnificent Shivalinga which was outside the temple. Though diminutive in size, its *jaladhari* was of impressive proportions, measuring nearly 10 ft in length. It appeared to have been left outside, perhaps once serving as a site of veneration for numerous ancient *rishi*s. There were people everywhere along the Narmada River who did not have the demeanour of a saint but had made a name for themselves among the temple communities nonetheless. The individual here in also wore a saffron robe but was anything but holy; he avoided meeting my gaze since he knew I may expose his actual nature if we conversed.

As I lingered in the vicinity, my thoughts were consumed with the fate of these ancient sites. I pondered what would become of them if they failed to reclaim their rightful place in our collective consciousness. With a heavy heart, I departed, haunted by the uncertainty of their future.

The vestiges of a rich historical past are retained by this temple, and I shall elaborate upon them in due course. Legend has it that the Kankariya River was created by a horde of demons who relentlessly hurled countless stones, resulting in the formation of this majestic waterway. As we drew near the river, a remarkable sight greeted us: a collection of stones, seemingly placed with a purpose, appeared before our very eyes. The remarkable aspect of the landscape bordering the river is that it conceals the existence of these comet-shaped heaps of rocks, which are only discernible when one is in close proximity to the river. Again I was watching the historical texts of Sanatana Dharma proving their points. Once more, I found myself engrossed in the historical texts of Sanatana Dharma, as they eloquently substantiated their arguments.

It was lunch time and as we were munching on our lunch, suddenly a slithery *baba* made an appearance. Now, in these parts, *baba* is not just a saintly title but also the name for a snake. One of the locals informed our *parikramavasi*s that *baba* had just left the premises. But, one of our team members quickly retorted, "No worries, all our *baba*s are still here!" The local guy looked confused and clarified, "I meant the *baba* that is a snake, not the saintly *baba*s. Keep your eyes open, folks!"

Bardha, a land imbued with age-old tales, was the next destination of our journey. Formerly referred to as Varah Nagar, this was the very place where Lord Vishnu, in his divine manifestation as Lord Varaha, had revealed himself. Although the temple remained hidden from our view, we persisted with unwavering determination until we finally uncovered its elusive location. As I explored the temple, I found myself captivated by the ancient remnants of Sanatana Dharma's historical narratives. It was a truly fascinating experience. It was here, according to Sanatana story, that during the Varaha Kalpa there was a demon named Jatasura who had done intense *tapasya* and got the blessings of Lord Shiva to be invincible. This is when he was drunk with proud, and after defeating the divine bodies was taken the Vedas to other world. Lord Vishnu took the form of Varaha and brought back the Vedas and destroyed the demons. After returning he had established Varaheshwar Mahadeva.[3]

As we embarked on our quest to discover the ancient *tirtha*s, we found ourselves taking numerous detours. Consequently, we found ourselves at a considerable distance from our intended destination of Bakaner, with the evening fast-approaching. As the sun began its descent, we prepared to embark on a journey of unprecedented proportions. After traversing a distance of approximately 26 km, we found ourselves in a difficulty. Our search for the *tirtha*s had been arduous, and the lack of a clear path had significantly slowed our progress. As the dusk was quite near, we found ourselves still a good 10 km away from our intended destination for the night – Bakaner.

We were joined on our trek by some folks from nearby Bakaner, but my confidence in their ability to complete the mammoth task at hand began to dwindle quickly. I urged Kumar to sing for me, signalling to everyone around that I was about to break into a speedy stride to make it to *arti* and *puja* on time. The travellers from Bakaner were so drained and drenched in perspiration that they vanished into thin air.

We arrived at Bakaner well past nightfall, the town's reception was magnificent. I had the opportunity to expound at length on the local *tirtha*s, and my words were met with great enthusiasm.

46

I Am Unknown

Today marked the beginning of our journey, as we embarked upon the path of the ancient *parikrama* – a route that has been largely neglected in favour of the fabricated tales of Mandu.

Our first stop was Shukleshwar Saur Teerth; according to Sanatana story, there was a *rishi* named Kusha who stayed here for long time and prayed to Lord Surya. Surya was pleased and asked for the boon that he wishes – *rishi* asked that he should always stay here and remove the sorrow of the people here who may come down to him. And this is what happened. Now here there is a beautiful temple and it seems that it has been well taken care of.[1]

Our next destination was Daruk Teerth,[2] as we arrived at Daruk Teerth, the aura of the place immediately transported us back in time to the era of Rishi Daruk's intense *tapasya*. The villagers remained unaware of the significance of their dwelling and the tale that bestowed the name upon their ancestral abode. It was quite intriguing to come across a man who was believed to be the most knowledgeable person in the village. These sorts of persons could be spotted frequently on the sacred banks. However, I felt compelled to remind him that he ought to revisit his lessons in history. It was quite intriguing to note that certain villagers, who had grown utterly weary of this man's demeanour, expressed great satisfaction with my presence.

Having journeyed through the revered Daruk Teerth, we arrived at Dharmapuri and sought lodging at the esteemed Bihari Das Maharaj Ashram. Our path crossed with that of a fascinating gentleman whose remarkable gift of gab and cleverness were quite impressive. Mahraj-ji seemed to be in a state of deep contemplation, perhaps pondering over the mysteries of the universe or deciding what toppings to get on his plate. Maharaj-ji's perspective on a certain *swami* who finished his *parikrama* last year was simply spellbinding. Bihari Das Maharaj played the role of a generous host to many hungry souls, but unfortunately, his kindness was met with a cold shoulder after the *swamiji* had completed his *parikrama*. Bihari Das Maharaj must have felt like a forgotten side dish at a fancy *bhandara*.

The experience left a profound impression on him. As he recounted the harrowing tale, his emotions surged to the surface, threatening to engulf him. I sensed an urgent need to intervene and extend a comforting presence. His efforts were evident, yet they remained unacknowledged.

As you journey along the *parikrama* path, it is fascinating to witness the diverse array of individuals who express their desire to attain the revered status of *guru*. Nevertheless, it is a frequent occurrence for such individuals to deviate from their intended path and unintentionally cause harm to themselves.

I have heard that, a gentleman is presently undertaking the sacred practice of *parikrama*, all the while dispensing Shivalingas to the nearby community, urging them to venerate these holy Shivalingas. It is impossible not to feel a certain uneasiness towards individuals like him. They seem to show little regard for the consequences of their actions, instead focusing on securing their own status within the community. During our recent encounter, I could not help but notice that the gentleman I crossed paths with seemed to be intentionally avoiding making direct eye contact with me.

As the sun began its descent, word was brought to my attention of the arrival of a holy persons. I was happy to welcome the holy men all along the *parikrama* path during *arti* and *bhandara*. But Yogesh informed me that the individual in question was none other than this man fraudulent individual, I notified Yogesh telling him to take away the *asana* designated for this man at the *arti*, and he complied. My words were firm and steadfast, conveying a sense of conviction and leaving little to no space for doubt or indecision. I deliberately chose to create some distance between myself and an individual whose moral fibre was tainted with a pervasive tendency towards deceit and dishonesty.

The man was experiencing a peculiar phenomenon. He was so consumed by fear that he adamantly refused to leave his chamber, even for meal.

Today witnessed yet another successful *bhandara* being organized. Bihari Das Maharaj promptly conveyed his gratitude, acknowledging my steadfast commitment to the *parikrama*. With a steadfast determination, my goal is to restore the once-impeccable standing of the *parikrama*, which suffered a significant setback a year ago when certain *swamiji* was on *parikrama*.

47

Dadhichi

This morning, we embarked on a journey with Bihari Das Maharaj towards the banks of Mother Narmada. It is the very place where Rishi Dadhichi had performed his greatest *tapasya* and selflessly offered his bones for the cause of divine work. The tale of Dadhichi has been recounted on numerous occasions, yet it is only through the *Skanda Purana* that the narrative is imbued with a sense of tangible history, as it offers a precise location for the occurrence of the entire episode. Dadhichi Rishi and his family (his son was Rishi Pippalada) are renowned in India for their various contributions, particularly in the realm of divine work. Pippalada Muni, through his rigorous *tapasya* on the banks of Mother Narmada, compiled numerous literary works that have endured through the ages.

Dadhichi, a revered saint, bestowed upon India the noble tradition of self-sacrifice. The Indian nation has been profoundly influenced by the exemplary acts of sacrifice for the nation's soul, culture and *dharma*. The credit for this can be attributed to the illustrious Dadhichi Rishi, who selflessly offered his bones to Indra. This act enabled Indra to vanquish Vritrasura, the demon and his accomplices. When Indra requested to kill Vritrasura, the *rishi* needed to sacrifice his life and acted without hesitation. In an instant, he surrendered his life, his thoughts consumed by neither his wife nor his unborn son.

Upon learning of the situation, Suvarcha, his cherished wife, was consumed by despair and found herself contemplating the possibility of ending her own life. Yet, the intervention of divine beings ensued, and they put forth a persuasive argument for her to continue living, given that she was carrying a child. Suvarcha eventually agreed, but her time was short-lived as she soon gave birth to Pippalada Muni and departed from this world, joining her beloved husband in the realm beyond.

Pippalada's early years were fraught with difficulty, as he resided within the confines of a *pipal* tree and subsisted on whatever sustenance he could find. This man's ascent to prominence was attributed to the blessings of his mother and *guru*. He even dared to challenge the deity Shanideva, imploring him to spare those under the age of 16 from his afflictions. As a result, children up to this age are believed to be immune to the influence of Saturn, one of the most dreaded planets in astrology.

Pippalada was a revered saint who dedicated himself to the study of the *Atharvaveda*. Through his diligent efforts, he achieved mastery over this complex text and even went on to compose his own Samhita based on it. Additionally, he is widely recognized for his authorship of the *Prashnopanishad*, a highly significant Upanishad within the rich tapestry of Indian tradition. Pippalada Muni had taken Padma as his wife, a woman of exceptional purity who had even cursed Dharma, the son of Brahma and the embodiment of righteousness on earth. With her curse, righteousness has gradually declined in each *yuga* – Satya, Treta, Dvapara and Kali Yuga. Pippalada Muni is renowned as one of the *avatara*s of Lord Shiva in his Rudra form. Therefore, worshipping both Pippalada and Shiva is of utmost importance, as their stature is beyond comparison.

The tale of Dadhichi and the rich history of Sanatana Kula, as recounted in several Puranas, make for a captivating narrative. It is possible that without a visit to Dharmapuri, one may not fully comprehend the significance of the concept of sacrifice. Perhaps this is why the Mandu story was introduced, to ensure that Dadhichi's memory and the matter of sacrifice did fade from the collective consciousness of India. It is my belief that the British introduced this narrative as a means of circumventing any potential challenges to their authority, thereby preventing the nation from being adequately prepared to make necessary sacrifices. A nation's actions are often shaped by its history, and it appears that the British have made a concerted effort to suppress certain aspects of ours past from our collective consciousness.

The confluence of the Kubja and the holy Narmada is revered not just because of the stories of Dadhichi and Bilvramak, but also because, as described by the Reva Khanda, it is comparable to the holy nectar that all divine beings seek.

The site of temple, currently under the care of the Department of Archaeology, appears to be in good condition. However, regrettably, the temple situated within the vicinity remains desolate, with scarce visitors. The department of archaeology responsible for the upkeep of the temple had made every effort to revive its former glory, yet its endeavours had failed to rekindle the ancient sentiments associated with it. I sat in the temple for a prolonged period, captivated by its distinctiveness and the space it provided. Nestled along the serene banks of Mother Narmada lies a place of great historical significance. It is said that during his visit, the revered Prabhu Dutt Brahmchari had informed the locals of the fascinating tale of this place.

This *tirtha*, called Bilvramak,[1] is located on an island in the middle of the Narmada River, which is why we did not visit it. According to legend, Mother Parvati invited her 108 closest friends to gather here. On one occasion, they got into a fight and, with the exception of Parvati, came here to settle their differences by praying to Lord Shiva with Bilva leaves and mango leaves, hence the name Bilvamrik Teerth. They were friends of Parvatiji, who subsequently became the Devi and was known as Chandika in Haridwar, Vishalakshi in Kashi, Lingadharini in Naimisharanya, Lalita in Prayag, Kamuka in Gandhamadan Mountain and Kramada in Mansarovar. In communion with the Divine Mother, I conveyed my fervent wish to remain in my present location – the hallowed grounds of your sacred land, surrounded by the sanctified *tirtha*s. but I was in *parikrama* which means I had to move.

After leaving Dharmapuri, we followed our trip to the beautiful Khalghat. In search of the holy Kapila Teerth,[2] we set out on our journey with great enthusiasm. Unfortunately, no matter how hard we tried, the *tirtha* eluded us. Once upon a time, in a land drenched in the mystical force of the divine, there was a realm cloaked in mystery and old legends. The great Brahmaji, the architect of the cosmos, set forth on a spiritual quest of profound introspection and repentance. The *yagya-kunda*, a sacred fire, burned brightly and with other-worldly force during this time of severe *tapa*. The majestic Kapila cow was born from the flames of this mysterious inferno. The gods and humans alike held this heavenly creature in high esteem because of its magical capacity to grant wishes and bring good fortune. The Kapila cow captivated the hearts of the gods as they gathered around her shining presence with reverence and wonder. They prayed and besought the majestic bovine, Kamadhenu, the one who grants wishes. The Kapila cow, ever inquisitive, probed for the innermost yearnings of her human visitors. The gods' voices rose in unison, each one expressing a different wish. Some pleaded with the Kapila cow to be at heaven with the heavenly beings, others pleaded her come to Earth, to shower humanity with her kindness. The Kapila cow listened patiently to every appeal, her eyes shining with a deep knowledge of what was being spoken. This was the conclusion reached. The Kapila cow would leave her heavenly home and travel to earth for a good cause. She would bring peace to a troubled globe, relief to those in need and prosperity to the prosperous. This is how the incredible history of this land began, a history knitted together by acts of kindness from deities and the infinite capacity for good in the hearts of humans. This is an ongoing narrative. Kapila chose a quiet, secluded place to sit down and prepare to begin her rigorous *tapasya*. The atmosphere was silent, as though waiting with bated breath for the holy encounter that was about to occur. With eyes closed and her thoughts clear, Kapila felt a wave of calm wash over her. At this same moment, the sacred river Narmada conferred upon Kapila her blessings as the Jagat Mata (mother of all).[3] The confluence of the Karam and Buti rivers with Mother Narmada, also known as Triveni Sangam, is located a short distance away. Sahasradhara, where Mother Narmada drops from a thousand little streams, is not far away. The rushing water may be heard from great distances. Not very far from here our intended destination was close to us, which was Jalkoti.

The day proved to be quite amusing as I strolled along and chanced upon a cluster of villagers. One of them approached me and offered a salute in the manner of the RSS organization. Initially, I was perplexed by this gesture, but soon surmised that he must have mistaken me for a revered *guru* among the RSS community, a misconception that several others have made during my travels.

48

Parashurama Temple

Our journey began in Jalkoti today, with our primary objective being the quest for the temple founded by Parashurama. Undertaking the task proved to be a formidable challenge, for despite my inquiries of those around me, not a single soul possessed any recollection. Numerous *tirtha*s situated along the banks of Narmada have been lost over time. The recollection of these sacred sites gradually fades away and their significance slowly diminishes. With a determined spirit, I made it my mission to locate the elusive temple. I began my quest by diligently questioning the inhabitants of Mandaleshwar, hoping to uncover any clues that would lead me to my destination. There was a town Maheshwar that we avoided since a great *sadhu* had passed away that day, and it was customary for us to refrain from passing by the *ashrama* on our way to Mandaleshwar.

Maheshwar has earned its place in history as the home of Queen Ahilyabai, who transformed numerous religious sites throughout India. Her legacy can be seen in the many temples that still stand today, as she was responsible for the construction of nearly every major temple in the country. As a former ruler of this small yet prosperous kingdom, Ahilyabai left an indelible mark on the region.

She was a remarkable queen, far ahead of her era. Her benevolent rule extended to all corners of her kingdom, from the weavers to the farmers. Her efforts to reduce crime in the capital and other cities were met with great success, as she provided a range of support to her people. Her major contribution lay in the realm of religion, where she played a pivotal role in preserving numerous temples and providing support for their management. Additionally, she contributed significantly to the construction of new temples, which was a remarkable achievement. Her memory lingers on in the town and throughout India.

Ahilyabai's life was marked by the duality of greatness as a ruler and tragedy in her personal life. However, it is possible that the divine had a hand in shaping her path towards a greater destiny. The untimely demise of her son Male Rao Holkar is a tragic tale. As per one account, he succumbed to insanity after realizing that he had punished an innocent person. Legend has it that an embroiderer once developed a close relationship with a servant in the household of Male Rao Holkar. However, this bond was met with disapproval and anger from Male Rao Holkar, who subsequently condemned the embroiderer to death. In the end, the establishment of his innocence had a profound effect on him. Some believe that the spirit of the embroiderer snatched away Ahilya's son by drowning him in his slumber. Ahilya was a mother who devoted herself to her son, made pleas to the spirits, promising to construct temples in their honour and ensure the well-being of her family. Despite her tireless efforts to care for her family, her endeavours proved fruitless and he eventually passed away. The historical event, which has unfortunately not received adequate attention in Indian history, served as the impetus for Ahilyabai's journey to the forefront of safeguarding the empire and her subjects. It was a time that gave rise to the manifestation of talent, virtue and energy, all of which were blessings to the nation and the empire under her reign.

Ahilyabai's ascent to power was far from easy. Her first test was a challenging one, but with the unwavering support of Mother Narmada, this great woman would go on to shape the history of modern India. Ahilyabai found herself in a difficult position following the death of her son, as her only surviving child was a daughter. Despite her daughter's capabilities, custom dictated that she could not ascend to the throne and participate in the administration of the kingdom. Thus, it fell upon Ahilyabai to take on the responsibility of ruling and governing her people. However, Gangadhar Jaswant, the minister in the administration, had a different idea. He played his cards shrewdly, proposing that a child from a distant relative be adopted and groomed to become the next king. This would have allowed the minister to gain control of the administration while the child grew up, eventually removing all members of the Holkar family from their positions of power. Perhaps Ahilyabai detected the scent of falsehood and firmly declared that no individual could replace her departed son. She emphasized that she had only one son, who was no longer with her. Ahilyabai's intellect remained untested, for the minister harboured ulterior motives. In the event of her rejection, he intended to seize control of the administration through force. Ahilyabai exhibited immense courage and a deep understanding of the needs of the common people. She was determined to prove that she was not just a mother and a wife of the king, but also possessed the qualities of a ruler. To demonstrate her resolve, she ordered the fitting of four bows, complete with quivers full of arrows, to the corners of her favourite elephant's *howdah*. This was a powerful political statement, showcasing her unwavering determination to lead her people into battle personally.[1]

Every day, Ahilyabai would diligently oversee the management of administration, instilling a much-needed sense of confidence that allowed for its growth and expansion. Her unwavering commitment to this task ensured the happiness and contentment of her citizens for an extended period. She had a penchant for listening to every complaint in person and exploring into the minute details of whatever was presented to her. This was the energy that she infused into the Holkar family. Ahilyabai is renowned for her multifaceted contributions to the society. Her accomplishments extend beyond the construction and maintenance of temples, as she also played a pivotal role in the development of infrastructure, including roads and lodgings such as *dharmashala*s. Her visionary spirit is evident in her efforts to establish niche industries, such as the creation of weavers' settlements that produced the highly sought after Maheshwari *sari*s, which remain popular to this day. Upon perusing the maps of India, one would undoubtedly observe the ubiquitous presence of Ahilyabai's masterful handiwork within the temples of the nation. In fact, there are several temples that have been restored by Ahilyabai where we can still offer our prayers. Not only was Ahilyabai responsible for the restoration efforts, but she also allocated a significant sum of money annually to numerous temples throughout India, spanning from Kedarnath to Rameshwaram. Further, she was always willing to share the expenses incurred in temples throughout India and much more.[2]

Ahilyabai was a woman who was eager to set an example for her town and its people. She dedicated herself to charitable causes, striving to make a positive impact on the lives of those around her. Everyday, she made it her duty to provide sustenance for the impoverished members of the society. Additionally, during special occasions and festivities, she hosted lavish feasts for those who were considered to be the most destitute. In the scorching months of the year, individuals were strategically positioned along the roads to provide weary travellers with refreshing water. As the chilly season approached, she generously distributed garments to a vast multitude of her loyal subjects and those who were physically frail. She had a tendency to amplify her emotions of empathy towards humanity to an extraordinary degree. The creatures that roamed the fields, soared through the skies and swam in the river were all recipients of her benevolence. She generously allocated portions of food to them, and even the labouring oxen were granted a respite from their toil to be revitalized with water brought by Ahilyabai's servants. The fields she had acquired were alive with flocks of birds, undoubtedly displaced by neighbouring farmers to deter them from feasting on the crops. Ahilyabai would often remark, "If we were to drive them, how would they survive?"[3]

Ahilyabai, a diligent individual, utilized every spare moment to immerse herself in the study of various Puranas and Sanatana Shastras. These texts served as her guiding force throughout her life. As she indulged in her favourite pastime of reading books, a brahmana presented her with a literary work extolling her virtues. Despite her initial patience while listening to the reading, she eventually came to the realization that the author's portrayal of her as a paragon of virtue was undeserved, given her own weaknesses and wrongdoings. Consequently, she ordered the book to be cast into the Narmada River and chose to ignore the author from that point forward. For a span of three decades, commencing from 1765 and culminating in 1795, she held a central position in India, her very existence altering the course of financial allocation from governance. When she was put in a position where she had to take drastic action, she would warn her fellow humans: "Let us, mortals, beware how we destroy God's creations".[4]

In his written account, Sir John Malcom describes the diligent efforts of Ahilyabai, who voluntarily undertook the task of not only ruling but also seeking inspiration from religious texts in her daily life. Before the break of dawn, she would rise and diligently attend to her religious duties of reading and *puja*. Following this, she would make her way to the court, often arriving around 2:00 p.m., where she would remain well into the late evening hours, sometimes even past 10:00 p.m. Throughout her time there, she remained steadfast in her commitment to ensuring the welfare of her subjects. If we were to summarize her life, we could say that it was characterized by prayer, abstinence and labour. Her routine was fairly consistent, with the exception of religious fasts and festivals, which she observed with great devotion and the occasional public emergency.[5]

Ahilyabai was a skilled leader, possessed with a remarkable ability to cultivate and nurture relationships both within her kingdom and beyond. It is noteworthy that throughout her thirty years reign, her domain was only subjected to invasion once by Rana of Udaipur. She was regarded by everyone in the same manner. The Nizam of the Deccan and Tipu Sultan accorded her the same reverence as the Peshwa. Both Hindus and Muslims alike offered prayers for her enduring well-being and success.[6]

As we journeyed through the town of Maheshwar, its rich history came to life before my eyes. From a distance, I could sense the profound legacy of a queen who had selflessly devoted herself to India, its people and the timeless principles of Sanatana Dharma.

In the enchanting town of Maheshwar lie numerous sacred *tirtha*s, each holding a unique allure that has beckoned pilgrims for centuries. Regrettably, our exploration of these divine sites was hindered by the untimely passing of a revered local *sadhu*. However, let us now rekindle our quest and delve into the *tirtha*s that have been meticulously chronicled in the ancient Shastras.

Matangeshwar Mahadev – In ancient days, the Ashokvanika Teerth was home to the revered Matanga Muni Ashram. There is a legend which states that Matanga Muni was formerly a member of one of the local tribes and that he was reborn as Matanga Muni after he prayed to Mother Narmada for a very long period. Matangeshwar Mahadev was founded by Matanga Muni after he performed extensive *tapasya* at this location.[7] Sahastrarjuna had made multiple pilgrimages to see Matanaga Muni, who served as his *guru*.

Jwaleshwar Teerth – According to legend, a king named Duryodhana wedded a queen named Narmada in the Satya Yuga, and the two had a daughter named Sudarshna. When she reached marriageable age, Agnideva requested the monarch for permission to marry her, but he was denied. After the king had made his preparations for *svayamvara*, a *yagya* was started in the same compound to mark the ritual's conclusion. This is when Agnideva appeared in the cloth of a brahmana, stood in front of the monarch and vanished. This is also when the fire in *yagya* stopped and the monarch realized his error and married his daughter Sudarshana to Agnideva.[8]

We were going towards Mandaleshwar, the neighbouring town of Maheshwar. Mandaleshwar, a quaint town, was the destination of our search for a temple. As we scoured the area, a kind stranger offered a suggestion that he believed could lead us to our desired location. This tip was relayed to us by the former MLA of the region, with whom we were enjoying a cup of tea while the search was underway. It was a unique experience, as this was the first time such a search had been conducted in the city for a temple. The atmosphere of the city was charged with a palpable sense of frenzy. As we arrived at the site, we were met with a scene of complete collapse and overgrowth. However, just prior to our arrival, the local (former) MLA had generously facilitated access to the area. Despite his assistance, he cautioned us that the condition of the site was dire and expressed uncertainty as to whether we would be able to proceed.

With a sense of urgency, I responded, emphasizing the crucial need for immediate action to prevent any future regrets that history may bring. As soon as I arrived at the site, I embarked on a quest to scour the ruins in search of any vestiges of its fabled history. As I chanced upon the Shivalinga, my gaze was immediately drawn to the elaborate well that encircled it. As I drew nearer to the walls, my eyes were met with a delightful sight – Sanskrit *shloka*s, etched onto the surface, just as I had read and researched. The site where Parashurama had undertaken his rigorous penance was a veritable embodiment of the vivid descriptions chronicled in a book published half a century ago. The Shivalinga exuded an air of antiquity, evident in the Sanskrit *shloka*s etched on its walls, now obscured by a thick layer of dust. The inscriptions proved to be a valuable source of information, shedding light on the historical context I had been fervently pursuing. Incredulity washed over me as I stumbled upon a location that had seemingly been overlooked by the local community. The bustling streets were filled with a diverse array of people, among them were journalists and prominent personalities. My very presence seemed to ignite a festive atmosphere throughout the premise, as if a grand celebration was underway. With elation in our hearts, we made a remarkable discovery.

Having defeated the warrior classes, known as the kshatriyas, on multiple occasions, Lord Parashurama proceeded to undertake a strenuous phase of penance. At long last, we have unearthed the very site where he engaged in his sacred practice and duly enshrined the Malashamneshwar Mahadev, as chronicled in the *Vasishtha Samhita*.[9]

The name in question carries great significance as it represents the divine entity responsible for purging the heart of all malevolent and envious tendencies. As I ventured along the banks of Mother Narmada, I chanced upon a number of *tirtha*s. Nevertheless, a specific one caught my attention, as it seemed to have been neglected by the inhabitants. By a fortuitous turn of events and under the watchful eye of Mother Narmada, we stumbled upon this concealed treasure. Amidst the august presence of the local municipal chairman, a solemn vow was extended to us, assuring that the requisite funds shall be procured to reinstate the *tirtha* to its former glory. In the event of his failure, it will be incumbent upon us to undertake the task of revitalizing it. After an exhaustive search, we finally arrived at the next *tirtha*, where we planned to take a break and enjoy our lunch.

The site held immense historical significance, much like several other locations along the banks of the Narmada River. It was here that Lord Shiva had undertaken his rigorous penance and the locals held it in high regard but only a few had the idea of the history. The *tirtha* in question bears the illustrious name of Gupteshwar Mahadev.[10] Its origins trace back to a bygone era when it was referred to as Daruk Vana, a sacred abode where numerous revered sages would engage in their austere penances. As Parvati gracefully traversed this sacred realm alongside Lord Shiva, her inquisitive spirit could not be contained. With a gentle curiosity, she ventured to inquire about the mystical *rishi*s who, amidst the dense foliage of the enchanting forest, had attained the desired *siddhi*s.

Lord Shiva, in his divine wisdom, graciously responded, acknowledging the profound significance of the wives who stand by their side, unwavering in their support and holiness, for the noble cause they champion. Mata Parvati then requested a test be administered to the women and she had Lord Shiva perform it on their behalf. Lord Shiva tried to explain to her that the outcome would be disastrous because the spouses of *rishi*s are extremely pure and committed to their purpose. But when Parvati was unyielding, Lord Shiva assumed the form of a Kapalika in the forest, stripped to his garments and began drumming the *damaru*. When the women of the forest laid eyes on Lord Shiva, they became transfixed by his extraordinary beauty and forgot about their labours. The *rishi*s witnessed the spectacle and cursed the Kapalika, saying that because he had crossed the boundaries of social interaction by appearing before women in Digambara Rupa (without clothes), his genital would shatter, and so it came to pass. The gods witnessed it and hurried to Brahmaji, who informed the *rishi* about the truth of the Kapalika as Shiva. Even though the *rishi*s have admitted that their *tapasya* was successful and the curse would take effect, the *linga* will now be venerated as the Rupa of Shiva. It is claimed that Lord Shiva, who originally established the Narmadeshwar, resides in this location in some unseen form.

After enjoying our midday meal, I was frequently interrupted by individuals who had become privy to the events surrounding *parikrama* and its impact on the town. After lingering for a while, I set out on foot towards our destination of Jalud.

On that day, we found ourselves at the sacred site of Baba Durgadas Samadhi, a revered soul who had devoted himself to spiritual practice on the banks of the holy Narmada River. As night fell, we remained at this enchanting location, surrounded by the natural beauty of the area and joined by local villagers who had gathered for a *bhandara*. Many years have passed since the departure of the great *sadhaka*, Baba Durgadas. However, the place where he once resided and devoted himself to his spiritual practices is still tended to by a dedicated local team. They diligently oversee all daily services and maintenance of the sacred site. I was requested to assume a position of quiet contemplation at the very spot where Baba Durgadas himself would engage in his spiritual practice, known as *sadhana*. Descending into the basement, I found myself in a cosy, albeit diminutive space. To my surprise, the room was adorned with exquisite decor that immediately caught my eye. As I settled into my seat, I could not help but feel as though I was in the presence of the great Baba Durgadas himself. Our conversation began to flow effortlessly, as if we were old friends catching up after a long absence. It seemed as though our conversation had been overheard by an unknown party. While Baba may no longer be present in the physical sense, it is widely understood that his presence remains palpable.

Jalud to Nemawar

49

Pipleshwar Mahadev

As the morning sun rose over the Baba Durgadas Temple, we embarked on our journey for the day. Our destination was the Pipleshwar Mahadev[1] Temple, where legend has it that Pippalada Muni once performed his rigorous *tapasya* here and establish the *tirtha*.

It was a tale that would remain etched in my memory forever. In the ancient Indian myth, it is said that Pippalada Muni's childhood was fraught with difficulty. His father, Dadhichi, had selflessly given his body for a divine cause. Following his birth, Pippalada's mother departed from the mortal world after giving birth to him, leaving him under a *pipal* tree. Pippalada Muni's early years were fraught with difficulty, as he resided within the confines of a *pipal* tree and subsisted on whatever sustenance he could find. This man's ascent to prominence was attributed to the blessings of his mother and *guru*. From a young age, he was cared for by others and his difficult childhood fostered a deep connection with children. He even dared to challenge the deity Shanideva, imploring him to spare those under the age of 16 from his afflictions. As a result, children up to this age are believed to be immune to the influence of Saturn, one of the most dreaded planets in astrology.

Pippalada Muni was a revered saint who dedicated himself to the study of the *Atharvaveda*. Through his diligent efforts, he achieved mastery over this complex text and even went on to compose his own Samhita based on it. Additionally, he is widely recognized for his authorship of the *Prashnopanishad*, a highly significant Upanishad within the rich tapestry of Indian tradition. Pippalada Muni had taken Padma as his wife, a woman of exceptional purity who had even cursed Dharma, the son of Brahma and the embodiment of righteousness on earth. With her curse, righteousness has gradually declined in each *yuga* – Satya, Treta, Dvapara and Kali Yuga. Pippalada Muni is renowned as one of the *avatara*s of Lord Shiva in his Rudra form. Therefore, worshipping both Pippalada Muni and Shiva is of utmost importance, as their stature is beyond compare.

Upon my arrival at the Pippalada Muni Temple, I was struck by an intriguing sight: a group of children performing the *puja* and *arti*. To my amazement, they informed me that they had taken charge of the temple a week prior, as the adults of the village had neglected their duties. It was a remarkable display of responsibility and devotion from these young ones. A group of children have formed a self-help collective, pooling their resources and efforts towards a common goal. After hearing this, I made a monetary donation and promised to send a bag of *puja* items the following morning. The children soon joined us on our *parikrama*. It proved to be a fascinating turn of events that my association with these children came about through the temple. Such is the enigmatic nature of the divine, how it can intersect with one's life in unexpected ways.

As the sun began to set, we arrived at the exquisite *ashrama* of Ma Anandamayi. The caretakers had clearly taken great care in maintaining the grounds, which emanated a serene and uplifting energy. The philosophy of Ma Anandamayi was something I was familiar with, but I had no idea that there was another story waiting for me when I got to Amarkantak.

The saint in charge exuded a gentle aura and the *ashrama*'s aesthetic was a feast for the senses, evoking a range of emotions with every detail. I was requested to retire for the night in a room which was overlooking the Mother Narmada and close to a temple of Kali Maiya, yet I found myself not at ease with the prospect of slumbering in such quarters. It was not until I arrived at Amarkantak that I finally comprehended the reason for my soul's reluctance to rest in that space.

On that day, a magnificent *bhandara* was held, drawing in individuals from distant villages to partake in the festivities.

50

No Passion for History

Departing from the *ashrama*, our next move was towards finding the Darukeshwar Mahadev Teerth.[1] The *tirtha* which is situated not very far from the *sangam* of the Khular River with the holy Narmada. During an ancient assembly of gods, the son of Vardhaman caused difficulties for the brahmanas which infuriated Indra. It was at this moment that Indra cursed Daruk, ensuring that he would be born into this mortal realm. Daruk then made numerous requests, but the curse had already taken physical form and could not be reversed by Indra. However, Indra promised that if Daruk performed *tapasya* on the banks of the Narmada, he would become Lord Krishna's charioteer. It was at this location that Daruk performed *tapasya* and founded the *tirtha*.

Upon arrival at the temple, a sense of dismay overtook me as I surveyed the scene. The temple, once revered and ancient, now lies in ruins. Its remnants scattered haphazardly, overtaken by unsightly cement and concrete. The temple's former beauty has been lost, replaced by walls constructed from its once-beautiful components. The vast expanse of the states lay before me, dotted with temples that once stood proudly in their designated locations, each with a rich history to tell. Alas, now they lay in ruins, destroyed and forgotten. In close proximity, a *katha* (traditional storytelling event) was taking place within a magnificent hall that had been erected. As I observed the scene, a thought crossed my mind – if the historical artefacts were to be destroyed, who would be willing to believe in the ancient Sanatana story that was being recounted?

Vimaleshwar Mahadev is located a short distance away. The history of this location dates back to a time of hunger, when many individuals were forced to consume foods forbidden by the Shastras. It was at this time that the *rishi*s met and decreed that those who had eaten forbidden foods should come here to perform *tapasya* in order to become *vimala* (pure). People from all over came to this spot to perform *tapasya* and become *vimala*.[2]

I experienced a surge of emotions as we travelled towards Barawaha, our intended destination for the night. The site was positioned directly opposite to Omkareshwar. Our accommodation was situated at Bhilat Dev Mandir, a destination that seemed to be an unusual selection for the majority of *parikramavasi*s. On the aforementioned day, we were joined by Dr Mohan Yadav, along with the esteemed presence of Mahant Mangal Das Tyagi. We experienced a moment of joviality with him.

Despite Mahant Mangal Das Tyagi's prior request for a secluded spot that he wanted us to stay, we found ourselves at Bhilat Dev Mandir, a place that seemed rather insignificant. The destination that Mahant Mangal Das Tyagi had in mind bore immense historical significance, as it was one of the age-old *tirtha*s situated on the banks of the revered Maiya Narmada. The one who established it was none other than Danu's son, the very entity from whom all demons were born. The location was situated quite far away, making it impossible to reach by foot on that specific day. As previously alluded to, it was Mother Narmada who held the power to dictate our place of repose.

I had informed Mahant Mangal Das Tyagi that I would capture a video of the location on my way out the following day. My video content, which showcases the ancient tales of the Narmada region, has been gaining popularity steadily. There was a growing audience eagerly anticipating the *tirtha*s that will be recounted in my latest narration.

On the last day of the year, there was a lively celebration with a continuous flow of individuals throughout the night. In the interim, I found myself situated within my improvised automobile, attentively listening to the perpetual drone of passing traffic.

51

Cat and the Tea

As the Gregorian calendar commenced, a peculiar calmness enveloped the atmosphere. The world appeared to be in a state of slumber, recuperating from the merrymaking of the preceding evening. We embarked on a journey towards the destination that Tyagiji had ardently recommended us to visit. The once well-trodden path had undergone changes, resulting in a decrease in foot traffic. Nowadays, travellers preferred the more accessible routes, disregarding the ones that led to sacred destinations. In my estimation, the Mahant had been eagerly awaiting my arrival, but to my surprise, he appeared to be unable to place me. The motive behind his conduct towards me remained ambiguous. The reason for his reluctance to acknowledge me as the intimate confidant that Mangal Das Tyagi had proclaimed me to be remains unclear. It is possible that my youth played a role in his hesitation or perhaps there were other factors at play.

Fortune smiled upon me as I basked in the divine aura of the Koteshwar Temple. Enraptured by the sheer magnificence of the scene before me, and as usual I made a video explaining the importance of the *tirtha*. This *tirtha* dates back to the time when Karanja, son of Danu, performed a *tapasya* here and established the *tirtha* of Koteshwar which was known as Kapila Teerth as well.[1]

Subsequently, I made my way to meet the *sadhu* who was looking after the premises. However, upon my arrival, I discovered that he was preoccupied with his responsibilities. As he emerged, a sense of disappointment washed over me, for it was clear that his eagerness to meet me did not match my own. He spoke incessantly and out of deference, I simply nodded along. During a particular moment in our dialogue, he inquired about my expectations for returns or the completion of the *parikrama*. "I conveyed my fervent wish to partake in the festivities of Holi and conclude my *parikrama* or return on the same day. However, the fulfilment of my aspirations rests solely on the benevolence of the revered Mother Narmada River", I responded. His response was a firm denial that the issues at hand had any connection to the holy Narmada. As soon as these words reached my ears, I felt compelled to interject with a personal observation that in the course of my own existence, it is the esteemed Mother Narmada who wields the authority to make determinations. Comparing it to a tense exchange, I swiftly took my leave.

As we left the area, a towering mountain loomed before us, presenting a formidable obstacle to our journey. We were fortunate that the water from the dam was not released, as it would have made crossing the little streams running to merge holy Narmada impossible had the gates been open. Further ahead, the way was obscured, leaving us with no discernible route. We were compelled to traverse the thickets of Barawaha, struggling all the while. Despite facing certain challenges, we ultimately succeeded in navigating our path.

One hour had passed when Nandlal Tayal approached me. He had ventured to Koteshwar, and upon his arrival, the *sadhu* had informed him of his failure to recognize me. I provided him with reassurance that the current predicament was not due to any inadequacies on his part. Instead, it arose from his inability to anticipate the possibility of befriending an individual as young as myself, who happens to be a close associate of Mahant Mangal Das Tyagi.

Mangal Das Tyagi arrived on the scene, tardy as he had promised to join us at 7 o'clock sharp in the morning. As soon as he arrived, our conversation turned to the topic of *parikrama* and our experiences with it. It was a joy to engage in dialogue with him. He walked with us for a considerable distance, accompanied by Suraj who had journeyed from Pura. Our abode was an *ashrama*, the setting for a remarkable tale.

Mangal Das Tyagi took us to an *ashrama*; I shall refrain from disclosing the name of the place, but it is frequented by a majority of the *parikramavasis*. We lingered there for a while and someone from the *ashrama* cordially invited us to partake a cup of tea. Mahant Mangal Das Tyagi graciously accepted the offer on behalf of our group and we patiently awaited the arrival of the tea.

As my eyes fixated on the surroundings, a feline gracefully appeared from the kitchen, its entire body soaked in creamy milk as it blissfully groomed itself. In that very moment, the esteemed Mahant of the *ashrama* made his arrival, acknowledging Tyagiji with a gracious nod and engaging him in conversation. He indulged in memories of his previous acquaintance with my *parikrama*. As the tea arrived, I could not help but wonder if it had been brewed with the same milk that a cat had taken a swim in? The tea was distributed among the group. Despite my usual reluctance, I felt compelled to accept a cup and took a small sip. As the tea service came to a close, the murmurs of satisfaction from my fellow *parikramavasi*'s caught my ear, each one expressing their delight at the delectable brew. Kumar, who abstained from both tea and coffee, was enticed by the aroma of the high-quality tea and eventually indulged in a cup. Interestingly, some individuals partook in the beverage twice.

I felt compelled to verify the veracity of what I had witnessed, so I made my way to the kitchen. Upon arrival, my suspicions were confirmed as I observed the unmistakable evidence of the feline's misdeeds – a tell tale paw print in the spilled milk. As I sat there contemplating, it dawns on me that the tea which has been the topic of much discussion for its exceptional flavour was infused with a unique ingredient – milk that has been expertly prepared by a male feline swimmer. I maintained a hushed demeanour, keenly watching as each individual took their leave from the *ashrama,* their praises for the tea ringing out in the air. I could not help but crack a witty remark about how the cat might have contributed to the tea's distinctive flavour by liberally dousing the milk with its saliva and else.

It must be noted that due to the dam of Omkareshwar, we were travelling from a different route for a few kilometres as the water of the dam had occupied the area and does not leave any portion to walk; also, the streams that merged in the Narmada are full mostly by the backwater which hinders the movement.

52

What Is Forgotten

As we made our way along the Narmada bank, we were compelled to venture further a field due to the gradual rise of the dam. Regrettably, this also meant that a number of *tirtha*s, as described in the Shastras, had been engulfed by the water. Our quest led us to a temple dedicated to the revered Sita Mata, said to be a sight of unparalleled beauty, adorned with sixty-four Yoginis idols and fifty-two Bhairavas.[1] However, upon our arrival, we were met with a disheartening sight. The temple, once a marvel of intricate design and artistry, had been marred by a garish coat of red paint. The once-beautiful idols and adornments were now obscured, their beauty lost to the overwhelming hue. I did not find all the sixty-four Yoginis and fifty-two Bhairavas.

Within the temple, a small number of priests maintain their duties. It appears that their focus is primarily on those devotees who are able to offer monetary contributions. Upon my arrival, the priests promptly congregated. However, upon surveying the temple and its current state, I refrained from offering any monetary contributions. This decision appeared to displease the priests, who likely assumed that as a spiritualist, I would be inclined to donate.

Dhavdi-Kunda was located nearby, but it has nearly completely disappeared due to rising dam levels. Additionally, the breathtaking vista of the Narmada tumbling down several feet below is obscured for the majority of the year. This is where according to the history of Banasura had sat with many millions of Shivalinga to worship and called by Shankaraji he had left abruptly leaving every Shivalinga in the river that were collected all through the ages and adored several temples of India.[2]

Chakra-Kundas[3] were last seen in this area, not too far from Bhetkheda. According to legend, Chakra-Kundas formerly stored all the rubbish from the river, allowing water to flow freely into the Dhavdi-Kunda, where Lord Shiva was said to live.

Since another Dam had been constructed in here, there are some more *tirtha*s that have been submerged in the water. One of them is Kaladeva which was in the head of Baranag Nala, now immersed in water and another a few kilometres away was known as Bharam Puri where the Pandavas had done the *tapasya* and *yagya*; in front of it there was Punyaghat, which is also submerged in water most of the year.

As we walked along the inner path, I diligently consulted my phone's digital map application, which was in the process of generating raw data. I took care to follow a route that was accessible to others on foot. As we traversed the countryside, our journey led us to the intersection of Khargone and Devas, where we encountered a formidable stream. Despite the challenge it presented, we were compelled to cross its waters, for no bridge had been erected by either district, given its location on the border. Such a phenomenon is not limited to Madhya Pradesh alone, but rather pervades the entire country. The border between two districts appears to be more akin to that between two distinct nations. The restriction of movement has caused great inconvenience to the locals, who are now compelled to take a long diversion of several kilometres to reach the neighbouring villages that are merely a few kilometres away. Many people have approached me with their grievances, urging me to escalate the matter to higher authorities. It is perplexing to ponder upon the inaction of the local politicians in this regard.

As we journeyed on, we came upon a quaint village by the name of Neemapura. It was adorned with an abundance of *neem* trees, their branches stretching far and wide. I could not help but ponder over the significance of the village's name, as it seemed to hold a special connection to the local community or perhaps even the region's rich history.

53

Ayodhyapuri

Our day began at the farm where we had spent the night. Our journey today took us towards Sirkiya, a path that we encountered frequently during the *parikrama*. We altered our route in an attempt to locate the most fitting path for the *parikrama* map. The chosen route necessitated the inclusion of every perspective, one of which stipulated that to avoid highways and remain accessible to fellow *parikramavasi*s.

In general, individuals tend to proceed towards the Pamakhedi, which can be likened to a descent, before ascending towards Nemawar. We had made the decision to traverse the direct route towards Kali Ratri, proceeding onward to Namanpura and ultimately to Nemawar. This course of action would not only spare us several kilometres of travel, but also provide a more enjoyable experience. Today, we have decided to forgo the usual route to Pamakhedi and instead traverse through the forest, eventually arriving near Sirkiya. From there, we shall proceed onwards, thus avoiding a few superfluous kilometres that would have otherwise been travelled. One of the reasons why Pamakhedi is a popular stop is because there are very few service areas offered to *parikramavasi*s on the alternative route, which will change in future.

As we began our leisurely walk, we traversed a forested trail that many find arduous, yet I found it to be the most tranquil path. The legend of Pamakhedi saint had reached our ears, warning us of his tendency to divert *parikramavasi*s. While the reasons for this were varied, I will refrain from delving into them. It is worth mentioning that a pair of youthful Pamakhedi locals were closely monitoring our movements, suspecting that our chosen path was unorthodox and that we may encounter difficulties such as a lack of water. Unbeknownst to them, our management team ensure that our needs were met. However, their gesture still managed to touch me deeply.

During our leisurely stroll, Kumar confided in me about his poignant experience from last year's *parikrama*. As fate would have it, they stumbled upon a lively function by a stream and were graciously invited to partake in the *bhandara*. Kumar could not resist the temptation and eagerly joined in. Looks like Kumar's vegetarianism saved him from becoming a part of the local *janya-jati*s' non-veg routine during the *bhandara*. He made a quick exit as soon as he realized what was on the menu.

In the same river crossing I stumbled upon a chap who seemed to be wobbling more than the river's current. He exclaimed "Hail Congress, Hail Indira Gandhi and Hail Sister-in-Law Sonia!". I dropped a spiritual bomb with "Jai Narmada Maiya" and he was left speechless. It was a curious discovery when he finally received the embrace he had been seeking, likely from none other than Nanga Baba, who had been walking behind me, Kumar told me this after several days when he saw the pictures in social media. "Two madmen always make for good company", I proclaimed.

The forest exuded a breathtaking beauty, with towering trees that seemed to have stood the test of time. We decided to pause for a midday meal and, during our stay, I chanced upon a plethora of lava stones. These findings served as a testament to the historical presence of volcanoes in the Narmada region. I took the liberty of collecting some of these stones as tangible evidence of the aforementioned theory.

A while ago, I encountered an individual affiliated with the Reva Foundation who extended an invitation for me to visit their establishment. However, I was left with a sense of unease and had no desire to partake in their hospitality, as it appeared they sought to exploit my *parikrama* for their own gain. Jitendra Sharma, the programme coordinator, had ventured to the very location I had wished to avoid, leaving me with a sense of unease. The day prior, I inquired with him to confirm whether the location in question was indeed not under the ownership of the Reva Foundation. He affirmed his certainty on the matter. It was ironic that Yogesh received a text late at night where we were welcomed for the next day. It prompted me to inquire of Jitendra Sharma in the morning what had transpired and immediately informed him that he must seek alternative accommodations, as I would rather reduce my daily commute than reside at the Reva Foundation's location.

As he moved forth, he came upon a new location known as Kali Ratri, or as locals call it Ratri. The forest earned its moniker due to its perpetual darkness and lack of vitality. As we journeyed along the path, the gracious members of the Reva Foundation arrived to offer us refreshments. However, despite their kind gesture, I opted to venture towards the quaint Ratri village. It was then that they became aware of my decision. As we embarked on the path towards Ratri, it became apparent that someone had attempted to thwart our journey through the use of dark magic. However, I refused to be deterred by such childish tactics, as I had already experienced enough of such nonsense in my life. With a determined spirit, I cast aside these obstacles and continued on towards our destination.

Ratri is a destitute location, scarcely frequented by anyone. However, it lies along the *parikrama* route and, in times past, travellers would traverse this region. I sensed that I had arrived at a destination that was imperative for individuals akin to myself. Performing the *arti* of Mother Narmaḍa in this hamlet, which is impoverished and scarcely traversed by individuals of my ilk, is of utmost importance. Amidst the plight of the village, we extended an invitation to each family to convene at *bhandara*. Our offer was met with gracious acceptance. As I stepped out of the shower and made my way back to my vehicle room, I received a text message accompanied by an audio recording. I promptly saved the recording to my cloud drive and listened intently as a representative from the Reva Foundation expressed their disapproval of my decision to select Ratri village, a locale deemed to be a wealthy man's heaven (which was not) and not to reach Sirkiya. The message was rife with derogatory language that ran counter to my personal code of ethics.

The individual asserted that I, the Rama of Kali Yuga, had opted for Ratri over Sirkiya, the sacred site. Unbeknownst to him, he was engaging in a dispute with an adversary of great consequence. Swiftly, I christened the village Ayodhyapuri and subjected him to a public examination, complete with audio evidence. The public's ire was palpable, yet they lauded my endeavours. Thus, the moniker Ayodhyapuri was born, its resonance reverberating throughout the entire *parikrama* route. It served as a reminder to all that engaging in unethical behaviour would not be tolerated, for I had no ulterior motive save for the completion of the *parikrama*.

54

Namanpura

On this auspicious day, we departed from the sacred land of Ayodhyapuri, accompanied by the entire village for the first 15 km of our journey. Our destination for the day was Namanpura. Kumar revisited the location where he had previously formed a bond with the family who accompanied him on the *parikrama* last year. The couple appeared sincere, yet struggled to grasp the essence of spirituality and the principles that I hold dear.

Jyoti, the wife of Dinesh, possessed a gift for gab and could effortlessly converse for hours. Her emotional nature was equally notable. In contrast, Dinesh was a straightforward and enthusiastic man who had the good fortune of being her husband. These landlords have established themselves in the area and are also involved in farming. However, of late, they have been dedicating their time to serving the *parikramavasi*s.

During my journey to Namanpura, I chanced upon one Kishore Patel who appeared to be contemplating the act of donating his land to the Reva Foundation. News of the preceding day's events had rapidly disseminated across a vast expanse. The man's decision not to generously offer the land for any purpose was ultimately reached. He conveyed a profound sense of appreciation towards me for safeguarding his well-being.

On this particular evening, we were graced with a grand *bhandara*. As we were fully equipped with all necessary provisions, including a team of skilled cooks, we found ourselves in no need of any assistance from Jyoti's family. The Patels hailing from this region were overcome with a sense of guilt, as they realized they had not contributed anything towards the betterment of *bhandara* or contributed towards it. Jyoti persistently requested for something and eventually presented Nandlal Tayal with a sack filled with wheat flour, which he accepted.

Nandlal was initially hesitant to accept the flour, but Jyoti insisted, claiming that she had obtained permission from me, which was not the case. Prior to embarking on my *parikrama* journey, I made a solemn vow to Mother Narmada. I pledged to refrain from accepting items such as these from others out of obligation, opting instead to exchange items as a token of appreciation for their kindness. This strategy proved successful and Mother Narmada recognized the unwavering commitment I held to my promise.

After approximately one week, the flour was utilized to prepare *chapatti* for me. Upon consumption, I experienced severe illness. Throughout the entire night, I experienced illness and was unable to comprehend the cause. The following day, we were required to traverse a considerable distance.

As the morning *arti puja* concluded, I inquired of Nandlal whether any oil had been replaced. His response was a simple negative. "Have you changed any flour?" I inquired. "No", he first replied but later recalled "The flour that you indulged in last evening has come from none other than Jyoti and Dinesh". My emotions stirred as I discovered that he had taken it without my consent. Nandlal explained that he had been under the impression that I had given my approval. I inquired of him as to why he had not consulted me directly. Silence was his only response. Despite being ill throughout the night and lacking energy to walk, we had no choice but to press on, and so I did.

I humbly implored Mother Narmada for forgiveness, despite the error not being of my own doing. With gracious benevolence, she granted me the ability to continue my journey with her divine blessings. Such is the way in which Mother Narmada guides and supports those who seek her aid.

55

Debts Repaid

On this particular day, we were en route to Nemawar, making our way towards the halfway point. Our intention was to rest in the very place where Kala Bhairavas had done his *tapasya*. The place is known as Bagdi Sangam, where Bagdi River meets with Holy Narmada. However, in order to reach our destination, we had to traverse the Datuni waterstream. Thankfully, Dinesh had made arrangements for us to cross the river by way of a boat.

From Bagdi to the illustrious Omkareshwar, the serene banks of the holy Narmada were plagued by a sense of trepidation during the early nineteenth century. Infested by a nefarious band of robbers, traversing this once sacred terrain became an endeavour fraught with danger. The marauding chiefs hailing from the formidable territories of Bakhatgarh and Salani were wreaking havoc upon the once tranquil lands of Indore, Ujjain, and various other regions. Not only did their audacious exploits extend to Asirgarh and Burhanpur, but these very locations served as their clandestine sanctuaries, where they sought refuge after their audacious acts of robbery. During the era of British rule, a multitude of these robbers found themselves gainfully employed, some serving a specific purpose while others met their untimely demise in fierce battles.[1]

The Datuni Sangam, a water body of considerable size, is not typically equipped with boats for crossing. However, on the occasion of our visit, arrangements had been made for our convenience. This proved fortuitous for other travellers who also required passage across the *sangama*, as they would otherwise have been forced to traverse great distances to reach a bridge spanning the Datuni River. On this particular day, Jitendra Sharma was attired in a striking ensemble of total black. It was only later that I became aware of an inexplicable presence, a certain call of Bhairava that seemed to emanate from within us. Curious, I inquired as to the source of this sensation. At that moment, I had not yet laid eyes upon Jitendra Sharma's attire. It was Kumar who pointed out that Jitendra Sharma's choice of clothing, indeed, was in keeping with the preferred colour of Bhairava – total black.

Today, Ujjwal Singh Chauhan graced us with his presence as we neared the vicinity of Nemawar. Although our initial intention was not to lodge in Nemawar that evening, the proximity of a mere 16 km prompted me to press on. Eventually, we arrived at the magnificent Nemawar Temple, a site I had frequented on numerous occasions before the *parikrama*. The Nemawar temples are imbued with the weight of history, their beauty captivating to the eye. However, they have not been spared the brutal impact of forces seeking to extinguish Indian civilization. Despite the severe damage inflicted upon the statues within the temples and temple walls, the sacred traditions persist. Nemawar and its sourroudings have witnessed various historical scenes of our times, Al-Biruni (970 CE-) mentions travelling from Dhar to Nemawar while he was in India. In the year 1801, Satwas which is not very far from here had witnessed a severe encounter between Jaswant Rao Holkar and Major Brownrigg, who was commanding a force of Sindhia's troops. A little later the Pindari leader Chitu obtained land in this area, and made Satwas and Nemawar his two principal places of residence.[2]

The day was bitterly cold, with a biting wind that whipped through the air. Despite the harsh conditions, I found myself seated at the *ghat*, participating in the sacred ritual of *arti*. The *pandala* was filled with a congregation of priests from the nearby temples, their voices raised in unison as they chanted their devotions. It was a deeply emotional moment for me, as I had come to this very spot before embarking on my *parikrama*, seeking the blessings of Mother Narmada to guide me on my spiritual journey. Gazing upon the very rock upon which I had offered my reverent prayers, I sensed a profound connection with the divine presence of Maiya Narmada, as if she were intently attuned to our entreaties.

Interestingly, there are many ways in which Maiya Narmada communicates with you, and it has happened once again. In the year 2021, I embarked on a journey with Dr Mohan Yadav from Bhopal to Omkareshwar. During our travels, we paused at a quaint spot to indulge in some roasted corn. It was then that we were approached by the esteemed MLA of the local region, Ashish Sharma. Dr Mohan Yadav engaged in a conversation with Sharma, and the two gentlemen conversed amicably. In the final moments, Dr Mohan Yadav was prevented from delivering the payment to the maize vendor, and I bore witness to this riveting conclusion. On that particular day, I experienced a sense of discomfort upon discovering that an unfamiliar individual had contributed funds towards the roasted corn I had consumed. In any case, we eventually left for Omkareshwar and Narmada Maiya.

Amidst the tranquil banks of the Narmada River in Nemawar, we performed a sacred *arti* ceremony. Consider the probabilities. On that fateful day, Ashish Sharma fortuitously found himself traversing through Nemawar, and subsequently made his way towards the banks of the revered Narmada River for the purpose of performing *achamana*. As his gaze wandered, he chanced upon the grand procession of our temple's vehicle, carrying the sacred *kalasha* of revered Mother Narmada. As we made our way back from the *puja*, we headed towards our overnight lodgings. Ashish Sharma's unwavering stare remained fixed on the vehicle in front of him as he deftly navigated to the place where we were staying.

As soon as he came into view, I swiftly offered him an invitation to partake in the exquisite culinary delights of *bhandara*. Although he had initially agreed to depart, I could not shake the feeling that his true desire was to engage in further discourse before bidding farewell. As our meeting drew to a close, I regaled him with the tale of the corn. I could perceive his reaction as he expressed astonishment that I still retained it in my memory. He appeared slightly unsettled that Maiya Narmada had brought him to this place only for this.

In that moment, I revealed to him the true purpose of Maiya Narmada's intervention – to alleviate the weight of debt that had been bearing down on me. Without a moment's hesitation, he lowered himself to the ground and reverently touched my feet, his feelings of intense emotion threatening to consume him. Urgently, he hurried towards the *bhandara* for food.

Once more, I offered my heartfelt thanks to Mother Narmada for relieving me of the weight of debts and monetary responsibilities. Thus, is the way in which she speaks to you.

Nemawar is currently witnessing the construction of a grand Jaina temple, which is set to be a magnificent structure. However, one cannot help but ponder over the lack of attention that the Jaina temple management has paid towards the very site that has brought them fame and recognition – Nemawar.

56

Nemawar

Since Nemawar[1] was a temple town with a history dating back several millennia, it still has several of its temples' ruins visible today. It was here that the moral ideals of *dharma* and many *ashrama*s in life got their beginnings. However, the location is stunning, and Mother Narmada flows out of it with such exquisite splendour that you almost feel you are in heaven.

There is one temple on the banks of Mother Narmada and another in just above on hilltop. If you examined this one closely, you would notice that an old temple was finished, despite what the archaeological department claimed as unfinished. The fact is that, Islamic conquerors had looted the temple, destroyed the roof and the surrounding area. The temple was magnificent; it had exquisite carvings, and if we attempted to reproduce it now, it would be expensive and challenging to construct. But history still weighs heavily here, even though the place is now empty. I lingered there for some time before ultimately rising to begin my journey to the temple on the banks of Narmada, which is known as Siddhanath Temple and then further to Turnal.

Siddhanath Temple is beautiful and has carving all around, but one would notice that every other image that may have taken ages to produce was mutilated by the Islamic conquests in the region. I felt pain that I have had every time I visit the temple.

As per the beliefs of Sanatana Dharma, this very location was once graced by the arrival of the *manas-putra*s, the sons of Lord Brahma who were born through the power of his mind. The four sons, viz. Sanaka, Sanandana, Sanatana and Sanatkumar, are said to have visited this sacred site. As the locals approached them, they shared with them the very essence of life, dividing it into four distinct stages that have since become widely recognized as *ashrama*. Maharshi Sanaka took centre stage and commenced an exposition on the very essence of the *brahmacharya ashrama*, the inaugural phase of life. With great wisdom, he shared invaluable insights on how to conduct oneself and prioritize actions. On the *grihasthya ashrama*, Maharshi Sanandana bestowed his wisdom and disseminated his teachings. The gentleman's words encapsulated the very essence of how to conduct oneself in the sacred bond of matrimony and fulfil one's obligations. With great wisdom, Maharshi Sanatana expounded upon the essence of the *vanaprastha ashrama*. His words were imbued with the sagacity of navigating life in one's later years. At long last, Sanatkumar made his arrival, bestowing upon us the very essence of the *sannyasa ashrama* and the responsibilities that come with it. According to legend, the temples known as Siddheshwar Mahadev were founded by the *manas-putra*s of Lord Brahma.

After leaving the great and magnificent temple of Siddheshwar Mahadev, where we did the *abhisheka* and *puja*, we went for the *samadhi* of Baba Atmaram. Since long I had planned to stop at the *samadhi* of Baba Atmaram, a revered saint in this region. This time, however, I wanted to make sure I visited his *samadhi* and this is when I again experienced how Maiya Narmada intersected with you.

The previous day, I had walked at a brisk pace and covered a considerable distance in a shorter amount of time. Had we adhered to our original itinerary for our journey to Nemawar and taken an additional day, we might not have realized the significance of our timely arrival. However, we managed to reach our destination just in one day and found ourselves at the *samadhi* of Baba Atmaram on a momentous occasion. This was the day when devotees of Baba Atmaram brought forth the *nishana* (flags) and commenced a procession. It was a pivotal day for the followers of Baba Atmaram and it was remarkable how Narmada Maiya had seemingly guided us to our destination. Baba Atmaram's *samadhi* is situated which was originally at the convergence of River Jambuvati (Jamner) with the Narmada.

It is worth noting that we were initially scheduled to remain in Nemawar. Ujjwal Singh Chauhan had suggested that we spend an additional day in the area. However, I made the decision not to do so. Had we stayed, we might have missed the significant *samadhi* ceremony that took place that day. Such is the manner in which the divine engages with each and every one of us.

During our time in Turnal, we resided in close proximity to a temple that holds great significance. It was situated near the very spot where

Lord Parashurama had performed the *tarpana* ritual in honour of his parents. The place is very close where the Goni River merges with the Narmada, now with the sand mining, many things are not visible.[2] In the location of our initial encounter, I happened upon an individual whom I affectionately referred to as Dawtha Naresh, owing to his origins in the eponymous village. Accompanying him was his uncle, who had recently completed a *parikrama* and proved to be the most amusing elder I encountered during my travels.

Dawtha Naresh's uncle claimed to have completed the *parikrama*, but it seems he treated it like a choose-your-own-adventure book – walking one minute, then hopping on a car or bus the next. I inquired about his *parikrama* experience and he replied with a lukewarm "fine", but it seems he won't be signing up for the next one anytime soon. "Why?" I inquired. "Oh, just a small desire to remain among the living", he quipped. I inquired as to how he braved the chilly weather. Well, apparently, he's found a new way to conserve water – just a handful of Narmada water and voila, he's showered!

When I inquired about the meal, he quipped that he made sure to keep his belly happy and if it was not up to par, he would give his dear Mother Naramda a tongue-lashing every night. When I inquired about the cuisine, he quipped that he had to resort to some divine intervention and plead with Mother Narmada to bless him with a satisfactory meal each night.

When I inquired about his *parikrama*, he replied with a clever quip: "I attempted to walk the path, but my feet had other plans. Alas! I missed out on the blessings that await us all. Now, I find myself trailing after those who are on foot, hoping to catch some of the blessings that eluded me before." I asked what he wants from me? He said "some of the blessings that I have collected during my *parikrama*".

Nemawar to Shokalpura

57

History Revisited

On that particular day, we departed from Turnal and encountered an elderly *sadhu*. I graciously presented my donation to him, and he responded with such humility that he extended an invitation for me to join him for tea. However, I respectfully declined his offer knowing it would be difficult to prepare the tea for such a large group. I ventured deeper and stumbled upon the very spot where Lord Parashurama had performed the sacred *tarpana* of his parents at the place where the Goni River merges with the Narmada. Even now, the stones bear the etchings of countless millennia, a testament to the enduring power of this ancient tradition. Once, an ancient temple stood in this very spot. However, it has since fallen under the jurisdiction of the archaeology department. Despite their best efforts, only a solitary stone remains, which they have been unable to excavate or remove. The area is rife with sand mining, and it is my belief that within the coming years, it will be expunged from the annals of the earth. Such is the plight of numerous *tirtha*s across the land of Madhya Pradesh.[1]

We crossed the Kankariya River and to our surprise it was exactly as it was mentioned in earlier Sanatana records. Interestingly, the river which in ancient record is called Kankariya has the story that many stones were thrown against the divine beings when they were walking on the banks of the Narmada River and we could still see the boulders in there, this is how the stripy of nation walked on the land of Mother Narmada.

Today, we found ourselves lodged in the quaint town of Chipaner. The area was originally called Sipaner since it is where the Seep and Narmada river meet. However, the term has since lost its original significance and is now known as Chipaner. This charming town is situated in close proximity to the meeting point of these two rivers. Now, in the aftermath of the complete annihilation of our history and the significance of its names, its memory has been lost to all.

Kumar's family had arranged a magnificent welcome for us, complete with gun salutes and other grand gestures that I had never before witnessed. The programme was splendid, and the *bhajana sandhya* in the evening was equally impressive. Mahant Mangal Das Tyagi Maharaj graced us with his presence and remained here for an extended duration.

58

Let Us Make a Final Plan

As we departed from the morning meeting with Kumar's family, a palpable sense of emotion hung in the air. Kumar himself appeared particularly moved, and it was clear that his family was similarly affected by the significance of the moment. As we bid him farewell, we embarked on our journey towards Nilakantha and Shilakantha. Two young children, around the same age as Kumar, had offered to guide us, but their uncertainty compelled us to take charge of the pathfinding ourselves. Everywhere we went, even the locals were unaware of the path we took, as it seemed to be one that nobody had ever traversed before. As time passed, I increasingly recognized the significance of digital mapping of the Narmada Maiya Parikrama *patha*.

On this particular day, I requested the presence of Kumar and Yogesh to engage in a planning session. As we journeyed along the route, our hearts were filled with determination to arrive at Omkareshwar at the time of Holi. Though the task may seem daunting, we were confident that with the grace of Mother Narmada, we will succeed in reaching our destination on the auspicious occasion of Holi.

During our stay in Shilakantha, which is situated at the convergence of the Kaushalya River with Mother Narmada, we stumbled upon an individual who was acquainted with the father of Ujjwal Singh Chauhan and Praveen Chauhan. I must admit, I was unaware of this connection, but once again, I found myself expressing gratitude to Mother Narmada for leading us to the precise locations we were meant to visit.

On this particular day, both brothers had made arrangements to convene and subsequently departed under the cover of darkness.

59

Cold Winter

The crisp morning breeze was merciless, piercing through our skin as we trekked on foot from the neighbouring farms where the wheat had been planted. As we made our way through the fields, the morning dew that had settled on the crops overnight clung to our clothes, dampening our steps. Shivanand Maharaj took the lead at first, but as the dew began to soak him, he graciously relinquished his position to me. As we traversed the farm, the dew that had settled in the wheat crop left me thoroughly drenched by morning.

As we arrived at the Amri Ghat, a curious incident unfolded. Nandlal Tayal approached us and shared an intriguing piece of information. "The local *pandit* claims that Lord Shiva once graced this very spot and indulged in the delectable Indian gooseberries, hence the name Amri Ghat", he revealed. I could not help but chuckle at the amusing anecdote. As I had taken the lead in providing details about the various temples on the Narmada bank, several members of our crew began to inquire about its significance and historical background in accordance with Indian traditions. Most of us, as laypeople, are unaware of the significance of the place, leading to a lack of appreciation for it.

60

Maidan-e-Kichad

On this particular day, we embarked from Amri Ghat, and I proceeded to expound upon the rich historical significance of the location, as per the tenets of Sanatana Dharma. Here is where the wives of celestial beings sought solace during the reign of Hiranyakashyapu, the demon who had seized control over much of the world. Here lies the sacred ground where the wives of *devata*s (divine beings) once performed their *tapasya*, seeking the blessings of Devi Parvati, who blessed and wives of the divine and prophesied that a child named Prahlada would be born into Hiranyakashyapu family, destined to make a tragic end of Hiranyakashyapu who eventually was killed in the Narsimha *avatara*. Since the divine *devi*s found the blessings from here and had made the divine Lord Amara (immortal) the place was called Amri Ghat.[1]

After explaining the history of the place, we left from the trails of the forest and farms. Having recounted the rich history of our departure point, we ventured forth from the verdant expanse of the forest and farmland, our journey taking us beyond the tracks. As we made our way through a farm, we encountered a treacherous irrigation system that we aptly dubbed the "sprinkler-killer". The narrow pathways proved to be quite slippery, especially during the winter months when the sprinkler was in operation. It was imperative that we navigate the terrain with utmost care to avoid getting drenched by the relentless spray.

One of the most significant issues in the Narmadapuram and Narsinghpur districts lies on the banks of the revered Mother Narmada. The farmers have taken up illegal farming practices without considering the impact on the *parikramavasi*s who frequent the area for when they do the *parikrama*. The prevailing trend of bypassing banks and opting for highways has resulted in a weird trend which also means that many *tirtha*s that are on the banks will get forgotten and with them the history of Sanatana Dharma.

On this particular day, while crossing the farmland where sprinkler irrigation was on, I conveyed to Maiya my reluctance to get wet. Despite my reservations, I had to traverse a distance of approximately half a kilometre while the sprinkler was in operation. Remarkably, I managed to cross without getting drenched, save for one unfortunate slip at a certain point. Kumar, who was present, documented the entire crossing episode, including the aforementioned slip, which remains vivid in my memory. I stumbled and quickly regained my footing. The scene appeared as though I had sustained a severe leg injury, yet to my relief, I emerged unscathed. Although I did not get wet, I did experience a sudden slip. Kumar has christened our muddy adventure as "Maidan-e-Kichad", which roughly translates to "The Great Muddy Plains".

61

Vanara Bhalu Vana – Bandrabhan

On the day of his birthday, Praveen Chauhan made the journey from Nagpur to Holipura. Despite the arduous journey from Nagpur, he persevered and successfully arrived at his destination. We journeyed to the *ghat* to perform the sacred *puja* in his birthday. The atmosphere was hushed, as if the preceding years had been bidding their time to converse with us on this very occasion.

We took our leave from his company and set out on our journey towards Shahganj. The muddy terrain posed a formidable challenge, especially since I had taken a tumble just the day before. The group was understandably hesitant to proceed on foot in the muddy farmland, but we continued our *parikrama* trying to find alternate route.

As we stumbled upon a *dargah* that coexisted with a *mandir*, I could not help but feel perplexed by what I saw. In the event that the gathering pertained to matters of religious concordance or commercial enterprise, wherein both faiths were represented, I merely observed from a distance out of inquisitiveness, yet promptly departed thereafter.

As we traversed the gentle waterstream and ventured into the realm of Bandrabhan, formerly referred to as Vanara Bhalu Vana (the forest of monkeys and bears), we were greeted by a sizeable congregation of primates eagerly anticipating our arrival. The steam was adorned with the graceful shade of an Indian *bera* tree, where mischievous monkeys frolicked and feasted on its succulent fruits with great delight. Struggling to traverse the stream, we could not help but notice the gazes of onlookers fixed upon us, perhaps even amused by our predicament.[1]

Upon our arrival in Shahganj, the town eagerly awaited our presence, greeting us with a rousing chorus of *bhajana*s in honour of Mother Narmada. The welcome I received was one that I deeply cherish, as a grand group sang the *bhajana* of Maiya Narmada. Upon arriving at the Shahganj guest house situated on the serene banks of Mother Narmada,

I hastily indulged in a refreshing shower to prepare myself for the customary evening *puja*.

On that fateful night, I consumed a portion of flour from Jyoti's residence, which resulted in a severe bout of illness. As I have recounted previously, the events of that evening remain etched in my memory.

62

Help Me to Walk

As the night wore on, a debilitating illness overtook me, leaving me feeling utterly depleted upon awakening. Despite feeling drained of energy, I persevered and took a refreshing morning shower. Without delay, I proceeded to carry out my daily ritual of performing the *arti* and *puja*. My body was consumed by an overwhelming sense of fatigue, causing me to question whether I possessed the strength to take even a single step further. Although my body yearned for a break, an inner drive pushed me to persist and keep moving forward. With a heart weighed down by fatigue, I implored Mother Narmada, beseeching her to relieve my pain. Despite being certain of my innocence, I humbly implored her to safeguard my bodily welfare, so that I could successfully traverse the 32-km path that loomed before me.

On that particular day, the auspicious occasion of Swami Vivekananda Jayanti coincided with our journey. Along the way, a few individuals expressed their desire for me to halt our journey and engage with the children. However, I had to respectfully decline their request, as it would have disrupted our carefully planned schedules and impeded our forward momentum. Thus, we continued on our path without interruption.

At every turn, an unrelenting issue loomed: individuals incessantly implored me to pause my schedule and engage in impromptu activities. Our daily itinerary was typically determined in the morning, with Jitendra Sharma taking charge of arranging our evening accommodations and ensuring that all vehicles were transported to the designated campsite. We would then make our way to the campsite on foot, following the predetermined route. If I were to venture into unexplored territories, it would certainly pose a challenge for those tasked with organizing my itinerary. I caught myself repeatedly murmuring the words "please do invite me next year", with the utmost earnestness.

On this day, from the early hours, Sahib Singh, a gentle soul from Nandner, joined us for the *parikrama*. During the height of the corona virus pandemic, he fell gravely ill and was hospitalized for a prolonged period of three months. However, through the grace of Mother Narmada, he miraculously recovered and returned to his loved ones, safe and sound. Despite his weak lungs, he valiantly walked alongside us for several days, though it was clear that each step was a great challenge for him.

Once again, we found ourselves traversing the roads. While it is commonly known as the path for *parikramavasi*s, it is primarily intended for vehicles. We were compelled to take precautions by ensuring that a vehicle trailed behind us, as walking on the road was fraught with peril. It is a challenge for me to convey to others that the *parikramavasi*s do not require roads, but rather "pathways" that are exclusively reserved for pedestrian use. Despite this, the general populace seems to prioritize the construction of roads. It is evident that those who have never undertaken the *parikrama* are unaware of the obstacles that it presents.

As I journeyed towards the quaint village of Jait, where the former chief minister of Madhya Pradesh resides, I could not help but notice the unassuming nature of the surroundings. As I strolled along the main road, a sudden downpour from the roof of the former chief minister's humble abode drenched passersby without discrimination.

63

Bharkacch

We lodged at the ancient Hanuman Temple adjacent to the remnants of the fabled Nainagarh kingdom during our stay in Nandner.

The tale harks back to a bygone era when the locale bore the name Nainagarh and was replete with opulence. The remnants it has scattered throughout bear witness to its presence. The village is overflowing with history, tucked away in every nook and corner. However, the locals seem to disregard these precious remnants, casting them aside as mere useless stones devoid of any value. It is quite unbelievable that I stumbled upon a massive heap of discarded objects outside the village. To my amazement, these objects were adorned with intricate carvings and resembled the very stones that make up the grand temples. The sight was enough to make me feel unwell, yet for the locals, it was a common occurrence. As they dug deeper into the earth, their shovels struck something hard and unyielding. Upon closer inspection, they discovered an ancient artefact of unknown origin, its purpose and significance shrouded in mystery. Every year, as the waters of the Narmada River recede and erosion takes place, a fascinating phenomenon occurs. Various statues emerge from the riverbed, each one a testament to the region's rich cultural heritage. Recently, a magnificent Shivalinga was discovered and is now being housed in a local temple, where it is sure to inspire awe and wonder in all who behold it.

The history of Nandner is one that is left to the whims of time to determine its level of intrigue. It appears that, at present, there is a lack of interest in this particular subject matter. It is worth noting that in close proximity to this location, an ancient skeleton dating back several millennia was discovered. Regrettably, the discovery was largely disregarded due to the construction of a dam, as there was a fear that archaeological investigations could impede the progress of the project.

As you depart from Nandner, a place called Bharkacch[1] comes into view, which holds a significant place in Indian Sanatana Shastras. In the *Vasishtha Samhita* and the *Srimad Bhagavata*, there is a tale of a sage named Saubhari Rishi who engaged in deep meditation on the banks of the Yamuna River. During his spiritual practice, he would immerse himself in a *kunda* within the river and concentrate on his meditation. Over time, the fish in the river grew accustomed to his presence and would fearlessly swim around him, even playing in his vicinity. In times past, Garuda would frequent this place in search of fish. However, this practice was met with disapproval from Saubhari Rishi. In response, he placed a curse upon Garuda, warning that if he were to return and take fish from the *kunda* of Yamuna, he would perish. Furthermore, the sage decreed that any individual who sought to harm another in this location would meet a similar fate and perish instantly. Garuda disregarded the warning and proceeded to retrieve the fish from Yamuna's *kunda*. However, he soon met the end of his life. As he beheld the lifeless form of Garuda, the revered vehicle of Lord Vishnu, a deep sense of sorrow overcame him. With great reverence and devotion, he chanted the powerful *sanjivani mantra*, and soon the mighty Garuda was restored to life, awakening from its unconscious state. The Garuda lacked the vitality and dynamism it once possessed. Saubhari Rishi imparted upon him the Harihara *mantra* and instructed him to embark on a journey to Bharkacch, where the mighty Garuda had once regained his lost vigour and energy through rigorous *tapasya*.[2]

There exists another tale of Bharkacch, one that speaks of the revered Bhrigu Muni. It is said that he arrived at this very place and performed the sacred Gayatri *purashcharana*, with the intention of benefiting Bali. As fate would have it, Bali emerged victorious in a battle against the gods, including Indra himself. Bharkacch, as it is known, owes its name to the fact that Bhrigu Muni once sojourned in this very place.

Further up there lies a place of great significance, as mentioned in the Shastras, known as Nardeshwar Mahadev. Despite our efforts to locate it, even at the *sangam* where it was believed to be, we were unable to find it. Here Narada Muni had done his *tapasya* and pleased Lord Shiva; Lord Shiva blessed the sage, proclaiming that he would henceforth be known as a Siddha Yogi – a perfected being who possessed the ability to traverse effortlessly through all realms. No longer bound by the limitations of mortal existence, divines and demons both will have respect for him and he will be able to see their wars. *Bhajana*s to please gods will be his one of the best kept blessings.[3]

As we journeyed forth, we stumbled upon a venerable temple steeped in history, beckoning us to delve deeper into its mysteries. The village was strewn with numerous old stones, seemingly abandoned and neglected, as if their presence held no significance to anyone.

64

Makara Sankranti

Makara Sankranti, the revered festival celebrated on the banks of the holy Narmada, witnessed a throng of people making their way to the river's shore. The air was thick with anticipation as devotees carried offerings of food to be presented to the River Goddess. The *bhandara* and *prasad* were to be shared among the other pilgrims present. The sight of the needle streams of people was a testament to the significance of the occasion. It was like a big, traditional celebration that did not require any planning but still had its own constraints.

As we strolled along the path towards the banks of Mother Narmada, it felt like we were wading through a sea of filth. It was as if we were traversing an infinite row of unflushed toilets, with no end in sight. Looks like we were on a holy pilgrimage following the footsteps of many, but little did we know that some folks had a different kind of "relief" in mind on the same path.

Amidst the fragrant air of the village, we stumbled upon a Shivalinga that bore a striking resemblance to the ones I had previously encountered in Nemawar and Devpath. Its central *linga* was flanked by four others, which seemed to envelop the sacred centrepiece. As we traversed the familiar path, I promptly pointed out the antiquated location. Before long, we stumbled upon a spot nestled beneath a sprawling tree. There, we discovered a plethora of ancient statues that took us back to the illustrious era of Indian history. However, they lay there motionless as if frozen in time.

Once again, we were unable to locate the significant *tirtha* site of Varuneshwar Mahadev,[1] which used to be situated on the convergence of the Varuna River with Mother Narmada. It is disheartening to witness the gradual disappearance of numerous *tirtha*s in Madhya Pradesh. As I was exploring, I chanced upon the Uttara Vahini Narmada – a place that is relatively obscure. According to Indian Shastras, this is the very spot where Yudhishthira had undertaken his *tapasya*, at one of the *sangams* where the Tendoni River converges with the mighty Narmada. In ancient records, this sacred site was referred to as Akashdipa Teerth. According to legend, the Pandavas illuminated oil lamps at this very location and performed their *yagya*. It is quite fascinating to consider that Yudhishthira specifically selected this spot for his spiritual practice, given that the Narmada River flows northward here, imbuing the site with great significance.[2]

65

Ketudhana

On one's *parikrama* of the Narmada, one will encounter numerous individuals who possess an immense dedication to the river. Many of these individuals can be found along the way. These individuals comprise the pool of supporters who provide a foundation for the *parikramavasis* embarking on their journey by foot. We spent the day in Boras, where a state government officer had established an *ashrama*. His wife managed the *ashrama* with their children, who returned from school to participate in the daily chorus.

As we journeyed towards Boras, our intended destination for the day, we embarked on a quest to locate Ketudhana[1] which is stated in the place where Khanda River merges with Narmada. Legend has it that Ketu, one of the nine celestial bodies in Indian astrology, had performed a rigorous penance at this very site, thereby earning a place of prominence among the planets. According to Hindu astrology, Ketu symbolizes the accumulation of karmic deeds, encompassing both positive and negative actions, as well as spiritual and other-worldly influences. The process of refining materialization to the spirit is symbolized by Ketu. This celestial body is known to be both malefic and benefic, as it brings about sorrow and loss, while simultaneously leading the individual towards God. To clarify, the process entails inducing a loss of material possessions with the aim of promoting a heightened spiritual perspective within the individual. Ketu, the celestial body, serves as a *karaka* (indicator) of various traits such as intelligence, wisdom, non-attachment, fantasy, penetrating insight, derangement and psychic abilities. It is widely believed that the veneration of Ketu can bestow prosperity upon the devotee's family, while also serving to alleviate the effects of snakebite and illnesses caused by poisonous substances.

66

Shokalpura

We departed from the banks of Narmada in the company of Jitendra Sharma, who would walk with us throughout the day which happened only once in *parikrama*.

The landscape stretched out before me, dominated by an endless sea of sand that imbued the environment with an ethereal essence.

Amidst the tranquil surroundings, the remnants of Jankateerth[1] lay before us, leaving us in a state of awe. The towering *ghat*, aged and grand, loomed before us, its splendour still apparent, while we absorbed the teachings of the Shastras, recounting its rich past. I had never before beheld a *ghat* of such grandeur, not on any of the riverbanks throughout the vast expanse of India. Maharaja Janak of Videha had performed numerous *yagya*s at this location and subsequently constructed *ghat*s for the benefit of devotees. Should you ever embark on a Narmada Parikrama and traverse the path as we did, you shall chance upon the remnants of an old *ghat*. Despite the passage of countless millennia, this structure endures, having been crafted through ancient techniques.

As we journeyed forth, we traversed the quaint town of Patai, renowned for the legendary figure of Patai Swami. It is said that he departed from this very place due to conflicts with the locals, but not before erecting a grand *ashrama*. Alas! this once-sacred abode has now been reduced to a heaven for drug users and other unsavoury characters.

Upon our arrival at Shokalpur, we were immediately transported to an ancient site imbued with the profound history of Sanatana Dharma. This was the very site where numerous divine deities, among them Lord Brahma and Prahlada, had undertaken their rigorous spiritual austerities. As per the tale of Sanatana history, the Shivalinga has existed since time immemorial and was established as Shukla Teerth by Lord Brahma. Upon arriving at this destination, one may feel as though they have reached the pinnacle of existence. However, this sentiment is ubiquitous along the banks of the Narmada River, as each *ghat* and location boasts an abundance of historical records from the ancient Sanatana tradition.[2]

At present, there exist two temples in this vicinity. The first, an ancient temple that has been renowned since time immemorial, is situated outside the walls. The second, a recently constructed temple dedicated to Radha–Krishna, is located within the confines of an *ashrama*.

I could not help but notice the stark contrast between two temples. The first, once revered by divine beings, now lay neglected and uncared for. A newer temple had been just a few metres away, meticulously adorned and maintained, yet lacking in the captivating stories of its predecessor. It was here that an ascetic had taken up residence centuries ago, undoubtedly drawn to the site for its spiritual energy. While the *ashrama* where he once resided still stood, the original temple had been left to wither away, a poignant reminder of the fleeting nature of all things. Compelled to recount the tale of the temple, I found solace in the fact that the locals were able to comprehend my narrative. Throughout the night, I had the unsettling feeling that the divine gods who are supposedly still guarding the temple's holiness were watching me from a few metres away where my sleeping van was parked.

Shokalpura to Gwarighat

67

Bilthari

After departing from Shokalpur, we arrived near Richavar, where the convergence of the Siddhavati River and the formidable Narmada can be found. In close proximity to this location, bereft of any notable settlements, we stumbled upon a treasure trove of ancient temples. The remnants of these sacred structures reverberate with the echoes of bygone eras. I was left spellbound by the resplendent temples, yet disheartened by the lack of regard shown by the local populace and administration. The exquisite idols, crafted with care and precision, are being repurposed brutally by individuals. Unfortunately, a significant number of these stunning creations are left to languish in storage rooms, accumulating layers of dust over time. The temple architectures evoke memories of the Parmara era. For an extended period, I remained in this location, utterly mesmerized by the stunning temples that graced the area, both on the riverbanks and beyond. Regrettably, many failed to fully appreciate their magnificence.

A profound sense of anguish overtook me as I pondered over the apparent neglect of the local administration towards the temple. Despite the possibility of private entities taking up the task of restoration, it appears that the archaeology department has shown little interest in the matter, leaving the temple to languish in a state of disrepair. Not only is it a tale of faith, but also a testament to the intricate cultural and architectural wonders that have been left to be swallowed by the sands of time.

We embarked on a boat to cross the deep waters and thus began our journey in Narsinghpur. Everyday, we found ourselves stranded in the fields along the banks of Narmada, owing to the irrigation practices of the farmers who had encroached upon the sacred land. The lack of space for *parikramavasi*s to walk was striking. It was in this very moment that I found myself scouring every nook and cranny for the renowned *parikrama* path.

On this particular day, we were graced with the presence of Raju from Gadarwara. He is a devoted follower of the esteemed Mahant Mangal Das Tyagi and arrived with much fanfare. Raju is a jovial and kind-hearted individual who also dabbles in the realm of politics.

As we gathered together, he inquired about the tea he had so kindly prepared for us. The atmosphere was electric, with a throng of people from Gadarwara who had come to see me. It felt as though we were perched on a tightrope, savouring our tea amidst the hustle and bustle of the great *parikrama*.

As the sun began its descent, we found ourselves settled in the quaint village of Balthari. Engaging with the local villagers, I delved into the topic of Narmada Yatra and Tirtha, and to my delight, the entire village had gathered to listen to our conversation. A year prior, a different saint had visited the village and requested that the locals prepare food and other offerings. However, the villagers were left dissatisfied as the expenses increased and they were unable to have a satisfactory glimpse of the saint. As Jitendra Sharma arrived to inspect the location, the villagers regaled him with their tale. Jitendra Sharma proceeded to inform the villagers that during our *parikrama*, we carry all of our belongings with us. The underlying principle of our journey is to refrain from imposing any burden upon the locals. Instead, we kindly request that the entire village refrain from preparing dinner and join us for the *arti* and *bhandara*. The villagers were taken aback by his proposal.

As the sun began to set, the villagers gathered together for a grand *bhandara*, one of the largest to date. The air was filled with the sweet scent of incense as they came together for the *arti*, followed by a hearty dinner that left everyone feeling satisfied. It is my belief that this has left a profound and enduring impact on individuals.

Balthari, or Bali Sthali as it is also referred to, has undergone a transformation over time. This location holds great significance as it was the site of numerous *yagya*s performed by the revered King Bali. Those who choose to reside in the *ghat*s of Balthari are said to be bestowed with an abundance of blessings.

68

State of Tirthas

Today, we traversed the Barman Ghat (earlier known as Brahman Ghat) only to be met with a sense of disillusionment. Barman, an ancient town steeped in history, is said to be the very place where Lord Brahma performed his rigorous penance and established the revered Brahmeshwar Mahadev.[1] Despite our ardent efforts to locate this sacred site, it remained elusive. In Madhya Pradesh, it was a woeful state of affairs as a significant number of *tirtha*s vanished from the banks without a trace.

Today Sunil Junankar and Pramod Bambal had come to see us and it looked like Sunil Junankar and Rahul Gandhi were in sync with their fashion choices! When Sunil Junankar showed up wearing the same shirt and trousers as Rahul's *pada-yatra* outfit, I could not help but wonder who was copying whom. But Sunil Junankar set the record straight and said it was actually vice versa.

Today, we were unable to take walks along the banks of Mother Narmada due to the irrigation that had been left on the fields without any thought on *parikrama*. This left us with no clear path to walk upon. Moreover, the use of sprinkler irrigation caused us to become drenched from head to toe.

69

Mrigkheda

The start of our journey took place in Manegaon, a delightful hamlet situated in close proximity to Barman. As we traversed the dense forest, a serene and tranquil ambiance enveloped us. As we made progress, a dilemma arose. The Narmada banks have fallen prey to the scourge of illegal landownership, resulting in the unfortunate occupation of its banks and obstruction of the *parikrama* path. Consequently, there are scarcely any trees along the banks upon which one may recline. The question lingers in my mind like a persistent melody: will the state government ever dare to venture upon these very paths?

It is interesting that Google Maps is completely incorrect in the Narmada Parikrama Belt, but Yogesh used to open it up for fun and check the places we assumed to go. Sometimes it will display the route as a motorized one from where we struggled to walk. The fact that individuals do not use these maps from becoming completely lost. It strengthened my conviction that I needed to provide a platform for the *parikrama* mapping, I was carrying out.

Upon our arrival at Murgakheda, it was revealed that the original name of this location was Mrigkheda, which denoted a significant presence of deer within the area. The location possessed an other-worldly quality that left me feeling quite peculiar, as though we had been transported to an entirely different planet. The sense of peculiarity arises from the fact that despite being on the *parikrama* route, a significant number of villages remain oblivious or indifferent towards it. It is plausible that even the *parikramavasi*s themselves have failed to engage with the local communities and raise awareness about the *parikrama*, as is customary along the rest of the route.

70

The Path

As the first light of day began to illuminate the sky, we set out from Mrigkheda and commenced a voyage along the vast network of highways. The expedition was a formidable and arduous undertaking. Earlier, our focus was captured by the presence of a swollen river that posed a challenging hindrance to cross. Consequently, we were left with no alternative but to alter our direction and embark on the highway, a path that has always evoked a sense of displeasure within me.

As our journey brought us closer to Jabalpur, the Jan Abhiyan team's excitement mounted as they made meticulous preparations to welcome us. Even amidst the dense forest, where I had sought respite, they were able to track us down with remarkable precision.

One cannot help but find it intriguing that Jitendra Sharma had embarked upon the very same path a mere day before. When inquired about the state of the traffic, specifically in regards to the presence of a vehicle safeguarding *parikramavasi*s from potential accidents, he confidently affirmed the absence of any such concerns. Furthermore, when queried about the level of convenience regarding pedestrian access along the pathway, he responded affirmatively. Contrary to what was anticipated, the reality unfolded in a manner that was markedly distinct. I had to make a call earlier than anyone had anticipated for two vehicles that could cover us on the road. Contemplating Jitendra's experiences during his voyages, I found myself lost in thought. It is possible that his understanding of the obstacles encountered by *parikramavasi*s is limited, owing to his unfamiliarity with walking.

71

Lamps to Shed Light On

Our journey began from Belkheda, with Bil Pathar as our destination. Along the way, we were compelled to pause by a village that beckoned us to visit the local temple and partake in some tea. It was there that we were regaled with the tale of Nanga Baba, a man who dispatched individuals to gather food and summon others to his cause as he journeyed onward. Having become acquainted with this man's character, people would often decline to welcome him specially seeing our preparations.

Once again, we found ourselves trudging along the highway, struggling to find respite from the sun and a spot to enjoy our midday meal. It was then that Sanjay Singh appeared with Indar Singh Jamnod and Ritesh Jaiswal, and I made the decision to veer off the beaten path towards the nearby banks. Though it was a challenging route, my exhaustion from walking on the highway made it a necessary diversion. Sanjay Singh, a bulky man, refused to walk with me when he saw my destination. He quickly turned and made his way to his vehicle, telling me that we would meet further ahead. I could not help but laugh at his reaction.

Today, we journeyed to the revered Saugandhikavan Teerth,[1] nestled in the picturesque vicinity of Sarraghat. This sacred site, situated on the banks of the revered Mother Narmada, exudes a serene and captivating aura. As the name suggests, this was once a breathtaking location, adorned with fragrant flora. Legend has it that this was the very site where hundreds of revered *rishis* performed their austere penance and offered homage to their ancestors. It was here that two distinct streams, known as Ganga and Yamuna (believed to be streams of the respective rivers), were summoned to converge and establish the sacred Triveni Sangam. Amidst the increasing development along the Narmada banks, one stream has become obscured from view. However, another stream continues to converge and, interestingly, this particular locale remains densely populated with verdant trees that serve as a testament to the rich history of Sanatana Dharma.

Further as we move forward, we come across another sacred site known as Brahmod Teerth.[2] This holy place is located a short distance from Gora village and is believed to have been the site of intense meditation and offerings by the revered *saptarshi*s. It is said that performing the rituals of *shraddha* and *tarpana* here can bring great benefits to one's ancestors. It was a regrettable circumstance that, despite my diligent efforts, I was only able to uncover the *gatha*s and not the revered Udamvar Shiva Temple. As per the ancient texts of Sanatana history, this temple was founded by the *saptarshi*s and was believed to be the abode of the deity who bestowed profound inner wisdom. A sense of unease took hold of me upon witnessing the complete collapse of *tirtha*s along the banks of Mother Narmada. It is my apprehension that if prompt action is not taken, we may soon be bereft of any ancient *tirtha*s on the banks of the Narmada in Madhya Pradesh.

By covering these *tirtha*s we closed in to Bil Pathar, a sacred location where Bali once performed a rigorous *tapasya*, as documented in the ancient Indian Sanatana Shastra texts.[3]

As we reached Bil Pathar we found ourselves enveloped by the *amavasya* (a night of the new moon). The tranquil Narmada River allured us to partake in the profound *dana* ceremony, where we offered lamps to the river as a sacred ritual. The mesmerizing view of the lamps drifting along with the gentle current of the river was truly a spectacle to witness. Performing the *amavasya dipa-dana* ritual is an incredibly personal and specific practice, which is why it was imperative that we carry it out on our own. Notwithstanding my sincere appeal, Jitendra Sharma and a handful of others opted to disregard my advice and, as a result, they may be required to endure a phase of rigorous atonement.

Amidst the serene banks of Mother Narmada, there stood a captivating figure who went by the name of Indar Singh Jamnod. His heart swelled with a profound yearning to make a significant impact on the numerous temples that adorned the hallowed banks of the river. I approached the revered Mother Narmada with a query regarding the true intention behind the wish that had been offered to me, and whether I should accept it. With a heart full of reverence, I implored Mother Narmada to reveal her thoughts on the character and sincerity of Indar Singh Jamnod. Should she find him worthy of notice, I pleaded with her to offer me a clue.

With an oil lamp clasped in his hand, Indar Singh Jamnod approached the sacred waters of Mother Narmada with great reverence. He then humbly presented the lamp to the holy river. It is a truly captivating phenomenon to witness the revered Mother Narmada accepting an individual's offering and transporting it from the depths to the very heart of her being, before ultimately returning it to the banks where the sacred temples are situated. On this particular day, we had offered nearly hundreds of oil lamps to the river. As fate would have it, all of the lamps, except for one, were carried away by the current and disappeared into the centre of the river. Interestingly, the lamp that was gifted to Mother Narmada by Indar Singh Jamnod defied the odds and made its way back to the shores. It is truly fascinating to observe the various ways in which a mother expresses her reactions.

The Bil Pathar Temple emanated an unmistakable Mughal flair, and what rendered it all the more captivating was the dearth of any other shrines in its proximity. One could behold the enduring legacy of Islamic architecture, a poignant reminder of the tumultuous era when Muslim rulers laid waste to the land, obliterating all other architectural styles. Consequently, the sole thriving genre of architecture in the region was Islamic, and each artist was proficiently trained in that distinctive style, leading to the construction of numerous temples where the style is not Sanatani.

72

Bil Pathar to Gopalpur

The town of Bil Pathar lies in close proximity to Jabalpur and Shahpura. Here, one can witness the fascinating amalgamation of Islamic architecture in Hindu temples. As I explored the area, this unique blend of cultural influences became increasingly apparent to me. I discovered that Islamic victories had made Shahpura a stronghold, and that the locals there had been instrumental in constructing new mosques and *haveli*s with the assistance of contemporary architects. Most of the works were commissioned by the Islamic armies that had conquered the area, leaving a lasting effect at a time when the locals had no alternative models from which to draw inspiration for their own constructions. The influence of Islamic design can still be seen in nearby temples.

The day prior, I had observed that Lokesh was not energetic and almost lost in his head which appeared to have been influenced by Saturn. Consequently, I requested that he offer some oil lamps to Mother Narmada on the *amavasya* on the new moon which happened yesterday. This ritual is believed to alleviate any obstacles that may have arisen due to the influence of Saturn. Today, we bore witness to the realization of a long-awaited event.

Upon our arrival at the lunch spot, a pack of dogs greeted us. To our amazement, they sat upright like humans as we enjoyed our meal. During the hour that we, the *parikramavasi*s, were partaking in our midday meal, it was intriguing to observe that they remained completely still and slumbered without so much as a glance in our direction. As soon as Lokesh settled down to enjoy his midday meal, these dogs rose from their seats and, in a manner of speaking, implored him for food.

It is said that dogs will grace your presence once Saturn has bestowed its blessings upon you. They are known to approach you during and after mealtime, as this act holds great significance. Dogs are believed to have a strong intuition and can sense positive energy, which is why they are attracted to people who have received Saturn's blessings.

On this particular day, we embarked on a journey along the entire length of Mother Narmada's riverbank. The scenery was breathtaking, but the trek was not without its challenges. At times, we found ourselves forging our own path, as it appeared that few had ventured this way before. While the journey was time-consuming, it was well worth the effort. As we arrived at Gomukh Ghat, a peculiar sensation overcame us. We noticed a group of cows lying lifeless nearby, yet that was not the most intriguing aspect of our encounter. To our surprise, a few individuals were cooking their meals in close proximity to the carcasses. I could not help but ponder over the kind of disposition they possessed, as they seemed impervious to the stench and had not taken any measures to perform the last rites. An *ashrama* existed, but it seemed to go unnoticed by many.

The atmosphere along the banks of the Narmada River struck me as peculiar. Revellers were indulging in libations and merrymaking, a sight I had never before witnessed and would never again encounter in the presence of the revered Mother Narmada. The area was inundated with a throng of visitors, many of whom seemed disoriented amidst the peculiarly attired individuals. Among them were those who appeared to be in poor physical condition, unable to traverse a mere 100 m despite being under the age of 45. The state of the nation's health is rapidly declining. It appears that people are not engaging in physical activity, as even a short 500-m walk can leave them feeling fatigued. The implications of this trend for our future remain unclear.

The flow of Mother Narmada was magnificent, and I found myself sitting on the bank for an extended period, completely entranced by her beauty and the gentle current. In many regions, the natural flow of the Narmada River has been disrupted by the presence of dams and mining activities. As a result, the once vibrant and lively Narmada can no longer be witnessed in its former glory.

On this particular day, our expedition took us on a path that traversed Bhedaghat, culminating in our arrival at the coveted destination of Gopalpur. In close proximity to this very location rests the quaint village of Tevar,[1] which holds a tale of immense significance in the annals of Indian history. Once known as Tripuri, this village is steeped in legend and lore. The tales of this locale have been recounted through various texts, among them is the revered *Srimad Bhagavata*. The *Vasishtha Samhita* notably recounts the tales of this place, wherein Lord Rama becomes acquainted with them.

In the tale recounted by Sanatana history, the vanquishing of the demons by the divine gods instilled a sense of apprehension within the latter, for it called into question their very survival.

In the interim, Mayasura crafted three magnificent cities, each fashioned from iron, silver and gold. These cities were embellished with an array of weaponry, showcasing Mayasura's extensive knowledge in this domain. Three cities, imperceptible and in constant rotation, rained down their arsenal upon the divine beings. However, due to their invisibility and rotation, the celestial gods were unable to retaliate. Beholding the divine deities beseeching him for salvation from the malevolent demons, Lord Shiva was implored to intervene.

Upon the entreaties of the other divine beings, Lord Shiva proceeded to engage in battle with the demons. The demons had made preparations in advance, constructing a *kunda* (tank) that contained the craved nectar of immortality. Whenever Lord Shiva vanquished a demon, Mayasura would take the fallen creature and submerge it in the *kunda*. After being bathed in the nectar and tasting its life-giving properties, the demon would be restored to life once more. The relentless cycle persisted, leaving Lord Shiva to ponder over how the demons were able to revive themselves time and time again. Despite the prolonged conflict, the war ultimately yielded no decisive outcome, prompting the deity to return to his abode in Kailasa. The divine deities implored Lord Brahma for salvation, to which he suggested seeking the counsel of Lord Shiva. Let us return to Lord Shiva and assess the situation, he proposed. Lord Shiva proceeded to recount the tale of Mayasura, emphasizing the elusive and deceptive nature of this individual. He suggested that only a deity as intelligent as Lord Vishnu, capable of employing similar tactics, could emerge victorious in any potential conflict.

Lord Brahma and Lord Shiva approached Lord Vishnu and recounted the tale to him. Upon hearing it, Lord Vishnu proposed that they engage in the game of Maya, or deception, once more with the demon. In a divine exchange, Lord Vishnu beseeched Lord Brahma to take on the form of a calf while he himself transformed into a cow. Together, they journeyed to the city of Mayasura where Lord Vishnu, in the guise of a bovine, began to imbibe the elixir of immortality. Some demons, observing the unusual sight, exclaimed in disbelief, while others cautioned against disturbing the cow. Unbeknownst to them, the cow was no ordinary creature, but

Lord Vishnu himself, who consumed all the nectar in the tank before departing. In that momentous era, Lord Shiva manifested himself and vanquished the cities of *asura*s and the demons. This is the very site where Lord Shiva wrought destruction upon the city of Mayasura, hence earning the name Tripuri. Over time, the name became distorted and evolved into Tevar. Lord Shiva is a truly exceptional deity, having even bestowed his blessings upon Mayasura and other demons. The latter had approached him with a plea and, in response, Lord Shiva imparted the *panchakshara mantra* to him. Together, they embarked on a spiritual journey, performing their *sadhana* at the banks of Mother Narmada. It was there that they established the Bahireveshwar and Tileshwar Mahadev.[2]

We spent a lot of time near Bhedaghat, on the magnificent banks of Mother Narmada, looking for Narmadeshwar, whom we wished to bring back with us from *parikrama*. We found numerous Narmadeshwars made of marble in the dried bed of the Narmada River.

Just before *arti* and *bhandara*, the local Judge Mr Mishra had come to see me. Our conversation was lengthy and centred around the topic of holy Narmada, including her health and future prospects. During our discussion, I took the opportunity to share my thoughts on the *tirtha*s and the various discrepancies surrounding it. Since we were closing in to Amarkantak, Lalaramji graced us with his presence and led us on our journey towards Amarkantak.

73

Gopalpur to Gwarighat

As we departed from Gopalpur, our hearts were set on discovering ancient temples steeped in history. Regrettably, our quest proved fruitless, and among the elusive sites was the revered Pippalada Rishi's temple. Amidst the residential abodes, we chanced upon several other ancient temples, albeit ensconced within private domains.

As we stumbled upon a temple, our curiosity was instantly piqued. A sense of awe and wonder enveloped us, as we could not help but ponder over if this sacred place was none other than the renowned Pipleshwar Mahadev?[1] We were shocked to see that the temple had been abandoned and that the revered icons had vanished. The temple's architecture showcased a unique blend of intricate carvings and vibrant colours, setting it apart from the Mughal era temples we had visited before. However, the presence of drug addicts and individuals seeking refuge from societal norms within the sacred space was disheartening, detracting from its overall sanctity. According to Sanatana mythology, this is where the Indreshwar Mahadev was established by Lord Indra following his *tapasya*. There was a Shani Temple nearby, and a small stream used to flow from Pipleshwar Mahadev that would merge with the Narmada River. All of the temples and their locations were visible until the 1970s, but during my pilgrimage, I was saddened that these locations from the great Sanatana mythology had vanished.

With unwavering determination, we pressed on, undeterred by the formidable obstacle that lay in our path, our destination of Gwarighat beckoning us with its allure. In our journey of *parikrama*, it appeared as though we were forging a fresh trail, slowly but surely.

As we ventured forth into the rugged terrain, our path led us to the awe-inspiring Trishul Ghat. According to the ancient Sanatana tales, it is said that this very site was where Lord Shiva brandished his formidable *trishula* (trident), thus creating this revered *ghat*.

Ramnagar, or Ramnagara Mukti Kshetra[2] as it is sometimes called, awaits beyond this juncture. According to the legend of Reva Khanda, it was at this very place where Lord Harishchandra undertook his penance. As per the legend, Lord Harishchandra exhibited great magnanimity by bestowing tens of thousands of cows, gold and several villages upon the brahmanas residing in Kurukshetra. By performing this noble and selfless deed, he secured a position in the esteemed Antariskha Puri.

In the annals of history, there existed a ruler by the name of Shashok who devoted himself to the practice of *tapasya* and the act of charity at the sacred site of Amarkantak. It is said that through the simple act of donating 1,000 cows to the revered brahmanas, he was able to attain the ultimate state of liberation. Harishchandra approached Brahmaji with a curious mind, seeking to understand the reason behind his inability to achieve liberation despite his numerous charitable deeds. Instead, he was only bestowed with a celestial city, which left him perplexed. According to Lord Brahma, the act of performing charitable deeds and enduring penance along the banks of the Narmada River held a greater significance than any other location. Upon discovering this, Harishchandra made his way to Ramnagar to commence his own acts of penance and charity. Through his relentless efforts, he attained liberation and the location was henceforth referred to as the Mukti Kshetra, i.e. the field of liberation.

As we ventured forth, my excitement grew at the prospect of beholding the renowned Tilabhandeshwar Mahadev,[1] an ancient *tirtha* situated on the banks of the revered Mother Narmada. However, to my dismay, this revered site appeared to have vanished without a trace. Despite my persistent efforts to locate the temple of Tilabhandeshwar, as recounted in the Sanatana tales, it remained elusive. As per the Sanatana history, it is said that a group of revered sages, including Rishi Bharadvaja, Yagyavalkya, Durvasa, Vamadeva, Vasishtha, Vishvamitra and Jamadagni, embarked on a sacred journey to perform the Narmada Parikrama. It is believed that they arrived at their destination on the auspicious day of Makara Sankranti. During the Sankranti festival, the customary offering of sesame seeds posed a challenge as they were nowhere to be found. Frustrated and unable to procure the essential ingredient, they resigned themselves to slumber. In the dream, the revered *rishi* was graced with the presence of Lord Shiva. The deity revealed that a Shivalinga, once worshipped by Banasura, lay submerged in the waters of Narmada. The Shivalinga bore the distinct marking of sesame (*tila*). Lord Shiva instructed the *rishi* to embark on a journey into the waters and retrieve the Shivalinga, so that it may be worshipped with due reverence.

They followed suit, located the Shivalinga, performed their *puja* and reaped the benefits of Sankranti *puja* with sesame seeds. The Sankranti festival, which is celebrated with great enthusiasm throughout India, appears to have originated from these tales and stories. The Narmada belt is a place of great celebration, where people gather to bathe, cook, share meals. The inability to find the temple in the nearby area was a discouraging experience for me.

It was a sombre day as we traversed the area, finding few temples to explore. My displeasure grew to the point where I found myself speaking more loudly than usual, expressing my disbelief to the Jan Abhiyan vice- president Dr Jitendra Jamdar about the lack of attention from the local government.

Our lodging was the ancient *ashrama* of Vikasanand Maharaj, a revered figure in the Tantrika tradition. I had the privilege of staying in the very room where he once resided and the ambiance was delightfully rustic. Kumar fancied himself quite the explorer as he traversed the entire *ashrama*, but was left scratching his head at the peculiar placement of the books. Kumar could not help but notice the pristine appearance of the books, as if they had just rolled off the printing press. The *ashrama* insisted that they had all been lovingly tended to by the wise *guruji*, but something about that claim did not quite add up.

The leader of the Jan Abhiyan Parishad arrived with his team and I recognized him from a previous encounter. During the period when the Madhya Pradesh government had launched the Narmada Abhiyan, I was cordially invited to deliver a speech at the programme held in Amarkantak. The esteemed Dr Jitendra Jamdar was appointed as the coordinator for the entire event.

As we concluded our *arti* and prepared for the *bhandara*, I took the opportunity to share some insights on the *tirtha*s situated along the banks of the holy Narmada River. I delved into the rich history of the *parikrama* and other relevant details. To my surprise, my audience member expressed his disappointment in not having known these facts earlier. Dr Jamdar publicly acknowledged that he had never given much thought to the *tirtha*s of the mighty Narmada and was deeply moved by my speech. He confessed that he had always believed the *tirtha*s mentioned in the Shastras to be mere stories, but my words had opened his eyes to the fact that they were indeed rooted in history and could still be explored.

Gwarighat to Amarkantak

74

Let Us Maintain Our Pace

As we embarked on our voyage from Gwarighat to Amarkantak, we were presented with a choice between two potential pathways. One option presented itself: to trace the winding path of the northern bank of Mandla. The other, however, offered a divergence from this route, bypassing Mandla entirely and forging ahead towards the destination of Amarkantak. We chose to take this specific route, as I had a suspicion that Nanga Baba, who was following us, might have been using a vehicle to advance ahead of me along a section of the path. I had an impression that he wanted to go ahead of me and for that he will do anything sinister.

I conveyed to Lalaram, the mastermind behind our travel plan, my eagerness to accelerate our voyage towards Amarkantak. At the outset, our intended path led us towards the northern expanse of Mandla, thereby requiring us to allocate extra days for our journey. Nonetheless, I was determined to maintain a consistent speed to reach Amarkantak before the person in question, whom I believed to be a dishonest and deceitful individual.

Opting for the abbreviated route, we wound our way through the dense forest. Our journey led us to the tranquil village of Dhanpuri, situated along the well-trodden path of the *parikramavasi*s. The construction of the Bargi Dam on the Narmada River has necessitated a slight deviation from the stream, as the water has engulfed several sacred *tirtha*s and eroded the ancient route of the *parikrama*. Our lodging was at the Nirankari Ashram, located on the outskirts of the village. It appeared that the Bhavan of Nirankaris had not been utilized for this intention in quite some time. The place was a sight to behold, meticulously maintained and yet, it seemed to be underutilized by the *parikramavasi*s and for other purposes. Our stay was simply delightful and we were fortunate enough to partake in a magnificent *bhandara* that was attended by the friendly local villagers.

Next day we left from here pretty early in the morning and in the evening we found ourselves staying in the heart of the forest, nestled in a serene location where a gentle river flowed nearby. Thanks to our meticulous planning and preparation, we had the freedom to choose our ideal spot for lodging, which was truly a testament to the capacity of the organization committee. Needless to say, I was overjoyed with our successful arrangements.

A throng of onlookers had congregated, their curiosity piqued by the unfolding spectacle. The initial glimmers of lights and the emergence of tents began to captivate their attention. Their astonishment was palpable as they laid eyes upon us, the *parikramavasi*s, the masterminds behind this meticulously orchestrated affair.

Once our tents were pitched, we gracefully settled into the embrace of the forest, as if we were intrepid pioneers forging a new settlement amidst the towering trees.

75

Future of the Nation

On the auspicious occasion of Basant Panchami, Sanatani joyously commemorate the advent of spring, a season that brings forth rejuvenation and vitality. This cherished day also serves as an opportunity to pay homage to the revered Goddess Sarasvati, the divine embodiment of knowledge, wisdom and the pursuit of learning. We conducted all the necessary rituals amidst the serene forest, in our tented city that our organizing team had made for our stay. As the day progressed, we eagerly awaited the development of our tented city where we would spend the night. As we journeyed along the path of Narmada Parikrama, our dedicated organizing team worked tirelessly to prepare the city for our return and much-needed rest. From the very outset, the organizing team had been attentive to every need, ensuring that all arrangements were made and all necessary purchases were secured for the *parikrama*. Amidst the forest and barren land, they had meticulously planned and executed every arrangement necessary to establish a city. In the years to come, it is quite probable that this particular organization will etch its name into the annals of the *parikrama* path, leaving an indelible mark on the collective memory of those who traverse its hallowed grounds.

On that particular day, I found myself engaged in a spirited conversation regarding the subject of toilets along the *parikrama* path. It struck me that this particular topic had scarcely been broached in the discourse surrounding the *parikrama* path. Upon the hallowed shores of Mother Narmada, a multitude of *parikramavasi*s embark on their sacred pilgrimage, traversing the length and breadth of this revered river. These devout souls find solace in the nourishment and shelter provided by their generous hosts, yet, alas! the humble lavatories have gone unnoticed, their significance overlooked. Additionally, I made donations towards this cause. The school was packed with pupils and their parents, and I was requested to speak to them on the occasion of Basant Panchami as we walked there. The people who make their homes on the banks of the holy Narmada, I said, have a special obligation to reflect on their past and plan for their future. I argued that it is crucial for the youth and the country's future to learn about the country's history, its political and religious systems and the significance of its faith, all of which provide not only an inner holiness but also the intellectual foundation the country so desperately needs. Since the next generation cannot come into being unless children are educated, I pleaded with their parents to provide them with new knowledge every day. We are not respecting our lives or our earth if we do not seek out fresh knowledge every day. I also suggested the institution host an essay contest on the topic and donated a sum for the competition.

As we pressed on from the hallowed halls of academia, our path led us into a desolate expanse, where the earth itself seemed to bear the weight of its inhospitable nature. The land, barren and unyielding, offered little solace to the toiling farmers who laboured tirelessly in hopes of reaping a bountiful harvest. Alas! their efforts were met with disappointment, as the meagre fruits of their labour served as a stark reminder of the unforgiving nature of their surroundings. The dire consequences of such circumstances left the local populace in a state of abject impoverishment. With great fervour, I implored all individuals within my reach to embark upon the noble endeavour of gathering seeds, meticulously selecting those of utmost quality and potential. It was my ardent desire that these precious seeds find their rightful place within regions blessed with the ability to retain water during the forthcoming monsoon season.

On a particular day, Deepak Bansal, Vinod Hisaria and other Delhi residents and part of organizing committee joined us for a few days. In our tented city the moon shone brightly on that particular evening, revealing to us a remarkable Shivalinga formation that remained visible throughout the duration of our *arti*. It was a powerful reminder of the immense support that the divine mother provided us on our *parikrama*.

76

Seeds to Be Sown

On that day, we had the opportunity to witness a plethora of fossils. As we explored the area, we stumbled upon a fossil park and I urged my companions to take a look and not miss out on the experience. While they stayed behind, I ventured out with Kumar and Yogesh to a nearby land, a mere few hundred metres away. To our amazement, we discovered fossils that were not present in the museum. Upon reuniting with the rest of the group, they expressed disappointment at not having witnessed such a remarkable sight.

On this particular day, a Member of the Legislative Assembly hailing from the nearby locality came to a halt in his vehicle while en route to his destination. However, it appeared that he was not acquainted with our identities. I was informed that he is the MLA. Upon meeting him, I detected a hint of arrogance in his demeanour. However, I have a particular method of handling such individuals. When he inquired if there was anything we required, I responded that he was unable to fulfil any of our needs as it is taken care by Holy Mother. Nevertheless, I suggested that he could participate in the daily *bhandara* and *arti* ceremonies.

As the sun gradually descended upon the town of Shahpura, we were greeted with a cordial welcome from the residents. During that moment, our paths again crossed with that of the MLA. As our gazes met, I could not help but be intrigued by the reaction that flickered across his face.

On this specific day, Lalaram and I got into a discussion about gathering as many seeds for planting as we could along the Narmada belt. The topic of our conversation revolved around the promising possibility of harnessing the power of these seeds to fashion seed balls, a clever method that would allow for their widespread distribution along the picturesque banks of the majestic Narmada River. With fervent anticipation, we held onto the hope that a handful of these seeds would gracefully awaken from their slumber and embark on the wondrous journey of germination, firmly establishing themselves in the fertile soil of our aspirations. In this way probably we would increase the awareness among the *parikramavasis* for their duty towards the banks of holy Narmada.

77

Ma Narmada Jayanti

Upon the propitious commemoration of Narmada Jayanti, I had conveyed my yearning to observe the occasion in a remote location, distanced from the commotion and glamour of the urban centre. I was overjoyed when Mother Narmada made arrangements for the festivities to be held at Takanghat. This charming *ghat* is nestled on the serene banks of the Narmada River. The entire community, including those who had made their homes in the neighbouring forests, came out for the *bhandara*. Celebrating the Jayanti amidst the *janya-jatis*, a people who reside in the forest and hold a special place in my heart, was a truly heartening experience.

On this particular day, we embarked on a journey through the dense forest, traversing its entire length. Our guide led the way, and during our trek, he presented me with a *kadua kanda* (a potent energy booster). Despite its bitter taste, a single bite could sustain one for an entire day. This particular plant had been sought after by Prabhu Dutt Brahmchari during his travels, but he had never been able to locate it. Remarkably, I stumbled upon it after half a century had passed.

In front of us stretched a grand *ghat*, where the tranquil current of the Narmada River unveiled its shallow depths and subdued might. Despite the knee-deep water and the absence of any bustling activity, the *ghat* exuded a serene and picturesque charm. The area was surrounded by a dense thicket of trees and in distance lived many *janya-jatis* and their families.

This particular *ghat* is known as "Takan", as the stones along the banks of the Narmada were inscribed with many things. Unfortunately, the darkness of night prevented me from seeing these inscriptions, which means I must return once more. Despite this setback, we were able to perform *dipa-dana* and witness a beautiful scene with the villagers and other individuals who are often overlooked by society. The local people were greatly appreciative of the recent *bhandara*, as it was an unprecedented event that left a lasting impression. As I basked in the beauty of my surroundings, nestled among the *janya-jatis*, I could not help but feel a sense of gratitude towards Mother Narmada.

Throughout the night, the entire village remained in our company and the *bhandara* was met with tremendous enthusiasm.

78

Kids Are Not Kids

As we departed for Takanghat, our sights were set on Nunkher as our final destination. Our journey took us along the banks of the Narmada, a challenging yet breathtaking path. The towering stone walls appeared to be guarding the river's entrance, preventing its flow into the surrounding area.

The entirety of the walk was a sight to behold, with the villages adorned in exquisite decorations that truly captured the essence of the *janya-jati* culture. Once again, Google Maps proved to be unreliable as it directed me towards the wrong direction or even towards a path that did not exist.

It is quite amusing that even the natives have not ventured into these uncharted territories. However, a group of young lads took it upon themselves to guide us through the wilderness. Alas! their enthusiasm waned when we reached a treacherous stream crossing. I must say, it was one of the most challenging experiences I have had. The rocks were like daggers piercing through our bones and the water was as slippery as a politician's promises. Yogesh beckoned them to lead the way, but the youngsters stood there like statues, petrified as if they were staring down the barrel of danger. Well, well, well, how fascinating!

We journeyed across most of the expanse, carving our own way and grappling to discover a fitting refuge from the scorching heat of the sun. We finally found a spot of shade next to the road and stopped there to have our lunch.

It was Gaurav's birthday who was part of our team and it started with an unforeseen twist of fate as he discovered himself stranded in the midst of a thick forest. He had a habit of walking a few steps behind us, but on this particular day, the path was filled with numerous sharp turns. As a result, he lost his way and ended up trailing off in a different direction. Undeterred by the difficult terrain, he persisted and, after covering several kilometres, he ultimately rejoined us. On this particular day, a certain individual by the name of Chaubeyji, hailing from the local vicinity, was observed traversing with sand in tow. He made a rather peculiar claim that people are capable of walking up to 70 km in a single day. This assertion was met with a round of laughter from those in his company including me.

Nunkher was the destination of our stay for the night. The village appeared to be inhabited by individuals of modest means, yet they had imparted their offspring with a rich cultural heritage. Upon my arrival at the village in the evening, I was struck by the remarkable nature of the children there. Without hesitation, they all eagerly joined in. Eager to capture the moment, they eagerly requested to take photographs with me and participate in the sacred *puja*s of Narmada Maiya's *kalasha*. As was customary, a *bhandara* (communal meal) was held. However, the attendees were of such refined character that they even offered to assist with various tasks around the camp. Nandlal Tayal, with graciousness, declined their offer and instead invited them to gather around me and pose any questions they may have had.

As night fell, I inquired about the attendees, who will be present for the morning *puja* and *arti*. To my surprise, every hand in the room was raised in response. The following day, they all arrived as promised and accompanied us on a journey spanning over 1 km.

79

Nunkher to Dindori North

We set out at the crack of dawn, accompanied by the little ones who joined us for a few kilometres. I graciously extended an invitation for them to indulge in a delectable breakfast at one of their preferred establishments which was a roadside eatery which they really liked and we bid farewell looking into eyes of each other.

It was lunch time and we were not seeing any place where we could have lunch but at the end we found a place which was not exactly great but still I thought better to have lunch here then delay. Lokesh arranged the place for us to have lunch and I went to rest after lunch this is when.

As I arrived at the serene location of Dindori North, a flawless automobile was already in place, having been sent from Delhi solely for my personal convenience. I was fortunate enough to witness a turn of events that brought a smile to my face. Prior to commencing the *parikrama*, Praveen Chauhan had procured a vehicle that was converted into a commodious chamber, replete with comfortable beds and other amenities to facilitate my repose. Additionally, another vehicle was designated for my exclusive use, equipped with restrooms and a cosy seating area, enabling me to operate my computer with ease. During my *parikrama*, I relied on two vehicles to accommodate my needs for both nightly rest and daily rituals. However, the vehicle that boasted a toilet began to experience issues over the course of several days. Fortunately, a replacement vehicle was dispatched from Delhi. This new vehicle was unique in that it combined the space of the two previous vehicles. It featured a bedroom, a toilet and even a workspace for me to utilize after completing my *parikrama*.

The recently obtained automobile was a remarkable improvement, equipped with all the necessary features for documenting the *parikrama* through written notes.

80

Book and Its Content

As I said that for quite some time, my van, which was equipped with a toilet, had been causing me trouble. However, on this particular day, a new vehicle that we had rented arrived from Delhi. It was so impressive that I found myself jotting down notes for this book. I could not help but think that I should have made this decision much earlier.

Now, I was able to both sleep and utilize the bathroom in the same location. Earlier, I possessed a pair of vans – one designated for toiletry purposes and the other intended for sleeping accommodations.

As we embarked on our journey from Dindori to Kachara Tola, the landscape that greeted us was reminiscent of a barren wasteland. The absence of trees was conspicuous, save for the occasional eucalyptus that had been planted. It was curious to note that the tree that had been chosen for plantation was one that had a reputation for being a water guzzler. In many regions, the practice of planting eucalyptus trees solely for aesthetic purposes in areas lacking water has become commonplace. Unfortunately, this practice has resulted in the depletion of already scarce water resources in these areas.

It is a curious circumstance that while the Narmada originates from this region, there appears to be a dearth of water in the vicinity. Kumar brought up an interesting point regarding the allocation of water from the Bargi Dam to the tribal communities. I nodded in agreement, but could not help but wonder who would take the initiative to address this issue.

81

Money Matters

Today, our journey led us to Damhedi, and as we embarked on our *parikrama,* I engaged in a thought-provoking conversation with the young individuals accompanying me. Our conversation revolved primarily around the subject of monetary matters, and I spoke about how I personally saw the functions that money serves. Instead of being something that can give and bring hops in life, money is a vehicle through which one can fulfil the responsibility that each person has towards their life, which is to achieve equilibrium and reach the sanctity of inner self.

On this particular day, we found ourselves resting after the *parikrama* in Kachara Tola, a hilltop location where our management team had made a tented city. Despite the windy night, the morning was a sight to behold. As an avid photographer, I took advantage of the picturesque scenery and captured many stunning images. The other travellers were taken aback by my photography skills.

What intrigued us the most was the ability to stay wherever we pleased, thanks to the comprehensive arrangements that covered all our needs. This afforded me the luxury of residing in serene locales, away from the hustle and bustle of the masses.

Once upon a time, the whole area was densely forested by *sarai* tree. However, in present times, it is quite challenging to witness the remnants of this once-thriving forest. The landscape was marred by the sight of numerous fallen trees, with no signs of new growth to replace them. The sight of more trees being felled than being planted was a disheartening one.

As we embarked on our journey, we came across numerous *parikramavasis* who had to undertake arduous journeys to far-flung locations, often beyond the *parikrama* route, in order to find food. The situation sparked a conversation about how we might offer aid to these individuals and prevent them from having to endure the strenuous trek of several kilometres to obtain food, only to repeat the process upon their return. The placement of the *ashrama*s holds significant weight in the decision-making process. With meticulous planning, aid can be extended in this regard.

82

Penance

It was still very dark in the morning when I got ready for the morning *puja*. I proceeded directly towards the *ratha* to perform the *puja*. It was customary for us and in daily ritual that flowers were presented to deities. However, on this particular day, an unusual occurrence took place – the customary offering of flowers were not there when I reached. Perplexed by this, I inquired as to the reason behind this forgetfulness, none had the answer. After a brief search, the much-needed flowers were eventually located, a mere five minutes later. As I delved into the matter, it became clear to me that the mistake in question demanded a thorough examination. It dawned on me that Mother Narmada was orchestrating this, testing our devotion to the rituals we perform, Moreover, I had the impression that our Panditji and the other members of the *parikramavasi*s had committed errors that call for *prayaschitta*.

With meticulous attention, I made certain that every individual within our collective comprehended their distinct duties. At first, only Panditji would go through the motions of performing penance by abstaining from food for the entirety of the day. However, after some consideration, I came to the conclusion that all *parirkamavasi*s including me should abstain from food while the campers continued with their normal activities. Embarking on a 32-km journey, we relied solely on our penance and the divine blessings of the mighty Narmada River to lead us in our pursuit of the sacred ritual of *prayaschitta* (penance). It was a fascinating experience to have refrained from consuming any food throughout the day. Although I believe that the mistake was made by Panditji, I also acknowledge that every mistake is a collective responsibility. As a result, all of us, the *parikamavasi*s, walked a distance of 32 km while fasting. It was intriguing that none of us felt weak, for it was Mother Narmada who bestowed upon us the strength to tread and aided us in comprehending the intricacies of the *parikrama*, which encompassed regulations and conventions.

As we made our way along the *parikrama* route, it became apparent that Mother Narmada had yet many more challenges in store for us. With a steady pace, we ascended the Maikal Mountain, the very birthplace of her existence. Soon enough, we found ourselves confronted with yet another test. For quite some time now, I have firmly held the conviction that Mother Narmada will have a way of testing the limits of one's *parikrama* endurance in unforeseen manners and at unforeseeable moments.

83

Jai Shri

Our journey began at Ferrisemar, a charming and picturesque village. Amidst the persistent chill of the season, I assumed the responsibility of distributing winter garments to the children. Having completed our task, we set out on our day's adventure – a walk further up into the Maikal Mountains. As our journey brought us closer to Amarkantak, Kumar's gaze was captivated by a breathtaking Shivalinga. Its exquisite beauty left me in a state of wonderment. Moved by the moment, I requested that Kumar to obtain the sacred Shivalinga. It was then that I felt the divine blessings of Mother Narmada, who had bestowed upon us this precious Shivalinga as we approached the very place of her origin.

I had the good fortune to meet Swami Milind on this auspicious day. Swami Milind was a well-known RSS *pracharak* in the past, but he is currently in his *sadhana* and is recognized for his enigmatic personality. In spite of his reputation, he kindly made an exemption and bestowed upon us the honour of his personal attendance. Much to our delight, he even graced us with his presence for a delightful dinner. Accompanying him was his revered *guruji* (a man of immense importance).

There is a story that I feel compelled to share. During our *parikrama*, I have had the pleasure of hearing from several individuals who were accompanying us on the journey. Swami Milind is renowned for his reclusive nature, as he refrains from venturing outside his abode to meet with others. Unbeknownst to me, we had arrived at the abode of Swami Milind where he currently resides and practises his *sadhana*. Upon our arrival, I eased myself into a comfortable chair to take a moment of repose. At that moment, my attention was drawn to a gentleman leisurely walking past, accompanied by Jitendra Sharma. After exchanging pleasantries, an irresistible urge took hold of me, prompting me to invite him to join me for a cup of tea. It was with joy that I observed him nodding in agreement.

Yogesh approached me and disclosed that the individual they had previously mentioned to was none other than the reclusive inhabitant of the diminutive hut, who had emerged to greet us. Once more, Yogesh explained that Swami Milind solely embarks on excursions to procure the essential vegetables for his personal culinary endeavours. I was pleasantly surprised by his unexpected visit. It is worth noting that during our conversation, I inquired about the agreed-upon time for tea. Swami Milind promptly responded, suggesting a window between 3:30 and 3:45. I acknowledged his proposal with a nod of agreement.

As I reclined in my caravan bed for a brief respite, time seemed to slip away from me. Suddenly, an inexplicable urge stirred within me, compelling me to rise from my repose. Without hesitation, I stepped out of the vehicle and called for a cup of tea. It was as if an inner voice whispered to me that Swami Milind's arrival was imminent. As I summoned the tea, my gaze fell upon Swami Milind and a companion in his company.

Swami Milnd's companion possessed a pair of striking eyes that immediately captured my attention. There was an enigmatic quality to his gaze that caught my curiosity and left me feeling intrigued. With unwavering confidence, I strode towards the pair and offered a courteous salutation of *Narmade har*. All of them replied, and I offered my apologies for the delay. Swami Milind expressed his awareness of my incomplete rest and had requested my attendants to knock on the door. However, my attendant, who is not accustomed to interrupting my rest, did not comply with Swami Milind's request.

With a gracious demeanour, I offered a cordial greeting to the two individuals before me and motioned towards my awaiting vehicle. With a solitary chair at our disposal, my attendants graciously extended it to me. It occurred to me that it would be discourteous to occupy the chair while Swami Milind and his companion were relegated to the stools. In light of this realization, I politely refused the offer. I made a polite request for stools to be provided so that all of us could be comfortably seated. I suggested that we all sit on stools together. The tea had arrived and we began conversing. It was then I became clear that the person whose gaze is so captivating must be the *guru* of Swami Milind. It was only *guruji*, who was engaged in dialogue with me and Swami Milind was quite all through, only sometime he would say yes or no or smile during the interaction we were having.

I was taken aback by Swami Milind's uncharacteristic reticence in the presence of his spiritual mentor. The *guru–shishya parampara* (tradition) is one that is steeped in mutual respect and deep affection between its participants.

We conversed for approximately an hour, during which time I attentively listened. As the tea time drew to a close, Swami Milind brought over the glasses in which the tea had been served. I requested that they be cleaned, but unfortunately, the cleaning was not thorough enough. Upon noticing this, I took it upon myself to wipe the glasses clean with my paper napkins. The *guru* of Swami Milind took note of this and remarked to Swami Milind that attention to detail was of utmost importance. Laughter filled the air as I extended an invitation to both *guru* and *shishya* for a dinner, which they graciously accepted.

As dinner time approached, Swami Milind was the only one to arrive and inform us that *guruji* was currently in the midst of a *havana*. He had requested that his dinner be brought to him. Later on, it was revealed to me that *guruji* had not consumed any solid food for the past five days, subsisting solely on milk.

Swami Milind sat next to me and, as we began to dine, we delved into a conversation about our respective pasts. He shared with me the rich tradition from which he began his *sadhana*, and I was pleased to inform him that I had previously engaged with this very same tradition on numerous occasions. Our exchange left us both feeling content and fulfilled. Jitendra Sharma, a former member of RSS, stood beside us with the demeanour of a diligent student. I promptly notified Swami Milind, who had previously served as a *pracharak* for RSS and was familiar with Jitendra. Upon receiving the news, Jitendra leaned back to divulge his personal information. It was at this moment that I observed Swami Milind's voice transform, as if the old *pracharak* had returned. I found it amusing to witness Jitendra Sharma near surrender to him. It was as though one could glean valuable lessons on conversing with RSS *pracharak*s from this encounter. It is an intriguing fact that Jitendraji and several members of *parikrama* had previously worked with the RSS. As a result, many individuals assumed that I was a member of the central team of *pracharak*s and would treat me accordingly. As I would enter the town, *pracharak*s would appear and began to provide me with information about their work. After encountering Swami Milind and engaging in a conversation with Jitendra Sharma, I occasionally found myself mimicking his acting for the sake of amusement. Without fail, it always proved to be a source of great hilarity.

As we concluded our meal, Swami Milind requested that we pack some dinner for his *guru*. With great care, I selected the *tikkad*, a plump wheat *chapatti* that has long been a staple in the Narmada region. I then prepared the *thali* for his revered *guruji*. Together, we made our way to the gate of his *guru*'s residence. As I approached the gate, I halted in deference to the no entry zone. However, Swami Milind beckoned me forward, assuring me that the rule did not apply to me. Together, we made our way to the presence of *guruji*, who was engrossed in performing a *havana*. Upon noticing our arrival, he warmly welcomed me to his *asana* and bade me to take a seat. Swami Milind was taken aback by the depth of affection shown to me by *guruji*. As I settled into my seat, he suddenly broke down in tears, overcome with emotion. Witnessing this, I could not help but feel a few tears well up in my own eyes. As we sat together, we found ourselves drawn to each other's feet, gently touching them in a shared moment of connection. It was a rare and profound experience, one in which we saw ourselves reflected in each other and felt a deep sense of unity.

As we sat in silence for some time, the *guruji* finally broke the stillness and requested that I retrieve the *bhasmi* from the *havana*. I respectfully asked if he would be willing to administer it himself, as it was his *havana* after all. I was aware of the customary practice that dictates that one must not handle the sacred substance without express permission from someone of his stature. The *guru*, recognizing my familiarity with tradition, proceeded to take some *bhasmi* for himself. Placing it on his own forehead, he then transferred it to mine before giving some more to be distributed it amongst the other members of our *parikrama*.

On a fateful night during his *parikrama*, Kumar was plagued by a haunting dream that left him feeling unsettled. It was during this moment of introspection that he came to the profound realization that his life's purpose was not solely centred around his spiritual practices and connection, but rather, it was equally important to cultivate meaningful relationships with those he held dear – his family and society at large. Kumar had spent much time contemplating the trajectory of his life, vacillating between the paths of a monastic existence or a domestic one. Though the notion was not yet fully formed, he felt a certain inclination towards joining the ranks of the *sadhus* and embracing their way of life. But Maikal Mountain had finally made it clear what I had been suggesting to him throughout the *parikrama* carry on domestic life with spiritual inclinations.

84

Amarkantak

On this particular day, we made our way from the northern banks of the Narmada River to the southern banks, as we had arrived at the sacred site of Amarkantak.

Amarkantak, nestled within the heart of India, has long been revered as a sacred place within the Sanatana fold. Its illustrious reputation has stood the test of time, drawing pilgrims and seekers from far and wide. In the enchanting month of February in the year 2023, I found myself standing at this very spot, having embarked on a remarkable journey of spiritual significance, while I traversed the sacred path on foot, immersing myself in the profound beauty and sanctity of this revered pilgrimage. This sacred place, steeped in rich history and revered by the devoted followers of Narmada, has perpetually captivated the minds of writers, philosophers and the esteemed *rishi*s, *muni*s and saints of our nation.

Amarkantak holds within its embrace the very origins of the majestic Narmada River. Not only that, but it also serves as the birthplace of the Son, Johila and Kamandal rivers, each with their own captivating history and local tales of their inception.

Amarkantak Mountain

Amarkantak, a place of profound significance, finds mention in the revered texts of the Sanatana Dharma. These ancient scriptures bestow upon the entire mountain range a sacred aura, elevating it to a realm of utmost holiness. Such is the sanctity attributed to this sacred land that even those who breathe their last in its embrace are deemed to have attained the pinnacle of spiritual fulfilment.

Within the illustrious epic of *Valmiki Ramayana*, there exists a captivating depiction of the majestic Vindhya mountains. Interestingly, the name of Amarkantak, a notable location, is conspicuously absent from the narrative. However, the resplendent allure of Vindhyachal is eloquently portrayed in the Uttarakanda, wherein the account of Ravana's expedition to Mahishmati unfolds. It is within this enchanting backdrop that Ravana, driven by his unwavering spirit, embarks on a formidable encounter with the courageous warrior Kartavirya Arjuna, renowned for his unparalleled prowess.

In Valmiki's *Ramayana*, the author beautifully captures the picturesque allure of the Vindhyachal mountain range. With vivid imagery, he describes the towering heights of these majestic peaks, their summits seemingly merging with the ethereal clouds above. It is as if these mountains, so high and grand, have shattered the very earth beneath them, reaching upward towards the heavens. The poetry of the *Ramayana* extends beyond mere words, for it encapsulates the very essence of the majestic mountains. It weaves a masterpiece in the heavens, as if the grand peaks themselves write lines across the celestial canvas.

The poet, Maharshi Valmiki eloquently draws our attention to the majestic Vindhya mountains, likening them to the revered Himalayas. Through this comparison, he highlights their towering heights and abundant caves, which, in the future, shall transform into sanctuaries for profound contemplation. These very caves shall serve as abodes for countless sages, who shall seek solace and enlightenment within their hallowed confines.[1]

In the *Kurma Purana*, Markandeya Muni offers Yudhishthira the awe inspiring locale of Amarkantak where he says that the place is revered by millions of sages and and divine alike as all have found the blessings here by doing their *tapasya*.[2]

In addition to this, the *Kurma Purana* elaborates on the many *tirtha*s that are reported to be located in Amarkantak, and it tells the account of how completing the circumambulation of the Amarkantak mountain range is equivalent to performing the Paundarika *yagya*. Mohini is referenced in terms of Amarkantak's renowned *tirtha*s in the *Narada Purana* as someone who, when travelling to other holy towns, seeks out *darshana* at Amarkantak's *tirtha*s. In the sacred text of the *Skanda Purana*, amidst the narration of the Chaturmasa Mahatmya, a significant mention is made of Amarkantak. Within the revered pages of the Reva Khanda, a wealth of knowledge is bestowed regarding Amarkantak, the very birthplace of the revered holy River Narmada.[3] In the enchanting verses of the *Padma Purana*, a profound exploration of Amarkantak unfolds, revealing the myriad sacred *tirtha*s that grace the majestic mountain.

For countless millennia, the story of Amarkantak and its rich history has been passed down through generations. As I reflect on this quaint town, it strikes me as a serene hill station, where the focus is not on the Narmada Parikrama, but rather on the various enterprises that Mother Narmada has enabled the locals to pursue. There is little I can add to the timeless narrative of this remarkable place. This particular location held immense significance, for a single misstep could result in crossing the Narmada River incorrectly and thereby breaking the sacred vow that had been undertaken. It was imperative to follow the designated path with utmost care. The Narmada River, though diminutive in size, can be easily traversed by wading through its shallow waters. However, it must be noted that there are no signboards or markers to indicate its presence. It is intriguing that even in the midst of dense jungles, I have come across signposts indicating the *parikrama* route, yet here, in this place, there seems to be no such indication.

We continued our journey towards the Mai ki Bagiya, a sacred site that marks one of the origins of the Narmada River. From there, the water flowed gracefully towards the *kunda*. Lately, a great deal of confusion and hostility has arisen between the Mai ki Bagiya and the priests of *kunda*, which has been at odds for sometime now due to the conflict between their respective priests. I made sure to visit Mai ki Bagiya and walk along the correct route of *parikrama*. One of the most significant events in *parikama* is the changing of the holy banks and it needs that much care.

As we arrived at Mai ki Bagiya, a place notorious for mistreating those on the *parikrama* pilgrimage, I braced myself for the worst. However, to my surprise, my personal encounter proved to be quite different. Accompanied by the *kalasha*, we embarked on a changing the banks of Holy Narmada from north to south banks with the *rudraksha* and Shivalinga in a tow, paying homage to Mother Narmada. The transport that bore the sizeable *kalasha* was required to remain at a distance of more than 1 km before rejoining us on the southern shore, having successfully traversed it. Over the course of this journey, we were tasked with transporting a multitude of items, including *kalasha* (6 in numbers), a sizeable container of sacred Narmada water which was also on *parikrama*, *rudraksha* beads divided into several packs and a Shivalinga, all the way to the southern banks.

Several children arrived, seeking funds that they typically receive from the *parikramavasis*. I advised them to maintain a low volume and retrieve the money. In fact, at both Vimaleshwar and Amarkantak, where one switches banks on the Narmada, the local residents have been known to engage in preliminary discussions and cause inconvenience to visitors by demanding money.

I bestowed upon them the sum they had been seeking, and with it came a sense of tranquillity. Together, we made our way to the temple where we will change the shores and it is the ancient place from where one would change the banks of Narmada from north to south. The priests, who were in attendance, graciously granted us access to the entire premises. With great reverence, we conducted the sacred ritual of *arti* and procured water from the holy Narmada Kunda. Each of our *kalasha*s, including our individual one, was filled with this blessed water. According to historical accounts, it is customary to blend the water one carries during the *parikrama* with the water at the confluence of the sea and Narmada, as well as at its source. After the temple ceremony had concluded, we offered the *prasad* to the visitors, which was prepared and sent by our cooking team here.

With all the *puja* materials and *kalasha* in hand, we made our way towards the another *kunda* which is currently known as *udgam* or origin of the Narmada. It was a popular spot for changing the banks, but I was hesitant to enter. I knew that one wrong step could easily break the *parikrama* or cause me to cross the small water channels underneath the current temple premises and results in accidentally breaking the *parikramka* by crossing the natural flow of holy Narmada.

Within the local community, there exist *pandit*s who had become privy to our *puja*. They were cognizant of the fact that our primary *puja*, which involved the changing of banks of the revered Narmada River, had taken place in the Mai ki Bagiya. The priest in question began to assert that Mai ki Bagiya was not the appropriate site for altering the banks of the Narmada River, and he displayed a discourteous attitude towards the priests of that area. The moment I proposed a financial incentive, a flurry of priests descended upon me with the fervour of diligent bees. The spectacle elicited delight in all those who laid their eyes upon it.

Having just finished another *puja* and bidding farewell to the now familiar Narmada Kunda, I stumbled upon the Narmada stream that flowed beneath the platform. The sight of numerous individuals unknowingly transgressing the boundary, thus violating their pledge of *parikrama,* was truly dispiriting. The scenario brought to mind a comparable occurrence outdoors, wherein the municipal authorities had erected a thoroughfare. A multitude of *parikramavasi*s were traversing the path without realizing that they were violating the sacred vows of *parikrama* by crossing over the diminutive holy Narmada stream that flowed beneath it. Jitendra Sharma engaged in a lengthy argument with the priests regarding their perceived lack of effort in safeguarding the spiritual pledge of *parikramavasi*s during the *parikrama*. He expressed his concern that the *parikramavasi*s were not sufficiently knowledgeable about the terrain and, therefore, it was their responsibility to erect signboards and other markers to guide the *parikramavasi*s along the correct path but I do not think they had any impact as it is unlikely that they have embarked on a journey of Narmada Parikrama by foot.

By ending all kinds of commotion and having seen the Amarkantak and feeling sad by the affair how it is managed, and totally commercial vibe that I never got anywhere, I felt that it is better to walk ahead.

As I arrived at Jagatpur, one of the most stunning forest rest houses, I was immediately struck by the serene atmosphere. My companions and I spent the night there, and departed the following morning. Here I posed a question to my team, curious to know what they would offer me after *parikrama*? Some offered their time, while others offered their very lives. It was a fascinating experience, one that left me with a sense of wonder. However, not everyone was able to provide an answer, and I could not help but feel that this was a reflection of how Mother Narmada interacts with us all.

Amarkantak to Gadarwara

85

Jai Hind

During our journey from Jagatpur en route to Gorakhpur we encountered several locations where eager crowds eagerly awaited our arrival. At one such stop in a small village Karanjiya, which was known as Mundamaharanya,[1] I had the pleasure of meeting a *panditji* who had established himself in the area for quite some time. As it turned out, his father had been a revered local priest. The work for priests here is quite challenging. He had a captivating tale to tell. Upon his arrival, a few were able to comprehend his Bagheli the language of Baghelkhanda. However, he chose to remain and now the entire community seeks his presence for various ceremonies, including *puja*.

As we journeyed forth, we traversed the Seoni River, once known as the Shastravahini River. Along the way, we happened upon a diminutive village by the name of Survasa, now vanished without a trace. It was here that the esteemed Shri Gaurishankar Maharaj had held one of his legendary *bhandara*.

While I was crossing one village, I encountered an individual who mistook me for a member of the armed forces and proceeded to salute me with a resounding "Jai Hind!". Probably was I too dressed and did not look like *parikramavasi*s?

After bidding us farewell, Alok Nahar and Rohan embarked on a journey to Mai Ki Bagiya in Amarkantak. Upon their return, Alok regaled us with a captivating narrative about the Amarkantak Mai ki Bagiya, a place where I had generously donated funds to the priests. The priests' conversation was overheard, wherein they expressed their desire for someone like myself to arrive, as it would provide them with sufficient funds to sustain themselves for several weeks.

86

Madman

Amidst the sacred Narmada Parikrama, a momentous occasion unfolded as I was joyfully reunited with my beloved parents. Their arrival on this auspicious day filled my heart with immense happiness and gratitude. They arrived, bringing with them a stunning bouquet of flowers. Undoubtedly, it was an emotional journey for my parents as they bore witness to my 3,000 km trek.

As the evening descended upon the school, I arrived to find a group of eager children awaiting my presence. With a warm smile, I distributed small candies to each of them, eliciting joyous expressions of gratitude. Engaging in playful banter, I shared moments of laughter and merriment with my young companions. I asked Nandlal Tayal to prepare for everyone some savoury *kachauri* or *samosa* the following morning, in the hopes that these children may like eating them. I had left the educational facility in the morning, but I subsequently learned that the children were overjoyed to eat the savoury *samosa*s and, as a result, they contacted their parents to ask them to join them in consuming them. I had the impression that Mother Narmada is showering us with blessings in this way.

Every day, we were blessed with remarkable experiences that could fill volumes of books. Today Jitendra Sharma recounted a delightful anecdote, wherein, during the transportation of the cavalcade of vehicles including our *rath* which carried all the *kalasha*'s as well as all the *puja* materials the vehicles were halted at a weighing station. In a playful manner, Jitendraji exclaimed, "How dare you charge for *maiya ka kalasha*!" However, he knew that it was weighing only for the vehicle and no charges were asked despite this clarification, Jitendra Sharma persisted in his jest, causing a great deal of confusion. In the end, the officials asked them to continue on with their journey since they believed that some crazy people were hiding among the *parikrama* support workers. These people had normal appearances but acted in a strange manner.

87

Mischievous Kids

As we made our way from Dindori to Rai, our pace was leisurely, allowing us to fully indulge in the various forms of amusement shared amongst ourselves about the individuals who remained behind. These individuals, whom we affectionately referred to as the "camp people", were not trekking alongside us, but rather were integral members of our management team.

As I strolled alongside my cook, Jadu, after a prolonged absence, we took the opportunity to inquire about the tales of those residing in the camps. Jadu had a plethora of stories to share, including his observations of the indolent nature of the camp inhabitants. He recounted how they scarcely laboured, opting instead to slumber throughout the afternoon. However, as the evening approached and my return drew near, they would rouse themselves and prepare for the arduous tasks ahead.

On this specific day, I made a request to Kumar to perform his singing for us once again. Nevertheless, he had neglected to bring his *manjira* along. I communicated to him that I would request his performance only in instances where he had overlooked something. This realization prompted him to recognize that my concern extended beyond his singing abilities and encompassed his level of preparedness and attention to detail in all aspects of his work.

As we journeyed along the path, without *manjira* but sooner we had the pleasure of encountering some truly remarkable individuals. These people were passing by and seeing our entourage felt like singing for us, they slowed the bike in which they were travelling and sang timeless classic:

> *thali bhari bhojana se, pani se bhari gilasa, maiya teri yada mein bhukha lage na pyasa.* (A plate full of food, a glass full of water, but in memory of Mother Narmada, no hunger or thirst do I bother.) Once I heard them I said *Narmade har*.

As we made our way through Sakka Market, it felt like a bustling carnival for the nearby villagers. It seemed as though everyone had gathered there, either to purchase goods or simply to peruse the various market offerings. The market's value is significant, as it offers a plethora of options for buying, selling or simply visiting for leisure. In my experience, it seemed to be primarily geared towards recreational activities.

My cook Jadu was again walking with us comes from Kolkata and had been my cook for last few years. He is very sincere and makes sure that he does his religious work before starting in kitchen. I asked him today how is he feeling after so many days in *parikrama*? He replied that his mind has found a transformation soon after Amarkantak, I felt he had at last able to get the blessing of Mother Narmada.

Until this moment, the existence of a camera within the vehicle designated for my overnight accommodations had remained a closely guarded secret. Its discreet presence allowed me to observe all that occurred within its confines without detection. Upon my return from my daily walk, I would promptly enter my vehicle and switch on the television. The camera was operational, allowing me to have a complete view of the campsite and its amusing happenings.

Word quickly spread among the people there, prompting them to hastily reposition vehicles in a manner that obstructed the camera's view. It was a day that left everyone acutely conscious of their surroundings. The mischievous kids!

88

Services Offered

Today's our journey began from Rai and led us to Andiyar, where we found lodging in a school that had been founded in 1954. I was filled with joy at the thought of a school having been established in the *janya-jatis* belt so long ago.

It was relayed to me that there was once a hostel present at this location, and it appears that it is still in operation. This location has a fascinating history, as it was once under the supervision of Christian missionaries. A hospital was established in this area, but its name has caused confusion among the locals. Many of them have mistaken it for a Hindu institution. Satchidananda, the hospital's name, was strategically chosen by the missionaries to entice individuals of diverse beliefs to embrace Christianity.

In the midst of the day's bustle, a cluster of people approached me with the conviction that I was affiliated with the RSS headquarters and held a prominent role within the organization. The message was conveyed that they were interested in meeting with me. Beforehand, they had disclosed to our fellow *parikramavasis* that we had crossed paths in the past, which was inaccurate.

I decided to have some fun with them which we did. I asked some of my fellow *parikramavasis* who had prior experience with RSS to demonstrate how the senior officials would conduct themselves. As they confided in me, I emulated their actions with precision. Additionally, I incorporated certain elements gleaned from Swami Milind's exchange with Jitendra Sharma. I could confidently assert that I was a consummate senior *pracharak* of the RSS, despite my relative youth. Surprisingly, throughout our conversation together, these folks never once picked up on the fact that I was pretending everything for laughs.

As I traversed through the diverse hamlets, I came across a plethora of young ones who graciously extended me a share of their rice. The tradition dictated that any *parikramavasis* who passed by would be presented with a gift, and I received it with sincere appreciation.

89

Forest Camp

Our expedition commenced in Andiyar, and as we traversed the terrain, we chanced upon a rivulet that was contaminated with petroleum. Upon delving deeper into the matter, it was revealed that a truck transporting oil had toppled over in the nearby area. The once pristine stream, flowing towards the Narmada, now bore the mark of contamination with a slick substance. The tragic event had taken the lives of numerous snakes and fish, their motionless forms scattered throughout the stream. Were such a scenario to have occurred in other regions, what would have been the resulting outcome?

On this day, while we were going forward we had the pleasure of encountering a self-proclaimed deity. A man comes to me and says he is God, I said good for him and walked ahead. While I was impressed by his confidence, I could not help but think that true gods have more on their plate than simply announcing their divine status to anyone who will pass. I suggested that he team up with Nanga Baba – they would make quite the pair!

As we arrived at the Burhar Sangam of the river, we reached upon the ancient temple of Jamdagneshwar.[1] Despite its age, the temple had been abandoned and left to decay. The local *baba*, who was present at the time, seemed disinterested in the *tirtha*. Moved by a sense of duty, I suggested that we take action to restore this sacred site. I conveyed my desire to install the missing *kalasha*'s on the *shikhara* (atop the *mandira*) with the disclaimer that it would be subject to the permission of Mother Narmada. The locals received it with great enthusiasm.

Once we left the Jamdagneshwar Temple, we traversed the river using a bridge that was cobbled together from whatever materials people could find. As I contemplated the various activities that require assistance, my attention was drawn to the annual construction of the bridge. In an effort to explore potential avenues for involvement, I consulted with the local *panchayat* to assess the feasibility of contributing to this endeavour.

Having crossed the stream, exhaustion weighed heavily upon me and we found a place for lunch. During our lunch, a man with a missing limb kindly brought us water, perhaps assuming we were in need of it. This act of generosity was quite intriguing. The location was a beautiful mango orchard, providing a serene and picturesque setting for a peaceful slumber. We took a brief respite before continuing on to camp.

Upon arrival, I discovered that the drivers and other members of the group were not receiving their meals in a timely manner. In response, I invited everyone to dine with us that day. At our camp, we encountered an issue where some individuals seemed to lack the enthusiasm and vitality that one would expect from those who were present for a spiritual purpose. Despite being in the presence of the holy Narmada River, they appeared unable to fully embrace the blessings that it offered. Today, we strayed into the forest, equipped with all the necessary amenities to facilitate our *parikrama*.

90

Brahmapuri

Departing from our forest camp, we embarked towards Maharajpur, situated on the opposite side of Mandla.

As we journeyed through the land, we came across numerous forts and assemblies that were erected by the illustrious Rani Durgavati and her predecessors. However, the state of these structures was quite disheartening. Neglect and encroachment had taken their toll, rendering them almost inaccessible. I believe that if we fail to acknowledge the significance of India's history beyond the Delhi and Mughal eras, we risk losing our faith in this great nation. As I embarked on the Narmada Parikrama, I could not help but notice the dilapidated state of the places along the way. It left me pondering over whether the present India solely focuses on the Mughal-influenced architecture and locations, without any regard for other noteworthy sites such as Ramnagar, which boasts of magnificent edifices. Lalaram revealed that a multitude of individuals frequent this location in pursuit of buried riches concealed beneath the numerous monuments. I was astounded by the fact that people overlook the treasure trove of history that lies above ground, instead opting to search beneath the earth's surface.

We set out today for Madhupuri Ghat, a legendary location. Here is where the horse from Lord Rama's Ashvamedha Yagya is said to have emerged from Mother Narmada after travelling to her depths. The horse, accompanied by Lord Rama's brother Shatrughana and Lord Hanuman, went to the Narmada River to quench its thirst, but then vanished without a trace. After witnessing this, Lord Hanuman and Shatrughana followed the horse's trail all the way to the river's bottom, where they encountered a large number of *yoginis*. When the *yogini* saw Shatrughana and Lord Hanuman, she grew concerned and wondered how the two of them had managed to get to a place where not even the gods themselves were permitted to enter. Shatrughana told them that he was the brother of Lord Rama and that the Ashvamedha Yagya horse they were accompanying had come down here and they followed. After listening to their tales and gaining their trust, the *yogini* handed Shatrughana and Lord Hanuman the *abhaya mantra* and then brought them on earth once more. Madhupuri, also known as Ghoda Ghat (Horse Ghat), is the location where the horse reappeared alongside Lord Hanuman and Shatrughana.[1]

The picturesque location on the banks of Mother Narmada was truly a sight to behold. The *ghat*, which is renowned for its breathtaking views, still remains one of the most serene places.

As we journeyed forth, we encountered a group of women who eagerly awaited our arrival, anticipating the melodious strains of our *bhajana*. They expressed their desire to accompany us on our path to the next village. The women's eyes sparkled with excitement as they shared their longing to experience the uplifting power of *bhajana* and *parikrama*. Their heartfelt request filled us with joy and we welcomed them wholeheartedly, knowing that their presence would add even more depth to our spiritual journey. Eventually, I discovered that it was a self-help group that provided mutual aid, and emotional and financial support to its members. The village was strictly prohibited from the consumption of alcohol. Any individual found indulging in such activities would be subjected to severe consequences. The self-help group was instrumental in fostering a sense of unity and empowerment among the women, as they shared stories of overcoming challenges and achieving personal growth. Additionally, their commitment to maintaining a alcohol-free environment showcased their dedication to promoting a healthy and responsible community.

As I approached Maharajpur, a woman selling coconuts caught my attention. She had recently completed the Narmada Parikrama and eagerly offered me a coconut, requesting that I present it to Mother Narmada on the *sangam* of the Vanjhar River (Banjar is the distorted name) on her behalf. With the innocence of a child, her eyes shone bright and her emotions carried her away. As I approached the sacred waters of Mother Narmada, I presented a coconut as an offering on her behalf.

One will find the settlement of Purva on the banks of the Vanjhar River; it was here that Sarasvati performed her *tapasya*, earning the area the name Sarasvati Devi Prastravan Teerth.[2] We came across a temple that seemed to match the description of the historical site, but nobody there seemed to know anything about it. Once upon a time, Purva was known as Vishnupuri, the famous city opposite the Maharajpur.

The air of antiquity surrounded us as we entered Maharajpur, formerly known as Brahmapuri. Vyasa Teerth is directly across from here. Here, at Maharshi Vyasa's pleading, the Narmada River's mother alters her course.[3] The story of this place dates back to ancient times. However, the present situation is far from ideal. There is a story that from Hemtakdi, which is a hill just 1,000 m from the banks of Narmada, it is said that many *yagya*'s have been performed here and the stream of *ghee* (clarified butter) flown from these *yagya*s merged with the Narmada River here, therefore the name Ghrit Sangam. The renowned Ghrit Sangam finds itself in a precarious state, with all access blocked. It is a stark reminder of the consequences of neglecting history. In ancient times, this place was known as significant *tirtha*s where the act of donating Granthas, Shastras, and performing Gayatri Patha was highly revered.

Maharajpur, also known as the ancient Mandla or Mahishmati, bears a significant weight of Indian history. However, regrettably, this place has gradually faded from the collective consciousness of the Indian people. In this locale, the Narmada River meanders through various bends, encompassing all three perimeters of the town. In Ramnagar, where Rani Durgavati's fort stands, a similar occurrence takes place.

In my observation, it was quite evident that Rani Durgavati harboured a profound reverence for the holy Narmada, as is apparent from her decision to dwell in close proximity to its tranquil banks. Her actions distinguished her from another queen Rupamati rumoured to have had her lover transport the Narmada River to her palace grounds.

Lalaram Chakravarti who had been with us since the beginning of the *parikrama* hails from Brahmapuri or Maharajpur. On that day, we made our way to Lalaram's ancestral abode – a modest dwelling. There, I had the pleasure of meeting his mother, who was deeply moved. Lalaram then regaled us with the rich history of his cherished homestead. Amidst the bustling city, there once existed a serene park adorned with ancient trees that were lovingly planted by the protagonist's grandfather. However, the government claimed ownership of the land and the park was lost forever. Yet, amidst the concrete jungle, a few trees stands tall, a poignant reminder of the legacy left behind by the protagonist's grandfather.

I have frequently traversed through Mandla/Maharajpur and have paid my respects to Mother Narmada at this location during my crossings. Although the place may be new to me, the *ghat*s hold a familiar significance.

We hosted a splendid evening programme during which I delivered a speech on the historical significance of Mandla/Maharajpur highlighting the town's notable landmarks and pilgrimage sites situated along the Narmada River. Several individuals arrived tardily, however, I had already retired for the evening.

91

A Village of Soldiers

We departed from Maharajpur and encountered a poorly maintained road. During our journey, we were presented with a handful of *kadua kanda*, the bitter potatoes previously mentioned. As soon as I was presented with *kadua kanda*, Brahmchariji, seeing me watch him, presumably felt I was going to feed him, turned away from me.

On this particular day, we were greeted in many places by the team Jan Abhiyan. Throughout our visit, I made inquiries regarding the nature of the work being conducted in specific regions. As the NGO (known as Prasphutan Samiti) chairperson was elaborating on their organization's activities, an elderly gentleman interjected, expressing nothing is being done. Despite the laughter that greeted his statement, I offered reassurance to the NGO that this was just the start and such incidents were not unusual. I urged them to maintain their concentration on their tasks.

As we journeyed forth, we chanced upon a village that was entirely dedicated to the valiant army and youth were doing everything possible to join the army. It was a humbling sight to behold the numerous *samadhi sthalas* (memorials), of the brave souls who had laid down their lives in service of the nation. Witnessing the people receive their rightful recognition I was filled with a sense of contentment.

After leaving Maharajpur, one will arrive at Sahastradhara, where legend has it Sahastrabahu sought to halt the flow of the Narmada with the help of his thousands of hands, only for the mother river to continue flowing unabated and transform into thousands of separate streams.

92

Truth Expresses

As we ventured forth, our steps took us farther from the revered Narmada. The construction of the Bargi Dam had caused the submergence of the ancient *parikrama* path, as well as several small streams, due to the backwater of the Narmada. This presented a challenge for us to cross.

As our journey led us towards Vinayki, we could not help but wonder what we might have come across had we taken the ancient path. It is said that along that path, a sequence of *tirtha*s once stood, but now lie submerged beneath the water's surface. Despite many obstacles, we persevered in our endeavour to narrate the stories of these hallowed locations.

Near the Medha Ghat, at a distance of 6 km from Padmi Teerth Ghat, lay the Lukeshwar Teerth. As per the *Vayu Purana*, there existed a sacred site where the mighty waters of Mother Narmada flowed with great force. It was here that a magnificent Shivalinga stood tall amidst the stream, known as Lukeshwar Mahadev. This holy abode was frequented by divine deities, celestial beings and even serpents who came to offer their worship to Lord Shiva. The appellation Lukeshwar Mahadev derives from the fact that Lord Shiva concealed himself at this very location.

On that particular day, I requested Kumar to express himself candidly regarding the positive and negative character traits of individuals that require modification for their personal growth. In the depths of his being, he bore the essence of timidity, a delicate disposition that shunned the act of causing harm or displeasure unto his fellow beings. However, I endeavoured to convey the notion that it is not a matter of causing offence, but rather an opportunity to articulate one's genuine sentiments and observations about the people in question. If one were to have failed to confer upon the matter the requisite degree of attentive consideration, it would inevitably imply a certain lack of concern or regard for the individuals in question. In that moment, Kumar embarked on an elaborate discourse, delving into the depths of the subject matter. With eloquence and insight, he proceeded to unveil the diverse array of positive and negative traits possessed by each individual present. I admired the perspicacity with which he perceived it all. Swami Shivananda joined the discussion and proceeded to jest about the mannerisms and potential futures of those present. Later, a lengthy conversation took place with the majority of the *parikramavasi*s.

Along the *parikrama* path, one encounters a multitude of individuals who contemplate the *parikramavasi*s with great depth. There have been numerous instances where we have had to graciously decline offers of assistance. I believed that the blessings of Mother Narmada provided us with everything we needed, and that offering our services to others would be just a way to honour her. On this particular day, though, I recall a couple trying to stop us. I did not understand what they were saying, so I continued walking, but they were buying some fresh vegetables for us. As soon as I arrived at the campsite, Nandlal informed me that someone had dropped off some fresh vegetables for us. I stared at him and pondered over whether he had invited the pair to attend *bhandara* or not when he abruptly shared that they would also be attending night *arti* and *prasad*. Such acts of devotion are a testament to the deep reverence that *parikrama* and its participants inspire.

In Vinayki, once we reached, our camp was ready and we settled in an open field equipped with all the necessary amenities. As we embarked on our *parikrama*, word of our efficient organization quickly spread, leaving those around us pleasantly surprised.

93

Green Efforts

We departed from the Vinayki Power Plant, located in a desolate area devoid of any vegetation. The barren landscape evoked a sense of desolation, as if nothing could thrive in such a place – and indeed, that was precisely the case. I found myself pondering over the curious absence of any noteworthy efforts by the local inhabitants to cultivate the vast expanse of barren land in close proximity to the Vinayki plant. Why, one might wonder, have they not undertaken any endeavours to enrich this desolate terrain with an abundance of lush vegetation and majestic trees? Curiosity compelled me to inquire of the local inhabitants, who had graciously gathered to greet me along my journey, as to why they seemed reluctant on the matter at hand. Should we fail to undertake the arduous task of regreening the area, it is highly probable that within a span of a few years, the very notion of inhabiting this land will become an insurmountable challenge. The dire state of this place necessitates immediate action, for its continued degradation threatens the very livelihood of its inhabitants.

As we journeyed forth, we encountered a diverse array of individuals. Some were actively seeking my presence, while others fortuitously crossed our path during our travels. As the sun began to dip below the horizon, we finally arrived at Bargi Nagar. Our lodgings for the night were at the humble abode of Reva Maharaj, a renowned local astrologer who had made quite a name for himself. He possessed an impressive stature and a well-toned physique, resembling that of a seasoned actor. He arrived with a gentle demeanour and we partook in the traditional *arti* ceremony. As our time together drew to a close, he recounted the tale of his family's ancestral land and the unfortunate acquisition of it by the Bargi Dam. Presently, only this small plot remains, recently granted some semblance of legal recognition. He reserves the spot for the *parikramavasi*s and it is also where he encounters individuals from various regions.

On this particular day, a grand *bhandara* was held, drawing a multitude of visitors who had come to pay their respects. Additionally, Reva Maharaj had extended invitations to individuals to partake in the festivities.

94

Spirituality

As we set out in the morning, Reva Maharaj accompanied us for a few kilometres. Along the way, we encountered numerous individuals who warmly greeted him.

Our conversation commenced with the topic of astrology and related subjects, and I must say, he displayed remarkable knowledge in the field of Sanatana philosophy. As our conversation progressed, we delved into the present state of our nation, where a significant number of individuals who claim to be saints seem to lack any substantial understanding towards the principles of Sanatana Dharma. During our conversation, the topic of a particular "Dham" arose, along with a discussion of a young man who has recently emerged as a national hero. However, Reva Maharaj expressed his disappointment, stating that if this is to be the future of our country, then we may have no future at all.

I conveyed that this nation was founded upon the principles of Shastras, and that even the deities adhered to the laws of *karma*. For instance, Lord Rama undertook a 14-year journey on foot, and despite having Krishna on their side, the Pandavas still had to engage in battle.

Together, we concurred that the present milieu is rife with storytellers who lack a true understanding of *dharma*. These individuals are solely motivated by financial gain, deceiving others for their own benefit. As a result, an increasing number of individuals are becoming disillusioned, causing their faith in *karma* to wane. When *karma* is disregarded, the nation cannot thrive and flourish.

Reva Maharaj had a captivating story to share about a renowned "Baba" from south India who once had a public encounter with Anand Jadugar. The Baba conjured an apple seemingly out of thin air and presented it to Anand Jadugar. In response, the Jadugar astounded the Baba by producing two apples from the ether and offering them in return. The Baba's fury was palpable as he demanded, "What is that?" Anand Jadugar spoke truthfully about his actions, which were similar to those of Baba. He said: "However, neither of their actions can be considered as righteous or spiritual." Anand Jadugar further stated "both are merely acts of tricks and magic, and it would be inappropriate for Baba to refer to himself as a spiritual figure".

Spirituality is devoid of any enchantment or sorcery. It is the unyielding cornerstone of ultimate divinity. Even if one attains this state, it remains a personal and private matter. As exemplified by Lord Krishna, who revealed his complete *avatar* to only a select few.

While we were in the midst of our in-depth conversation, someone approached and asked Swami Shivananda, "Where do you think all these people are going?" His response was to gobble up *jalebi*. The shock of having this answer stuck with them forever, although it was typical of Swami Shivananda; he frequently had fun while on walk.

As we arrived at the hospital, it became apparent that we were in the presence of a remarkable establishment. Dr Sthapak, the mastermind behind this medical heaven, had created a space that was not only blessed by his *guru*, but also a testament to his unwavering commitment to his calling.

Once again, Dr Jamdar and his wife graced us with their presence today. We engaged in a fruitful discussion about our plans after Narmada Parikrama. I shared my thoughts on mapping and re-establishing the *tirtha*s, which were well-received. As we bid farewell, we pledged to do whatever it takes to make our plans a reality.

95

None Knew the Distance

At the break of dawn, we embarked on a tour of the hospital in the company of Dr Sthapak and his family. The hospital specialized in eye care and was under the good doctor's stewardship. It was heartening to learn that the hospital catered to the needs of people from far-flung villages and offered free surgical procedures to those in need. Upon inquiring about his management of the hospital, he divulged that he also oversees another medical facility within the city that operates with great success. The profits garnered from this establishment are then allocated towards the charitable efforts of the hospital in question. It is organized in a great manner.

After departing from the hospital, our initial destination was Mrigvan Teerth,[1] presently recognized as Seoni. It is said that Lord Vishnu perpetually manifests in the form of Chaturbhuja Rupa in this location. Engaging in spiritual introspection and practice in this sacred space is believed to yield great rewards. Once known as Mrigvan Teerth, the Seoni region has a fascinating history. According to the Reva Khanda, a skilled hunter had taken down numerous antelope before seeking respite in the area. Tragically, a sudden blaze consumed him, but after the rain, his remains were carried to the Narmada River where they merged. It was believed that dying on the banks of the Narmada and having one's ashes merge with the river granted liberation. This ultimate release was consequently given to the hunter and was given access to the holy realm in this way. The act of performing *pitr puja* and honouring one's ancestors is strongly encouraged. The *ghat* owes its existence to the trident of Lord Shiva, and as a result, both the *ghat*s on the north and south banks are known as Trishul Ghat. In ancient times, it was referred to as Trishul Bhed Teerth.[2]

Beyond Trishul Ghat lies the Lamheti Ghat, where both banks are referred to by the same name. Legend has it that Indra once performed *tapasya* here, and as such, the revered Indreshwar Mahadev and

Pipleshwar Mahadev[3] temples have stood here since ancient times. The Pipleshwar Mahadev Temple was successfully located, however, our search for the Indreshwar Mahadev Temple proved to be futile. It is likely that this particular *tirtha* has been lost amidst the ongoing developments in the area.

Despite the dilapidated condition of Pipleshwar Mahadev, we opted to pause and catch our breath at this spot. It was here that Pippalada Muni performed his *tapasya* in order to receive a vision of Lord Shiva. The Shivalinga dedicated to Pipleshwar Mahadev was erected in his honour by Pippalada Muni.

Our true ordeal commenced at this juncture, as we were confronted with an absence of clarity regarding the distance for the upcoming days. Despite consulting with several experts, including Lalaram, who were well-versed in the subject matter, we were unable to obtain the distance between one village and the next in the banks of holy Narmada. This was due to the fact that the villages were not interconnected from the Narmada banks. The well-known route that most individuals were familiar with was the distance between two destinations, traversed by the majority of *parikramavasi*s, who embarked on their journey along the highways. However, I had made the resolute decision to embark on a journey from the tranquil banks. This choice, though filled with determination, presented a formidable challenge, for the knowledge of the exact distances between the villages and the sacred banks eluded all. The intended distance of approximately 110-25 km was exceeded, as it turned out to be a daunting 175 km. It is my belief that very few of the *parikramavasi*s have been able to traverse from this route. It felt as though several decades had passed since anyone had walked this path, but as we continued on, more and more people joined us.

There are no roads linking the hamlets along the holy banks to one another. The villagers must traverse the entire distance all the way to the highway and then return back in order to reach a nearby settlement in the absence of interconnected roads. As we strolled along the banks, it became apparent that few ventured this way, leaving us uncertain of the precise distance. Fortunately, I had a book with me from the early nineteenth century that contained valuable information in miles. The written piece dates back to the 1848 and features the names of the villages and their distance in miles.

After Lalaram, who walked with us for a while, told me the distance in kilometres from one place to another, I checked his work and found that he and Yogesh had made a mistake. I promptly shared the detailed findings with them. As we had provided the dates for the Gadarwara programme, organized by Mahant Mangal Das Tyagi, we realized the urgency to arrive on time. Consequently, we began walking with great vigour, knowing that these upcoming days would require us to cover a significant distance without any respite.

As we traversed towards Bhadpura, we chanced upon the mining zone that lay adjacent to Bheraghat of south bank. Here, the extraction of marble was underway. The operation seemed to be conducted in secrecy, as the labourers had modified the route in a way that made it impossible for passersby to traverse, thus enabling them to carry out their tasks without interference. Through my personal observations, I have come to notice that those who partake in illicit behaviour in the vicinity of Mother Narmada tend to dissuade the presence of *parikramavasi*s. This is due to their apprehension that any dubious activities may be reported to the appropriate authorities.

The challenge was palpable as we journeyed through uncharted territory, our destination shrouded in mystery. The rugged hills loomed before us, presenting an additional challenge to our journey. The scarcity of pedestrians in the area only served to heighten the sense of confusion and bewilderment among many in our group. A fascinating observation arises, from the slightest deviation from the established path of the marked *parikrama*, as it piques the curiosity of onlookers regarding our intentions. As we embarked on our journey, we were compelled to seek out a fresh course, venturing beyond the familiar paths that had likely been charted by previous travellers.

As we journeyed, we encountered a remarkable *maharaj* whom Yogesh had previously encountered while exploring the paths one evening. Despite his lack of hands, the *baba* greeted us and Yogesh with great enthusiasm, exclaiming *narmade har*. His passion for the *parikramavasi*s touched me greatly, and I believe that it represents his passion for the sacred journey of Sanatana Dharma.

As the day wore on, we found ourselves traversing great distances on foot. As the sun began to set, two individuals, who had been directed by Lalaram, kindly offered to escort us. Their presence proved to be a stroke of good fortune, as the path we were on was treacherous, with only a few scattered footholds separating us from the raging waters of the Narmada River.

These individuals initially abandoned us en route, but upon realizing the challenges ahead, they retraced their steps and escorted us all the way to our final destination atop the hill. Our tents were already pitched, awaiting our arrival. We had our *arti* and *puja* and as usual another *bhandara* awaited the locals.

96

The Parikrama of Two Dogs

We began sooner since we were aware that the distance we were supposed to cover was greater than what had been estimated by books and our data team's analysis, Yogesh and Lalaram.

I had warned them that their anticipated distance of 24 km would actually be 36 km, and it ended up being about the same. It was a miserable trek because there was nowhere for trees or other vegetation to grow along the Narmada River banks and one had to travel through the crops while being doused in water from sprinkler irrigation. People don't typically walk from the banks in the Narsinghpur district since it takes skill to do so, as I discovered when I was on the northern bank. There is no way you can walk without problems; on one occasion, a participant in a *parikrama* had eye damaged because she was unable to notice the objects tossed onto the banks in the dark, and they landed within her eyes.

Within the depths of Mother Narmada's sacred embrace, a myriad of intricate machinery hummed with purpose. Alas! it is a sombre truth that the mining industry, driven by its own surreptitious motives, vehemently discourages individuals from traversing the hallowed shores and bearing witness to the illicit mining operations clandestinely unfolding within the river's very core. Over time, the trail or *parikrama* path underwent a gradual relocation, leading it away from the serene banks of the Narmada River. Its new course now meanders along a motorway, situated at a considerable distance from the tranquil waters and the sacred ambiance they hold. In the midst of it all, the clandestine enterprise of illicit sand mining persists unabated. The government, in its wisdom, has granted permission for the extraction of sand through legal means. However, it is imperative that this process be carried out with utmost care and deliberation, ensuring that the sacred essence of the river is preserved. However, the scourge of illegal mining, carried out with the aid of machinery and causing significant alterations to the river, is an undeniable affliction. Regrettably, the *parikramavasis*, who traverse great distances away from the river's edge, remain blissfully ignorant of the grievous harm being inflicted upon the sacred Narmada.

On this particular day, I engaged in a conversation with Lalaram. It became apparent to me that his contributions to the Narmada belt had gone unnoticed and unappreciated. Overwhelmed with emotion, Lalaram began to weep. And thus, I proceed to dismantle my perspective and present to him my proposed path ahead. In encountering an individual such as himself, I could not help but perceive a certain air of appreciation for the labour he had undertaken, coupled with an unwavering willingness to extend any necessary aid he may require.

On that particular day, we were accompanied on our journey by a pair of dogs. At first, I refrained from feeding them, for I feared that doing so would only foster unrealistic hopes and prolong their stay in search of sustenance. As we embarked on our expedition, our loyal canine companions joined us and during the lunch time I offered nourishment to my companions, enabling them to recuperate their vigour for the rest of our journey. With a newfound energy, they continued their journey alongside us. As we laid our eyes on the female canine, we could not help but notice her curious predicament. She seemed to be struggling with one of her legs, causing her to limp as she moved. To the astonishment of those in attendance, she made a sudden leap into the sacred Narmada River, only to resurface moments later, moving with confidence on all fours. The miracles performed by the divine Maiya Narmda are of a subtle yet indispensable nature.

The loyal dogs remained by our side like devoted *parikramavasi*s, refraining from barking at anyone and slumbering close to our *ratha* where the *kalasha*s of Mother Narmada were stored. They exhibited remarkable patience, never demanding food but rather waiting for it to be provided, as if they possessed an innate understanding of their role. It was a curious sight to behold as they accompanied us on our journey for a few days, only to come to a halt at a particular location, Muranch. As they gazed intently into our eyes, it became clear that this was their intended destination, and we bid them farewell before continuing on our way.

During the *parikrama*, one is put to the test. On this particular day, Girish was tested. For the past two days, we had been walking nearly

35-38 km each day. Today, Girish felt defeated and approached me with a request. He asked if he could sit on the bike for remaining 6 km till our todays destination. I agreed to his request, as he had already presented a solution. I have a policy of not interfering when a solution has already been proposed to me. The following day, I reminded Girish that if he had not lost his inner strength and faith in Mother Narmada, he would not have needed to ask for assistance.

From that day forward, he never lost his inner patience, even when faced with extreme discomfort from his ankle. He persevered and continued to walk.

As we embarked on our journey, we were accompanied by some friendly locals who expressed their desire to join us on our trek. However, despite their eagerness, they seemed unfamiliar with the path ahead and attempted to lead us astray. Despite our warnings, they remained resolute in their belief that they knew the way. After several kilometres of walking, they eventually conceded and looked to us for guidance, following the path we had originally suggested. I instructed them to refrain from interfering with our path as we embarked on a journey to discover the optimal route along the banks.

As we traversed the countryside, we passed by countless farms and sparsely scattered homes atop the rolling hills. However, one particular hilltop abode caught our eyes, emanating a certain charm that beckoned us closer. As the aroma of freshly baked bread wafted through the air, we could not help but feel a sense of contentment wash over us, as if we had stumbled upon the idyllic life we had always yearned for.

97

Shumbha and Nishumbha

Today, we departed from Brahmakunda, a place steeped in the rich history of Indian Shastras. Our journey led us to the sacred temple of Bhrahmakunda Teerth,[1] where the locals appeared to be unaware of its significance. After performing my *puja* in the *tirtha*, I took the opportunity to enlighten them with its rich history. According to Reva Khanda, it is so. After the gods and their divine realm were conquered by Shumbha and Nishumbha, they found themselves defeated and in dire need of assistance. Seeking aid, they turned to Lord Brahma. The gods were in dire need of Lord Brahma's assistance in their battle against a formidable foe. This was because Lord Brahma had bestowed a boon upon them during their *tapasya* in Pushkar.

Accompanied by Lord Brahma, they journeyed to the serene banks of Narmada, where they embarked on a rigorous period of *tapasya*. It was here that their unwavering devotion and penance caught the attention of Lord Shiva, who was pleased with their efforts and granted them the boon they had so fervently sought. This is the very location where Lord Shiva granted the boon that the demon brothers Shumbha and Nishumbha would meet their demise at the hands of Goddess Parvati. Along the banks of the revered Mother Narmada lies a sacred stone, once known as Devashila. Today, this hallowed site is adorned with a humble temple.

After leaving from the Brahmakunda and traversing a distance of approximately 130 km over the course of the past four days, my weariness had begun to set in.

Consequently, we proceeded at a leisurely pace along and our first stop was Budhgaon where the planetary being Budha had done his *tapasya* to remove his bodily disease; this is here Budheshwar Mahadev Temple still is.[2] Further we started walking along the canal. However, to my surprise, the canal was completely devoid of water. Upon inquiring about this, I was informed that the canal had once been a source of water, but now, with the advent of bore wells, it had become obsolete. The canal's condition was dire, lacking any lining and purported maintenance work had yet to be executed.

On the auspicious occasion of Shivaratri, we arrived at a quaint village where we partook in a splendid *puja* and indulged in a grand *bhandara*. As we settled in for the night, I could not help but notice the dogs that had accompanied us on our journey. They seemed to have found their home in this charming little town of Muranch. As I departed the following morning, the memory of their eyes lingered in my mind. Gratitude and affection were the only emotions that radiated from their gaze. Despite numerous attempts by others to persuade them to join us, they remained steadfast in their decision. I bid them farewell and continued on my way.

98

Farmers Knowledge

Today, as we journeyed from Muranch to Linga, we encountered a group of farmers along the way. One of them imparted some valuable insights regarding the art of farming. According to him, the key to a successful sugar-cane crop lies in the meticulous execution of three rounds of tilling and thirteen rounds of watering. In Hindi its said that *terah pani, tina jutai, tab ganne ki fasal hai ayi.*

As far as the eye can see, the landscape is dominated by sprawling sugar-cane fields. This crop reigns supreme in the area due to the abundant water supply, which is a vital requirement for its growth. Thanks to Mother Narmada's assistance, the region has flourished greatly. As I embarked on the *parikrama*, I was struck by the significance of culture and the narratives that unite us.

The route leading to the Narmada River is in a deplorable state, rendering it difficult to traverse. I imparted to the nearby villagers the necessity of embarking on foot to reach the river. It is intriguing to note that the people of Narsinghpur embark on *parikrama*, albeit mostly by car or buses. However, this mode of transportation has left them oblivious to the predicament that has arisen for the *parikramavasis*. Not only is *seva* required, but also the path. As I broached the topic, I expressed my readiness to embark on a walking journey once more if the needs come only in the region. However, I proposed that in order to facilitate this *parikrama*, farmers ought to allocate a mere 5 ft of their land and leave it unobstructed for pedestrian passage. The notion was met with unanimous agreement, and I am confident that this task will come to fruition.

Umariya village was the setting for a memorable encounter. At the junction, a magnificent *bud* tree and a great banyan tree stood tall, providing a picturesque backdrop. I engaged in a lengthy conversation with the locals who had gathered under the banyan tree to listen. I implored them to preserve the *parikrama* path, if at all possible, as it was a matter of utmost importance.

I emphasized the significance of preserving the *parikrama* path as a means of safeguarding history. With great emphasis, I conveyed the notion that any deviation from the intended path of the *parikrama* would undoubtedly result in the gradual erosion of the rich historical legacy of Sanatana Dharma. This is due to the cultural significance that supports the *parikrama*, which would inevitably fade away if not upheld.

Our destination was Devkachar, a place where the locals had suggested we rest and have lunch. It was not a typical spot, but rather a few trees in the school that provided shade and respite from our journey. As we settled into the school, a magnificent *jamun* tree caught our attention. We gathered beneath its shade to enjoy our lunch, and I could not help but marvel at the abundance of food before us. In spite of our numbers reaching a grand total of fifty, it became evident that the camp's preparations had been made with a more modest figure in mind, a mere twenty-five. Nevertheless, true to our nature, we found a way to distribute our offerings among all those in attendance.

As we traversed the Devkachar, a group of individuals approached me with a pressing matter. They expressed their belief that the government should allocate significant resources towards the *parikrama marga*. However, I firmly disagreed, asserting that it is the responsibility of the religious community to oversee such a sacred function. I proposed that if all the *ashrama*s and saints were to unite, we could construct the *parikrama marga* within a year's time. Rather than focusing on the construction of grandiose *ashrama*s, we could prioritize the maintenance of the ancient temples and the development of the *parikrama* path itself.

99

Longest Route

On this particular day, our journey commenced from Linga. Initially, I had reservations about our ability to arrive at our intended destination, the Pitambara Peeth. This visit had been arranged well in advance and we had the privilege of meeting with the esteemed priests of Pitambara, who also happened to have a familial connection with Jitendra Sharma and I have met his parents in Omkareshwar before the beginning of my *parikrama*. Despite the challenges, I successfully covered a distance of 39 km and arrived at our destination at around 8:30 p.m. Our next stop was Gadarwara, where we were eagerly awaited by the esteemed Mahant Mangal Das Tyagi.

As we journeyed through the Narmada belt, we encountered a curious phenomenon. The locals, upon sighting us, extended warm invitations to their homes and farmland. One such encounter was with a farmer who directed us towards an alternate path, citing water on the original route which hinder our movement. However, it became apparent that his true intention was to lead us to his sugar factory or jaggery unit. As we journeyed to the suggested path leading to the jaggery unit, I implored my companions to partake in the refreshing nectar of sugar cane. After all, we had traversed an additional 2 km to reach our current location, and such an effort surely warranted a well-deserved treat. The farmer expressed his desire to offer us some jaggery for the way. I suggested that he join us for lunch and bring the jaggery along. Only then would I be willing to accept his kind offer. I elucidated that I possess specific regulations.

Nonetheless, we appreciated his kind gesture and enjoyed the refreshing beverage. Hailing from Narsinghpur, he firmly stated, "No, Vivekji, I am a local and we possess the knack of accomplishing our tasks". He then proceeded to challenge me, "You won't be able to sway me and walk further if you won't take the jaggery that I am offering" in response, I calmly asserted, "Throughout the last 100 days, I have crossed paths with countless individuals, yet not a single one possessed the ability to impose their will upon me". The weight of his quietude was palpable, a testament to the realization that he had come face-to-face with an individual of unparalleled uniqueness.

On our journey, we encountered an individual by the name of Ramesh Yadav. He exuded a great deal of emotion and was dedicated to the noble cause of serving the *parikramavasis*. Upon seeing us, he was nearly moved to tears. We spent some time in his company before bidding him farewell, as we had a long journey ahead of us.

Once more, we found ourselves in a barren landscape, devoid of any trees to provide us with shade. Despite the challenging circumstances, we persevered and eventually stumbled upon a spot that offered respite from the scorching sun. We were overjoyed to have found a place to enjoy our lunch. It was intriguing to observe how some individuals merely cast a fleeting glance in our direction, only to depart once we commenced our midday meal.

On this day, Raju graced us with his presence and accompanied us on a walk leading to Pitambara Peeth. It was there that we had the pleasure of meeting the Maharaj. During our conversation, I mentioned the arduousness of the journey, but I persevered as I had made a promise and I am one to keep my word.

From this point, we shall embark towards Gadarwara, as per the wishes of Mahant Mangal Das Tyagi. It is his hometown, which he has not visited in many years.

100

Gadarwara

Our day began later than anticipated, as our destination was only Gadarwara. Once Mahant Mangal Das Tyagi gave us the green light, we set out on our journey. It was during this time that we encountered a large crowd of people, eagerly welcoming us to Bhatera, a village that would take us quite some time to traverse. It was here that we had the pleasure of meeting Mangal Das Tyagi. We arrived at the designated spot and that was when I felt the unmistakable presence and aura of Mahant Mangal Das Tyagi. Bhatera is situated along the banks of holy Narmada, the *ghat*s of this place were most ancient. I heard from Mahant that people of Gadarwara used to come here when they needed to immerse themselves in holy Narmada. The village was adorned with our banners, posters and every corner had been prepared for our arrival. The crowd was so dense that we had to form a heavy security ring to keep them at bay.

As we embarked on our journey from Bhatera towards Gadarwara, we were greeted with a warm reception at every turn of the road. The entire town was adorned with our banners and posters, and it seemed as though there was not a single spot that had not been marked with a welcoming gesture. Despite having traversed this path before, I could not help but feel the overwhelming presence of Mahant Mangal Das Tyagi's devoted followers, whose unwavering support was palpable at every step of the way. The few kilometres that lay ahead of us took several hours to cross, but the experience was nothing short of humbling. As we arrived at Gadarwara, it seemed as though the entire town was eagerly anticipating our presence. The excitement persisted throughout the night, with the programme.

After our evening *arti* and *puja*, I found myself scheduled to speak on stage. However, I could not help but notice the overwhelming presence of vibrant banners that adorned the entire grounds. The sight was nothing short of awe-inspiring, as if the very essence of our collective spirit had been captured and displayed for all to see. In this discourse, I delve into the profound significance that Gadarwara holds within the annals of our nation's history. Moreover, I shed light upon the disheartening reality that Gadarwara, despite its hallowed status, fails to bestow due reverence upon its revered saints. In addition, I said that it is worth noting that among the saints who were born or raised in Gadarwara none has done so quite like Mahant Mangal Das Tyagi to dedicate life for holy Narmada. During the course of my discourse, I delved into the intricacies of the Narmada Parikrama, expounding upon its significance and the profound experiences it offers to those who embark upon this sacred pilgrimage. Additionally, I devoted considerable attention to the *tirthas*, the holy sites along the Narmada River, elucidating their spiritual essence and the transformative power they hold for devotees. Furthermore, I expounded upon the communal food practices observed during this journey, highlighting the communal harmony and our responsibility. As I reflected upon the Narmada Parikrama, it felt as though I was encapsulating the essence of this sacred journey. The weighty responsibility of Gadarwara for this noble cause loomed large in my thoughts.

Gadarwara to Kokhsar

101

Walks in Gadarwara

The morning progressed slowly, with a relaxed and unhurried mood permeating the air. There was no urgent need to leave the area right away, so a sense of calm and relaxation could take hold. We started our morning rituals and went about our regular routines as the sun rose and shed a pleasant glow over the landscape. I supposed to go to Mahant Mangal Das Tyagi's birthplace, which was a significant part of my plan. People in Gadarwara were surprised to find only him and I going about by ourselves. They could not believe that it was me because the day before, the entire town had been waiting for us, but today, we were walking alone and not letting anyone to join us.

When I visited the ancient house, the locations where Mahant Mangal Das Tyagi had studied, and the locations where he had played games, it was like visiting an old friend's home and town. Mahant continued taking me to the places and things that held special meaning to him. Many people stopped to talk to him, including some old friends from before he became a *sannyasi*.

It is interesting to note that when I asked Mahant if I might visit his home earlier, before arriving in Gadarwara, he said that his sister, who serves as his carer, wanted to see me. He said it was lucky that I asked this issue in person since he was hesitant to inquire about my willingness to travel 4 km within the town while engaged in *parikrama*, when I had made a vow not to use any automobiles for movement.

Mahant graciously led me through the winding streets of Gadarwara, a town steeped in history. It was here, many years ago, that the renowned Acharya Rajneesh had resided and pursued his studies. As we strolled along the paths, it felt as though we were retracing the very footsteps that the esteemed Acharya Rajneesh had once taken, imbuing the atmosphere with a sense of reverence and nostalgia. The town seemed to come alive with whispers of his presence, as if the echoes of his laughter and the melodies of his childhood games still lingered in the air.

After spacing quite a bit of time in his hometown we along with Mahant Mangal Das Tyagi left further towards Shokalpur, Mahant walked with us for some kilometres and seeing his tiredness, I asked him to return; also it would mean that we could maintain our pace and walk towards our intended destination which was Shokalpur. When we got to Shokalpur, we stayed in a little *ashrama* (a humble place). The *ashrama* was nestled amidst the banks of holy Narmada.

102

Jai Shri Dadaji

This morning, we departed from the Shokalpur Temple and encountered the Maharaj. He requested funds for his temple, to which I expressed my willingness to contribute. However, I am unable to commit a specific amount or timeline due to my existing obligations to other temples. During my *parikrama,* individuals would approach me for financial assistance upon observing the number of vehicles and preparations under my direction. They perceived me as a wealthy saint, unaware that I do not solicit financial assistance from anyone and it was only Mother Narmada's blessings that such kinds of arrangement are in place.

As I embarked on my *parikrama,* I received a request from Mahant Mangal Das Tyagi and was reminded of the wise words of Swami Satchidananda, who had recently departed for the divine realm. I was advised to graciously receive any *dakshina* tendered by the devotees during the *parikrama* period, as these *dakshina*s are infused with profound sentiment. Embarking on the Narmada Parikrama is a deeply transformative journey, one that has the potential to elevate an individual to the status of a revered deity in the eyes of the local populace. This was the only time that anyone who would offer anything monetary I would take and at the end this was used for the last *bhandara* at Omkareshwar.

The day held a certain intrigue, a sense that something significant was on the horizon, destined to etch itself into memory for years to come. Despite my usual lunchtime being around or after 12-12:30 p.m., I curiously found myself experiencing a sense of fatigue. Consequently, I resolved to pause and relax on the Mother Narmada's edge around 11 o'clock in the morning. The arrival of the food was imminent and it was precisely at this moment that it made its appearance. Our resting spot was situated exactly on the serene banks of the Narmada River. Should you trace a line from our present whereabouts, it would unswervingly guide you to the quaint hamlet of Saikheda. It was here that the legendary Dhuniwale Dadaji once resided, and where his captivating tales came to life. Prior to commencing the *parikrama*, I took a solemn oath to present *prasad* to Dhuniwale Dadaji as we approached Saikheda.

Just as I was about to quench my thirst (before taking food) with a refreshing sip of water, a resounding splash in the nearby Narmada River jolted, and I felt we are near Saikheda I verified our proximity to Saikheda, and upon consulting the map, Yogesh confirmed that we were indeed in close proximity, directly in queue. My irritation with Yogesh was palpable as I realized that we had nearly reached Saikheda without his timely reminder.

In that fleeting moment, I declared that the plates ought to be readied for Dadaji. Once the plates had been meticulously arranged, I reverently presented them to the sacred waters of Mother Narmada. I was astonished as I offered the brimming plate to Mother Narmada on behalf of Dhuniwale Dadaji, and observed that none of the food items was afloat in the water. However, it was not long before the mighty river devoured it whole. As I beheld the scene before me, a feeling of deep satisfaction and happiness washed over me. As I sat down to enjoy my midday meal, my thoughts turned to the many blessings bestowed upon me by Mother Narmada. It was she who had reminded me of the location of Saikheda, which Yogesh had forgotten to mention. As I pondered over these things, another resounding splash echoed through the air, a testament to the power and majesty of this great river. It was as if she were nodding in agreement.

As I retired for the afternoon following a hearty lunch, I humbly beseeched Mother Narmada for her blessings. Should the Holy Mother have accepted the food for Dadaji, another splash in the water would be required, to occur while I am lying on my left-hand side. It occurred precisely as I shifted my repose from the right to the left, and a resounding splash occurred. It seemed as though the divine presence of Maiya was conveying a message to us through her distinct and singular means of communication.

When we sat down to enjoy our midday meal, a canine companion made an unexpected appearance. Moved by his presence, I offered him a portion of our *chapattis*, which he eagerly accepted. To my surprise, he consumed the food with a level of etiquette and grace that one might expect from a human diner. Once he had finished his meal, he bid us farewell and went on his way. It was like a saint had come to have lunch with us and then left.

103

Sandiya

Amidst the lush greenery of the surrounding terrain, lies the charming hamlet of Jhikoli. It was here that we discovered a haven of serenity in the form of the revered Dadaji *darbar*. The property and temple located in Saikheda are under the diligent care of a particular family, who are also responsible for the administration of this premises. As the first rays of sunlight illuminated the horizon, we set out on our expedition. To our great fortune, we chanced upon Jagdish Goswami during our travels. Despite being in his seventies, he engaged me in conversation in English. In reply, I mirrored the same vernacular. After some time had passed, he conveyed his difficulty in understanding my words, which resulted in a jovial outburst of laughter. Afterward, we enjoyed a pleasant walk through his farm.

As I beheld his immaculately smooth countenance, I found myself compelled to inquire about his meticulous grooming practices. He confirmed that he does not shave on a daily basis, but rather ensures that he maintains a clean-shaven appearance by shaving regularly. His gaze then shifted towards my own facial hair, which had grown out in all directions.

I inquired about his barber's fee, to which he replied, "five *pansari*!" I inquired about the nature of his statement, wherein he mentioned giving five *pansari* of wheat to the barber for his entire family for a year. Curious to know more, I sought clarification on the term *pansari*, to which he responded that 5 kg equate to one *pansari*. In the village, a barter system is still in practice where a service is exchanged for goods. For instance, a family may offer 25 kg of wheat in exchange for the services of a barber. As I traversed the Narmada belt, I was struck by the sight of a well-organized bartering system. While it is possible that such practices are commonplace in other villages, my firsthand experience came to light here.

As we ventured beyond the customary path taken by the *parikramavasis*, the locals were perplexed and inquired about the commotion surrounding the Narmada Parikrama. It is quite surprising that many individuals are not familiar with the Narmada Parikrama, even if they reside in close proximity to it. This is particularly true for those whose villages are not situated along the regular path of the *parikrama*.

As we journeyed through Dudhi Sangam, the expanse of sand before us seemed endless, as if we were crossing an insurmountable barrier. Here, the Dudhi River converges with the revered Mother Narmada. Dudhi River originates from Satpura range, pretty far away, and then travels for around 130 km before joining the Narmada.

After crossing the Dudhi Sangam we walked for several kilometres and the local farmers have cordoned off much of the surrounding land, leaving little room for leisurely repose and scarce tree coverage. After an arduous search, we finally chanced upon a shaded spot where we partook of our midday meal, though we refrained from lingering. I inquired of a young lad named Dhaniram, who happened to be present in our midst, as to the distance of Hosangabad. His response was an estimate of around 500 km, but it was erroneous as it is only a day's journey away from our present location. This is how people form ideas about their surrounding environment.

Despite the scorching sun, we resumed our journey after a brief lunch break, as we aimed to reach the banks of the holy Narmada in Sandiya. However, upon arrival, we were disappointed to find the area in a state of disarray. The once pristine waters were now murky and littered with debris, while the local farmers had taken up most of the space, leaving us with little room to walk. In ancient times, Sandiya was well known since it was here that Rishi Shandilya performed his *tapasya*. The *Vasishtha Samhita* contains a legend of Jamadagni, Vasishtha and Yagyavalkya who decided to perform a *yagya* together. They sent invitations to all the *rishi*s, and all but Kashyapa arrived. Kashyap Rishi was a brilliant *rishi* and since he did not show up for the *yagya*, all the other *rishi*s created an image that was thought to be Kashyap in his place. When Kashyap Rishi arrived, he observed the *rishi*s performing *puja* on the grass-made idol of Kashyap. When the *rishi* was asked why, they replied that it was for him because he was not physically present. When Kashyap noticed this, he laughed and grabbed some water from his *kamandala*. While saying the *mantra*, he then tossed the water on that persona of graas-idol. Soon after, a man manifested in physical form and was given the name Shandilya by Kashyap Rishi. Shandilya Muni performed *tapasya* here after his arrival for a considerable amount of time, thus, the name Sandiya, formerly known as Sandiya Teerth.[1]

104

Kubja Sangam

The day had dawned with an intense heat that persisted throughout. Our group had determined that we would not be able to endure a lengthy walk under such conditions. Our journey began from Canal Road, which was scarcely deserving of its name as no water flowed through it. As we walked along the road, there was a sense of being in a green desert. The absence of any tree cover on the roadside made the surroundings seem barren. The belt of Narmada banks was occupied by farmers, making it impossible to walk through. It felt as though the biggest hurdles that humans could put on the *parikrama* were already in place.

On this auspicious day, we embarked on a journey to the hallowed confluence of Kubja and Narmada, renowned as Kubja Sangam. The *Vasishtha Samhita* contains a narrative about the Kubja River. As per the tale, Devi Sarasvati was on her way to meet Lord Brahma when she chanced upon Marichi Muni, a man who was not bestowed with physical attractiveness. As her eyes fell upon Marichi Muni, a chuckle escaped her lips, much to his dismay. As a retort, he let out a vehement curse directed towards her, foretelling her inevitable reincarnation on this mortal plane, where she would be compelled to serve others.[1]

Upon hearing this, Devi Sarasvati implored the *muni* for forgiveness. However, he regretfully informed her that he was unable to intervene, as he had already uttered the word which would inevitably take effect. But *muni* said that in the course of two lifetimes, she would be granted the divine vision of the Lord, and in her subsequent life, she would be liberated from the curse that had befallen her. According to the Sanatana story, during the time of Lord Rama, she was born as Manthara. After listening to Narada Muni, she performed *tapasya* here. In her second life, she was known as Kubja. By attending Lord Krishna's *satsanga*, she was liberated from the mortal world. As per the Sanatana story, this is the very place where she performed her *tapasya* and it is now known as Kubja Sangam.

After crossing the Kubja Sangam, we were looking for the spot where we could have lunch, and we sought refuge under the canopy of a *babul* tree. Its sparse foliage provided a modicum of shade, shielding us from the scorching sun. Despite its lack of leaves, the tree's shelter was a welcome respite from the usual intensity of the midday sun. I attempted to rest amidst the sweltering heat. Upon rising, I caught sight of individuals scouring the area for my presence, eager to make my acquaintance. Despite their search efforts along the main road, they failed to recognize that I had no intention of traversing the bustling thoroughfare amidst the constant flow of vehicles. In their quest, they scoured the land for an elderly gentleman, a description that does not fit my personage. This scenario has unfolded on numerous occasions, where search parties have combed various locales in pursuit of my whereabouts. However, due to my unassuming nature and youthful countenance, I have eluded their detection.

As we journeyed, we happened upon a locale where the Narmada Purana was being observed. However, to our dismay, the event solely consisted of devotional hymns, lacking any narration or anecdotes pertaining to the venerated Mother Narmada. If this is to be the way of the future, it seems we have lost it.

Sahib Singh from Nandner reappeared amongst us today, expressing his concern over the lack of activity amongst the locals. He attributed this to the decline of this particular district. As we strolled along the opposite side of the Nandner, his approach became more convenient.

As I journeyed towards Satvasa, I could not help but notice that the path had significantly improved. The farmers had left a generous 5 ft space, allowing for easy navigation even during irrigation periods. Gone were the days of struggling to cross a narrow, precarious footpath.

As we arrived at Satvasa, we found ourselves in the midst of an *ashrama*. The locals, who were incredibly kind, showed their reverence from a distance rather than approaching us directly. One individual even humbly requested that assembled people shall refrain from taking all of the blessings of Mother Narmada from my feet.

105

Satvasa to Sangakheda Kalan

On this fateful day, as we prepared to bid farewell to the tranquil haven of Satvasa, a whirlwind of eager visitors descended upon us from the neighbouring regions. News of my imminent arrival had spread like a flame, igniting a fervent curiosity among the locals who were now scouring the area in search of my elusive presence. As the day unfolded, a steady stream of locals gracefully traversed the path that led them to our humble abode, their faces adorned with warm smiles and eager anticipation. Each arrival brought with it a palpable sense of camaraderie and a genuine desire to extend a heartfelt welcome. On this particular day, we embarked on a journey that saw us traverse a distance of nearly 28 km before the midday meal, a feat that had never been achieved by our group before. We arrived at Sangakheda Kalan quite late, with even some folks from Nagpur, such as Arvind Patankar, Hemant Patil and Shailesh Mahajan making an appearance. They all wanted to walk in Narmada Parikrama, but when I saw their efforts I could not help but chuckle at the notion of walking every day.

106

Shri Gaurishankar Maharaj

On this particular day, our destination was Kokhsar. However, our journey began with the task of crossing the Tava River, which eventually converges with the mighty Narmada River near Sangakheda Kalan.

The expanse of the Tava River was so immense that our journey across it required a significant amount of time. Joining us on this expedition was a talented photographer named Dinesh. As we prepared to enter the Tava River, he quietly mentioned a discomfort in his leg and turned to Maiya Narmada, requesting her assistance in easing the pain. Upon emerging from the Tava River, Dinesh made a remarkable observation – his pain had completely dissipated.

I could not help but express what I was thinking to him when I realized how important it was. I asked the question, "Why do you bother with such insignificant details?" because it seemed like a waste of your time. "There are significantly more profound questions and requests for blessings that can be made and requested."

The Tava River, formerly known as Tapa (short form of *tapasya* which means austerities) is a significant waterway that merges with the Narmada River, much like the revered confluence at Prayagraj. In bygone times, amidst the enchanting aura of Karttik Purnima, a magnificent fair graced this very spot. As per the Sanatana legend in the *Vasishtha Samhita*, there existed a king by the name of Vaishvanara. His kingdom was seized by his adversaries, and after being vanquished, he retreated to the Mandranchal Mountain to perform his penance. As he arrived, the king was greeted by Narada Muni, who imparted a wealth of wisdom upon him. Narada Muni encouraged the king to delve into the profound values of life and pursue inner knowledge, urging him to relinquish his attachment to his kingdom and his current way of life. However, the king failed to give Narada Muni his undivided attention, prompting the *muni* to bestow upon him a curse that would transform him into a monkey, as his behaviour mirrored that of a monkey. The king implored Narada Muni with a sorrowful countenance, beseeching his pardon. With great kindness, Narada Muni suggested to the king that he embark on a journey to the confluence of the Tapa and the Narmada, where he could engage in his *tapasya*. Through this action, all of his desires were granted. The king followed suit and ensured that his wishes were fulfilled. Ever since that momentous occasion, the location has been renowned as Vanar Bhalu Teerth.[1]

Kokhsar, located farther away from the convergence, was our final goal. A sacred site that serves as the final resting place of the revered Shri Gaurishankar Maharaj. This spiritual luminary was a towering figure in the Mother Narmada's region and his contributions to the area are immeasurable.

Shri Gaurishankar Maharaj, a devoted follower of Shri Kamal Bharti Maharaj, participated in the *jamat* of Shri Kamal Bharti Maharaj for the Narmada Parikrama. Shri Kamal Bharti Maharaj embarked on Narmada Parikrama, completing the three *parikrama*s of Mother Narmada. Following this, he founded an *ashrama* in the vicinity of Markati Sangam, situated around Mandaleshwar. However, after a while, he departed from the Markati Ashram and established a new one near Chaubis Avatara Temple, in the vicinity of Omkareshwar. Due to the submergence of its original location by a dam, the original temple had to be relocated. As per certain sources it is believed that Shri Kamal Bharti Maharaj entered *samadhi* in the year 1912, having lived for more than a century, and his *samadhi* was also located here.

Shri Kamal Bharti Maharaj, after performing three *parikrama*s of Mother Narmada, handed over leadership of the *jamat* to Shri Gaurishankar Maharaj, who led a large congregation of *sadhu*s on foot, accompanied by hundreds of elephants, horses, camels and other animals. With great care and precision, he opened the intricate system of *sadavrata,* which to this day provides *parikramavasi*s with the necessary rations to cook along their journey. It was around the year 1887 when he took *samadhi* in Kokhsar, marking a significant moment in his spiritual journey.[2]

Indeed, it was Shri Gaurishankar Maharaj who established the *parikrama* in its current form, by the aides of his *guru*, Shri Kamal Bharti Maharaj, a testament to the immense respect he commanded in the Narmada belt. He would traverse the land amidst a throng of thousands, bearing all the necessary provisions and tending to the needs of those he encountered along the way.

In my humble opinion, he is the saint whose footsteps and manner I endeavoured to emulate within myself. Although I am but a mere mortal in the presence of the esteemed Shri Gaurishankar Maharaj, I remain steadfast in my commitment to upholding the values he espoused. It is with great reverence that on my *parikrama* I was going to Kokhsar and paying homage to his *samadhi* which holds a special place in my heart.

Prior to my *parikrama,* I begged Mother Narmada to make it possible for me to get a satisfying stay in the *samadhi* and my request was duly honoured. A grand communal feast, *bhandara,* was organized by us. The entire village was cordially invited to partake in the festivities. The profundity of the experience was undeniable, as a powerful spiritual connection to Shri Gaurishankar Maharaj was established at his *samadhi* site, where his presence could be felt with great intensity.

There were but a handful of destinations that necessitated our arrival by way of fasting. It was not our original intention, but as the day progressed, we found ourselves unable to partake in a midday meal. And so it came to pass that the same circumstance befell us again. On this day, we all arrived at *samadhi* while fasting.

As I sat in stillness, a feeling of *samadhi* enveloped me. At the pinnacle of this sacred space stood a magnificent Shivalinga and as my gaze met its form, I beheld a wondrous sight – the Shivalinga was adorned with a resplendent *jaladhari.* Whenever I visit the Shiva Temple, I have a customary ritual that I follow. I offer my prayers and humbly receive the holy water from the *jaladhari,* which I then gently apply to my eyes and head. Finally, I bow down in reverence to the divine deity. As I gazed upon the Shivalinga atop the *samadhi,* I noticed the absence of water and pondered over how I would perform my customary practice in this state. Lost in thought, I gazed out into the open space for a brief moment before turning my attention back to the Shivalinga. It was then that I noticed the presence of water in *jaladhari.* As I laid my eyes upon it, a wave of emotions washed over me. With reverence, I accepted the water from *jaladhari* and proceeded with my ritual. It was at this moment that I sensed the divine presence of Shri Gaurishankar Maharaj bestowing his blessings upon me.

Near the *samadhi* there is a room where all the belongings of Maharaj are still kept. As I stepped into the chamber, I found myself surrounded by Maharajji's cherished belongings. Among them were several *vigraha*s, each one a divine representation, as well as his *paduka*, conches and an array of other precious items. Before me, a sight of great historical significance lay in plain view. They were not mere depictions of the divine, but rather the vestiges of a magnificent entity who once adorned the Narmada Khanda, ranking second only to the venerated Markandeya Muni.

Two magnificent conches, grand in size and resembling five fingers, caught my eyes. I had never laid eyes on such a sight before. It was as if I was touching something that had been graced by the divine touch of Shri Gaurishankar Maharaj himself.

As the evening drew to a close, we performed our *arti* with great reverence. Following the ceremony, those in attendance expressed a desire to hear my thoughts. I was overcome with emotion, having arrived at this momentous occasion. At first, individuals had positioned my *asana* in close proximity to *samadhi*, which left me feeling uneasy. As a result, I relocated it to a lower position beneath his *samadhi*, as I found it inappropriate to sit adjacent to such a sacred site.

At the location, I had the pleasure of encountering Sumit Patel. His family had been entrusted with the care of Shri Gaurishankar Maharaj and his *samadhi* for generations. Sumit was a remarkable and rational individual.

Earlier before reaching to *samadhi* while entering the Kokhsar village, my attention was immediately drawn to a poster featuring a Nanga Baba. I could not help but feel a sense of disappointment upon realizing that this individual had equated himself with the revered Shri Gaurishankar Maharaj. I could not help but ponder over why the local villagers had not taken issue with this and removed the banner prior to my arrival. As it turned out, the banner was taken down after I had left the area.

Kokhsar to Omkareshwar

107

Cultural Obliteration

In the morning, we departed from Kokhsar Ghat, having spent time in close proximity to the *samadhi* of Shri Gaurishankar Maharaj and the divine energy that permeated the area. Shortly thereafter, we encountered Sumit Patel, whose family has been taking care of the *samadhi* of Shri Gaurishankar Maharaj.

We briefly spoke during our *arti* and *bhandara* yesterday evening, but this morning he went out of his way to see me because he knew I had gone early and he wanted to talk to me about his feelings from last evening. He was obviously moved by what had occurred that evening, as earlier he had not counted on my sincere devotion to Shri Gaurishankar Maharaj. Sumit had seen many people come and go from this place, along with many famous saints, yet the aura of *samadhi* prohibited them from staying or offering *bhandara*. But we had stayed here and had given the great *bhandara* what we did on a regular basis, which was totally an unexpected event. He thought it was all the blessings of Shri Gaurishankar Maharaj, which exactly was the case. After a lengthy discussion, we felt as though we had made a divine bond.

As we continued our journey, we chanced upon a notable landmark that bore the inscription "Bhela". The intended name was "Bhola", a name held in high esteem as a reference to the revered Lord Shiva. The temple's history is steeped in the annals of Indian Shastras, rich with stories and significance. Across the country, a disheartening pattern has arisen wherein indigenous appellations are being modified without proper regard for their historical import. This practice not only corrodes the intricate storytelling of the terrain, but also diminishes the essence of its inhabitants. From my perspective, expunging names that hold significant historical value is akin to committing a grievous offence of cultural obliteration.

As we journeyed forth, we came upon the Hathner River, known in ancient times as the Hatyaharan River. It was at this very site that the

Pandavas, burdened with the weight of fratricide, sought to absolve themselves of their heinous crime. In close proximity lies Kuntipur, the very place where Kunti resided with Panchali and Rukmani. Rukmani had arrived at this very spot to rendezvous with Draupadi, also known as Panchali. Once upon a time, there existed a sacred *kunda* in Mother Narmada known as Lakshmi Kunda. However, upon our recent visit, we were unable to locate any remnants of the aforementioned *kunda*.[1]

As we embarked on our journey further, we were delighted to discover a quaint village nestled in a picturesque setting. To our delight, in the same village there was a big godown which our team promptly made as our temporary dwelling for the night. On the morning, our itinerary included a visit to the home of the proprietors, who hailed from a prominent Patel family, boasting one of the most expansive joint families I had ever chanced upon. The page could be filled with an impressive list of family members, all of whom resided together.

As we neared Omkareshwar, it seemed as though Mother Narmada would once again put us to the test, and a feverish feeling began to take hold of me; in fact, most of the *parikramavasi*s became ill at this time. Nonetheless, I was determined to get to Omkareshwar on time, and that determination inspired the people travelling with me. As the sun beat down relentlessly, my body grew weaker with each passing step. However, the allure of Omkareshwar's spiritual energy and protection of Mother Narmada propelled me forward, fuelling my determination to overcome any obstacles in my path.

108

Bhandara for Patels

In the morning, we departed from Banada after acquainting ourselves with the joint family. I had never seen or heard such a big joint family and still living altogether. Their residence resembled a grand castle, as every member of the family resided under its roof. The dwelling possessed a certain charm, and as I surveyed the premises, my gaze fell upon magnificent bulls with a fondness for equine creatures. At first I mistook them for a paired group of horses, but as I got closer I saw that they were actually bulls. They were stunning, standing as tall as a horse, with an air of calm confidence.

Despite the early hour, the entire family had gathered, their eager faces brimming with anticipation. They had come together to extend a warm welcome, to meet me and take part in a delightful photoshoot. Adorned with veils, the women of the house gracefully arranged themselves, their heads modestly covered, in preparation for the captivating photoshoot. In this particular locale, it is customary for the women residing within a household to gracefully drape a covering over their heads when in the esteemed company of their elders. Nevertheless, the patriarch, whose seniority demanded reverence, requested to the womenfolk, urging them to discard their *parda*. He believed that the picture would turn out better without it.

On that fateful day, our expedition led us through the treacherous terrain of Ganjal, until we finally arrived at the pivotal Harda district. At the confluence of the Ganjal River and the revered Mother Narmada lies the Ganjaleshwar Mahadev Temple, a site steeped in legend as recounted in the *Skanda Purana*. In this very place, Somvanshi Maharaj from Kanyapura, by the name of Maharaja Devanik and son of Hrishikesh, undertook the sacred Narmada Parikrama. Upon fulfilling his religious obligations and reaching the Triveni Sangam, where the Ganjal and Gomati streams converge with the holy Narmada River, he was absolved of all his prior offences. As the story goes, during his *yagya* ceremony at

Mallikarjuna, the *yagyashala* was engulfed in flames, leading to a tragic incident in which both cows and brahmanas lost their lives. Consumed by a sense of guilt, King Devanik believed that he had made a grave mistake. He discovered a path to redemption at the Triveni Sangam. It was there that he found the means to absolve himself of his wrongdoing and start anew. This is here Ganjaleshwar Mahadev Temple is situated.[1]

After crossing Ganjal we were entering Harda district and this was a momentous occasion for us, as it signified our passage into the last district in our *parikrama*. Thenceforth, we shall advance towards Khandawa district, the abode of the venerated Omkareshwar, culminating our *parikrama* at this very place.

As we traversed the path, we paused for a brief respite. It was then that a genial farmer caught sight of us and kindly proffered a handful of fresh green *chana* for our consumption. I declared that the acquisition of the said item was contingent upon the acceptance of monetary compensation by the individual in question, who, being a prominent farmer, possessed a commensurate level of pride. Upon his refusal to accept said compensation, I was compelled to inform him that none of my *parikramavasi*s would be in possession of the said item. It is doubtful that he comprehended the situation, as it was likely the first instance in his life that a *parikramavasi* had offered payment for the items being provided.

I conveyed to him that in order for him to offer me something, he must either take payment or take part in a meal. This would enable us to engage in a fair exchange and within my rule of *parikramavasi*s. He was welcome to enjoy a cup of tea or a hearty lunch, after which we could proceed to consume his green *chana* without any monetary compensation. However, if he declined to partake in the meal, I would be compelled to prohibit my team from partaking in his offering. He proceeded to take some money, and we acquired a small quantity of *chana* that was available to all. Throughout the *parikrama*, we encountered difficulties in conveying our preferred method of completing the journey without incurring unnecessary debts. Many individuals struggled to comprehend our intentions.

Kumar's birthplace, which is located on the northern bank of the holy Narmada, is not very far away from here. They had seen him a month and a half ago, but we had travelled thousands of kilometres since then, so I could understand their concern. When Kumar first caught a glimpse of his mother and the rest of his family, he was immediately filled with an array of feelings.

In the midst of this period, a distinguished gentleman graciously presented us with a delectable offering of *kachauri*, urging us with utmost insistence to relish in its savoury delights. I cordially extended an invitation for him to participate in the pleasure of joining us for tea, prior to savouring the delectable offering he had presented. Despite his solemn vow to come back, he failed to fulfil his promise, thereby granting me the fortunate reprieve from indulging in the delectable *kachauri*.

Our dwelling was nestled within the expansive Prahlad Patel household complex, affording us ample space to house all of our managerial vehicles. The estate was a magnificent spectacle, exuding an aura of grandeur that testified to its owner's distinguished standing as a prominent landlord. The atmosphere, ionized and charged, imbued the surroundings with a captivating appeal, adding an extra layer of fascination to the scene. On that particular day, there was no necessity for the family of Prahlad Patel to unveil their kitchen as we had taken it upon ourselves to prepare meals for all. The encounter with the Patels was a singular experience, for it appeared that we were the ones providing *bhandara* to them, a reversal of the customary dynamic. The Patels in the vicinity had likely never encountered such generosity before, as they were known for providing food to those who continuously sought their financial assistance.

109

Hanuman Tekri

As the time came to bid farewell to the esteemed Patel family, a wave of intense emotions washed over the gathering. Prahlad Patel boasts a sizeable and illustrious dairy as well as farms, which has garnered a reputation throughout the region. With hearts brimming with anticipation, we set forth on our grand expedition to the enchanting town of Harda. Our destination held the promise of a fateful encounter with Pravin Saranga, a figure of great renown in these parts. The air crackled with excitement as we ventured forth, each step bringing us closer to the moment we had long awaited.

Having departed from Rundhlai, our journey was now directed towards Handia. Handia is an old town located on the banks which used to be one of the important centres in early times. For Sanatani it was the place which was dotted with temples. There are various locations in and around Handia where you can still see old ruins. During the reign of Akbar, Handia served as the capital of the *sardar*s, *fauzdar*s, *diwan*s and Mughal armies stationed there. The Gond kings kept their kingdom in the area to the east of the district, which the Mughals never invaded because they considered it too dangerous.[1] Harda is not far from Handia, a former commercial centre that boasted four cotton ginning and pressing mills in the late eighteenth century.[2] Both Handia and Harda were famous throughout the country for their brass production. Once a major metropolis, Handia is now just a little village; the Mughals placed a high value on it, which is likely why the Marathas destroyed it so severely during their occupation.

I had visited Handia on numerous occasions prior to embarking on this *parikrama*, but being there as part of this sacred pilgrimage held a special significance for me. Upon our arrival in Handia, we were cordially greeted by Pravin Sarang. Our initial destination was the Riddhanath Temple, situated in Handia and nestled along the serene banks of Mother Narmada. The Riddhanath Temple was founded by none other than Kubera himself. Kubera, a devout follower of Lord Brahma, was bestowed with the golden city of Lanka as a reward for a life well-lived and various austerities that he had performed. Envious of Kubera's prosperity, Ravana engaged him in battle and emerged victorious, subsequently claiming Lanka as his own. It was at this moment that Kubera began to worship Lord Shiva with great devotion. Through the benevolence of the deity, Kubera was bestowed with the grand Alkapuri, a city as vast and impressive as the legendary Lanka. Once Ravana inquired of Narada regarding Kubera's whereabouts, to which Narada recounted the tale of Alkapuri. This only served to further enrage Ravana, who subsequently emerged victorious in his conquest of Alkapuri. Overwhelmed with sorrow, Kubera sought refuge in Nemawar and began his spiritual practice at the Siddhanath Temple situated on the northern banks. With a sense of joy, Lord Shiva appeared before Kubera and spoke of his divine presence at the Siddhanath Temple as Siddheshwar Mahadev on the northern bank, but instructed that he must venture to the southern bank to establish Riddheshwar Mahadev. By following thorough with this task, all of his desires would be fulfilled. Kubera executed precise actions to establish the Riddheshwar Mahadev and subsequently regained possession of his Alkapuri.[3]

Following a visit to the Riddheshwar Mahadev and a brief respite, we embarked on our journey towards our intended destination amidst the sweltering heat of the day. As the sun gradually descended below the horizon, we arrived at Hanuman Tekri – a desolate site ensconced in the heart of the woods. Upon our arrival, a multitude of monkeys greeted us, but they scattered hastily, much to the relief of Nandlal Tayal. He had been concerned for the safety of his kitchen staff and the food provisions. As the campsite was being arranged, we made ourselves comfortable for the night.

In the night, *arti* and *puja* of Mother Narmada were performed and a grand *bhandara* was set up once again, which was truly wonderful. On this day, I had the pleasure of interacting with Ajay Vijayvargiya, Mamta Vijayvargiya and Nina Vijayvargiya, who had travelled from Nagpur to see me. Unfortunately, their visit was brief due to their late arrival. As I reflected on the situation, I could not help but feel regrettable that my visitors had journeyed such a great distance solely to see me. Despite my sincerest intentions, my busy schedule had left me with no choice but to retire early, leaving them to depart for Nagpur without proper meeting.

Not long after *bhandara* was done, a figure came up to me and held me a phone, signalling that the highly respected local minister was calling and would like to speak with me. I picked up the phone and said, *Narmade har*, but the other person on the other end did not recognize my voice. Following a short pause, a call came in, this time from the minister and said he was sorry he could not recognize my voice and asked if there was anything he could do. I graciously declined, explaining that thanks to Mother Narmada, we have more than enough food to feed everyone in this area.

110

Punyaghat

We had to use the road from Handia to Omkareshwar because the dam water had flooded the historic path of the *parikrama*. Another issue that causes difficulty in crossing tiny streams is the presence of backwater.

For the next few days, we traversed along the road, contemplating the many *tirtha-sthalas* that lay submerged beneath us. It was a poignant realization that these sacred sites may soon fade from memory, lost to the depths of time. I am compelled by my duty to share some of these places. Had we strolled from the age-old sacred bank of the Narmada, we would have come across the Uchavan Ghat where Uchavan Rishi[1] had performed his penance at this very site, infusing it with an alluring fragrance. This picturesque *ghat*, ensconced within the verdant forest, was truly a sight to behold.

Had we traversed the ancient path of *parikrama*, we would have arrived at Jogikila Ghat, a locale nestled in the midst of the Narmada River. Here, a diminutive island bears witness to a storied past, wherein a fort once stood and a revered *sadhu* performed his austerities, ultimately receiving a divine boon from Mother Narmada. Thus, the site came to be known as Jogikila Ghat.

Venturing beyond Jogikila, one would come across first the Ajnal River and then the Machack River, which converge with the revered Mother Narmada. At this juncture lies the hallowed Punyaghat Teerth, an ancient pilgrimage site. The original site now lies submerged in water, which has risen following the construction of the Indira Sagar Dam.

The name Punyaghat (near Punasa, which actually derived the name from these *ghats*), the *ghat* of the virtue, is a combination of two sources that describe this place. One tale claims that Gautama Rishi founded Gautameshwar Mahadev[2] there after being falsely accused of cow-killing by the brahmanas. According to the tradition, during a horrible time for crops, the entire region was engulfed in famine. In Gautama Rishi's *ashrama*, where there was food for everyone, many brahmanas spent twelve years. They all survived the famine, but when they were prepared to depart, they made a fictitious cow and left it at the door of Gautama Rishi. When the *rishi* opened the door in the morning and inadvertley did not see the cow and the image was broken, the brahmanas condemned Gautama Rishi to have made the sin as he had killed the cow which was not the case. However, Gautama Rishi asked those brahmanas what sort of penance or *prayaschitta* he could carry out. They claimed that if he could bring the Ganga, which flows in the north, you would be absolved of the sin.

In the sacred realm where Gautama Rishi diligently engaged in his austere *tapasya*, his unwavering devotion caught the attention of none other than Lord Shiva himself. The divine deity, pleased by the *rishi*'s unwavering commitment, graciously manifested before him. With an air of compassion, Lord Shiva gently conveyed to the venerable sage that his arduous efforts were, in fact, unnecessary. The cow that Gautama Rishi believed he had inadvertently taken the life of was, in truth, a mere illusion, a figment of his imagination rather than a tangible creature. As a response, Gautama Rishi said, "I am aware of that, but I still want to fulfil my promise and bring majestic Ganga here". In a divine encounter, Lord Shiva graciously bestowed upon him a few strands of his illustrious *jata*, the sacred locks that adorned his divine form. With utmost reverence, he was instructed to delicately sprinkle the holy *gangajala* (sacred water from the Ganges), through these sacred strands. It was believed that this sacred ritual would invoke the presence of the revered River Goddess Godavari Ganga herself. In a remarkable display of divine power, the revered Gautama Rishi effortlessly conjured forth the majestic Godavari Ganga. Gautameshwar Mahadev, a manifestation of the divine whose divine presence resembled that of the famed Jyotirlinga Trayambakeshwar, was founded by him at this propitious period.[3]

In the era when the majestic temple of Gautameshwar Mahadev graced the landscape, a remarkable stone inscription adorned its sacred walls. This inscription proudly proclaimed that the temple had undergone a splendid renovation under the patronage of the illustrious Uday Bhanu king during the auspicious Vikram Samvat year 1720, which corresponds to the year 1663 in the Common Era.

Legend has it that during their exile, the Pandavas established

Dharmapuri on the northern shore and performed numerous charitable deeds on the southern banks, giving rise to the name Punyaghat. The surrounding region was once adorned with numerous temples, all of which now lie submerged beneath the water's surface.

Beyond Punyaghat Teerth lies a location renowned as Balkeshwar Mahadev. As per the Sanatana legend, it was here that Maharaj Bali performed his penance and enshrined the Shivalinga, known as Balkeshwar Mahadev. Now it lies submerged beneath the waters of the Indira Sagar Dam.[4]

While we were going in the roadside and I was thinking about the ancient path and the repucusion of the Indira Sagar Dam, I also noticed that the prominence of agriculture in this region is undeniable and probably the dam has helped it.

During our travels through the region, we happened upon a charming Vishnoi village. Each modest dwelling in the village dutifully upheld the sacred tradition of *annakshetra*.

As the sun began to set, we arrived at Chakdi, a quaint village with a vibrant ambiance. Our lodging for the night was the local school, where I had the pleasure of meeting some individuals who expressed interest in accompanying me on my journey to Omkareshwar. However, come morning, I found myself unable to locate them as I set out on my *parikrama* for the day.

111

Weather Changes

As we journeyed through the enchanting landscapes of Khirkiya, our path unexpectedly crossed with a fascinating individual. This person had played a crucial role in the life of Yogesh, during his time as a dedicated *vistarak* in the esteemed organization known as the RSS. In the depths of my intellectual pursuit, I find myself grappling with the enigmatic nature of the organizational framework that lies at the heart of the RSS. It is a conundrum that has persistently eluded my understanding, leaving me in a state of perpetual bewilderment.

There were dark clouds covering the sky and it looked like they may start pouring any second. To our great fortune, the digital forecast bestowed upon us a glimmer of hope, predicting a delightful shift in the weather. It was a true blessing, for the sweltering heat had reached a point of unbearable intensity.

The morning had been marked by a gentle rainfall, and I had taken advantage of the soothing sound to indulge in a few hours of restful slumber.

112

Maa Narmada Put to the Test

In Bundi, we had the pleasure of meeting Surendra Patel for the remainder of the day. He was a deeply emotional man, yet his demeanour was fitting to his cultural background. Surendra Patel, a local resident of Bundi, warmly welcomed and graciously shared stories about the rich history and traditions of the town. His expressive nature and genuine passion for his heritage made our time with him truly memorable. As we explored Bundi together, it became evident that Surendra's emotional depth was not only a reflection of his individual character but also a testament to the profound connection he felt towards his cultural roots.

Over the course of the last few days, I have mentioned to everyone in the group that last some days are important and Mother Narmada will test us and we shall be ready to take sure we follow the same set of rules and regulation that we have followed all through *parikrama*. I had spoken these words a day before and today the test came to our light.

I had set a personal policy right from the beginning of the *parikrama*, stating that we would only venture into farms that were not fenced and if we have to enter in some farms for lunch and if we find they are fenced we would avoid unless the farmer himself requests us to come and rest.

It was today that Lokesh found himself in a predicament as he searched for an appropriate venue for our lunch. He did not find any place and frustrated, he resorted to making slight modifications to the fence in order to gain access to a particular location in farm which had beautiful tree cover. As I arrived, an overwhelming feeling of disbelief washed over me. The scene before me appeared too perfect to be real. As I delved deeper into the matter, I discovered that the fence had not been left open by happen stance, but rather had been deliberately opened by Lokesh. I seized the opportunity to remind Lokesh of our mutual agreement to abstain from engaging in such actions as he had for all through the *parikrama*.

In the final days, I took extra precautions to ensure that our *parikrama* would withstand Mother Narmada's test. Mother Narmada put us through multiple tests, but with her help, we always came out on top.

This evening we took up residence in the tranquil Gulab Das Maharaj Ashram, where we were joined by Indar Hisaria and his family. Despite they could not walk with us until we completed the *parikrama*, they remained steadfast in their commitment to be around us in the *parikrama*, accompanying us every step of the way by car.

113

Submerged Tirthas

As we embarked on our journey towards Omkareshwar, a wave of emotions washed over us. With the first light of dawn, Surendra Patel appeared, bearing a pot of tea that exuded a comforting warmth. Savouring the warmth of the beverage, we relished in the tranquillity of the moment. In the midst of our arduous journey, fate led us to cross paths with none other than Narayan Patel, the brother of Surendra Patel and local Member of Legislative Council. He had made large banners of mine, which would be awaiting my arrival at Omkareshwar the following day.

Beneath the sprawling branches of a *ber* tree, we indulged in a meal. Adjacent to us stood an ancient *baoli* (water reservoir), its age is evident in its weathered appearance. The sense of history surrounding us was palpable, as if we were in the presence of a cultural relic. Despite our awe, we did not tarry long and departed expeditiously. As we journeyed, we had the pleasure of encountering Narendra Singh, a prominent figure in the area. He had been diligently seeking me out for days, having recognized me from my online presence on Facebook and other social media platforms.

We were getting close to Omkareshwar and it was like reaching to a destination that everyone of was waiting. Since we had crossed one dam Indira Sagar and another is being built in Omkareshwar. In between these tow dams many ancient *tirtha*s are submerged and some are lost, we could not find any of them but still the story must be written.

Had we strolled along the ancient path of the *parikrama*, undisturbed by the reservoir's submergence, we might have chanced upon the sacred Saptamata Teerth, nestled in close proximity to Bayphal. And Kotkheda which was on the eastern side of the temple premises.[1]

The seven Matrikas, known as Saptamata, included Varahi, Chamunda, Brahmani, Vaishnavi, Indrani, Kaumari and Maheshwari. In my perusal of various articles dating back to the early twentieth century,

I chanced upon an archive that offered me a tantalizing glimpse into the grandeur of a temple that once graced this very location. In the temple the south-facing deities were Brahmani, Vaishnavi, Indrani. The deities that looked on western side were Varahi, Chamunda and Kumari.

In addition to the revered temple of Saptamatrika, a host of other idols adorned the sacred space, including those of Bageshwari, Bhairava, Ganesha, Hulkadevi, Mahavira and many more (outside of the temple facing east according to the historical accounts of the time). Omkareshwar lay a mere 12-14 km from this location.

Around 5 km from this point, the revered Kaveri once met with the Narmada.[2] However, she maintained her separate flow and continued for a few more kilometres before dividing again to form the Omkareshwar Island. The northern flow belonged to the Kaveri, while the southern flow belonged to the Narmada. They would reunite after traversing a couple of kilometres and converge once more, marking the second confluence of the Kaveri with this sacred River Narmada. The Kubera Bhandari Teerth marked the site of the initial confluence, a place of great significance akin to the revered Prayagraj's Ganga–Yamuna confluence. It is belief that the place has six times more merit than the Prayagraj confluence.[3] In this sacred abode, Kubera, with unwavering determination, embarked upon his arduous *tapasya*, seeking to attain the divine blessing that would grant him the coveted position of ruling over the *yaksha*s.

Beyond this *sangam*, there were once four additional *tirtha*s known as Varahi Sangam, Chandavega Sangam, Arandi Sangam and Pitr Teerth or Brahma Teerth.

Varahi Ganga, a celestial river of profound origins, gracefully came into existence through the divine perspiration of Lord Vishnu, who had assumed the magnificent form of Varaha (boar incarnation).[4]

Chandavega Sangam[5] was very pious and it was here that the king of Ayodhya Chandasena in Svarochit Manvantara had his *tapasya* to get free from the curse of Saudamani, the wife of Shandilya. The story goes back that once Chandasena, having embarked on a hunting expedition, arrived at the serene Ashram of Shandilya. It was there that his eyes fell upon the enchanting figure of Saudamani, igniting within him a forbidden desire. Consumed by his lustful yearnings, Chandasena contemplated forcefully claiming Shandilya's wife as his own. However, fate intervened in the form of Saudamani, who, perceiving his immoral intentions, cast upon him a curse. In her divine wisdom, she likened his behaviour to that of a *chandala*, a lowly outcaste, decreeing that he would henceforth embody the very essence of his immoral thoughts.

It was at this juncture that his countenance took a sharp turn towards the horrible, rendering him almost unrecognizable. As he made his way back to his regal domain, a disheartening truth unfolded: even his once-devoted wives and kinsfolk held themselves at a distance, unable to bear the sight of his altered visage. On asking from Vasishtha the way he could repent his wrongdoing he was suggested to go back to Saudamani and ask forgiveness.

Once more, the king made his way to Saudamani's abode, his heart heavy with remorse. He sought her forgiveness, knowing that he had wronged her deeply. In her wisdom, she proposed a course of action that would begin the process of healing their fractured relationship. She advised the king to approach her husband and humbly request a remedy for the pain he had caused. It was at this juncture that the venerable Shandilya Rishi, in his wisdom, proposed that it was imperative for him to seek the guidance of the esteemed Sage Markandeya. The king, burdened by his curse, sought the wisdom of the venerable Markendaya Muni. It was in the presence of this sage that he received a profound suggestion. Markandeya Muni advised the king to embark on a spiritual journey to the sacred confluence of the Chandavega River and the revered Mother Narmada. It was at this sacred site that the king was instructed to engage in deep meditation and fervently appeal to the divine Chandikeshwar Mahadev. Only then, Markendaya Muni proclaimed, would the king find liberation from the shackles of his curse. In a grand display of humility and devotion, the illustrious king made his way to the sacred confluence, a place of profound significance. With a heart heavy with remorse, he sought solace and redemption in the divine presence of Chandikeshwar Mahadev. It was this benevolent deity who, in his infinite mercy, absolved the king of his transgressions, liberating him from the burden of his sins. Such was the magnitude of this extraordinary *tirtha*, a place revered for its unparalleled sanctity and transformative power.

In the immediate vicinity, there lay another sacred site known as Erandi Sangam. Legend has it that in this very hallowed ground, Bhadra and Rudra, the two ethereal *gandharvas*, embarked upon a demanding journey of penance. Their unwavering devotion led them to seek solace and sanctuary in the celestial abode of Erandeshwar Mahadev. In a moment of divine inspiration, they laid the foundation for the magnificent Bhadreshwar Mahadev.

The establishment of this sacred *tirtha* can be traced back to the decree of none other than the esteemed father of Durvasa (Lord Shiva). It is worth noting that the revered Sage Erandi, too, chose this very place to embark on his arduous spiritual journey, engaging in rigorous *tapasya*. This particular locale had gained a reputation for its sacred rituals of *pindadana* and *tarpana*, which were performed either individually or with the assistance of learned brahmanas.

Some images I had seen from the period of the dam building and progressively rising water showed many temples in the water, rendering them inaccessible to the public for all time. Although they are no longer physically present, their spirits remain, and it is up to our collective memories to keep these sites alive in our hearts even when we cannot see them. All these *tirtha*s that have been buried under water will eventually be discovered by a future generation.

This evening we reached Karoli and had our night in an *ashrama*; the vexing brought some rains and we felt that Mother Narmada was blessing us in our final days when we were so close to Omkareshwar.

114

Returning to Omkareshwar

It was a day filled with emotion for me, and we got going on time, making our way by villages full of happy youngsters playing Holi on the way to Omkareshwar.

My prayer to return from the *parikrama* to Omkareshwar on the day of Holi was granted by Mother Narmada, which I had asked for shortly after passing the point where Mother Narmada meets the ocean. After receiving the holy Narmada's graces, a task that seemed impossible to many was finally accomplished.

A few kilometres before Omkareshwar, we reached Mangal Das Tyagi's Shri Jod Ganapati Temple Ashram, he greeted us with a large parade and a band. Here I saw the *ratha* bearing the holy *kalasha*s filled with water from the holy Narmada River.

Several months ago, in Omkareshwar, we filled the *kalasha*s, and today, as we returned with them, I thought that the bands who were playing had done the justice to it; they played for the sacred *kalasha*s.

As the sun began its descent, casting a warm golden glow over the ancient city, we made our way to the sacred Brahmapuri Ghat. It was a momentous occasion, for the *parikrama*, a spiritual circumambulation, was about to conclude with the sacred *kalasha*s, water given to holy Narmada in the same *ghat*.

The *arti* (a devotional ritual of offering prayers to the divine) was the centrepiece of this evening's gathering. Many people were there who had come to be part of this ceremony when we had returned back to Omkareshwar after travelling 3,000 km.

After Mangal Das Tyagi had finished speaking at the end of the *arti* and ceremony, I was called upon to do likewise. When Mangal Das Tyagi remarked that he had witnessed my *parikrama* and found it to uphold the principles established by the great Shri Gaurishankar Maharaj, I felt a flood of emotion.

As a wave of emotions crashed over me, I found myself on the precipice of tears. In the depths of my consciousness, I had never fathomed that this particular moment would culminate in such an unforeseen manner. That day, I spoke again as I often do, but this time it was out of gratitude to Mother Narmada rather than any sort of discourse. The focal point of my discourse was that one *parikrama* is concluded but many more are starting to take shape and this is when I shared that Ma Narmada Gyan Peeth, an organization solely devoted for the cause of holy Narmada, has been founded.

115

Omkar Maharaj

It was on 8 March when we arrived at Omkareshwar, having reached our destination a day earlier. As the sun began to set, we made our way to Brahmapuri Ghat. There, we immersed ourselves in the spiritual atmosphere and took part in a captivating *arti* ceremony. Today, our intention is to present the water of *parikrama* to Omkar Maharaj, the presiding deity of Omkareshwar. As we embarked on our journey, we were joined by the esteemed Dr Mohan Yadav, the current chief minister of Madhya Pradesh, accompanied by a sizeable group of talented band members. As our journey commenced, a cascade of rose petals descended upon us, producing a grand spectacle in Omkareshwar, reserved only for those who had completed the *parikrama* and offered water. It is customary for individuals to commence the *parikrama* with grandeur, but conclude it in a tranquil manner. Contrary to Mahant Mangal Das Tyagi's statement, our experience was quite the opposite. The conclusion of our *parikrama* was truly magnificent.

Our journey commenced at the sacred Jod Ganapati Temple, accompanied by the lively sounds of bands. Our destination was Omkareshwar Temple. We presented the *parikrama* water to Omkareshwar Maharaj and the temple resounded with the melodious strains of the band, fulfilling my heart's deepest desire. As soon as we presented Omkarji with the vibrant *gulal* powder, this is when our Holi commenced.

Upon my arrival at the temple, I was greeted by the familiar faces of priests, who immediately recognized me. They eagerly informed me that their faith had been affirmed and that the *parikrama* path was soon to be realized. As I spoke to them, I implored them to relay my request to Omkar Maharaj that I yearned for his permission to reside in the sacred presence of Mother Narmada for a span of three years. With their gracious blessings, I envisioned undertaking numerous endeavours. "We have already asked that", the priest said.

Upon presenting the *parikrama* water to Omkar Maharaj and offering the *gulal* we departed from temple premises, and thus commenced the celebration of Holi for our entire group. Undoubtedly, it was the grandest Holi ever witnessed in Omkareshwar, marking the conclusion of our *parikrama* journey.

With great determination, I set my sights on returning to the Holi festivities in Omkareshwar, despite the seemingly insurmountable obstacles that lay ahead. As I embarked on this challenging journey, I fervently wished that my success would serve as a testament to the divine blessings bestowed upon me by the revered Mother Narmada. I fulfilled my commitment and was met with a familiar sensation.

Before reaching Omkareshwar, I had notified the group of *parikramavasi*s that, in the event of our timely arrival, I would offer them *bhang*.

Upon my arrival at Omkareshwar, I had arranged for the preparation of *bhang*. It was a captivating scene as we found ourselves enclosed with my parents and a multitude of individuals, including *parikramavasi*s. Suddenly, a commotion arose outside as the *bhang* arrived. The offering was presented to Omkar Maharaj first, and subsequently, the majority of the *parikramavasi*s took part in it, with the exception of a select few, including me.

Gradually, the town too had its fair share of *bhang*, which was openly distributed in the market. As we embarked on the *parikrama* of Omkar Parvat, a gradual realization dawned upon us. With the exception of a select few, the majority of individuals were indulging in the merriment of *bhang*, completely oblivious to their surroundings. While I was disheartened by their behaviour, I chose to let it go, recognizing that the *parikramavasi*s and the team had overcome a significant obstacle and deserved to revel in their triumph.

As we arrived at the *ashrama*, a peculiar scene unfolded before us. The majority of the *parikrama* team appeared to be under the influence of *bhang*, their senses seemingly dulled by the substance. Meanwhile, the festivities of Holi were in full swing within the *ashrama*'s grounds, with copious amounts of *gulal* being used to partake in the traditional *parikrama*. The situation was undeniably amusing, to say the least.

It was day after 9 March 2023 that a grand *bhandara* and *kanya-pujana* were organized, after the *bhandara* I left from Omkareshwar.

I found that the *parikrama* had concluded. However, my existence has since become a perpetual circumambulation around the divine Mother Narmada, a journey without end.

In Appreciation

Planning my Narmada Parikrama in detail was one of the most challenging tasks at hand before I even set out on my journey. Initiated by Mother Narmada, the *parikrama* committee included

Ajay Vijayvargiya, Dr Mohan Yadav, Chandrashekhar Bawankule, Praveen Chauhan, Deepak Bansal, Nandlal Tayal, Sujeet Gade, Indar and Vinod Hisaria. Jitendra Sharma was tasked with coordinating things during the *parikrama*. Nandlal Tayal were in charge of everything related to food and *bhandara* on the banks of the holy Narmada, while I was walking in *parikrama*, arrangements were being made on our behalf.

There were a lot of people who had put in a lot of work to make the *parikrama* happen and I want to make sure they know how much I appreciate it.

I think it was great that Ajay Vijayvargiya and Praveen Chauhan visited us nearly every other week while we were on *parikrama*. In addition, it aided them in realizing the difficulties *parikramavasi*s experience. This allowed them to spend a few brief days walking along the sacred banks of the Narmada River, which no doubt had a profound effect on their spiritual development. I have to mention that Shreya, Ajay Vijayvargiya's daughter, made sure I always had fresh *salad* greens and sourdough bread – both of which were incredibly important to me on my journey but were not favourites of the other *parikramavasi*s with whom I shared these provisions.

Along with Vinod Hissaria, Nandalal Tayal and Deepak spent months in Delhi shopping for a massive amount of merchandise. They shopped for us so that we would have everything we needed and people used to be startled to learn that we even had a generator and could use it if we stayed in the woods. Each day as I returned to the camp after a day of walking, I was struck by how thoroughly the planning of purchase had been done, as not a single thing was missing that was essential for us.

Vinay Chauhan took the initiative to adapt the vehicles to our requirements, to source local materials and print banners that were displayed on a wide variety of vehicles and other locations. Vinay would almost live with us for weeks at a time, helping out at the camp and seeing to the needs of the *parikramavasi*s.

Rajeev Hissaria was our point man in Gujarat; he coordinated our every move and even made sure I got to eat some of my favourite French food while on *parikrama*. I cannot thank Ashita, enough for her diligence in taking care of all the additional shopping that had to be done in Gujarat.

All of the bookkeeping for the Narmada Parikrama was handled by Deepak Bansal and Rohan Junankar, both before and after the walk. I had assigned them the enormous duty of keeping meticulous records of all money spent on *parikrama*. Both of them are chartered accountants, but conducting accountancy for the *parikrama* was not easy, therefore, I think they did quite well and I am sure they learned a lot from it!

Nishu Agrawal performed an excellent job of packing the *shringara*, putting everything in a box that we opened every night and decorated with a new *sari* before presenting it to Maiya Narmada.

Others stayed behind in camps to ensure that we had everything we needed while I walked 3,000 km with Swami Brahmachari and Swami Shivananda and others like Yogesh Azad, Kumar (my namesake Vivek Panwar), Atul Shukla, Vikas Tiwari, Girish Kapse, Sahibrao Tahkeet, K. Khandelwal, Gaurav Pavar, Lal Bahadur, Yam Bahadur and Dinesh Devvasi. This was our *parikrama* team, to which were added every day scores of others who would walk with us for a day or leave us off at various points along the way.

Nandlal Tayal oversaw daily catering with the help of Mukesh Sharma, the head cook, Raju Banna, Bipin Sharma, Pawan Sharma, Yograj Sharma, Raju Soni, Munna Paswan and Rahul Soni. In my opinion, they did a great job every day and served out delicious *bhandara*. The cooking crew used to rise early to get started on the *prasad* for morning *puja*, which they would then follow up with our breakfast and lunch. After they have prepared the food, they will wash the dishes, reload the tractor truck and head to the site where they will set up camp for the night. Once they arrive at the spot, they will reopen everything that was stored in the tractor lorry, brew the tea that Lokesh transported and then make night *bhandara*. Balkrishna Paradkar Roshan and Jadu Burman both contributed to the preparation of food and *bhandara*.

Jitendra Sharma was in-charge of coordinating and scouting out potential campsites, while Vikas Parasar was on the ground providing whatever assistance was required, including documentation. Dileep Jadhav and Vishal Shitole were in charge of the vehicle, which served as our moving storehouse by transporting all additional amenities. In addition to finding us to give lunch, tea and snakes along our lengthy walks, Lokesh Jharbade took care of the on-the-way purchase. As we were making our way out from the holy banks, Lokesh would ride on his bike, checking for us and making sure we were well-fed and watered. Our chief priest, Pandit Nirnay Vyas, ensured that morning and evening *puja*s were performed precisely. He also ensured that our *puja-ratha* was properly prepared when travelling through towns and permitted anyone who wanted to perform *puja*s. During his monthlong stay with us, Kaushal Sharma took care of a number of the camp's needs.

We had a whole team of drivers who were in charge of moving the vehicles that were following me around. While I was on my walk along the holy banks and in the forest, these drivers delivered all of the necessary items that were in the vehicle to the location where I would be in the evening. For the first two months, Mohan Uikey was in-charge of my two vehicles, one of which included my bed at first and another, driven by Vijay Dhurve, which contained my workroom and restrooms. When one of the vehicles with a toilet started having minor issues during our *parikrama* two months later, Deepak provided another fantastic vehicle from Delhi that was driven by Tarsen Singh and Rana. Vasudev Dhurve was responsible for transporting the *puja-ratha*, Nilesh Jaiswal and Krishna Pawar alternated driving the water tanker and Sohan Singh was in-charge of the vehicle that Nandlal Tayal used to get around and make purchases. Ram Dhurve was behind the wheel of our largest vehicle, a truck where all the amenities were kept. Our food tractor was driven by Sukhdev Varma and it had a lorry attached that served as a temporary kitchen with a pure water filter, a water heater and a sizeable battery for lighting. Dinesh was responsible for guarding the campsite if we were in forest or other such locations.

This was our *parikrama* team, to which were added everyday scores of others who would walk with us for a day or leave us off at various points along the way; their names might fill another book, but some resonated in my mind as they walked for days at a time, including Pramod Bambal, Rahul Tompe, Alok Nahar, Arvind Patankar, Hemant Patil, Amit Sethi, Ritesh Jaiswal, Sunil Junankar, Sanjay Singh, Vaibhav Yadav, Indar Singh Jamnod, Lalaram Chakravarti, Sujeet Gade, Shailendra Tomar, Surendra Gahlot, Suraj Jat, Ashok Rawat, Dhansing Vasava, Vijay Chaudhari, Nilesh, Lalit Mukati, Bunty Sharma, Jaideep Patel, Jaipal Rajput, Ujjwal Singh Solanki, Ujjwal Singh Chauhan, Sahib Singh Rajput, Sanjay Dhote, Shailesh Mahajan, Raju Lodhi, Praveen Saranga, Surendra Patel, Monu Rai, Yogesh Sadaranga, S.R . Patil, Sanjay Jainansaria, Dinesh Chaudhary, who accompanied me for many kilometres of walk around the holy banks of Narmada, Om Soni, Manu Hisaria, Arun Jain, Ghansyam Mittal, Vinod Deshmukh, Trilok Chanda and Bunty Bansal were constantly in touch with our support staff and provided every assistance that was needed.

End Notes

Prologue

1. W.W. Hunter, 1881, *Imperial Gazetteer of India*, vol. 7, p. 55.
2. Unni K. Sankaran, 1996, *Ecology of River Narmada*.
3. Chakrabarti, Dilip K., 2006, *The Archaeological Foundation of Ancient India*, pp. 10-14.

Holy Narmada in Indian Shastras

1. चक्रवाकैः सकारण्डैः सहंसजलकुक्कुटैः । सारसैश्च सदा मत्तैः कूजद्भिः सुसमावृताम् ॥ – *वाल्मीकि रामायण*, उत्तरकाण्ड, श्लोक 21, गीता प्रेस, गोरखपुर
2. फुल्लद्रुमकृतोत्तंसां चक्रवाकयुगस्तनीम् । विस्तीर्णपुलिनश्रोणीं हंसावलिसुमेखलाम् ॥ २२॥

   पुष्परेण्वनुलिप्ताङ्गीं जलफेनामलांशुकाम् । जलावगाहसुस्पर्शां फुल्लोत्पलशुभेक्षणाम् ॥२३॥

   पुष्पकादवरुह्याशु नर्मदां सरितां वराम् । इष्टामिव वरां नारीमवगाह्य दशाननः ॥२४॥

   स तस्याः पुलिने रम्ये नानामुनिनिषेविते । उपोपविष्टः सचिवैः सार्धं राक्षसपुङ्गवः ॥२५॥

   – *वाल्मीकि रामायण*, उत्तरकाण्ड, सर्ग 31, श्लोक 22-25, गीता प्रेस, गोरखपुर
3. सिवप्रिय मेकल सैल सुता सी । सकल सिद्धि सुख संपति रासी ॥

   सदगुन सुरगन अंब अदिति सी । रघुबर भगति प्रेम परमिति सी ॥

   – रामचरित्मानस, तुलसीदासकृत, बालकाण्ड, गीता प्रेस, गोरखपुर
4. नर्मदां तु समासाद्य नदीं त्रैलोक्यविश्रुताम् ॥ तर्पयित्वा पितॄन् देवानग्निष्टोमफलं लभेत् ॥ ५२ ॥
5. शोणस्य नर्मदायाश्च प्रभवे कुरुनन्दन । वंशगुल्म उपस्पृश्य वाजिमेधफलं लभेत् ॥

   – रामचरित्मानस, तुलसीदासकृत, बालकाण्ड, गीता प्रेस, गोरखपुर
6. त्रैलोक्ये यानि तीर्थानि पुण्यान्यायतनानि च । सरिद्वनानि शैलेन्द्रा देवाश्च सपितामहाः ॥ ३ ॥ – Ibid.

   नर्मदायां कुरुश्रेष्ठ सह सिद्धर्षिचारणैः । स्नातुमायान्ति पुण्यौघैः सदा वारिषु भारत ॥ ४ ॥ – Ibid.

   – वेदव्यास, *महाभारत*, भाग 2, गीता प्रेस, गोरखपुर
7. नर्मदायामुपस्पृश्य तथा शूर्पारकोदके । एकपक्षं निराहारो राजपुत्रो विधीयते ॥ ५०॥

   – *Mahabharata*, vol. 6, Gita Press, Gorakhpur
8. ततः सुराणामसुरै रणः परमदारुणः । त्रेतामुखे नर्मदायामभवत् प्रथमे युगे ।।

   – *Srimadbhagavata Mahapurana*, vol. 1 (Skanda 1-8), Gita Press, Gorakhpur

9. तं नर्मदायास्तट उत्तरे बलेर्य ऋत्विजस्ते भृगुकच्छसंज्ञके । प्रवर्तयन्तो भृगवः क्रतूत्तमं व्यचक्षतारादुदितं यथा रविम् ॥२१॥
– Ibid., vol. 1, Skandha 8, Gita Press, Gorakhpur

10. प्रविश्य रेवामगमद् यत्र माहिष्मती पुरी। मनुतीर्थमुपस्पृश्य प्रभासं पुनरागमत् ।
– *Srimadbhagavata Mahapurana*, vol. 2, Gita Press, Gorakhpur

11. पूर्वप्रवाहे यः स्नाति गङ्गास्नानफलं लभेत्। प्रवाहे दक्षिणे तस्या नर्मदा सरितां वरा।।
– *Vamana Purana* 7, Gita Press, Gorakhpur

12. इत्थं तयोस्तु वदतोर्नर्मदायास्तटे मुने। जलवासाद् विनिष्क्रान्तौ चण्डमुण्डौ च दानवौ ॥
– *Vamana Purana*, Gita Press, Gorakhpur

13. स्नात्वा कपिलधारायां संतर्प्यार्च्य पितॄन् सुरान्। दृष्ट्वा स्कन्दं समभ्यर्च्य नर्मदायां जगाम ह।।४७।। – Ibid.

14. वीरं कुवलयारूढं शङ्खचक्रगदाधरम् । श्रीवत्साङ्कमुदाराङ्गं नर्मदायां श्रियः पतिम् ।।१८।। – Ibid.

माहिष्मत्यां त्रिनयनं तत्रैव च हुताशनम् । अर्बुदे च त्रिसौपर्णं क्षमाधरं शूकराचले ।।१९।। – Ibid.

15. तैश्चोक्तं पुरुकुत्साय भूभुजे नर्मदातटे। सारस्वताय तेनापि मह्यं सारस्वतेन च।।
– *Vishnu Purana*, Gita Press, Gorakhpur

16. नर्मदायै वरं ददुः । यस्तेऽनुस्मरणसमवेतं नामग्रहणं करिष्यति न तस्य सर्पविषभयं भविष्य-तीति।।११।।
अत्र च श्लोकः ।।१२।। नर्मदायै नमः प्रातर्नर्मदायै नमो निशि। नमोऽस्तु नर्मदे तुभ्यं त्राहि मां विषसर्पतः ।।१३।।
– Ibid.

17. *Agni Purana*, chapter 13, English translation and annotation by N. Gangadharan, 4 vols, 1954.

18. *Narada Purana*, Uttarabhaga.

19. *Bhavishya Purana*, Brahma-Parva.

20. *Brahmavaivartta Purana*, Ganapati Khanda.

21. पुण्या कनखले गङ्गा कुरुक्षेत्रे सरस्वती। ग्रामे वा यदि वारण्ये पुण्या सर्वत्र नर्मदा ॥ ७ ॥
त्रिभिः सारस्वतं तोयं सप्ताहेन तु यामुनम्। सद्यःपुनाति गाङ्गेयं दर्शनादेव नार्मदम् ॥ ८॥
– *Kurma Purana*, 38th chapter, Gita Press, Gorakhpur

22. *Padma Purana*, Shrishti Khanda, Gita Press, Gorakhpur.

Historical Literature on Narmada

1. Schoff, 1912, *The Periplus of the Erythraean Sea*.
2. Iyangar (ed.), 1942, *Krityakalpataru of Bhatta Lakshmidhara*.

Chapter 4

1. *The Gazetteer of the Central Provinces of India*, 1870, ed. Charles Grant, p. 258, Bombay: Education Society's Press.
2. *The Gazetteer of the Central Provinces of India*, 1870, p. 259.
3. Ibid.

4. *The Gazetteer of the Central Provinces of India*, 1870, p. 261.
5. Ibid.
6. 1904: viii-xiii, 333-34, note.
7. Kielhorn 1895; Mittal 1979, 86-91; Neuss 2014, 124; and Trivedi 1978, 61-64.
8. Neuss 2014: 125.
9. Malcolm, 1823, *A Memoir of Central India*.

Chapter 9

1. Matanga Muni, *Padma Purana*, Prabhu Dutt Brahmchari, *Narmada Darshan*, p. 145.

Chapter 12

1. *Vayu Purana*, Reva Khanda, 44; Prabhu Dutt Brahmchari, *Narmada Darshan*, p. 147.
2. Prabhu Dutt Brahmchari, *Narmada Darshan*, p. 148; *Skanda Purana*, Reva Khanda, p. 144.
3. *Skanda Purana*, Reva Khanda, p. 144, Prabhu Dutt Brahmchari, *Narmada Darshan*, p. 148.
4. *Vayu Purana*, Reva Khanda, 9, Prabhu Dutt Brahmchari *Narmada Darshan*, pp. 148-49.
5. *Vayu Purana*, Reva Khanda, 10, Prabhu Dutt Brahmchari, *Narmada Darshan*, pp. 148-49.
6. *Vayu Purana*, Reva Khanda, 65, Prabhu Dutt Brahmchari, *Narmada Darshan*, p. 150.
7. *Vayu Purana*, Reva Khanda, 65.
8. *Vayu Purana*, Reva Khanda 64.

Chapter 14

1. *Vayu Purana*, Reva Khanda 32; *Skanda Purana*, Reva Khanda 31.
2. *Padma Purana*, Svarga Khanda; *Kurma Purana* 39-40.
3. *Padma Purana*, Svarga khanda; *Skanda Purana*, Reva Khanda 32.

Chapter 15

1. *Padma Purana*, Prabhu Dutt Brahmchari, *Narmada Darshan*, p. 158.
2. *Vayu Purana*, Reva Khanda 69.
3. *Vayu Purana*, Reva Khanda 17.
4. *Skanda Purana*, Reva Khanda 127.

Chapter 16

1. *Imperial Gazetteer of India*, vol. 7.
2. *Indian Foresters*, 1895, vol. 21, pp. 16-17.
3. *Vayu Purana*, Reva Khanda 115; *Skanda Purana*, Reva Khanda 108-09.

Chapter 17

1. Prabhu Dutt Brahmchari, *Narmada Darshan*, p. 167.
2. *Skanda Purana*, Reva Khanda 35; *Vayu Purana*, Reva Khanda 73; *Padma Purana*, Svarga Khanda.

Chapter 18

1. *Vasishtha Samhita* 48.

Chapter 24

1. *Padma Purana*, Svarga Khanda; *Kurma Purana*, Reva Khanda 39; *Skanda Purana*, Reva Khanda 44-58; *Vayu Purana* 80-92.
2. *Transactions of the Bombay Geographical Society 1836-1838*, vol. 1, 1844.
3. Ibid.

Chapter 26

1. *Vayu Purana*, Reva Khanda 79; *Padma Purana*, Svarga Khanda.
2. *Skanda Purana*, Reva Khanda 138; *Kurma Purana* 39-40; *Padma Purana*, Svarga Khanda.
3. *Padma Purana*, Svarga Khanda.
4. *Skanda Purana*, Reva Khanda 96; *Vayu Purana*, Reva Khanda 65.
5. Prabhu Dutt Brahmchari, *Narmada Darshan*, p. 188.
6. *Skanda Purana*, Reva Khanda 67; *Vayu Purana*, Reva Khanda 96.
7. *Skanda Purana*, Reva Khanda 67; *Vayu Purana*, Reva Khanda 96.
8. *Skanda Purana*, Reva Khanda 148.
9. *Skanda Purana*, Reva Khanda 75; *Vayu Purana*, Reva Khanda 99.
10. Prabhu Dutt Brahmchari, *Narmada Darshan*, pp. 201-04.
11. *Vayu Purana*, Reva Khanda 99; Prabhu Dutt Brahmchari *Narmada Darshan*, pp. 201-04.
12. Prabhu Dutt Brahmchari, *Narmada Darshan*, p. 204.
13. Ibid., p. 205.
14. *Skanda Purana*, Reva Khanda 84.
15. Prabhu Dutt Brahmchari, *Narmada Darshan*, p. 206.

Chapter 27

1. *Skanda Purana,* Reva Khanda 83; *Vayu Purana,* Reva Khanda 83.
2. *Skanda Purana,* Reva Khanda 89; *Vayu Purana,* Reva Khanda 106.
3. Prabhu Dutt Brahmchari, *Narmada Darshan,* p. 214.
4. *Skanda Purana,* Reva Khanda 99; *Vayu Purana,* Reva Khanda 111.
5. *Skanda Purana,* Reva Khanda 167.
6. *Skanda Purana,* Reva Khanda 96; *Padma Purana,* Svarga Khanda.

Chapter 28

1. Prabhu Dutt Brahmchari, *Narmada Darshan,* p. 217.
2. *Skanda Purana,* Reva Khanda 111; *Kurma Purana* 39.
3. *Skanda Purana,* Reva Khanda 124.
4. *Skanda Purana,* Reva Khanda 118.
5. Ibid.
6. *Vayu Purana,* Reva Khanda 10; *Skanda Purana,* Reva Khanda 61; *Padma Purana,* Svarga Khanda; *Kurma Purana* 39-40.
7. *Skanda Purana,* Reva Khanda 150; *Kurma Purana* 39-40.
8. *Skanda Purana,* Reva Khanda 158; *Padma Purana,* Svarga Khanda.
9. *Skanda Purana,* Reva Khanda 159.
10. *Skanda Purana,* Reva Khanda 161.
11. *Skanda Purana,* Reva Khanda 170-71.
12. Prabhu Dutt Brahmchari, *Narmada Darshan,* p. 233.
13. Prabhu Dutt Brahmchari, *Narmada Darshan,* p. 236.
14. *Skanda Purana,* Reva Khanda 174.
15. *Skanda Purana,* Reva Khanda 199.
16. *Skanda Purana,* Reva Khanda 66; *Vayu Purana,* Reva Khanda 96.
17. Prabhu Dutt Brahmchari, *Narmada Darshan,* p. 243.
18. Ibid., p. 242.
19. *Kurma Purana* 39-40; *Skanda Purana,* Reva Khanda 221; *Vayu Purana,* Reva Khanda 10.
20. *Skanda Purana,* Reva Khanda 222.
21. *Skanda Purana,* Reva Khanda 222; *Vayu Purana,* Reva Khanda 68.
22. *Skanda Purana,* Reva Khanda 222-23.
23. *Skanda Purana,* Reva Khanda 225; *Kurma Purana* 39-40.

Chapter 29

1. *Skanda Purana*, Reva Khanda 223; *Padma Purana*, Svarga Khanda.
2. *Skanda Purana*, Reva Khanda 218; *Kurma Purana* 39-40.
3. Mayananda Saraswati, *Narmada Panchanga*, p. 173.
4. *Skanda Purana*, Reva Khanda 220.
5. *Skanda Purana*, Reva Khanda 174.

Chapter 30

1. *Padma Purana*, Svarga Khanda; *Kurma Purana* 39-40; Mayananda Saraswati, *Narmada Panchanga*, p. 179.
2. Mayananda Saraswati, *Narmada Panchanga*, p. 179; Prabhu Dutt Brahmchari, *Narmada Darshan*, p. 264.

Chapter 31

1. Forbes, Alexander Kinloch, *Rasmala: Hindu Annals of the Province of Geozerat*.
2. *Kurma Purana*, Chapter 39-40, cited in Prabhu Dutt Brahmchari, *Narmada Darshan*, p. 267.
3. *Skanda Purana*, Reva Khanda 212.
4. *Skanda Purana*, Reva Khanda 211; Mayananda Saraswati, *Narmada Panchanga*.
5. Mayananda Saraswati, *Narmada Panchanga*, p. 180.
6. Mayananda Saraswati, *Narmada Panchanga*, p. 181.
7. *Skanda Purana*, Reva Khanda 214.
8. *Skanda Purana*, Reva Khanda 209; *Padma Purana*, Svarga Khanda; *Kurma Purana* 39-40.
9. *Padma Purana*, Svarga Khanda; *Kurma Purana* 39-40; *Skanda Purana*, Reva Khanda, 209.
10. *Skanda Purana*, Reva Khanda 208; *Kurma Purana* 39-40.
11. *Skanda Purana*, Reva Khanda 207; *Padma Purana*, Svarga Khanda; *Kurma Purana* 39-40.

Chapter 32

1. *Skanda Purana*, Reva Khanda 206; *Kurma Purana*, 39-40.
2. *Skanda Purana*, Reva Khanda 181-84, 187; *Vayu Purana*, Reva Khanda 09, *Padma Purana*, Svarga Khanda, *Kurma Purana*, 39-40.

Chapter 33

1. *Vayu Purana*, Reva Khanda 69; *Skanda Purana*, Reva Khanda; *Padma Purana*, Svarga Khanda 156.

2. *Vayu Purana,* Reva Khanda 69; *Skanda Purana,* Reva Khanda; *Padma Purana,* Svarga Khanda, 156.
3. *Skanda Purana,* Reva Khanda 157; *Padma Purana,* Svarga Khanda.
4. *Skanda Purana,* Reva Khanda, 157; *Padma Purana* Svarga Khanda.
5. *Skanda Purana,* Reva Khanda 153; *Vayu Purana,* Reva Khanda 94.
6. *Skanda Purana,* Reva Khanda 152.
7. *Skanda Purana,* Reva Khanda 151.
8. *Skanda Purana,* Reva Khanda 115; *Padma Purana,* Svarga Khanda; *Kurma Purana* 39-40.
9. *Padma Purana,* Svarga Khanda; *Kurma Purana* 39-40; *Skanda Purana,* Reva Khanda 146.

Chapter 34

1. *Skanda Purana,* Reva Khanda 140; Prabhu Dutt Brahmchari, *Narmada Darshan,* p. 290: Nanda Devi Teerth; Mayananda Saraswati, *Narmada Panchanga,* p. 197.
2. *Skanda Purana,* Reva Khanda 85; *Vayu Purana,* Reva Khanda 105; *Kurma Purana* 39-40.
3. *Skanda Purana,* Reva Khanda 138.
4. *Skanda Purana,* Reva Khanda 137.
5. *Skanda Purana,* Reva Khanda 134; Mayananda Saraswati, *Narmada Panchanga,* p. 198.
6. *Skanda Purana,* Reva Khanda 133; *Padma Purana,* Svarga Khanda.
7. *Skanda Purana,* Reva Khanda 132.
8. *Skanda Purana,* Reva Khanda 219.
9. *Skanda Purana,* Reva Khanda 128.
10. *Skanda Purana,* Reva Khanda 129.
11. *Skanda Purana,* Reva Khanda 114.
12. *Skanda Purana,* Reva Khanda 34.
13. *Skanda Purana,* Reva Khanda 123.
14. *Skanda Purana,* Reva Khanda 124.
15. *Skanda Purana,* Reva Khanda 122.
16. Ibid.

Chapter 35

1. *Vayu Purana,* Reva Khanda 114; Prabhu Dutt Brahmchari, *Narmada Darshan,* p. 290.

2. *Skanda Purana,* Reva Khanda 122.
3. *Skanda Purana,* Reva Khanda 120.
4. Prabhu Dutt Brahmchari, *Narmada Darshan*, p. 296.
5. *Skanda Purana,* Reva Khanda 117.
6. *Skanda Purana,* Reva Khanda 116; *Padma Purana,* Svarga Khanda.
7. *Padma Purana,* Svarga Khanda; *Skanda Purana,* Reva Khanda 115.
8. *Skanda Purana,* Reva Khanda 119.
9. James Forbes, *James Forbes Oriental Memoirs: A Narrative of Seventeen Years Residence in India,* around 1765-84.
10. Ibid.
11. *Skanda Purana,* Reva Khanda 110; *Vayu Purana,* Reva Khanda 116; *Padma Purana,* Svarga Khanda; *Kurma Purana* 39-40.
12. *Skanda Purana,* Reva Khanda 111; *Vayu Purana,* Reva Khanda 116.
13. Prabhu Dutt Brahmchari, *Narmada Darshan*, p. 296.
14. *Skanda Purana,* Reva Khanda 184.
15. *Skanda Purana,* Reva Khanda 167.
16. *Skanda Purana,* Reva Khanda 111; Prabhu Dutt Brahmchari, *Narmada Darshan,* p. 292.
17. *Vayu Purana,* Reva Khanda 97.
18. *Skanda Purana,* Reva Khanda 106; *Vayu Purana,* Reva Khanda 114.
19. Prabhu Dutt Brahmchari, *Narmada Darshan*, p. 296.
20. Ibid.
21. *Skanda Purana,* Reva Khanda 105.
22. Mayananda Saraswati, *Narmada Panchanga*, p. 206.
23. *Skanda Purana,* Reva Khanda 104; *Vayu Purana,* Reva Khanda 114; *Padma Purana,* Svarga Khanda.
24. *Skanda Purana,* Reva Khanda 103: Erandi Sangam; *Vayu Purana,* Reva Khanda 113.
25. *Skanda Purana,* Reva Khanda 102; *Vayu Purana,* Reva Khanda 112, 102.
26. *Vayu Purana,* Reva Khanda 18.
27. *Skanda Purana,* Reva Khanda 101; *Vayu Purana,* Reva Khanda 112, 101.
28. *Skanda Purana,* Reva Khanda 98; *Vayu Purana,* Reva Khanda 110.
29. Mayananda Saraswati, *Narmada Panchanga*, p. 208.
30. *Skanda Purana,* Reva Khanda 96; *Vayu Purana,* Reva Khanda 109; Mayananda Saraswati, *Narmada Panchanga*, p. 208.

31. *Skanda Purana,* Reva Khanda 95.

Chapter 36

1. *Skanda Purana,* Reva Khanda 178.
2. *Skanda Purana,* Reva Khanda 92; *Vayu Purana,* Reva Khanda 108.
3. *Skanda Purana,* Reva Khanda 91; *Vayu Purana,* Reva Khanda 107-09.
4. Mayananda Saraswati, *Narmada Panchanga,* p. 210.
5. Prabhu Dutt Brahmchari, *Narmada Darshan,* p. 300.
6. *Skanda Purana,* Reva Khanda 88.
7. *Skanda Purana,* Reva Khanda 87.
8. *Vayu Purana,* Reva Khanda 105.
9. *Skanda Purana,* Reva Khanda 140; Mayananda Saraswati, *Narmada Panchanga,* p. 211.
10. *Skanda Purana,* Reva Khanda 121.
11. *Skanda Purana,* Reva Khanda 108.
12. *Skanda Purana,* Reva Khanda 82; *Vayu Purana,* Reva Khanda 102.

Chapter 37

1. *Skanda Purana,* Reva Khanda 80; *Vayu Purana,* Reva Khanda 101.
2. *Skanda Purana,* Reva Khanda 79; *Vayu Purana,* Reva Khanda 101.
3. Prabhu Dutt Brahmchari, *Narmada Darshan,* p. 314
4. Prabhu Dutt Brahmchari, *Narmada Darshan,* p. 315.
5. Prabhu Dutt Brahmchari, *Narmada Darshan,* p. 315.
6. *Skanda Purana,* Reva Khanda 179.
7. Prabhu Dutt Brahmchari, *Narmada Darshan,* p. 316.
8. Mayananda Saraswati, *Narmada Panchanga,* p. 215; *Skanda Purana,* Reva Khanda 72.
9. Prabhu Dutt Brahmchari, *Narmada Darshan,* p. 313.
10. Mayananda Saraswati, *Narmada Panchanga,* p. 215; *Skanda Purana,* Reva Khanda 71.
11. Mayananda Saraswati, *Narmada Panchanga,* p. 215.
12. *Skanda Purana,* Reva Khanda 64; *Vayu Purana,* Reva Khanda 95; *Padma Purana,* Svarga Khanda; *Kurma Purana* 39-40.
13. *Skanda Purana,* Reva Khanda 63; *Vayu Purana,* Reva Khanda 95.

Chapter 39

1. *Skanda Purana*, Reva Khanda 62; *Vayu Purana*, Reva Khanda 95.
2. *Skanda Purana*, Reva Khanda 81.
3. Prabhu Dutt Brahmchari, *Narmada Darshan*, pp. 306-07.
4. Mayananda Saraswati, *Narmada Panchanga*, p. 216; *Padma Purana*, Svarga Khanda; *Kurma Purana* 39-40.
5. *Padma Purana*, Svarga Khanda; *Kurma Purana* 39-40; *Skanda Purana*, Reva Khanda 60; *Vayu Purana*, Reva Khanda 93.
6. *Skanda Purana*, Reva Khanda 43; *Vayu Purana*, Reva Khanda 80.
7. *Skanda Purana*, Reva Khanda 50; *Vayu Purana*, Reva Khanda 80-93.

Chapter 40

1. Mayananda Saraswati, *Narmada Panchanga*, p. 218; Prabhu Dutt Brahmchari, *Narmada Darshan*, p. 326.

Chapter 41

1. Mayananda Saraswati, *Narmada Panchanga*, p. 219.
2. *Skanda Purana*, Reva Khanda 41; *Vayu Purana*, Reva Khanda 78.

Chapter 42

1. William Stirling, *River of Paradise and Children of Sham*, p. 5.
2. Ibid., p. 20.
3. Ibid., p. 4.
4. John Malcom, 1823, *A Memoir of Central India.*

Chapter 43

1. *Vayu Purana*, Reva Khanda 69; *Skanda Purana*, Reva Khanda 130; Prabhu Dutt Brahmchari, *Narmada Darshan*, p. 336.
2. Mayananda Saraswati, *Narmada Panchanga*, p. 219.
3. *Vayu Purana*, Reva Khanda 69; *Skanda Purana*, Reva Khanda 130; Prabhu Dutt Brahmchari, *Narmada Darshan*, p. 336.
4. *Vayu Purana*, Reva Khanda 67.

Chapter 45

1. *Vayu Purana*, Reva Khanda 71, Prabhu Dutt Brahmchari, *Narmada Darshan*, p. 336.
2. *Padma Purana*, Svarga Khanda; *Kurma Purana* 39-40.
3. *Vayu Purana*, Reva Khanda 68; *Padma Purana*, Svarga Khanda.

Chapter 46

1. *Padma Purana,* Svarga Khanda; *Vayu Purana,* Reva Khanda 10.
2. *Skanda Purana,* Reva Khanda 30; *Vayu Purana,* Reva Khanda 39.

Chapter 47

1. *Vayu Purana,* Reva Khanda 21-25, 61, 63-64.
2. *Vayu Purana,* Reva Khanda 94; *Skanda Purana,* Reva Khanda 39.
3. *Vayu Purana,* Reva Khanda 94; *Skanda Purana,* Reva Khanda 39.

Chapter 48

1. Sir J. Malcom's *Central India,* p. 160.
2. Sir J. Malcom's *Central India,* p. 187.
3. Sir J. Malcom's *Central India,* p. 186.
4. Sir J. Malcom's *Central India,* p. 177.
5. Sir J. Malcom's *Central India,* p. 179.
6. Sir J. Malcom's *Central India,* p. 189.
7. *Vayu Purana,* Reva Khanda 56.
8. *Skanda Purana,* Reva Khanda 33.
9. *Vasishtha Samhita* 30-31; Prabhu Dutt Brahmchari, *Narmada Darshan,* p. 351.
10. *Skanda Purana,* Reva Khanda 38; *Vayu Purana,* Reva Khanda 76.

Chapter 49

1. *Skanda Purana,* Reva Khanda 42; *Vayu Purana,* Reva Khanda 79.

Chapter 50

1. *Skanda Purana,* Reva Khanda 36; *Vayu Purana,* Reva Khanda 74.
2. *Skanda Purana,* Reva Khanda 43; *Padma Purana,* Svarga Khanda.

Chapter 51

1. *Skanda Purana,* Reva Khanda 40; *Vayu Purana,* Reva Khanda 77.

Chapter 52

1. Prabhu Dutt Brahmchari, *Narmada Darshan,* p. 365.
2. Ibid., p. 365.
3. Ibid., p. 366.

Chapter 55

1. John Malcolm, 1823, *A Memoir of Central India.*
2. *Imperial Gazetteer of India*, vol. 22, 1908.

Chapter 56

1. *Vasishtha Samhita* 49; Prabhu Dutt Brahmchari, *Narmada Darshan*, p. 368.
2. Prabhu Dutt Brahmchari, *Narmada Darshan*, p. 374; Mayananda Saraswati, *Narmada Panchanga*, p. 232.

Chapter 57

1. Prabhu Dutt Brahmchari, *Narmada Darshan*, p. 374; Mayananda Saraswati, *Narmada Panchanga*, p. 232.

Chapter 60

1. *Vasishtha Samhita* 21; Prabhu Dutt Brahmchari, *Narmada Darshan*, pp. 377-78.

Chapter 61

1. Prabhu Dutt Brahmchari, *Narmada Darshan*, p. 386.

Chapter 63

1. Prabhu Dutt Brahmchari, *Narmada Darshan*, p. 389; *Vasishtha Samhita* 20.
2. *Vasishtha Samhita* 20.
3. *Skanda Purana*, Reva Khanda 78; *Vayu Purana*, Reva Khanda 101.

Chapter 64

1. *Skanda Purana*, Reva Khanda 81; *Vayu Purana*, Reva Khanda 102.
2. Prabhu Dutt Brahmchari, *Narmada Darshan*, p. 391.

Chapter 65

1. Prabhu Dutt Brahmchari, *Narmada Darshan*, p. 391.

Chapter 66

1. *Vayu Purana*, Reva Khanda 18.
2. *Vayu Purana*, Reva Khanda 69-70; *Padma Purana*, Svarga Khanda.

Chapter 68

1. *Skanda Purana*, Reva Khanda 129.

Chapter 71

1. *Vayu Purana,* Reva Khanda 68; Prabhu Dutt Brahmchari, *Narmada Darshan,* p. 400.
2. *Vayu Purana,* Reva Khanda 68; Prabhu Dutt Brahmchari, *Narmada Darshan,* p. 400.
3. Prabhu Dutt Brahmchari, *Narmada Darshan,* p. 400, *Padma Purana,* Svarga Khanda.

Chapter 72

1. *Skanda Purana,* Reva Khanda 26-28; *Vayu Purana,* Reva Khanda 8-9.
2. *Skanda Purana,* Reva Khanda 26-28; *Vayu Purana,* Reva Khanda 8-9.

Chapter 73

1. Prabhu Dutt Brahmchari, *Narmada Darshan,* p. 39.
2. Prabhu Dutt Brahmchari, *Narmada Darshan,* p. 40.
3. Ibid.

Chapter 84

1. *Valmiki Ramayana,* Uttara Kanda, Sarga 31.
2. *Kurma Purana,* chaper 38.
3. *Vayu Purana* 2-7; *Skanda Purana,* Reva Khanda 21-28.

Chapter 85

1. *Vayu Purana,* Reva Khanda 43.

Chapter 89

1. *Skanda Purana,* Reva Khanda 218.

Chapter 90

1. Prabhu Dutt Brahmchari, *Narmada Darshan,* p. 82.
2. Ibid., p. 83.
3. *Skanda Purana,* Reva Khanda 87; *Vayu Purana,* Reva Khanda 109.

Chapter 91

1. Prabhu Dutt Brahmchari, *Narmada Darshan,* p. 88.

Chapter 92

1. Prabhu Dutt Brahmchari, *Narmada Darshan,* p. 89.

Chapter 95

1. *Vayu Purana*, Reva Khanda 56-57.
2. Prabhu Dutt Brahmchari, *Narmada Darshan*, p. 91.
3. Prabhu Dutt Brahmchari, *Narmada Darshan*, p. 91.

Chapter 97

1. *Skanda Purana*, Reva Khanda 37; *Vayu Purana*, Reva Khanda 75; *Padma Purana*, Svarga Khanda.
2. Prabhu Dutt Brahmchari, *Narmada Darshan*, p. 93.

Chapter 103

1. *Vayu Purana*, Reva Khanda 20; *Vasishtha Samhita* 55.

Chapter 104

1. *Vasishtha Samhita* 56; Prabhu Dutt Brahmchari, *Narmada Darshan*, p. 110.

Chapter 106

1. *Vasishtha Samhita* 54; Prabhu Dutt Brahmchari, *Narmada Darshan*, p. 112.
2. Prabhu Dutt Brahmchari, *Narmada Darshan*, p. 118.

Chapter 107

1. Prabhu Dutt Brahmchari, *Narmada Darshan*, p. 119.

Chapter 108

1. *Skanda Purana*, Reva Khanda 12; Prabhu Dutt Brahmchari, *Narmada Darshan*, p. 120.

Chapter 109

1. *Imperial Gazetteer of India*, vol. 13, p. 187.
2. Ibid., p. 48.
3. Prabhu Dutt Brahmchari, *Narmada Darshan*, p. 116; *Vasishtha Samhita* 53.

Chapter 110

1. Prabhu Dutt Brahmchari, *Narmada Darshan*, p. 116; *Vasishtha Samhita* 53.
2. *Skanda Purana*, Reva Khanda 74.
3. *Vasishtha Samhita* 52; Mayananda Saraswati, *Narmada Panchanga*, p. 121; Prabhu Dutt Brahmchari, *Narmada Darshan*, p. 133.
4. Prabhu Dutt Brahmchari, *Narmada Darshan*, p. 134.

Chapter 113

1. Prabhu Dutt Brahmchari, *Narmada Darshan*, p. 135.
2. *Skanda Purana*, Reva Khanda 29.
3. Prabhu Dutt Brahmchari, *Narmada Darshan*, p. 124.
4. *Skanda Purana*, Reva Khanda 132; Prabhu Dutt Brahmchari, *Narmada Darshan*, p. 136.
5. *Vayu Purana*, Reva Khanda 42.

Bibliography

A Bombay Subaltern: *History of Mandu*, 1879.

A Study of Skanda Cult, South Asia Books, 1995.

Baillie, Joanna, 1849, *Ahalya Baee*, printed for private circulation [Spottiswoods and Show 1849].

Bal, Hartosh Singh, 2013, *Waters Close Over Us*.

Banerji, Rakhal Das, 1931, *The Haihayas of Tripuri and Their Monuments*.

Baviskar, Amita, 1997, *In the Belly of the River*, Oxford University Press, USA.

Beglar, J.D., 1878, *Report of a Tour in the Bundelkhand and Malwa, 1871-72; and in the Central Provinces, 1873-74*.

Bhattacharya, P.K., 1977, *Historical Geography of Madhya Pradesh*.

Bombay Geographical Society, 1850, *The Transactions of the Bombay Geographical Society, from 1847-1849*, vol. 8.

———, 1844, *Transactions of the Bombay Geographical Society 1836-1838*, vol. 1.

Choubey, M.C., 2006, *Tripuri, History and Culture*.

Clunes, John, William Raban and Sir Michael White, 1818, *Origin of the Pindaries*.

Cousens, Henry, 1897, *Lists of Antiquarian Remains in the Central Provinces and Berar*, Calcutta: Archaeological Survey of India.

Deshpande, N.A. (tr.), 1993, *The Padma-Purāṇa*, Motilal Banarsidass.

Elwin, Verrier, 1970, *A New Book of Tribal Fiction*, Shillong: North-East Frontier Agency.

———, 1993, *Din-Sevak*, I.S.P.C.K.

———, 1964, *The Tribal World of Verrier Elwin*.

Fisher, Ronald C., M.E. Sharpe, 1995, *Toward Sustainable Development*, Routledge.

Forbes, Alexander Kinloch, 1856, *Râs Mâlâ*.

Forbes, James, 1834, *Oriental Memoirs*.

Forsyth, J., 2018, *The Highlands of Central India*, Franklin Classics.

Grewal, Royina,1994, *Sacred Virgin*, Penguin Books India.

Guha, Ramachandra, 1999, *Savaging the Civilized*, University of Chicago Press.

Hunter, William Wilson, n.d., *Imperial Gazetteer of India*, vols. 1-21.

———, 1908, *Central Provinces District Gazetteers*.

India International, Centre, 2010, *Water*, Pearson Education India.

Iyangar, K.V. Rangaswami (ed.), 1942, *Krityakalpataru of Bhatta Lakshmidhara*, vol. VIII; Thirthavivechanakanda (Gaekwad's Oriental Series XCVIII), Baroda: Oriental Institute.

Kalidasa, 2015, *The Works of Kalidasa*, CreateSpace.

Kaye, Sir John William, 1856, *The Life and Correspondence of Major-General Sir John Malcolm, G.C.B., Late Envoy to Persia and Governor of Bombay; from Unpublished Letters and Journals*, London: Smith Elder.

Khandelwal, S.N., 2017, *Sribhavisyamahapuranam*, CSP.

Kurma Purana, Anuwad Sahit, Sanskrit Hindi (Hindi edn), Gorakhpur: Gita Press.

Malcolm, John, 1823, *A Memoir of Central India*.

Mehta, Gita, 2018, *A River Sutra*, Penguin, UK.

———, 1995, *Narmada Sutra*, LGF/Le Livre de Poche.

Mill, James, 1858, *The History of British India*.

Monier-Williams, Monier, 1883, *Religious Thought and Life in India*, part I: *Vedism, Brāhmanism, and Hinduism*, London: John Murray.

Mountains of India, Indus Publishing Company, n.d

Myths and Traditions in India: A Fusion of the Past and the Present, BPI (India), n.d.

Naidu, G. Dhananjaya, 2012, *Deep Crystal Structure of the Son-Narmada-Tapti Lineament*, Springer Science & Business Media.

Narada Purana, Hindi (Hindi edn), Gorakhpur: Gita Press.

Neuss, Jürgen, 2012, *Narmadāparikramā: Circumambulation of the Narmadā River*, Brill.

———, 2014, "Omkareshvar-Mandhata: A 'Blind Spot' in the Study of Paramara History and Culture", *Patrimoine Culturel de L'Eau: Cities and Settlements, Temples and Tanks in the Medieval Landscape of Central India*, ed. Michael Willis, Pankaj Rag and O.P.Mishra, Bhopal: Directorate of Archaeology, Archives and Museums.

Omkareshwar and Maheshwar, 2011, Goodearth Publications.

Padma Purana, Hindi (Hindi edn), Gorakhpur: Gita Press.

Pargiter, F.E., 1904, *Mārkaṇḍeya Purāṇa*, Calcutta: Asiatic Society of Bengal.

Patil, Rajaram D.K., 1973, *Cultural History from the Vayu Purana*, Motilal Banarsidass.

Rana, S.S., 1995, *A Study of Skanda Cult*, South Asia Books.

Roy, Mahendra Prakash, 1973, *Origin, Growth, and Suppression of the Pindaris*, New Delhi: Sterling Publishers.

Russell, Robert Vane, 1916, *The Tribes and Castes of the Central Provinces of India.*

Sankshipt Brahmavaivartta Purana, Gorakhpur: Gita Press.

Schelling, Andrew, 2017, *The Cane Groves of Narmada River.*

Schoff, Wilfred H., 1912, *The Periplus of the Erythraen Sea*, New York: Longmans, Gren & Co.

Shah, Vidya, 2010, *Narmada*, Pratham Books.

Sharma, R.K., Shiv Kumar Tiwari and Anuradha Khandekar, 2017, *The Eternal Narmada.*

Sharma, R.K., 1979, *Art of the Paramāras of Mālwā*, Agam Kala Prakashan, original from University of California.

Shastri and Tagare, 2000, *Ancient Indian Tradition and Mythology*, vol. 20, Motilal Banarsidass.

Shastri, J.L. and G.P. Bhatt, 1999, *The Skanda Purana*, New Delhi: Motilal Banarsidass.

Sleeman, Sir William Henry, 1893, *Rambles and Recollections of an Indian Official.*

Sri Vishnu Purana, Anuwad Sahit, Gorakhpur: Gita Press.

Stirling, William, 1855, *The Rivers of Paradise and Children of Shem: With a Copious Appendix.*

The Agni Purana, Motilal Banarsidass, 1984.

The Divine (ed.), 2013, *Brahmavaivartta Purana: A Concise Guide*, Mocktime Publication.

The Gazetteer of the Central Provinces of India, 1870, ed. Charles Grant, p. 258, Bombay: Education Society's Press.

The Mahābhārata, tr. and ed. J.A.B. Van Buitenen, University of Chicago Press, 1973.

Tulasīdāsa, 1978, *The Rāmāyaṇa of Tulasīdāsa* Motilal Banarsidass.

Tyagi, D., 1998, *Narmada Basin: Land and People*, Anthropological Survey of India.

Unni, Sankaran K. (ed.), 1996, *Ecology of River Narmada*, Ashish.

Valmiki Ramayana, Anuwad Sahit Bhag 1-2, Gorakhpur: Gita Press.

Ved Vyas, *Mahabharata*, Hindi Anuwad Sahit (Bhag 1-6), Gorakhpur: Gita Press.

Ved Vyas, *Skanda Purana*, Gorakhpur: Gita Press.

Ved Vyas, *Sri Vaman Purana*, Gorakhpur: Gita Press.

Ved Vyas, *Srimad Bhagavat Mahapurana*, Vyakhyasahit Bhag 1-2, Gorakhpur: Gita Press.

Vegad, Amrit Lal, 2006, *Saundarya Ki Nadi Narmada* (Hindi), Penguin India.

Watawe, Shrikant, 2020, *Maa Narmada Parikrama: A Spiritual Journey*, Xpress Publishing, 2020.

Wood, John R., 2007, *The Politics of Water Resource Development in India*, Sage Publications India.

Index

Aashapuri Devi Teerth 177
Aashita 151, 408
Abhishek 126
Abraham, homeland of 218
Adi Shankaracharya 36
Aditi 68, 111, 145, 147
Adityas 146
Adityeshwar Kambaleshwar Teerth 211
Adityeshwar Mahadev/Teerth 173, 211
Adivaraha Teerth 178
Agastya 201
Agastyeshwar 201
Agastyeshwar Mahadev 201-02
Agastyeshwar temple 201
Agni Purana 14
Agni Teerth 78
Agni/Agnideva 178, 194-96, 211, 222, 242
Agnishwar Mahadev 222
Agrawal, Nishu 408
Ahilyabai, Rani 6, 31, 69, 199, 238-41
Ahilyapuri 177
Ajastra 200
Ajastreshwar 200
Ajnal River 393
Akashdipa Teerth 285
Akbar 390
Alauddin 30
Al-Biruni 264
Alika Teerth 149
Alikabet 150
Alikeshwar Mahadev 150
Alkapuri 391
Amahak Teerth 174
Amara, Lord 275
Amareshvara Temple 33, 35
Amarkantak 4, 9-10, 14-15, 17, 25-27, 250, 302, 304-05, 309, 324, 328-29, 331-32, 338
Ambheta 162
Ambika 188
Ambikeshwar Mahadev 188
Amri Ghat 274-75
Amritasya Ma Narmada 24
Amritasya Ma Narmada Pada-Parikrama v
Anadwahi River 120
Anandeshwar Teerth 120
Anandeshwara Shivalinga 120
Anangeshwar Mahadev Temple 85
Anarkeshwar Mahadev 139
ancient
- *ashrama* of Vikasanand Maharaj 305
- *rishis* 69
- Shivalingas 187
- *tirthas* 73, 88, 230

ancient Sanatana
    history 120
    tales 303
Andhakasura 112
Andiyar 339-40
Angareshwar/Angareshwar Teerth 174, 183
anjan tree 80
Ankleshwar 142, 144
Annapurnabai 210
Antaji 60
Anusuya Mata 181, 189
Anusuya Mata Mandir 189
Apsareshwar Mahadev 165
Arandi Sangam 400
archaeological sites 7
Arjan River 131
arti of *kalasha*s 52
Arundhati 187
Ashapuri Devi 179
Ashokvanika Teerth 242
ashrama of Ma Anandamayi 250
*ashrama*s 4, 31, 35, 47, 54, 116, 362
Ashvamedha Yagya 342
Ashvaparna 198
Ashvaparni River 198
Ashvinikumaras 120, 124, 146
Asirgarh 263
aspects of the Narmada Parikrama 108
Atharvaveda 235, 249
Atri Rishi 181
Atul our esteemed cameraman 100-101, 197
Aurangzeb 30, 59
    passing of 60
Aurobindo, Sri 174, 192, 194
Avanti 171
Avasgarh 79
*avatara*s of Lord Shiva 235, 249
Ayodhya/Ayodhyapuri 177, 220, 260-61
Ayonij Teerth 178, 183
Azad, Yogesh 408

Baba and Babi 125, 127
Baba Atmaram 267
Baba Durgadas 245
    Samadhi 245
    Temple 249
Baba, Siyaram 63-64
Badrikashram 191
Badwani Rajghat 80
Bagad Sangam 224
Bagad, waters of 224
Bagdi River 263
Bagdi Sangam 263
Bageshwar Teerth 224
Bageshwari 400
Bagheli 335
Baghelkhanda 335
Bagu 224
Bahuroma 16
Bajirao Peshwa, *samadhi* of 56, 62
Bakaner 230
Bakhatgarh 263
Balaji Vishwanath 59-61
Balakhilya Rishi 177
Balarama 12, 190
Balbala-Kunda 144
Bali 282, 292, 297
Bali Sthali 292
Balkeshwar Mahadev 395
Balthari 292
Bambal, Pramod 50-51, 102, 293, 410

Banada 387
Banasura 256, 304
Bangali Baba 49
Bangash, Muhammad Khan 59
Banna, Raju 408
Bansal, Bunty 410
Bansal, Deepak 312, 407-09
Banvariya 217
Bappa Rawal 79
Bapu, Sitaram 179-81
Baranag Nala 257
Barawaha 252
  thickets of 254
Bardha 230
Bargi Dam 309, 319, 347, 349
Bargi Nagar 349
Barman Ghat 293-94
Barwani 79-81
Barwani Rajghat 81
Basant Panchami 311
Batkal Teerth 190
Bavanavahini 73, 81-82, 85
Bawankule, Chandrashekhar 42, 97-98, 407
Bayphal 399
Baz Bahadur 219
Belgaon 103
Belkheda 296
Benares 58-59, 184
Bhabri 97
Bhadbhut 166
Bhadpura 354
Bhadra 401
Bhadrashila 15
Bhadreshwar Mahadev 402
Bhagavata Purana 11
Bhagavati (Bhavati) Devi 85, 87-88, 109, 142, 166, 178
Bhagavati Siddha Pitha 166
Bhairava 120, 176, 400
Bhanumati 200
Bharadvaja 304
Bharam Puri 257
Bharat 187, 193
Bhargal 173
Bhargaleshwar 173
Bhargava Rishi 78
Bhargeshwar 174
Bharkacch 281
Bharteshwar Teerth 187
Bharti, Kamal 50
Bharti, Somnath 115, 119
Bharuch 6, 25, 113, 165, 169
Bhasmasura 121
Bhatera 365
Bhattayan 65
  journey to 63
Bhaumik, Tapan 48-49
Bhavishya Purana 15
Bhedaghat 5, 300, 302
Bheraghat 354
Bhetkheda 256
Bhilat Dev 71
Bhilat Dev Mandir 252
Bhima 33, 109, 210
Bhimkulya Sangam 210
Bhishma 10
Bhogeshwar 185
Bhopal 264
Bhopali Baba 63
Bhrahmakunda Teerth 359
Bhrigishwar Teerth 178

Bhrigu Rishi 178, 195, 282
Bhrigu Parvat 113
Bhrigu Teerth 165
Bhrigukaccha 12, 165
Bhrigukshetra 169
Bible 219
Bihari Das Maharaj 232-34
Bijasen Teerth 88
Bijaseni 88
Bil Pathar 296-97, 299
Bil Pathar Temple 298
Bilvramak 235-36
Bilvramak Teerth 236
Boras 286
Brahma, Lord 13, 74, 111, 113, 123, 134, 136-37, 139, 143, 148, 152, 178, 181, 196, 213, 227, 229, 266-67, 287, 293, 301, 304, 359, 375, 390
Brahma Svarupa 222
Brahma Teerth 400
Brahmadutt, Maharaj 224
Brahmakunda 359
Brahmana 195
Brahmanda Purana 16
Brahmani 400
Brahmaprasada Teerth 178
Brahmapuri 344
Brahmapuri Ghat 42, 403, 405
Brahmavaivartta Purana 15
Brahmavart Teerth 74
Brahmchari, Prabhu Dutt 236, 314, 413-25
Brahmeshwar 124
Brahmeshwar Mahadev 293
Brahmeshwar Shiva 74
Brahmi 66
also known as Sarasvati 178
Brahmod Teerth 297
Brahmshila Teerth 136
Brihaspati, Devaguru 124, 136
British rule, era of 263
Brownrigg, Major 264
Budheshwar Mahadev Temple 359
Budhgaon 359
Bundelkhand 58, 61
Bundi 397
Burhanpur 263
Burhar Sangam 340
Burman, Jadu 409
Buti River 237

Chaitra Maharaj Chaitreshwar 200
Chakdi 395
Chakrabarti, Dilip K. 411
Chakra-Kundas 256
Chakratirtha 113, 186, 193
Chakravarti, Lalaram 55, 302, 309, 313, 342, 344, 353-54, 356-57, 410
Chakreshwar 124
Chakshu Manu 200
Chamunda Devi 228, 400
Chanayaka, King 171
Chanda and Munda 13, 193
Chanda, Trilok 410
Chandasena 400
Chandatiya 193
Chandavega River 401
Chandavega Sangam 400
Chandika in Haridwar 236
Chandika Tirtha 193
Chandikeshwar Mahadev 401
Chandod 113, 184, 193
Chandra 181, 195, 198

Chandrachuda 15
Chandrapida 120
Chandraprabhash Teerth 181
Chandrayana Vrata 67
Chandreshwar Mahadev 181
Chandreshwar Mahadev Temple 198
Chaturbhuja Rupa 352
Chaturmasa Mahatmya 329
Chaubis Avatara Temple 379
Chaudhari, Vijay 98-99, 101, 103, 105, 410
Chaudhary, Dinesh 410
Chauhan, Praveen 86, 96, 98-99, 102, 151, 273, 277, 318, 407
Chauhan, Ujjwal Singh 264, 267, 273, 410
Chauhan, Vinay 179, 408
chauth and *saradeshamukhi* 60
Chaya 145
Chhatrapati 59
Chikhaldha Teerth 221
Chipaner 271
Chitrasena Gandharva 74
  one of the rulers of *gandharvas* 149
Chitu, Pindari leader 264
Chota Vardha Ghat 78
Chyavana Rishi 12, 196
communal
  food 1, 36
  meal 75
cook Jadu 337-38
Cousens, Henry 32
Curzon, George Nathaniel 32-33

Dab Ganga 114
Dab River 111
Dabhade, Khande Rao 60
Dada Darbar 51
Dadhichi, Rishi 161, 234-35, 249
Dadhi-Madhu Kshetra 198
Dahej, city of 161
Dahi 216
Daksha 13, 80, 134, 195
Dakshayani 67
Damhedi 320
Dananjaya 140
Danu 252-53
Danvantari 144
darshana puja 13
Daruk 251
Daruk, Rishi 232
Daruk Teerth 232
Daruk Vana 244
Darukeshwar Mahadev Teerth 251
Dashan or Dashkanyeshwar Teerth 169
Dattatreya, Lord 189, 202, 204
  Mandir 202
Datuni River 263
Datuni Sangam 263
Dawtha Naresh 268
Delhoste, E.P. 113
Deshmukh, Vinod 410
Dev Path Linga 222, 224
Dev Path Linga Teerth 221
Deva Ganga River 109-11
Deva ka Talab 145
Deva River 113
Deva-Kunda 144
Devanadi River 78
Devanik, King 387-88
Devaraja 142
Devashila 359
Devimahatmya 33

Devkachar 362
Devmay Teerth 222
Devvasi, Dinesh 408
Devyani 67
Dhabades 58
Dhadgaon 103-05
Dhanakubera Teerth 187
Dhaneshwar Mahadev 122
Dhaniram 374
Dhanpuri 309
Dhar to Nemawar, travelling from 264
Dharma 249
  son of Brahma 235
Dharmapuri 232, 235-36, 395
Dharmarai 216
Dharmaraja 172
Dharmashala 174
Dharmeshwar 124
Dhaumya Rishi 11
Dhavdi-Kunda 256
Dhoot, Satyanarayan 126
Dhote, Sanjay 410
Dhruva 68
Dhuniwale Dadaji 162, 371-72
Dhurve, Ram 409
Dhurve, Vasudev 409
Dhurve, Vijay 409
Dhutpapeshwar, temple of 185
Digambara Rupa 244
Dindeshwar Teerth 165
Dindori 319, 337
Dindori North 318
Dinesh, photographer 261-63, 378, 409
Diptikeshwar Teerth 227
Diti 68, 111, 147
Draupadi 16, 386
Dudha Dhara 5
Dudhi River 374
Dudhi Sangam 374
Durgavati, Rani 342, 344
Durvasa 304, 402
Duryodhana 242
Dusharavan 168

eleven Rudras and Rudranis, *puja* of 88
era of British rule 263
Erandeshwar Mahadev 402
Erandi, Sage 402
Erandi Sangam 163, 189, 401, 418

Farrukhsiyar 60
Ferrisemar 324
fifty-two Bhairavas 256
Fleet, John Faithful 33
Forbes, James 183

Gadarwara 292, 354, 363-66, 369
Gade, Sujeet 407, 410
Gahlot, Surendra 410
Gajasura 209
Galav Rishi 15
Gamona 210
Ganapati 228
Gandhi, Indira 259
Gandhi, Rahul 293
Ganesha 400
Ganesha, Lord 179, 228
Ganeshvari Arundhati 68
Ganga, River 16, 55, 131, 135, 192, 296, 394
Gangadharan, N. 412
Ganga–Yamuna confluence 400
Gangeshwar Mahadev 54-55, 192
Ganglade Ghat 224

Ganita Teerth 166
Ganjal River 387-88
Ganjaleshwar Mahadev Temple 387-88
Garuda 123, 140, 202, 209, 282
Garudeshwar 170, 202, 204, 209-10
Garudeshwar Teerth 209
Garudeshwar Temple 204
gathering of *rishis* and *munis* 135
Gaumukha 156
Gaurav 316
Gauri River 85
Gauri Somnath 30-31
Gauri Somnath Temple 32
Gaurishankar Maharaj 1, 50, 67, 335, 379-81, 385, 403
Gautama Rishi 176, 199, 393
Gautameshwar Mahadev 393-94
Gautameshwar Teerth 199
Gayatri Patha 344
Gayatri *purashcharana* 282
Ghoda Ghat 343
Ghodi 145
Ghrit Sangam 344
Girish 357-58
Godars and Dashnamis 31
Godavari Ganga, River Goddess 394
Gomukh Ghat 300
Goni River 268, 271
Gopal 211
Gopalpur 300, 303
Gora Colony 114-16, 119
Gora village 297
Gorakhnath 171
Gorakhpur 335
Goswami, Jagdish 373
Grant, Charles 412
Gregorian calendar 253
Gujarat 61, 77, 114-16, 126-27, 154, 214, 408
Gulab Das Maharaj Ashram 398
Gupta Prayag 198
Gupteshwar Mahadev 244
Gwarighat 5, 303, 309
Gyarahalingi Teerth 73

Handia 390, 393
Hansheshwar Mahadev 148
Hansot 148
Hanuman 107, 128, 342-43
Hanuman Tekri 391
Hanuman Temple 179, 281
Hanumanteshwar Teerth 128
Hapeshwar Teerth 213-14
Harda 142, 387-88, 390
Hari ka Dham 26
Harihara *mantra* 282
Harihareshwar Mahadev 222
Harishchandra, Lord 304
Hathner River 385
Hathnora 7
Hatyaharan River 385
Hela Dab 109-10
Hemtakdi 344
Hindu Pad Padshahi 58
Hiranyagarbha River 69
Hiranyakashyap 14
Hiranyakashyapu 181, 275
Hisaria, Indar 126, 398
Hisaria, Manu 410
Hisaria, Purushottam 126
Hissaria, Rajeev 408
Hissaria, Vinod 312, 407
Holi 273, 405-06
Holipura 277

Holkar, Jaswant Rao 264
Holkar, Male Rao 239
Holkar, Malhar Rao 58
Hosangabad 374
Hrishikesh 387
Hulkadevi 400
Hunkar Teerth 173
Hunkareshwar Teerth 172
Hunter, William Wilson 27, 407

illustrious era of Indian history 284
Imperial Gazetteer of India 27, 414, 422, 424
impressive collection of *tirtha*s 127
Indian
- history, illustrious era of 284
- *rishi*s 121
- traditions, rich tapestry of 52

Indian Antiquary 32
Indian Foresters 414
Indian Sanatana
- Shastra 223, 281, 297
- traditions 121

Indian Shastras 284
- annals of 385
- rich history of 359

Indira Sagar Dam 393, 395
Indore 263
Indra 119, 136-38, 152, 176, 187, 234, 251, 303
Indrani 67, 112, 400
Indreshwar Mahadev 136-37, 303
Indreshwar Mahadev Temple 353
intersection of Khargone and Devas 257
intricacies of the Narmada Parikrama 366

Jabali 149, 173
Jabalpur 299
Jadhav, Dileep 409
Jadugar, Anand 350-51
Jagadamba, Mata 163
Jagat Mata 237
Jagatpur 332, 335
Jageshwar 162
Jain, Arun 410
Jain, Vijay 39
Jaina temple 265
Jainansaria, Sanjay 410
Jaiswal, Nilesh 409-10
Jaiswal, Ritesh 296, 410
Jalkoti 237-38
Jalud 245
Jamadagni 16, 155, 304, 374
Jambavan 129
Jambhasura 119
Jambudvipa 178
Jambuvati (Jamner), River 267
Jamdagneshwar Temple 340
Jamdar, Jitendra 305, 351
Jamnod, Indar Singh 296-98, 410
Jan Abhiyan 346
Jan Abhiyan Parishad 305
Janak, Maharaj 190, 287
Janakeshwar Teerth 190
Jankateerth 287
Jaswant, Gangadhar 239
Jat, Suraj 410
Jateshwar Teerth 122
Jayant 176
Jayasimha I 33
Jeemut 125
Jhanor 174

Jharkhand 95
Jhikoli 373
Jija Bai 60
Jod Ganapati Ashram 48
Jod Ganapati Temple 405
Jod Ganapati Temple Ashram 403
Jogikila Ghat 393
journey
    from Sondhwa to Dahi 215
    to Bhattayan 63
Jrimbhasura 138
Judge, Mr Mishra 302
Junankar, Rohan 335, 408
Junankar, Sunil 50, 293, 410
Jwaleshwar Teerth 242
Jyoti 261-62
Jyotirlinga 25-26, 29, 36
Jyotirlinga Trayambakeshwar 394

Kachara Tola 319-20
Kadru 200
Kailasa 104, 301
    sacred journey to 128
Kailasha, Shulpani 104
Kala Bhairavas 263
Kaladeva 257
kalasha 50
    pujana 126
    sacred of 24
*kalasha*s 42-43
    arti/puja of 52
Kalavashpa 121
Kali 193-94
    temple of 250
Kali Mata Temple 194
Kali Ratri 258-59
Kamadeva 189
Kamadhenu 167, 236
Kamal Bharti Maharaj 379
Kambaleshwar 211
Kambhukeshwar Mahadev 182
Kambhukeshwar Teerth 181
Kambuka 181
Kameshwar Ganapati 200
Kamuka in Gandhamadan Mountain 236
Kanjetha 187
Kankariya River 229, 271
Kantheshwar Temple 166
Kanthishikha 148
Kapalamochana Teerth 78
Kapaleshwar/Kapaleshwar Teerth 163, 165
Kapalika 244
Kapardeshwar Mahadev 179
Kapil Teerth/Tirtha 194, 211
Kapila 236
Kapila Dhara 5, 13
Kapila Muni 163, 182, 194, 200, 211
Kapila Teerth 236, 253
Kapileshwar/Kapileshwar Teerth 78, 182
Kapisthitapura 129
Kapse, Girish 408
Karam River 237
Karanj Rishi 188
Karanja 253
Karanjatarani 131
Karanjeshwar/Karanjeshwar Teerth 187-88
Karanjiya 335
Karkateshwar Mahadev 176
Karnali 194
Karoli 221, 226-27, 402

Karoteshwar Mahadev 209
Karoteshwar Rupa 209
Kartavirya Arjuna 15-16, 329
Karttik Swami 146
Karttikeya, Lord 134, 202
Kashi 15, 178-79, 188
Kashyap Rishi 111, 144-45, 147-48, 173, 194, 374
Kasrawad 80
Kathi 107
Kathora 129
Kaumari 400
Kaushalya River 273
Kaveri 400
Kedara Mahalaya 176
Kedara, Lord 186, 201
Kedareshwar Mahadev temple 201
Kedareshwar Temple 185
Kedarnath 201
  to Rameshwaram 240
Ketu 286
Ketudhana 286
Khadag Ghat 71-73
Khadak stream 62
Khalghat 236
Khan, Abdullah 60
Khan, Hussain Ali 60
Khanda River 286
Khandawa 388
Khandelwal, K. 408
Khandesh 79
Khapparmal 99-100
Khargone and Devas, intersection of 257
Khirkiya 396
Khular River 251
Kielhorn 413
king of
  Ayodhya 400
  Kashi 176
Kinioch, Forbes Alexander 416
Kinkaid, W. 218
Kohan Rishi 180
Kohna 179-80
Kokhsar 378-81
Kokhsar Ghat 385
Kolkata 338
Kolyada 163
Koral 177-79
Kosava 166
Koteshwar 127, 132, 149, 151, 191, 254
Koteshwar Kundeshwar Teerth 216
Koteshwar Mahadev 132, 149
Koteshwar Teerth 191
Koteshwar Temple 253
Kotinarpura 132
Kotitirtha 178
Kotkheda 399
Kovind, Ram Nath 21, 170
Kramada in Mansarovar 236
Krishna, Lord 251, 350-51, 375
Krittika 146
Kubera 122, 124, 177, 195, 216, 390, 400
Kubera Bhandari Teerth 400
Kubera Teerth 177, 179
Kubereshwar Mahadev Temple 195
Kubja River 235, 375
Kubja Sangam 375-76
Kumar 255, 258-59, 261, 263, 272-73, 276, 305, 313, 319, 324, 327, 337, 347, 388-89, 408
Kumaraswami 209
Kumareshwar, Lord 202, 209
Kumbha Mela 21-22

Kumbhabhisheka 125
Kumbheshwar 124
Kumudini 142
Kundhar 216
Kunti 386
Kuntipur 386
Kurma Purana 15, 329, 412-20
Kurukshetra 304
Kusha 232
Kusumayudha Kamadeva 139
Kusumeshwar 139

Ladva 139
Lakhaṅ Giri Maharaj 93
Lakhi 156-57
Lakshmana 17, 125
Lakshmaneshwar 125
Lakshmi Kunda 386
Lal Bahadur 408
Lal, Hira 89
Lalita in Prayag 236
Lamheti Ghat 352
Lanka 391
Lingadharini in Naimisharanya 236
Linkeshwar Mahadev 174
Lodhi, Raju 410
Loharaya 155
Lohariya Ghat 78
Lokesh 37, 52, 63, 71, 76, 90, 120, 132, 197, 299, 397, 409
Lopamudra 68
Lukeshwar Mahadev 347
Lukeshwar Teerth 122, 347
Luntheshwar Teerth 156
Luvara 155

Ma Anandamayi, *ashrama* of 250
Ma Narmada Gyan Peeth 404
Ma Narmada Pada-Parikrama 23
Machack River 393
Madhuparna 198
Madhupuri 343
Madhupuri Ghat 342
Mahabharata 10-11, 109, 411
Mahadeva, Lord 202
Mahajan, Shailesh 377, 410
Mahakala 21, 181
mahamrityunjaya patha 180
Mahant Seetasharan 138
Maharajpur 342-44, 346
Mahashivaratri 23
Mahavira 400
Mahesh 227
Maheshwar 6, 33, 69, 219
Maheshwar, town 238, 242
Mahgana 166
Mahishasuramardini 176
Mahishmati 12, 15, 33, 329, 344
Mai ki Bagiya 330-31, 335
Maidan-e-Kichad 276
Maikal Mountain 323-24, 327
Makara Sankranti 284, 304
Malashamneshwar Mahadev 243
Malcolm, John 32, 79, 241, 413, 420-22
Malegaon 210
Mallikarjuna 388
Malsar 182
Malwa 61
Mamleshwara 34
Man River 200
Manad Temple 166
Mandaleshwar 238, 242, 379
Mandavya Ashram 67, 142
Mandavya Rishi 142-43

Mandavya Teerth 143
Mandavyeshwar 142
Mandhata 30, 33-34
Mandhata-Omkareshwar 28-29, 35
Mandla 5, 309, 342, 344
Mandleshwar 7
Mandranchal Mountain 378
Mandu 218, 220-21, 226-27, 232
Mandu and
  Baz Bahadur, chronicle of 218
  Maheshwar, temples of 28
  Reva-Kunda, theory of 219
Manegaon 294
Mangala 123, 174, 183
Mangaleshwar 173
Mangaleshwar Teerth 123
Mani Nag 200
Maninageshwar Teerth 200
Manknak Rishi 66
Mankneshwar Mahadev Temple 66
Manmatheshwar Mahadev 189
Manthara 375
Maratha
  Chhatrapati 58
  elite, members of 61
Marichi Muni 375
Markandeshwara Shivalinga 132
Markandeya Rishi/Muni 16, 26, 113, 124, 132, 134-35, 166, 178, 186, 210, 214, 329, 381, 401
Markandeya Purana 33
Markandeya Teerth 132, 134, 166, 178
Markandeyeshwar Mahadev 186
Markandeyeshwar Teerth 186
Markat Teerth 66
Markateshwar Teerth 67
Markati Sangam 379
Marshall, John H. 32
Maru ki Chichli 77
Marudha 198
Matanga Muni Ashram 242
Matanga Rishi/Muni 54-55, 242
Matangeshwar Mahadev 242
Mathasar 114
Matrika Teerth 146-47
Matruka Temple 146
Matsyak Muni 125
Matsyakeshwar 125
Mauni Baba Ashram 49
Mayasura 301-02
Mayura Kalpa 198
Medha Ghat 347
Meera Ashram 197-98
Megheshwar 125
Meghnath Teerth 85, 216
Menaka 74
Mesh 219
Mithitalai 153
Mittal, Ghansyam 413, 410
Mogi Mata 109, 111
Mogi Mata Temple 109-10
Mohini 15, 122, 329
Mokhdi 113, 211
Moksha Ganga 113
Molgi 105, 107-08
Monier-Williams, M. 27
Mother 174
Mother Narmada, *tirtha*s of 65
Mothiya 146
Mount Sumeru 201
Mrigkheda 294-95
Mrigvan Teerth 352
Mukati, Lalit 410
Mukti Kshetra 304
Mukuteshwar Teerth 134

Mundamaharanya 335
Munyalaya Teerth 166
Muranch 357, 360-61
Murgakheda 294
Murti, Vishnu 173

Nagaraja 14
Nageshwar 130-31
Nageshwar Teerth 187
Nageshwar Temple 131
Nagpur 277, 377, 391
Nahar, Alok 335, 410
Nahili River 78
Nainagarh 281
Nakalpura Gurukul 212
Nal 130
Naleshwar Mahadev Teerth 130
Naleshwar Mahadev Temple 130
Namanpura 258, 261
Nanda Devi 194
Nanda Devi Teerth 176
Nandahad Tirtha 194
Nandgram 176
Nandi 121, 129, 156, 185, 198, 224
Nandikeshwar Teerth 198
Nandner 279, 281, 376
Nandoriya 191
Nanga Baba 93, 171, 259, 296, 309, 340, 381
Nara and Narayana 191
Narada Muni 121, 178, 282, 375, 378-79
Narada Purana 14, 329
Narasimha Purana 16
Narayan Swami 210
Narbuda or Nerbudda 3
Nardeshwar Mahadev 282
Nareshwar 179
Narmada Abhiyan 305
Narmada Bachao Andolan 81
Narmada Ghat 121
Narmada Jayanti 314
Narmada Kunda 331
Narmada Kurukshetra 155
Narmada Maiya Parikrama patha 273
Narmada Parikrama 21-22, 25, 30, 47, 54, 62, 73, 95-96, 154, 217, 219, 287, 304, 330, 332, 336, 342-43, 351, 371, 373, 377, 379, 387, 407-08
  aspects of 108
  Belt 294
  cause of 108
  history of 93
  intricacies of 366
  path of 186, 311
  significance of 225
  Teerthas of 2
Narmada Samagra 69
Narmada
  Devi 126
  udgam of 331
  *tirtha*s 18
  Yatra and Tirtha 292
Narmadapuram 5, 275
Narmadashtakam 36
narmade har 162, 325, 337, 392
Narmadeshwar 179, 245, 302
Narmadeshwar Mahadev 136
Narmadeshwar Teerth 134, 147
Narmadeshwar Varuneshwar and Shivayogeshwar, temples of 78
Narsimha *avatara* 275
Narsinghpur 275, 291, 356, 361, 363
Navetha 165
Neel 129
Neemapura 257
Nemawar 258, 263-67, 284, 391

Nemawar Temple 264
Neuss 413
Nikora 174
Nilakantha 273
Nilkantheshwar Mahadev 222
Nimar 28-29, 32, 35, 56, 215, 217, 219
Nirankari Ashram 309
Nishkalankeshwar 186
Nizam of the Deccan 242
Nunkher 316-18

offering of *prasada* 52
Old Testament 219
Omkar Maharaj 41, 405-06
Omkar Mountain 41
Omkar Parvat 406
Omkareshwar 7, 25-27, 31, 35, 37-38, 40-41, 48, 52, 209, 252, 255, 263-65, 273, 363, 371, 379, 386, 388, 393, 395, 399-400, 402-03, 405-06
Omkareshwar Dharmashala 39
Omkareshwar Maharaj 405
Omkareshwar Mountain 50
Omkareshwar Temple 405
Omkarnath Temple 173
Ori 127
Oz 177

Pada-Parikrama 24
Padma 249
Padma Purana 17, 329, 413-24
Padmi Teerth Ghat 347
Padshah of Delhi 58
Pakshiraja 176
Palkhed 61
Pamakhedi 258
Panchakubera 179
Panchakunda Teerth 221
Panchali 386
Pandavas 214, 285, 350, 386, 394
Panditji of Pura 215
Pandu 182
Pandutirtha 182
Paradkar, Balkrishna 409
Parasar, Vikas 409
Parashara Rishi 13
Parashurama 15, 71, 155, 186, 238, 243, 268, 271
Pargiter, Frederick Eden 33
parikrama
    act of 39
    certificate of 53
    kalasha 152
    pilgrimage 38
    sacred
        journey of 23
        pilgrimage of 53
    sankalpa of 42
    three kinds of 26
    virtues of 39
    walk on 54
parikramavasi 255
    band of 90
    fellow 64
*parikramavasi*s 2, 41, 50, 53-54, 63, 68, 75-76, 86-87, 89, 93-94, 97, 108, 114, 125-26, 138, 142, 145, 153-54, 162, 164, 170, 199, 205, 213-14, 217-18, 225-27, 230, 252, 254, 258, 261, 275, 280, 286, 291, 294-95, 299, 309-11, 313, 322, 330, 332, 335, 339, 348-49, 353-54, 356-57, 361, 364, 373, 379, 386, 388, 406-08
Parmara era, memories of 291
Parvati 14, 34, 85, 109, 111-13, 121, 131, 134, 179, 236, 244, 275, 359
Pashupati 146
Paswan, Munna 408

Patankar, Arvind 377, 410
Patel, Jaideep 410
Patel, Mufatbhai 169, 171
Patel, Narayan 399
Patel, Prahlad 390
Patel, Sobhag Chandra 55
Patel, Sumit 381, 385
Patel, Surendra 397, 399, 410
Patels of Dharmpuri 219
Patidar community 217-18
Patil, Hemant 377, 410
Patil, S.R. 410
Patkar, Medha 102
Patreshwar Mahadev Teerth 74
Pavakeshwar Mahadev 195-96
Pavar, Gaurav 408
Pawar, Anand Rao 58
Pawar, Krishna 409
Peshwa, Baji Rao 57-58, 61
pilgrimage sites 1
Pimpalkhunte 108
Pindaris 6
Pingaleshwar Teerth/Tirtha 178, 194
Pipaliya 217
Pipleshwar Mahadev 303, 353
Pipleshwar Mahadev Temple 249, 353
Pippalada Muni/Rishi 119, 234-35, 249, 353
Pippalada Muni Temple 250, 303
Pippalada Teerth 119
Pitambara Peeth 363-64
Pitr Teerth 400
pitri-tarpana 113
Prabha Teerth 190
Prahlada 12, 275, 287
Prajapati 148
prasada, offering of 52
Prashnopanishad 235, 249
Prasphutan Samiti 346
Pratinidhi, Shripat Rao 58
Prayag/Prayagraj 58, 378, 400
Priyavrat Mahraj 200
Priyavrateshwar 200
Ptolemy 3
puja of
    all the *kalasha*s 52
    eleven Rudras and Rudranis 88
Puloma 195
Punasa 393
Pundarika, Nag 187
Pundarika, Trilochana 182
Punyaghat 257, 395
Punyaghat Teerth 393, 395
Pura 221, 226
Puranas 137, 235, 241
    old temples mentioned in 199
Puri, Antariskha 304
Purnapathaka Mandala 33
Purtikeshwar Mahadev 129
Purukutsa 13-14
Pushkar 359
Pushkarni Teerth 211

Radha–Krishna 288
Rahul 102
Rai 337, 339
Rai, Monu 410
Raingan 200
Raivata Manu 200
Rajiv 126, 151, 212
Rajneesh, Acharya 369
Rajpipla 6
Rajput, Jaipal 410
Rajput, Saheb Singh 410

Raju 292, 364
Rama, Lord 17, 124-25, 128-29, 132, 199, 220, 260, 300, 342, 350, 375
Rama Teerth 155
Ramabai 210
Ramacharitmanasa 10, 64
Rama-Kunda 144
Ramalala 107
Ramayana 329
Ramdas 108
Rameshwar Mahadev 125
Rameshwar Shivalinga 177
Rameshwaram 119, 125, 127
Ramnagar 5, 342
Ramnagara Mukti Kshetra 303
Rana 409
Rana of Udaipur 242
Ranapur 181
Rang Avadhut 179
Rashtriya Swayamsevak Sangh (RSS) 82, 237
Ratnavali 68
Raudri known as Narmada 178
Ravana 88, 125, 128, 130, 328-29, 391
Raver 57
Raverkhedi 62
Ravi Teerth 173, 179
Rawal, Deepak 151
Rawal, Manish 151
Rawat, Ashok 410
Renuka 155
Reva 149
Reva Foundation 106, 259-60
Reva Maharaj 349-50
Reva Sagar Sangam 26
Reva Sangam 155
Reva-Kunda 219
rich
    historical legacy of Sanatana Dharma 362
    history of Indian Shastras 359
    tapestry of Indian traditions 52
Richavar 291
Riddhanath Temple 390
Riddheshwar Mahadev 391
Rinmochan Teerth/Tirtha 168, 194
Rinmukteshwar temples 168
*rishi*s
    and *muni*s, gathering of 135
    revered 3
Rohineshwar 186
Rohini 67, 81, 186, 195
Ruchka Rishi 178
Rudra 123, 176, 401
    Kunda 113, 131
    patha 180
    puja 74
Rukmani 386
Rundha 131
Rundhlai 390
Rupamati 219, 344

Saat Pipli Ghat 65
sacred
    journey to Kailasa 128
    of *kalasha* 24
    pilgrimage of *parikrama* 53
    *tirtha*s 17, 119, 144, 177, 180, 242
        multitude of 181
    *tirthasthala*s 120
sacred journey of
    parikrama 23
    Sanatana Dharma 354
Sadaranga, Yogesh 410
Sagar 200
saha-bhojana 1-2

Saharanpur 219
Sahasradhara 237
Sahastrayagkhya Teerth 78
Sahjot 144
Saikheda 371-73
Sakka Market 337
Sakratirtha 119, 176
Sakreshwar 139
Sakreshwar Mahadev 138
Sakreshwar Shivalinga 119
Sakreshwar Teerth 137-38
Salani 263
samadhi of Bajirao Peshwa 56, 62
Sambhaji, King 59
Sambharayani 67
Samjna 145
Sanaka 266
Sanandana 266-67
Sanatana
  Kula 235
  mythology 303
  philosophy 350
  Shastras 241
  son of Brahma 266-67
  tradition 288
Sanatana Dharma 23, 36, 41-42, 52, 57, 68, 78, 107, 115, 122, 155-56, 161, 165, 180-81, 183, 187, 206, 215-16, 227-28, 230, 242, 266, 275, 287, 297, 328, 350
  rich historical legacy of 362
  sacred journey of 354
Sanatkumar 266-67
Sangakheda Kalan 377-78
sangama 14, 42, 67, 113, 198
Sangameshwar Teerth 139
Sanjroli 200
sankalpa of *parikrama* 42
Sankaran, Unni K. 411
Sankarshan Teerth 190
Sankranti *puja* 305
Saptamata Teerth 399
Saptamatrika 199, 399
  temple of 400
Saranga, Praveen 390, 410
Sarasvat 13
Sarasvat Teerth 66
Sarasvati Devi/Goddess 13, 16, 66, 182, 311, 343, 375
Sarasvati Devi Prastravan Teerth 343
Sarasvati Ganga 113
Saraswati, Mayananda 416-20, 422, 424
Saraswati, Vasudevanand 202, 210
Sardar Patel, statue of 115
Sardar Sarovar Dam 7, 72, 78, 81, 104, 111, 113, 210-11, 213, 216, 222-23, 228
Sarpeshwar Mahadev 140
Sarpeshwar Teerth 142
Sarraghat 296
Satak River 72
Sataklingi Ghat 72
Satchidananda 339
Satpura
  Mountains 6
  range 374
Satvasa 376-77
Satyak Maharaj Satyakeshwar 200
Satyanarayana Katha 178
Satyasena 66
Saubhagya Sundari Mata 187
Saubhari Rishi 282
Saudamani 400
Saugandhikavan Teerth 296
Savitri 68
Sawariyadigar 102
Seera 147

Semalda 227
Semlet 91, 97
Senapur 183-86
Seoni River 335, 352
Seth, Bhila 108
Sethi, Amit 410
Shahganj 277
Shahpura 299, 313
Shahu Maharaj 59-61
Shakreshwar 124
Shakti 119, 166
Shakuntala 187
Shalivahana 65, 69
Shalivahana Temple 70
Shalivahaneshwar Mahadev 70
Shalivahaneshwar Temple 69
Shandili 143
Shandilya, Rishi 374, 400
  Ashram of 400
Shandilya *gotra* 201
Shandilya Teerth 374
Shanideva 124, 235, 249
Shankhchuda snake 123
Shankhchudeshwar Mahadev Temple 123
Shantiraj Shantireshwar 200
Sharma, Ashish 264-65
Sharma, Bipin 408
Sharma, Bunty 410
Sharma, Jitendra 37, 51, 119, 132, 137, 153-54, 179, 215, 259, 263, 279, 287, 292, 295, 297, 324, 326, 332, 336, 339, 363, 407, 409
Sharma, Kaushal 409
Sharma, Mukesh 408
Sharma, Pawan 408
Sharma, Vishnu 167
Sharma, Yograj 408
Shashok 304
Shastras, *tirtha*s mentioned in 305
Shastravahini River 335
Shatrughan Maharaj 200
Shatrughana 342-43
Shatrughaneshwar 200
Shaunik Rishi 178
Shilakantha 273
Shipra Parikrama 22
Shitole, Vishal 409
Shiva, Lord 10, 14, 21, 34, 63, 66, 68, 74, 86, 88, 104, 112, 119-21, 123, 125, 128-29, 131-32, 134, 137-40, 143-45, 147, 149, 152, 156, 163, 167-69, 176-79, 182, 184-85, 189-90, 194, 198, 200, 202, 209-11, 213, 216, 224, 230, 236, 244, 256, 274, 282, 301-04, 347, 353, 359, 385, 391, 394, 402
  *avatara*s of 235, 249
Shiva Temple 380
Shivaji 58-60
Shivalinga 31, 52, 63-64, 74, 85, 93, 107, 111, 113, 123, 125, 131, 134, 140, 144, 148, 154, 156, 163, 166-67, 171, 177-78, 182, 189, 196, 201, 210, 223, 227-29, 256, 281, 284, 287, 304, 312, 324, 330, 347, 353, 380, 395
Shivalingas 233
Shiva-Mahimna Stotram 34
Shivanand Maharaj 274
Shivaratri 108, 360
Shokalpura 287, 291, 370
Shokalpura Temple 371
Shoolpaneshwar 111, 113, 120
Shoolpaneshwar Temple 109-11
Shraddha-*kalpa* 14
Shreya 407

Shringaravallavi 66
Shringi Rishi 152
Shukla, Atul 408
Shukla Teerth 171-72, 287
Shukleshwar Saur Teerth 232
Shulbhed 211
Shulpani 6, 82, 85-93, 97, 100, 103-04, 107-09, 111, 113, 115, 141, 211, 213-14
  Bhils 93
  hills 110
  Temple 211
Shumbha and Nishumbha 359
Siddhanatha Temple 32, 266, 391
Siddhavati River 291
Siddheshwar 78
Siddheshwar Mahadev 30, 144, 267, 391
Sindia, Ranoji 58
Singh II, Rana Mohan 79
Singh, Bhim 79
Singh, Chandra 79
Singh, Gajendra 85
Singh, Jaswant 80
Singh, Mohan 79
Singh, Paras Ram 79
Singh, Parsan 79
Singh, Sahib 279, 376
Singh, Sanjay 296, 410
Singh, Sohan 409
Singh, Tarsen 409
Sinore 184
Sirkiya 258, 260
Sita 17
sixty-four Yoginis 256
Skanda 123, 184, 186
Skanda Purana 18, 29, 111, 234, 329, 387, 413-25
Skanda Swami 134
Skandeshwar Mahadev 134
Skandeshwar Teerth 134
Solanki, Sumer Singh 72, 76
Solanki, Ujjwal Singh 410
Soma 176, 195
Somaj 176
Somasharma 17
Somatirtha 176
Someshwar Mahadev 195
Somnath Tirtha 194
Son Johila and Kamandal rivers 328
Sondhwa 214
  to Dahi, journey from 215
Soni, Om 126, 410
Soni, Rahul 408
Soni, Raju 408
Sri Hari 15
Srimad Bhagavata / Srimadbhagavata Mahapurana 282, 300, 411-12
Statue of Unity 115, 170, 210-11
Sterling, Major William 218-19
Sthapak, Dr 351-52
Sthulashira 16
Sudarshna 242
Sugriva 124
Sunda and Upasunda 172
Suparna 198
Suraj 225, 254
Surantaka 120
Survasa 335
Surya 145, 152, 190, 193, 200-201, 211, 232
Surya-Kunda 145
Suvarcha 234
Suvarnashila Teerth 188
Suvarneshwar 168

Suvarneshwar Teerth 168-69
Svarochit Manvantara 200, 400
Svayambhuva Manvantara 200
Svetavarah Teerth 174
Swami Brahmachari 408
Swami Brahmananda 192
Swami Milind 324-27, 339
Swami Satchidananda 371
Swami Shivananda 348, 351, 408
Swami Vivekananda Jayanti 279
Swarnadipa Teerth 69-70

Tahkeet, Sahibrao 408
Takanghat 314, 316
Talamegha 193
Tapas Manvantara 200
Tapti 6
Tara 68
Tava River 378
Tayal, Nandlal 114, 132, 168, 180, 254, 261-62, 274, 317, 336, 348, 391, 407-09
Teerthas of Narmada Parikrama 2
Tejomaya Teerth 123
Tejonath or Vaidyanath Teerth 123
Tembe, Ganesh Bhatt 210
temple of
- Dhutpapeshwar 185
- Kali 250
- Saptamatrika 400
- Tilabhandeshwar 304

temples of
- Mandu and Maheshwar 28
- Narmadeshwar, Varuneshwar and Shivayogeshwar 78

Tendukheda 6
Tevar 300
Thakur, Usha 41
theory of Mandu and Reva-Kunda 219
thickets of Barawaha 254
three kinds of *parikrama* 26
Tijyananda 183
Tilabhandeshwar Mahadev 304
Tilabhandeshwar, temple of 304
Tiladeshwar Mahadev 149
Tiladeshwar Teerth 149
Tilakbada 199
Tilakeshwar 200
Tilakeshwar Mahadev 199
Tileshwar Mahadev 302
Tipu Sultan 242
*tirtha*s
- age-old 252
- ancient 73, 88, 230
- countless 16, 134
- holy 120
  - pilgrimage 171
- impressive collection of 127
- inaugural 54
- map of 127
- mentioned in the Shastras 305
- of Mother Narmada 65
- surrounding 185

Tiwari, Vikas 408
Tomar, Shailendra 410
Tompe, Rahul 410
Trilochan Teerth 182
Tripuri 300, 302
Tripushkar Teerth 15
Trishira 152
Trishul Bhed Teerth 352
Trishul Ghat 303, 352
Trivedi 413
Triveni Sangam 237, 387-88
Turnal 266-67, 271
Tvasta 136, 152, 187
Tyagi, Mahant Mangal Das 37-38, 41,

43, 47-49, 53, 209, 220, 252-54, 272, 292, 354, 363-66, 369-71, 403, 405

Ucchaishrava 198
Uchavan Ghat 393
Uchavan Rishi 393
Udamvar Shiva Temple 297
Uday Bhanu 394
udgam of the Narmada 331
Uikey, Mohan 409
Ujjain 22, 210, 263
Uttama Manu 200
Uttara Vahini Narmada 284

Vadava 167
Vaidyanath Teerth 120, 145
Vaidyatanath 124
Vaikuntha 17, 168
Vaishnavi 400
 affectionately referred to as Bhagirathi 178
Vaishvanara 378
Vaivasvata Manu 199-200
Vakataka dynasty 28
Valmiki, Maharshi 329
Valmiki Ramayana 9, 328
Vamadeva 304
Vamana Purana 12-13
Vamanadeva 12
Vanar Bhalu Teerth 379
Vanara Bhalu Vana 277
Vanavasi *samaja* 105-06
Vandariya 124
Vanjhar River 343
Vanreshwar Teerth 124
Vanshagulm Teerth 10
Varah Nagar 230
Varaha, Bhagavan 174, 178, 230, 400
Varaha Kalpa 181, 230
Varaheshwar Mahadeva 230
Varahi 400
Varahi Ganga 400
Varahi Sangam 400
Vardhaman 251
Varkhad Sangam 73
Varma, Sukhdev 409
Varuna 124, 177
Varuna River 284
Varuneshwar 124, 177
Varuneshwar Mahadev 284
Vasava, Dhansing 410
Vasavatirtha 149
Vasaveshwar Mahadev 149
Vasishtha 304, 374, 401
Vasishtha Samhita 18, 88, 243, 282, 300, 374-75, 378, 414, 422, 424
Vasna, village of 200
Vasnoli 149
Vasuki Naga 131
Vatveshwar Mahadev 198
Vayaveshwar 177
Vayu 177
Vayu Purana 18, 111, 347, 413-25
Veda Sangam 66-67
Vedavyasa 120
Vibhandaka Muni 67, 152
Videha 287
Vidyananda 150
Vijayvargiya, Ajay 151, 154, 391, 407
Vijayvargiya, Mamta 391
Vijayvargiya, Nina 391
Vimleshwar 25, 152, 331
Vimleshwar Mahadev 251

Vimleshwar Teerth 152, 211
Vinayki 347-48
Vinayki Power Plant 349
Vindhya mountains 6, 328-29
Vindhyachal 201
virtues of the *parikrama* 39
Visaji 60
Vishalakshi in Kashi 236
Vishnoi village 395
Vishnu Purana 12-13, 412
Vishnu, Lord 13, 17, 112-13, 122-24, 137, 144, 162, 178, 181, 187, 193-94, 227-30, 282, 301-02, 352, 400
    took the form of Varaha 230
Vishnu Teerth 228
Vishnudas 178
Vishnupuri 343
Vishok Sangam 67
Vishokeshwar Mahadev 67-68
Vishvamitra 304
Vishvarupa 136
Vishwakarma 145-46
Vivekananda 206
Vrauna 213
Vritrasura 137, 213, 234
Vyas Rishi 132, 190-91, 344
Vyas, Pandit Nirnay 409
Vyasa Sukeshwar 131
Vyasa Teerth 344
Vyaseshwar Teerth 190
Vyasheshwar Mahadev 120
Vyasheshwar Teerth 120

Welcom, Major General John 219

Yadav, Mohan Dr 37, 42, 72, 252, 264, 407
Yadav, Ramesh 364
Yadav, Vaibhav 222, 410
Yadu 190
Yagyagarbheshwar Mahadev Temple 69
Yagyavalkya 304, 374
Yaha Mogi 109
Yam Bahadur 408
Yama 177
Yamaraja 124, 139, 145, 192
Yameshwar 177
Yamhas Temple 192
Yamuna River 16, 282, 296
Yayati 125, 190
Yogesh 53, 55, 63, 80, 90, 132, 146, 197, 233, 273, 294, 313, 316, 324-25, 354, 356, 372, 396
Yudhishthira 11, 16, 26, 284, 329